DISASTERS
IN HISTORY

A GRAPHIC NOVEL COLLECTION

by Jane Sutcliffe, Donald B. Lemke, Heather Adamson, Scott R. Welvaert,
Kay Melchisedech Olson, Matt Doeden, B. A. Hoena, and Jessica Gunderson

illustrated by Bob Lentz, Keith Tucker, Brian Bascle, Ron Frenz, Charles
Barnett III, Phil Miller, Steve Erwin, Keith Williams, and Dave Hoover

CAPSTONE PRESS
a capstone imprint

Published by Capstone Press, an imprint of Capstone
1710 Roe Crest Drive, North Mankato, Minnesota 56003
capstonepub.com

Library of Congress Cataloging-in-Publication Data is available
on the Library of Congress website.

ISBN: 9781666315325 (paperback)

Summary: Eight true–life tragedies jump off the page in this dynamic collection
of graphic novels. Included are the Donner Party, Shackleton's lost Antarctic
Expedition, the Apollo 13 mission, the space shuttle Challenger explosion,
the Great Chicago Fire, the Triangle Shirtwaist Factory fire, the Hindenburg
disaster, and the attack on Pearl Harbor.

Designed by Heidi Thompson

Printed and bound in China. 5588

DISASTERS

IN HISTORY

A GRAPHIC NOVEL COLLECTION

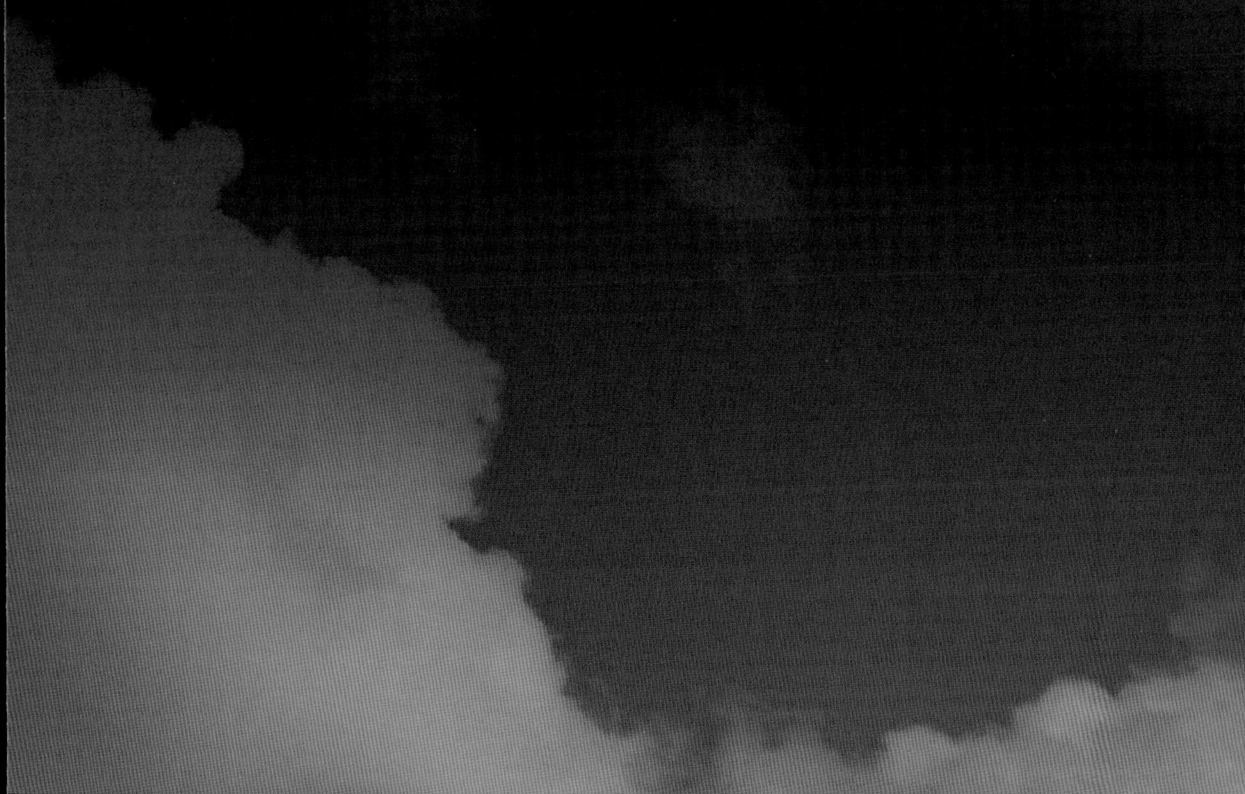

TABLE OF CONTENTS

PART 1

Throughout the book, direct quotations
are indicated by a yellow background.

PART 2

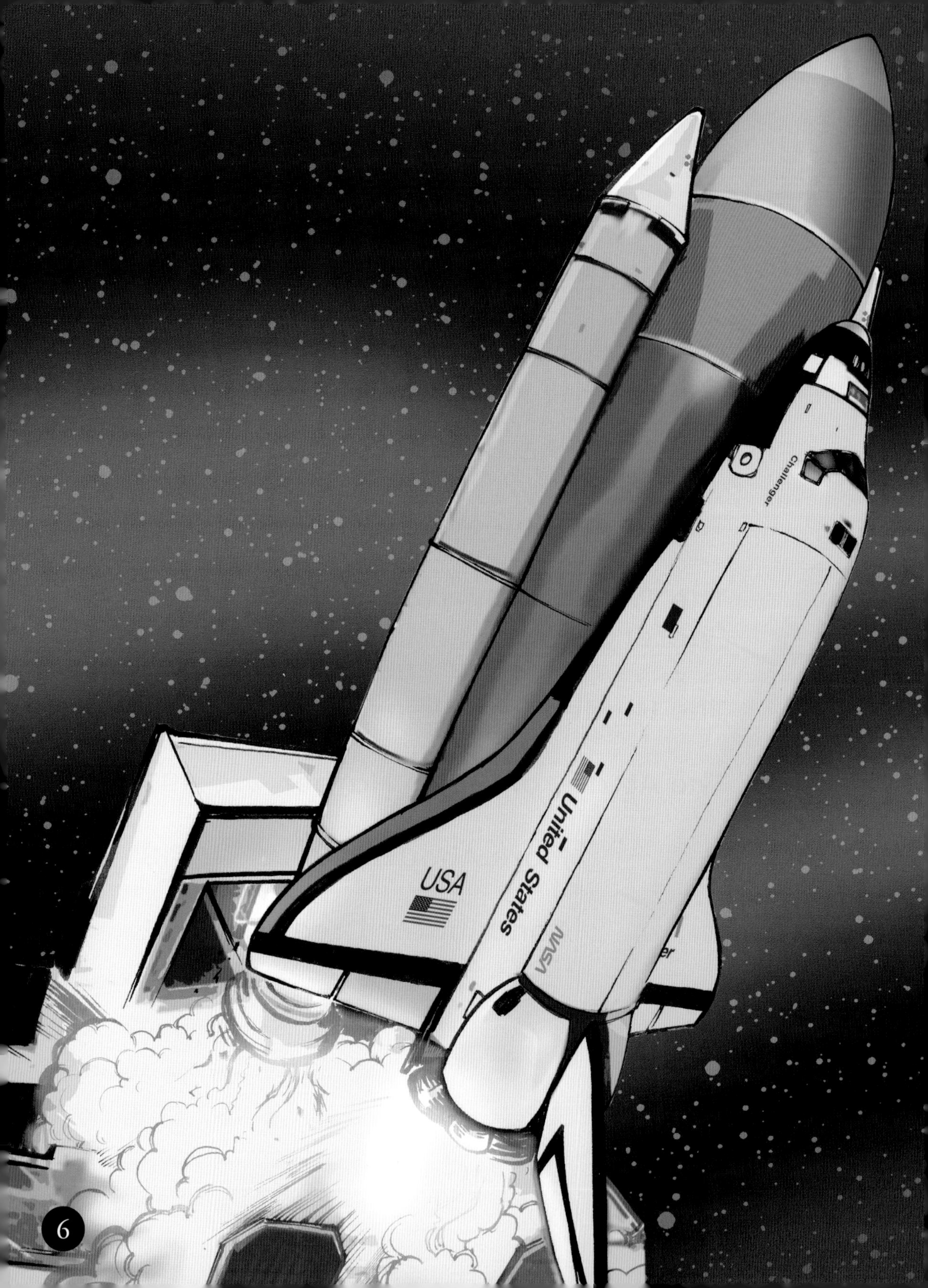
Challenger
USA
United States

PART 1
EXPLORATION & SPACE DISASTERS

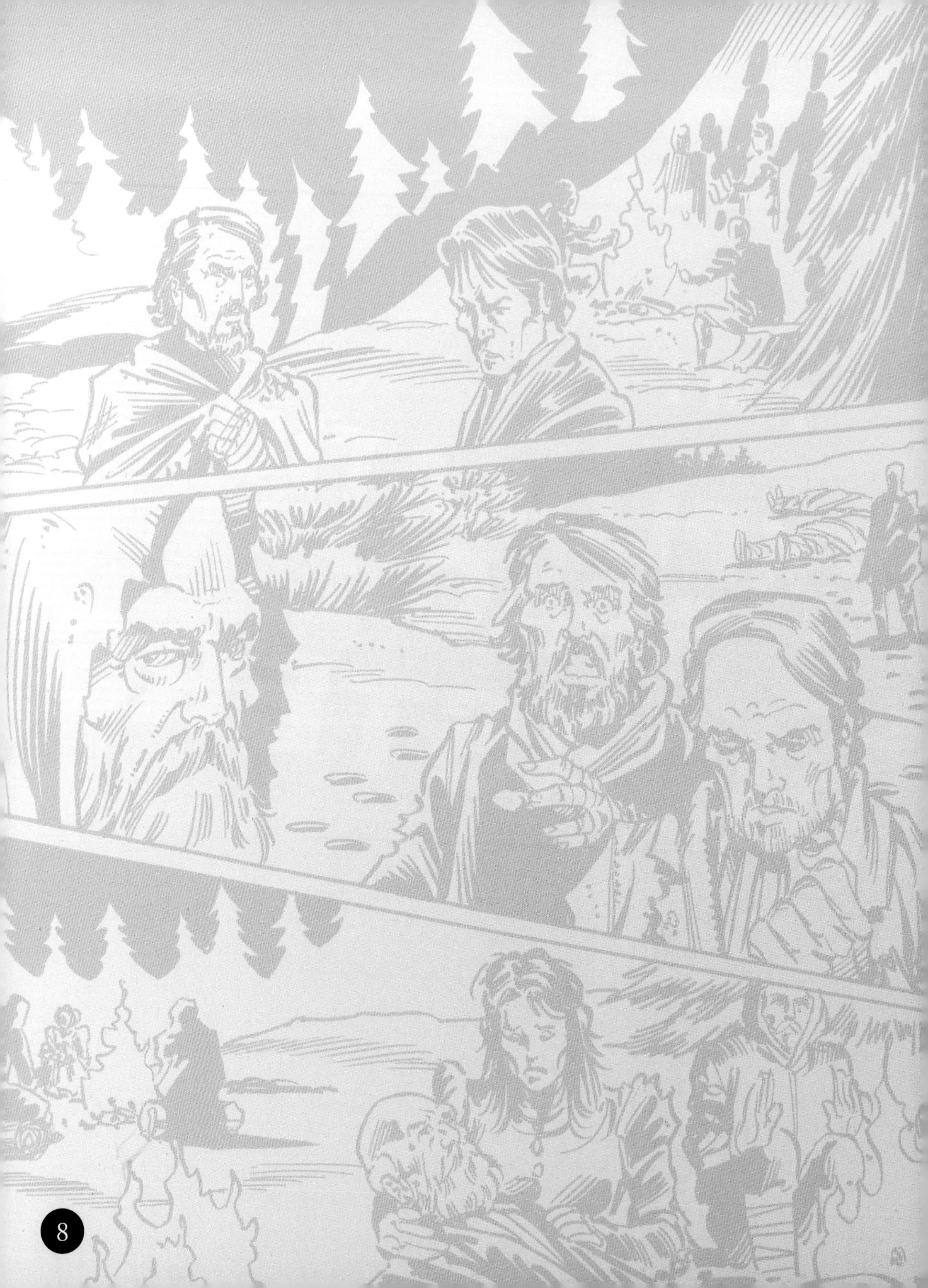

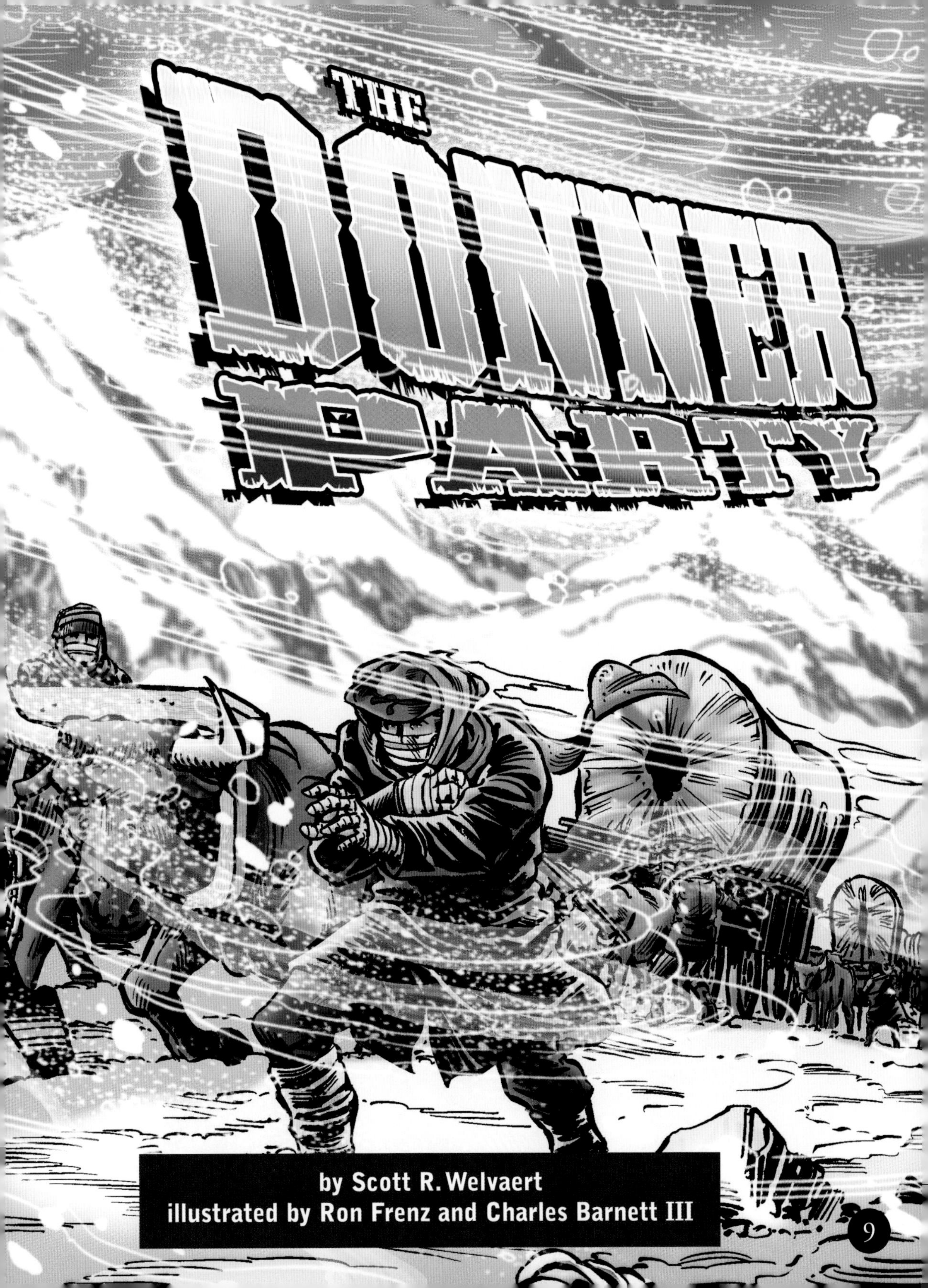
THE
DONNER
PARTY
by Scott R. Welvaert
illustrated by Ron Frenz and Charles Barnett III

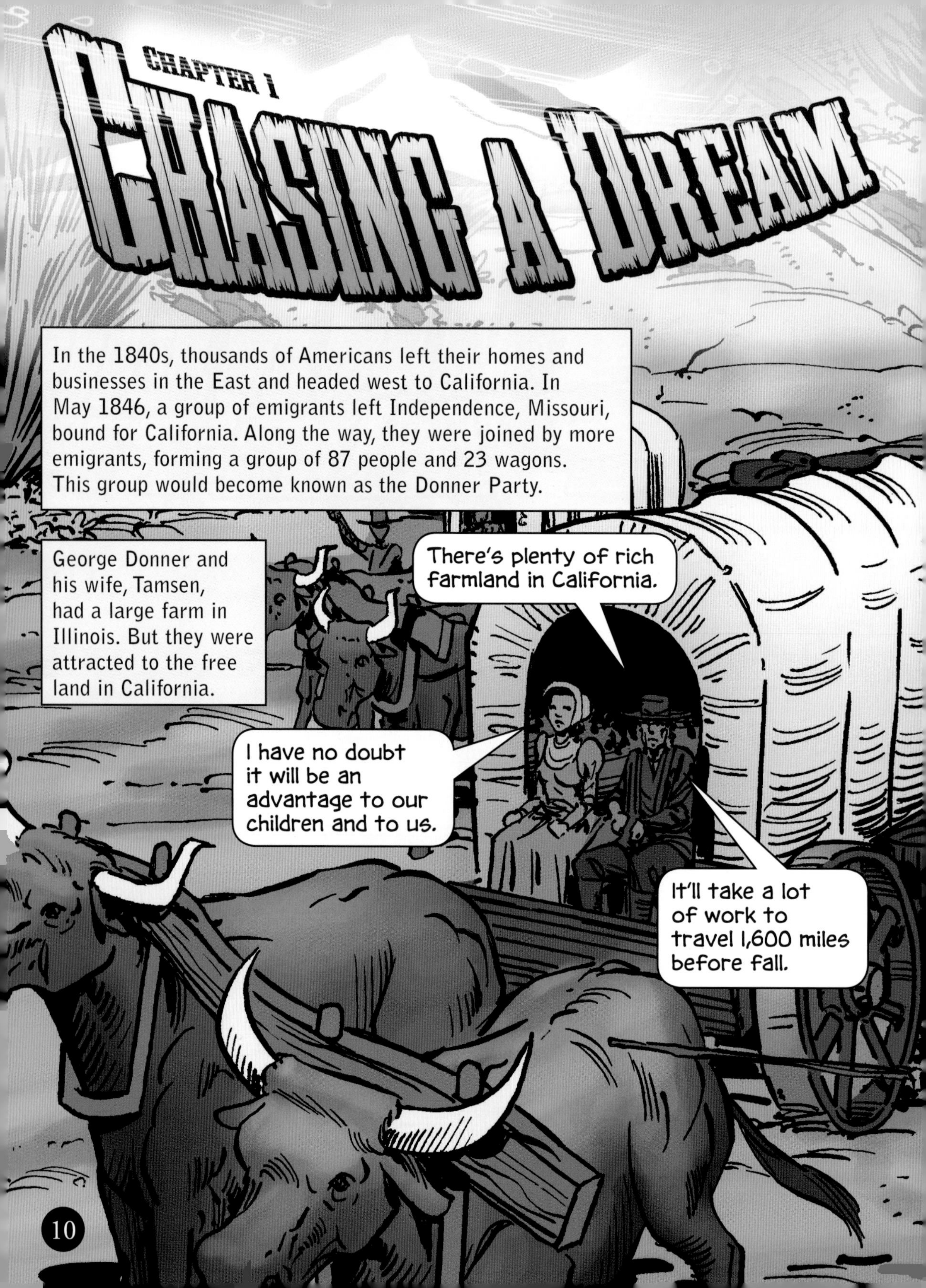
CHAPTER 1
CHASING A DREAM
In the 1840s, thousands of Americans left their homes and businesses in the East and headed west to California. In May 1846, a group of emigrants left Independence, Missouri, bound for California. Along the way, they were joined by more emigrants, forming a group of 87 people and 23 wagons. This group would become known as the Donner Party.
George Donner and his wife, Tamsen, had a large farm in Illinois. But they were attracted to the free land in California.
There's plenty of rich farmland in California.
I have no doubt it will be an advantage to our children and to us.
It'll take a lot of work to travel 1,600 miles before fall.

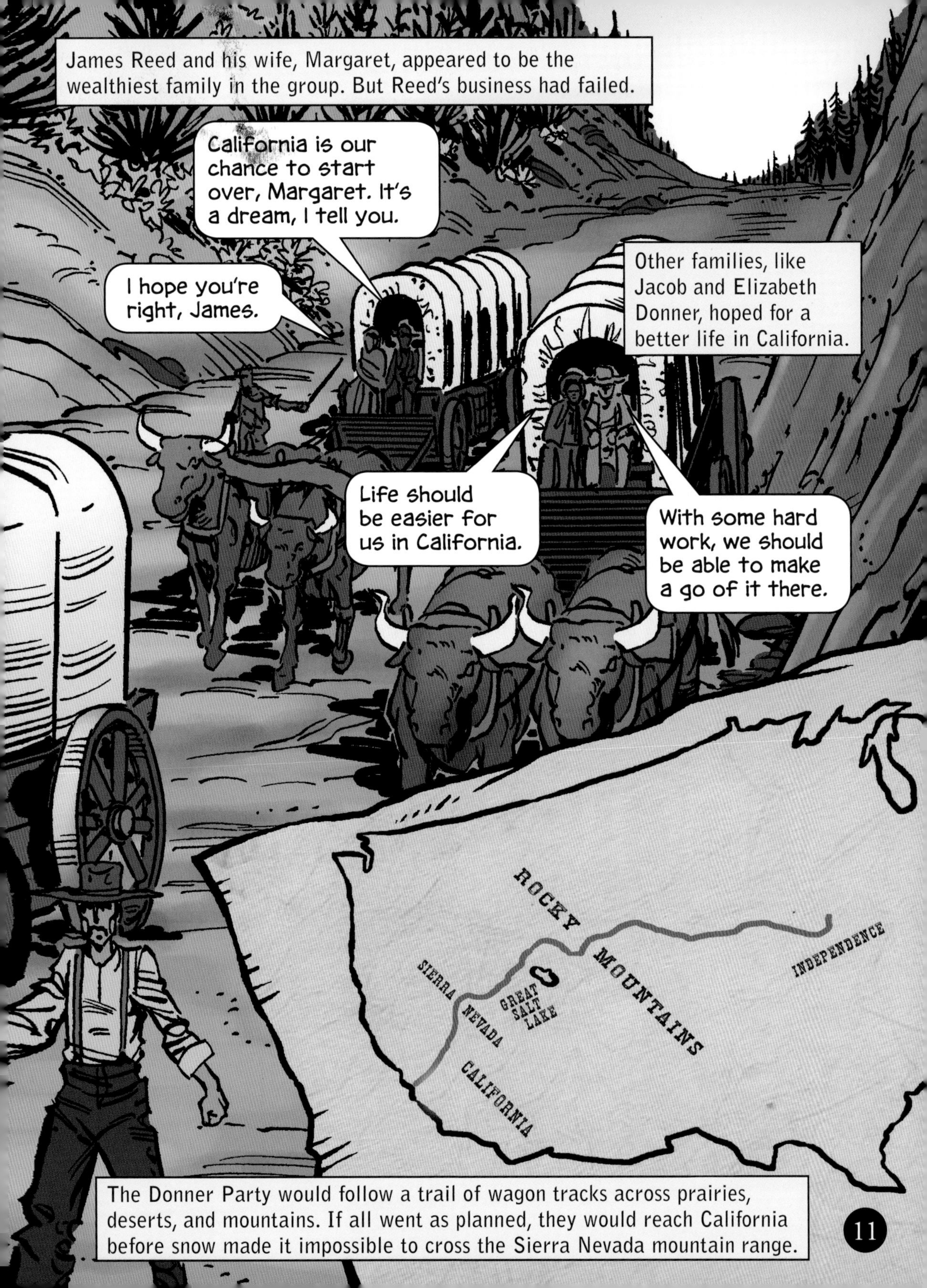
James Reed and his wife, Margaret, appeared to be the wealthiest family in the group. But Reed's business had failed.
California is our chance to start over, Margaret. It's a dream, I tell you.
I hope you're right, James.
Other families, like Jacob and Elizabeth Donner, hoped for a better life in California.
Life should be easier for us in California.
With some hard work, we should be able to make a go of it there.
ROCKY MOUNTAINS
INDEPENDENCE
SIERRA NEVADA
GREAT SALT LAKE
CALIFORNIA
The Donner Party would follow a trail of wagon tracks across prairies, deserts, and mountains. If all went as planned, they would reach California before snow made it impossible to cross the Sierra Nevada mountain range.

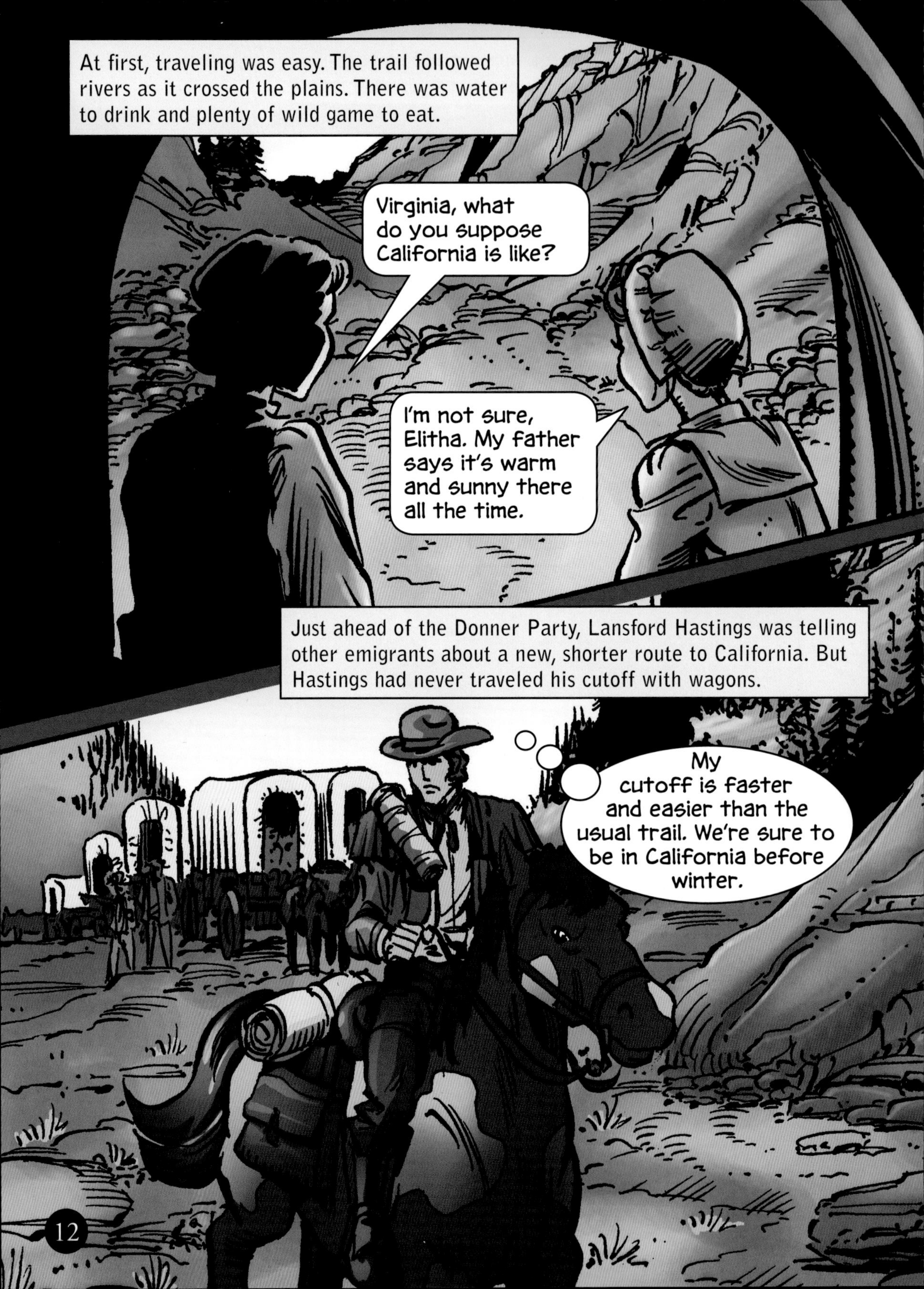
At first, traveling was easy. The trail followed rivers as it crossed the plains. There was water to drink and plenty of wild game to eat.
Virginia, what do you suppose California is like?
I'm not sure, Elitha. My father says it's warm and sunny there all the time.
Just ahead of the Donner Party, Lansford Hastings was telling other emigrants about a new, shorter route to California. But Hastings had never traveled his cutoff with wagons.
My cutoff is faster and easier than the usual trail. We're sure to be in California before winter.

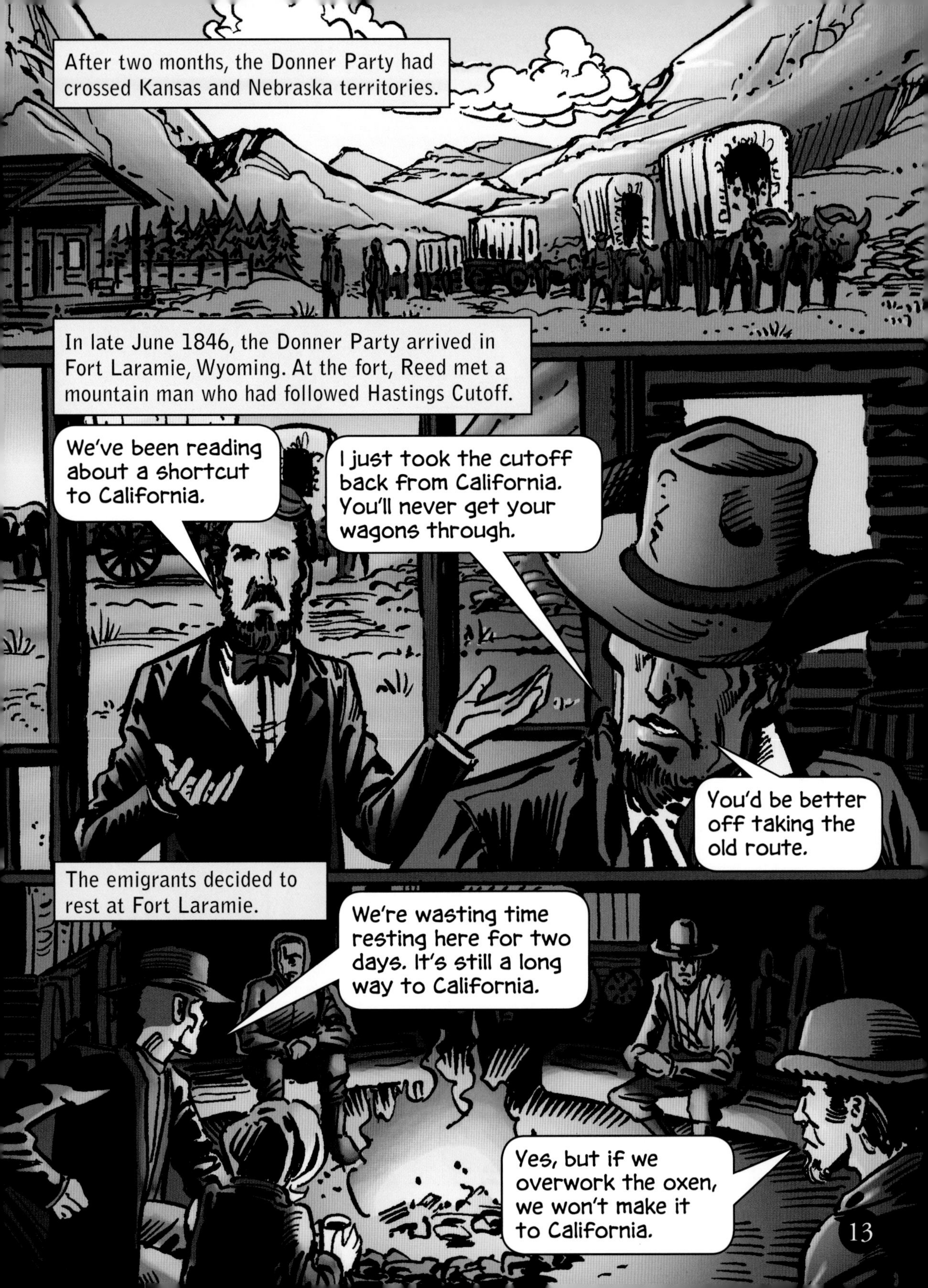
After two months, the Donner Party had crossed Kansas and Nebraska territories.
In late June 1846, the Donner Party arrived in Fort Laramie, Wyoming. At the fort, Reed met a mountain man who had followed Hastings Cutoff.
We've been reading about a shortcut to California.
I just took the cutoff back from California. You'll never get your wagons through.
You'd be better off taking the old route.
The emigrants decided to rest at Fort Laramie.
We're wasting time resting here for two days. It's still a long way to California.
Yes, but if we overwork the oxen, we won't make it to California.

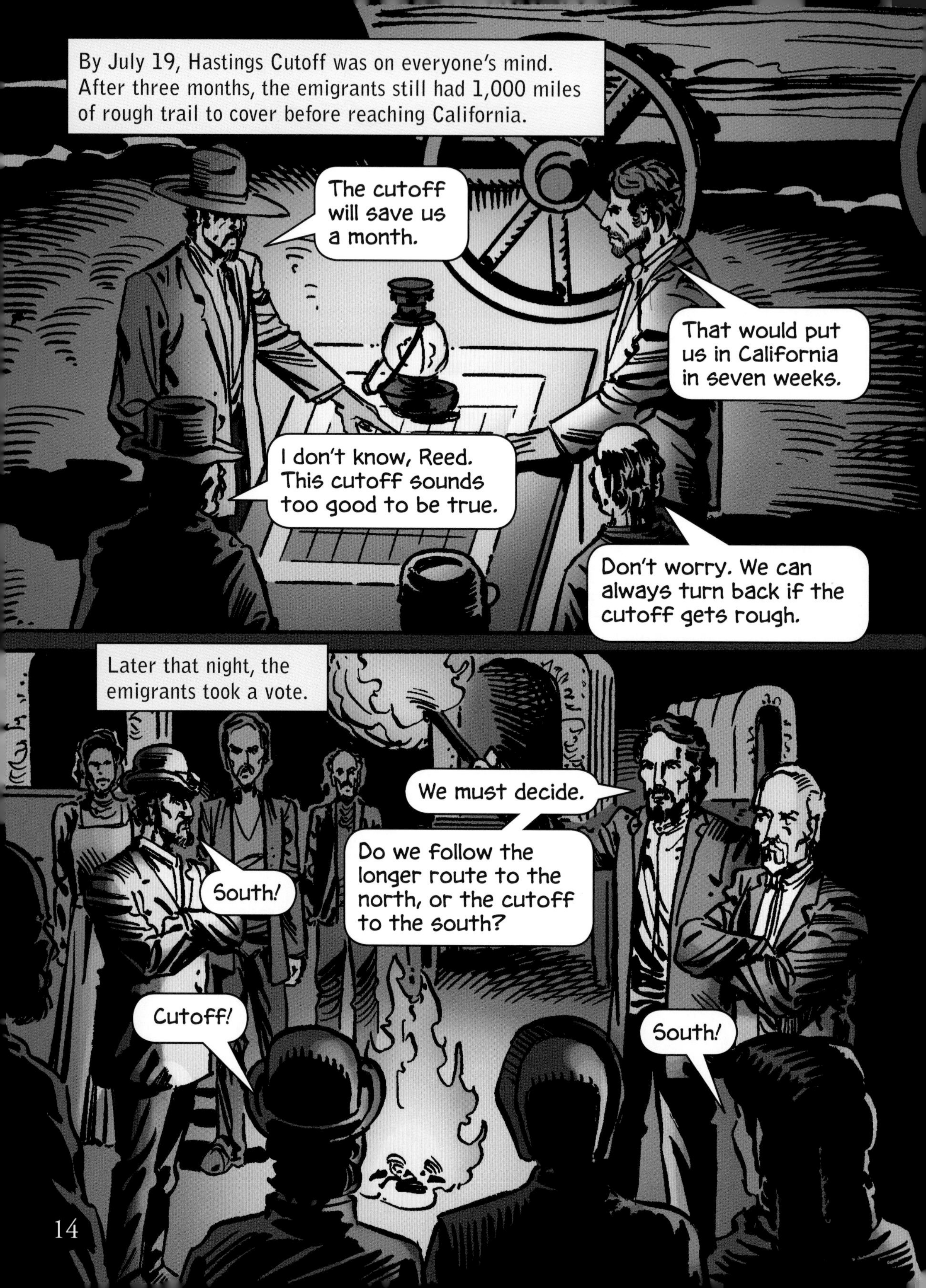

By July 19, Hastings Cutoff was on everyone's mind. After three months, the emigrants still had 1,000 miles of rough trail to cover before reaching California.
The cutoff will save us a month.
That would put us in California in seven weeks.
I don't know, Reed. This cutoff sounds too good to be true.
Don't worry. We can always turn back if the cutoff gets rough.
Later that night, the emigrants took a vote.
We must decide.
Do we follow the longer route to the north, or the cutoff to the south?
South!
Cutoff!
South!

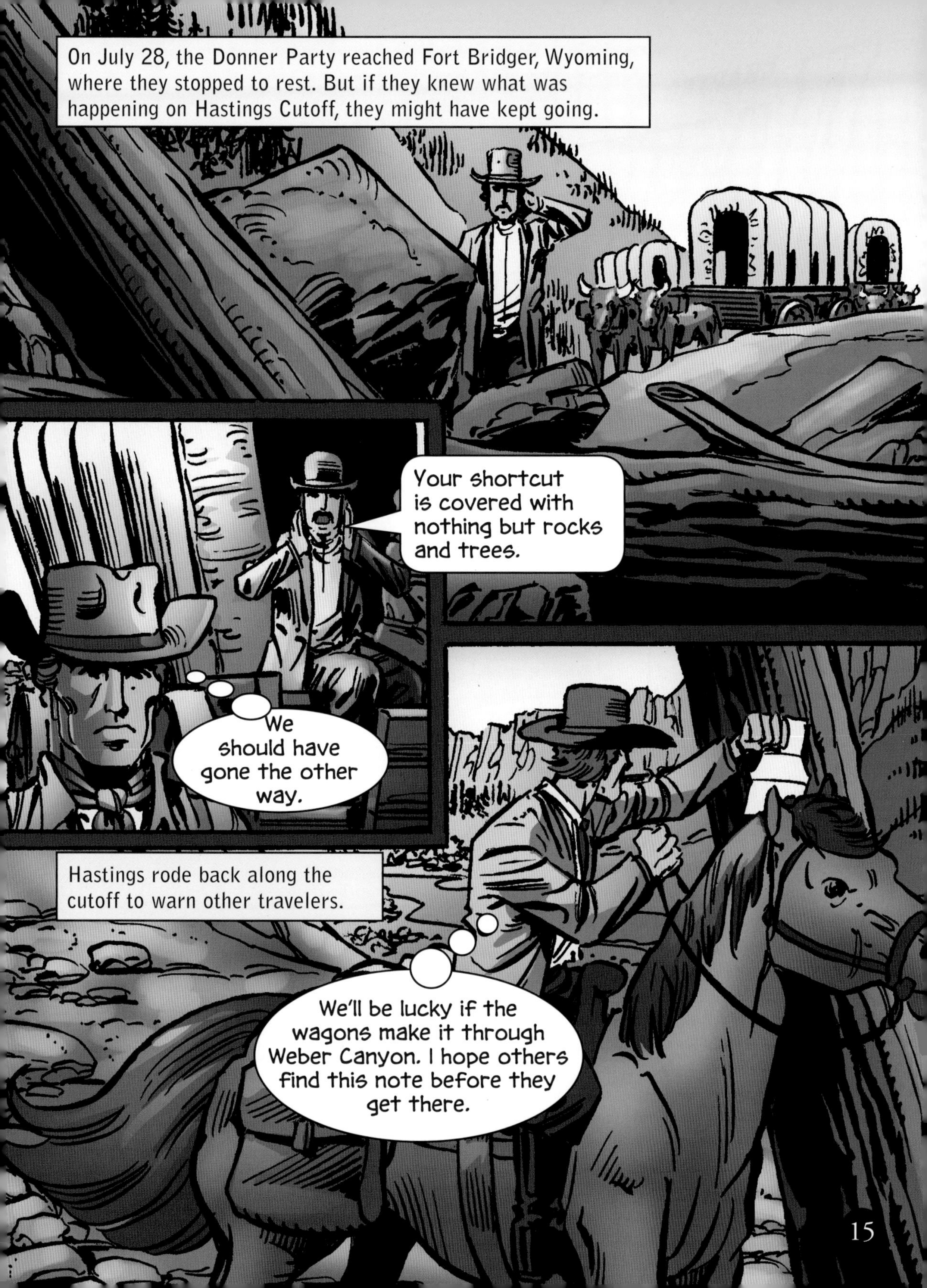
On July 28, the Donner Party reached Fort Bridger, Wyoming, where they stopped to rest. But if they knew what was happening on Hastings Cutoff, they might have kept going.
Your shortcut is covered with nothing but rocks and trees.
We should have gone the other way.
Hastings rode back along the cutoff to warn other travelers.
We'll be lucky if the wagons make it through Weber Canyon. I hope others find this note before they get there.

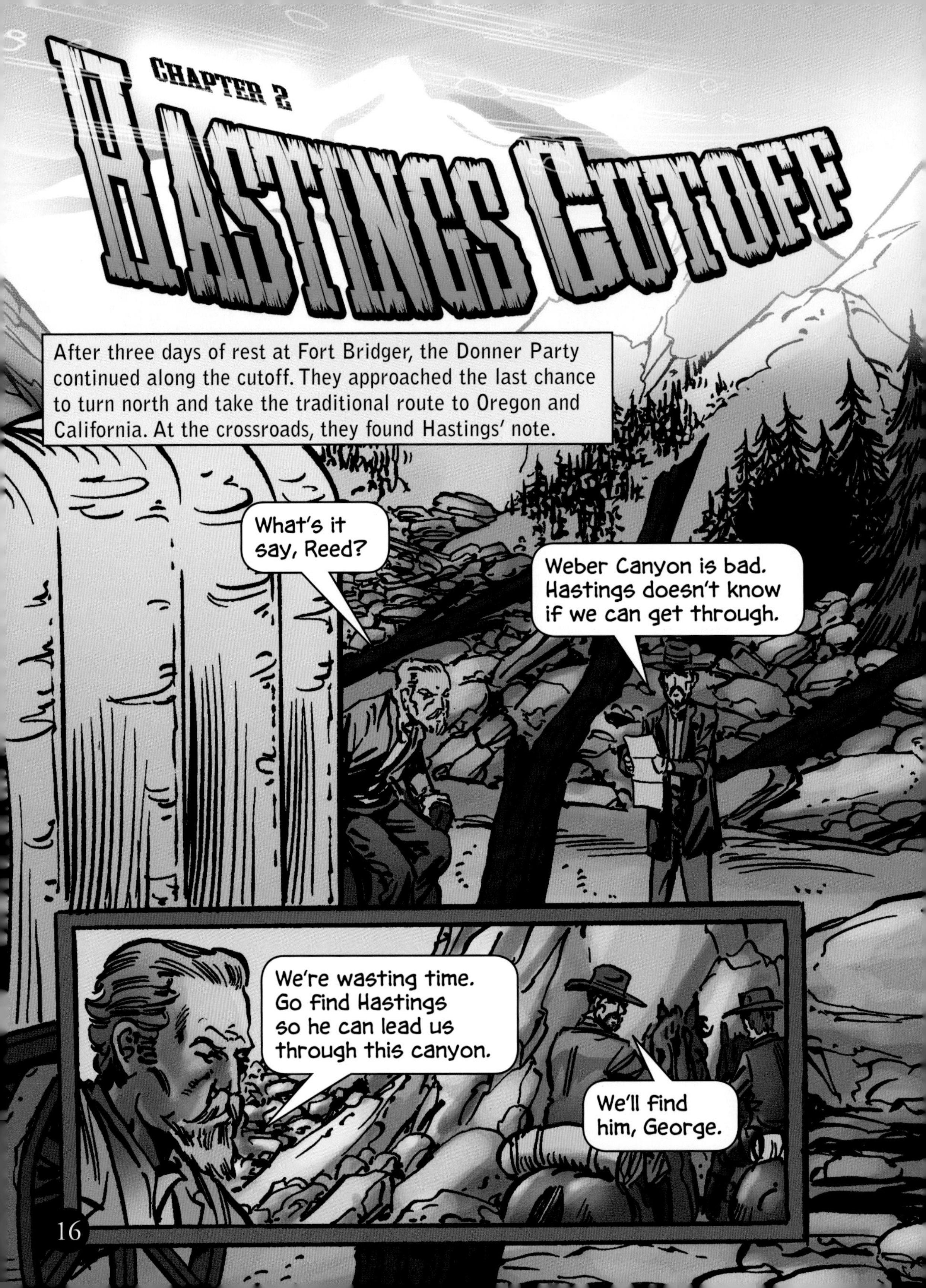
CHAPTER 2
HASTINGS CUTOFF
After three days of rest at Fort Bridger, the Donner Party continued along the cutoff. They approached the last chance to turn north and take the traditional route to Oregon and California. At the crossroads, they found Hastings' note.
What's it say, Reed?
Weber Canyon is bad. Hastings doesn't know if we can get through.
We're wasting time. Go find Hastings so he can lead us through this canyon.
We'll find him, George.

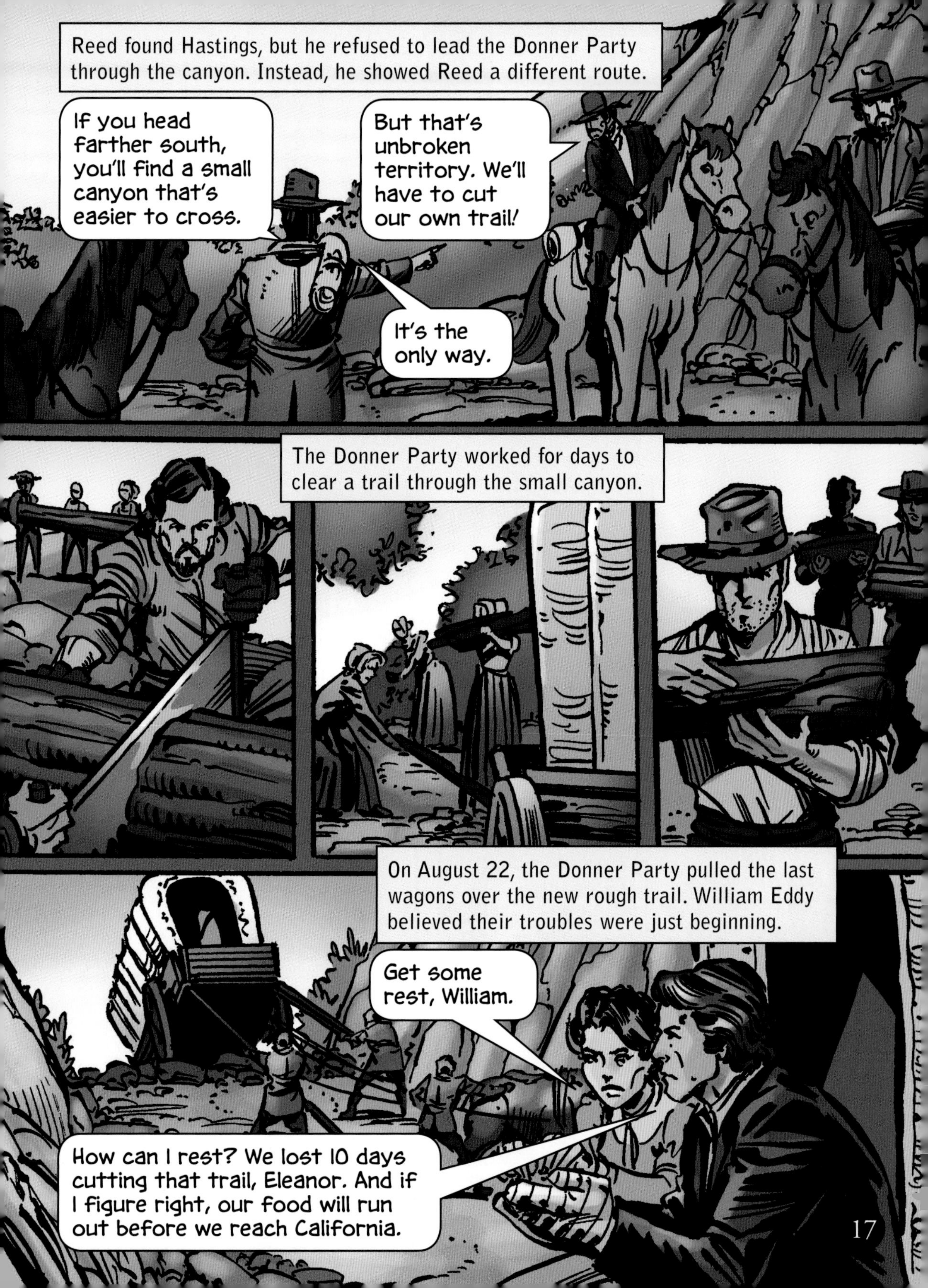
Reed found Hastings, but he refused to lead the Donner Party through the canyon. Instead, he showed Reed a different route.
If you head farther south, you'll find a small canyon that's easier to cross.
But that's unbroken territory. We'll have to cut our own trail!
It's the only way.
The Donner Party worked for days to clear a trail through the small canyon.
On August 22, the Donner Party pulled the last wagons over the new rough trail. William Eddy believed their troubles were just beginning.
Get some rest, William.
How can I rest? We lost 10 days cutting that trail, Eleanor. And if I figure right, our food will run out before we reach California.

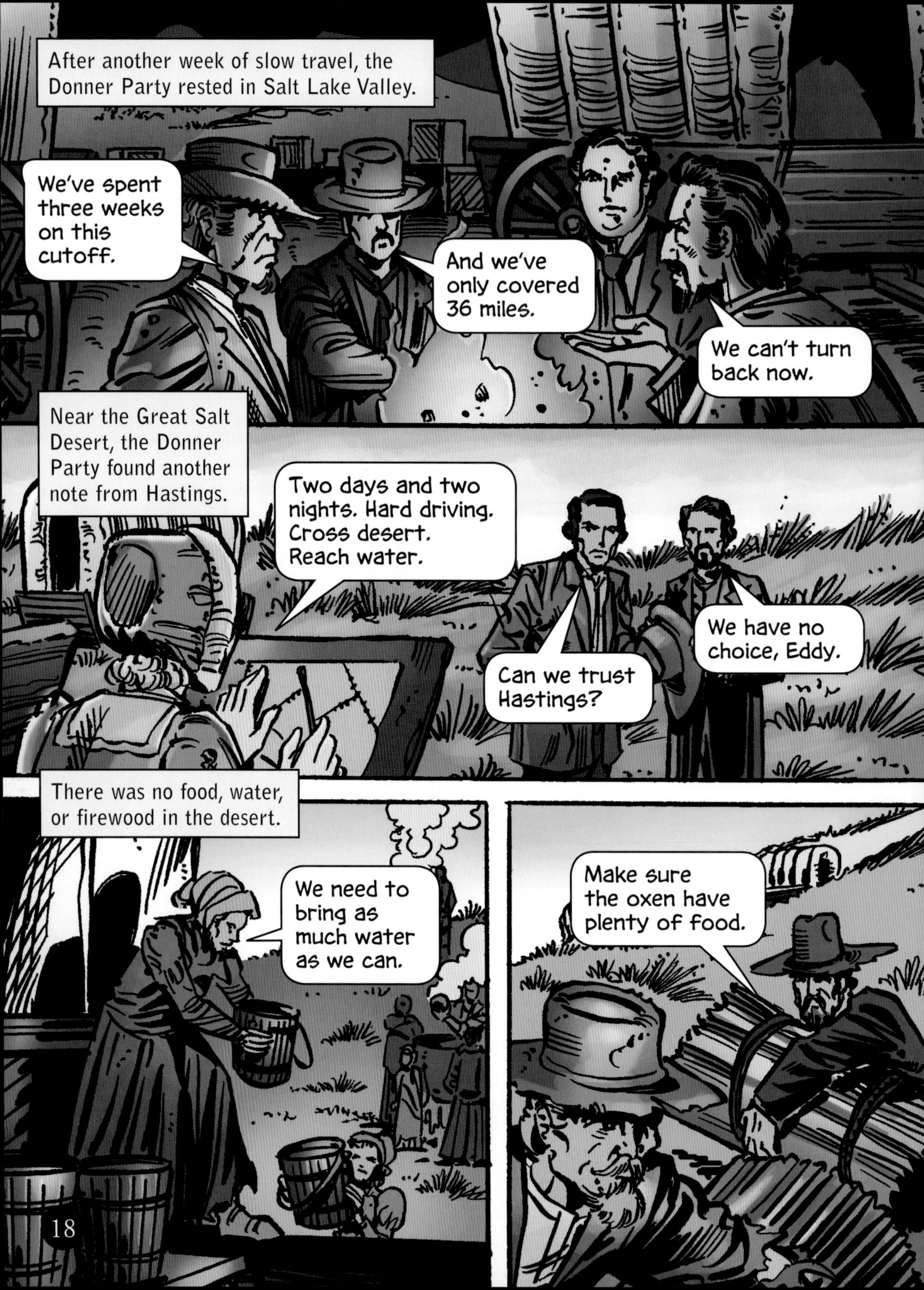
After another week of slow travel, the Donner Party rested in Salt Lake Valley.
We've spent three weeks on this cutoff.
And we've only covered 36 miles.
We can't turn back now.
Near the Great Salt Desert, the Donner Party found another note from Hastings.
Two days and two nights. Hard driving. Cross desert. Reach water.
Can we trust Hastings?
We have no choice, Eddy.
There was no food, water, or firewood in the desert.
We need to bring as much water as we can.
Make sure the oxen have plenty of food.

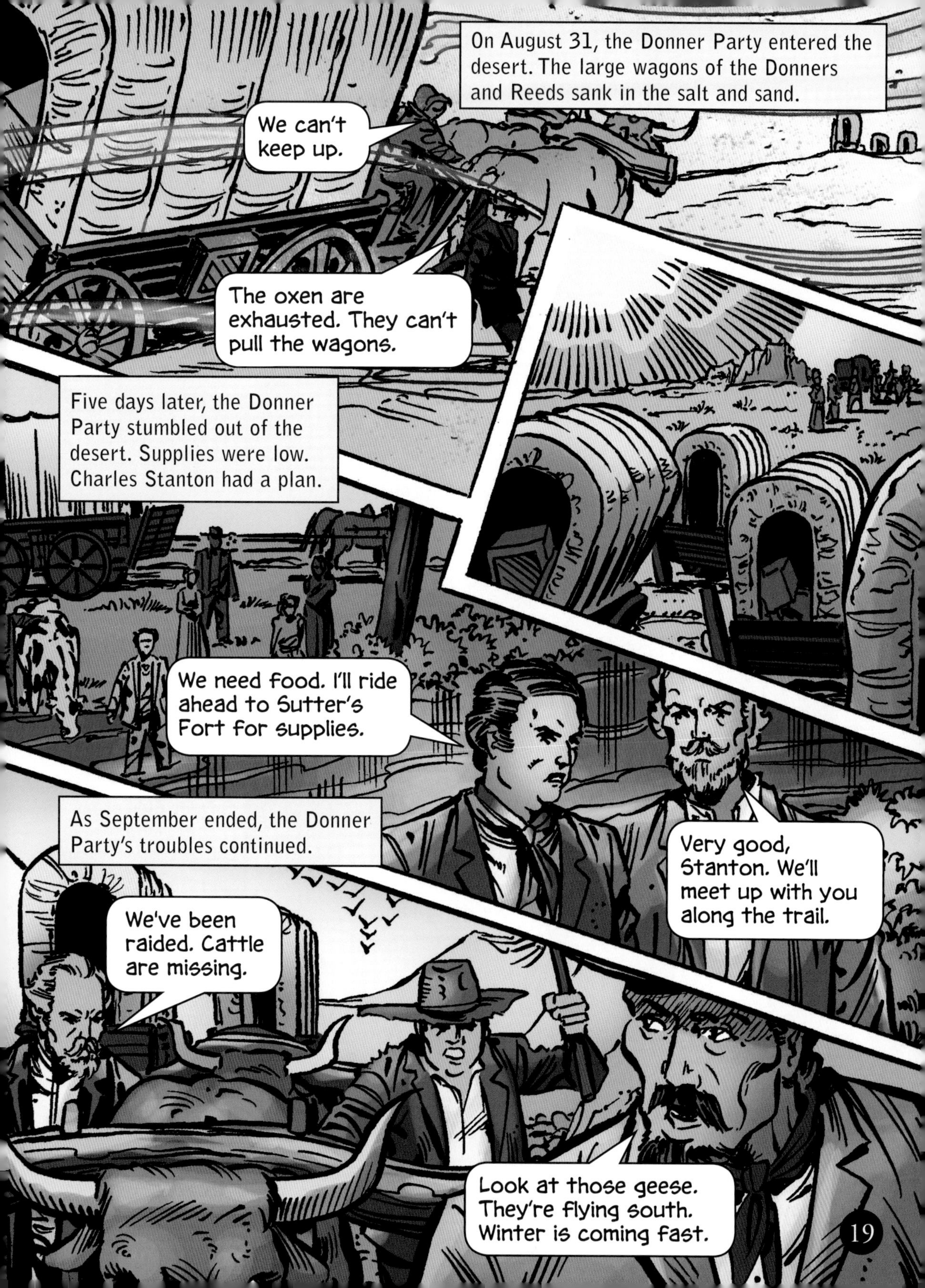
On August 31, the Donner Party entered the desert. The large wagons of the Donners and Reeds sank in the salt and sand.
We can't keep up.
The oxen are exhausted. They can't pull the wagons.
Five days later, the Donner Party stumbled out of the desert. Supplies were low. Charles Stanton had a plan.
We need food. I'll ride ahead to Sutter's Fort for supplies.
Very good, Stanton. We'll meet up with you along the trail.
As September ended, the Donner Party's troubles continued.
We've been raided. Cattle are missing.
Look at those geese. They're flying south. Winter is coming fast.

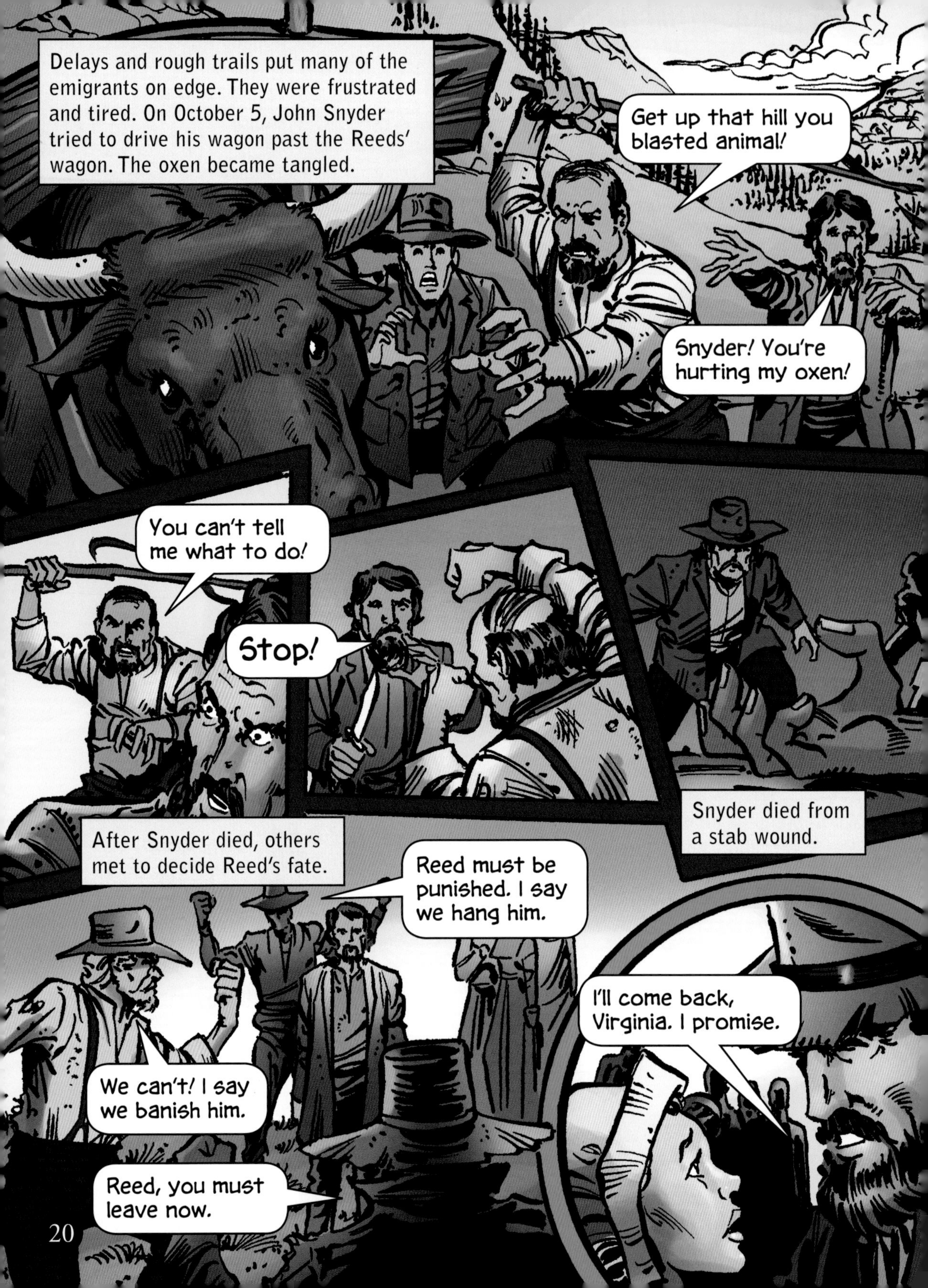

Delays and rough trails put many of the emigrants on edge. They were frustrated and tired. On October 5, John Snyder tried to drive his wagon past the Reeds' wagon. The oxen became tangled.
Get up that hill you blasted animal!
Snyder! You're hurting my oxen!
You can't tell me what to do!
Stop!
Snyder died from a stab wound.
After Snyder died, others met to decide Reed's fate.
Reed must be punished. I say we hang him.
We can't! I say we banish him.
Reed, you must leave now.
I'll come back, Virginia. I promise.

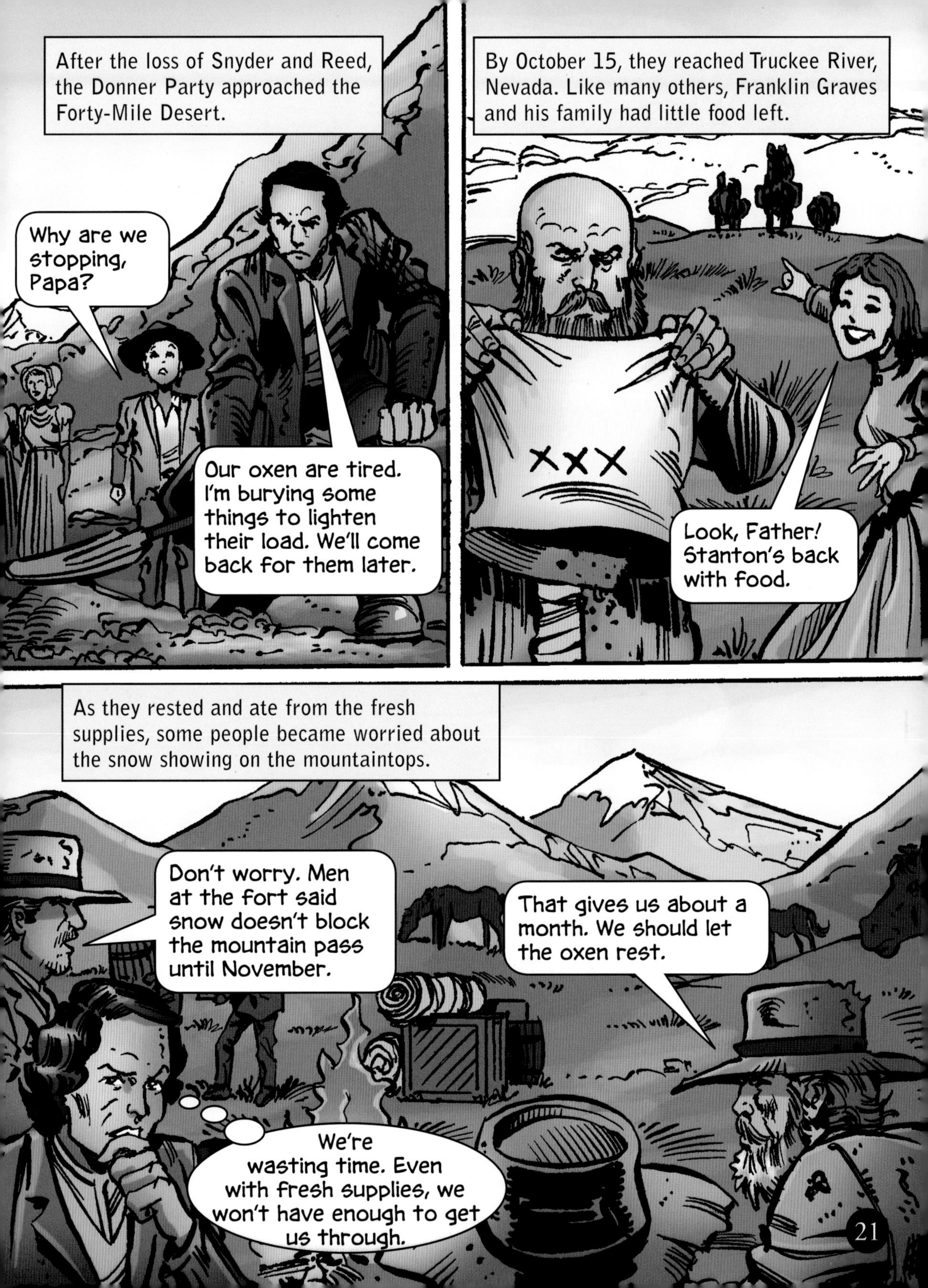
After the loss of Snyder and Reed, the Donner Party approached the Forty-Mile Desert.
Why are we stopping, Papa?
Our oxen are tired. I'm burying some things to lighten their load. We'll come back for them later.
By October 15, they reached Truckee River, Nevada. Like many others, Franklin Graves and his family had little food left.
XXX
Look, Father! Stanton's back with food.
As they rested and ate from the fresh supplies, some people became worried about the snow showing on the mountaintops.
Don't worry. Men at the fort said snow doesn't block the mountain pass until November.
That gives us about a month. We should let the oxen rest.
We're wasting time. Even with fresh supplies, we won't have enough to get us through.

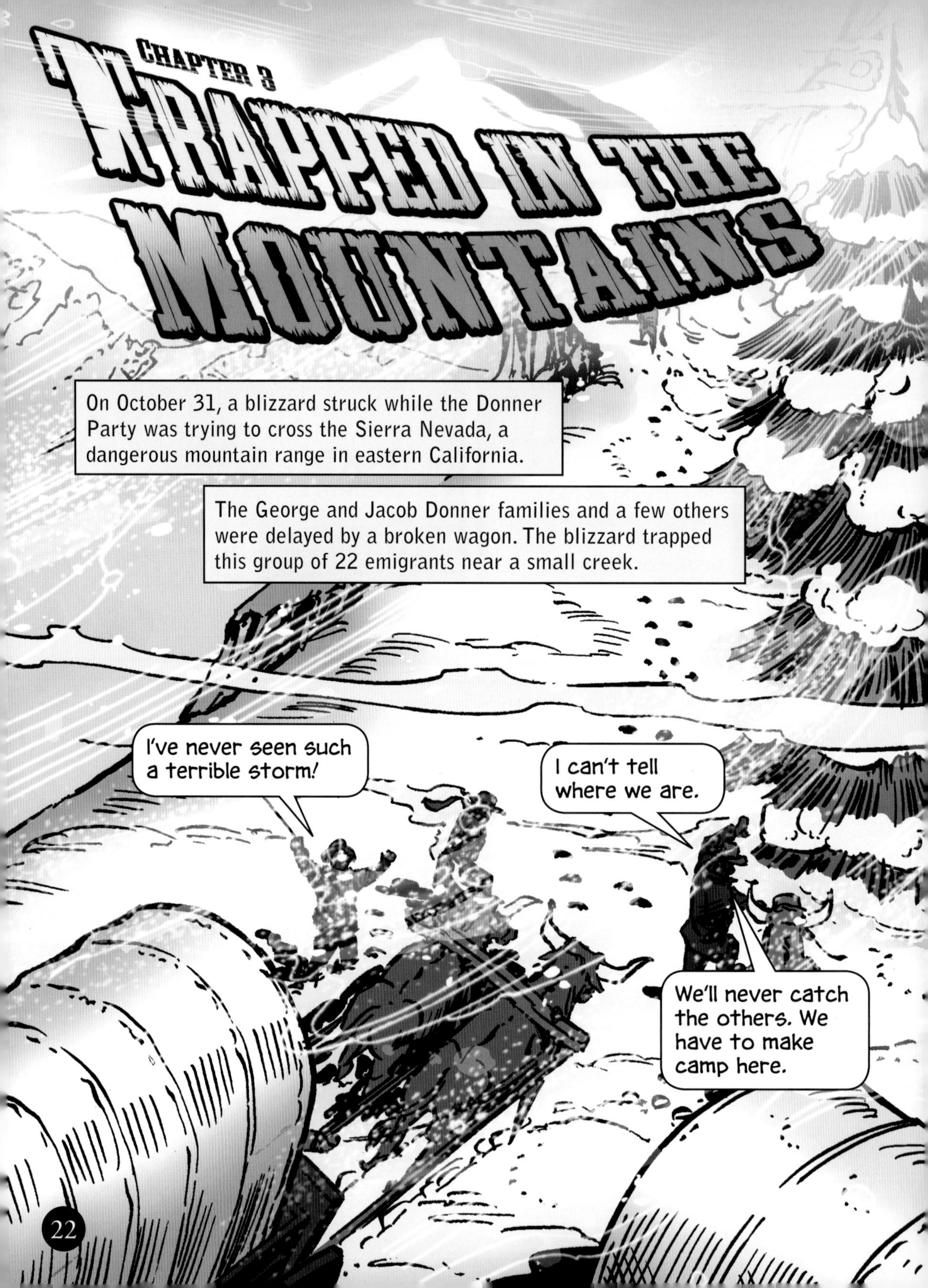
CHAPTER 3
TRAPPED IN THE MOUNTAINS
On October 31, a blizzard struck while the Donner Party was trying to cross the Sierra Nevada, a dangerous mountain range in eastern California.
The George and Jacob Donner families and a few others were delayed by a broken wagon. The blizzard trapped this group of 22 emigrants near a small creek.
I've never seen such a terrible storm!
I can't tell where we are.
We'll never catch the others. We have to make camp here.

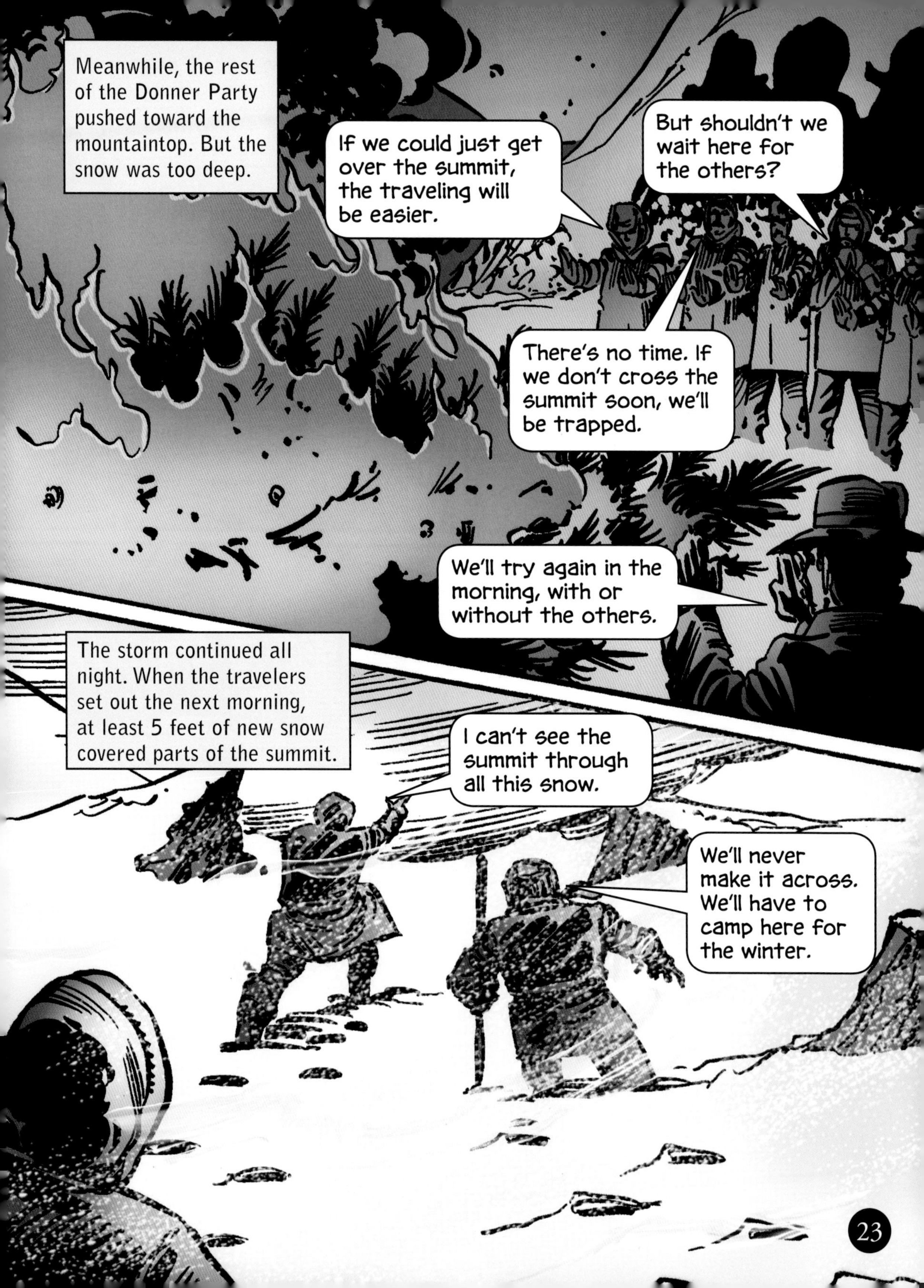
Meanwhile, the rest of the Donner Party pushed toward the mountaintop. But the snow was too deep.
If we could just get over the summit, the traveling will be easier.
But shouldn't we wait here for the others?
There's no time. If we don't cross the summit soon, we'll be trapped.
We'll try again in the morning, with or without the others.
The storm continued all night. When the travelers set out the next morning, at least 5 feet of new snow covered parts of the summit.
I can't see the summit through all this snow.
We'll never make it across. We'll have to camp here for the winter.

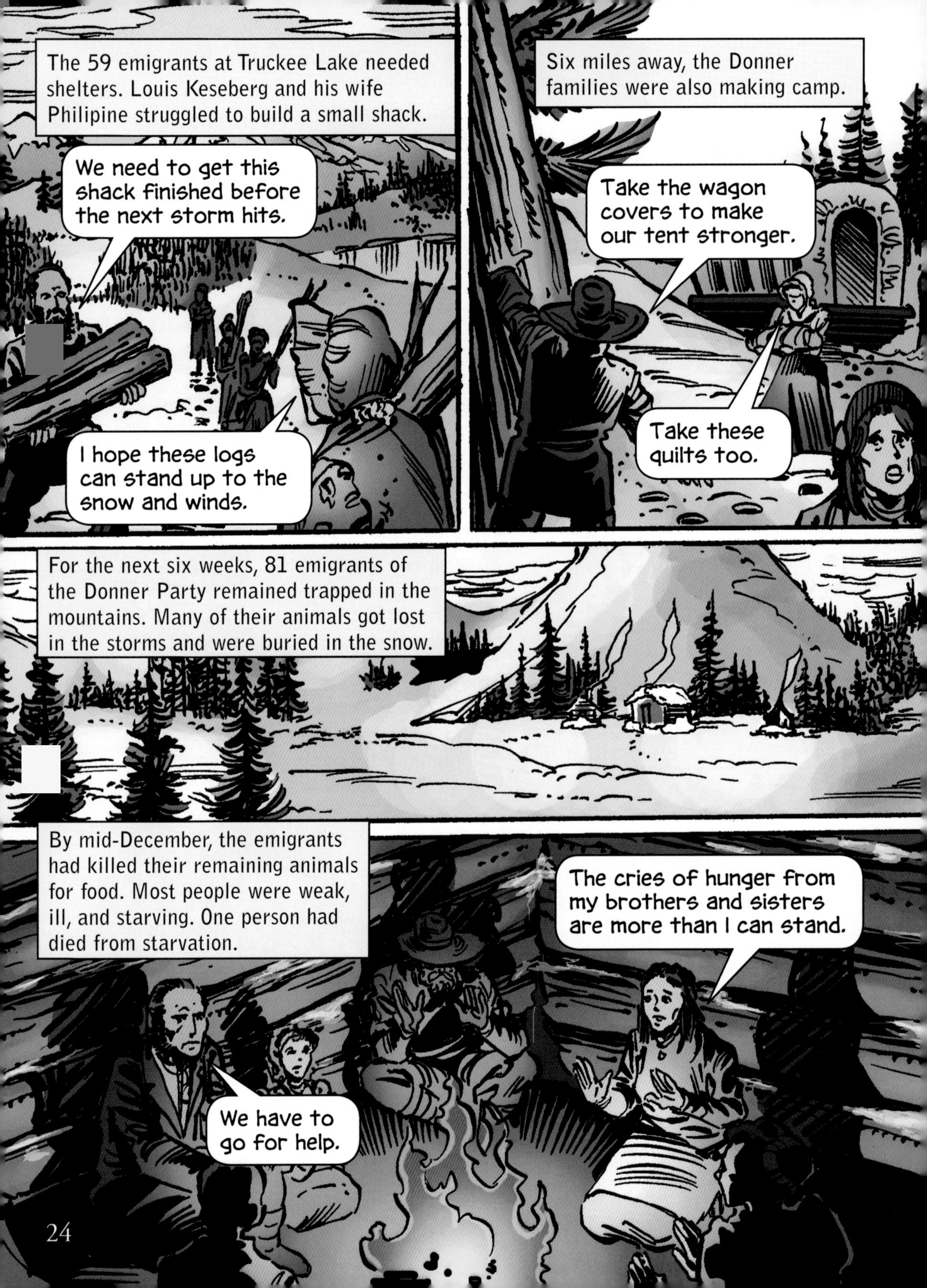
The 59 emigrants at Truckee Lake needed shelters. Louis Keseberg and his wife Philipine struggled to build a small shack.
We need to get this shack finished before the next storm hits.
I hope these logs can stand up to the snow and winds.
Six miles away, the Donner families were also making camp.
Take the wagon covers to make our tent stronger.
Take these quilts too.
For the next six weeks, 81 emigrants of the Donner Party remained trapped in the mountains. Many of their animals got lost in the storms and were buried in the snow.
By mid-December, the emigrants had killed their remaining animals for food. Most people were weak, ill, and starving. One person had died from starvation.
The cries of hunger from my brothers and sisters are more than I can stand.
We have to go for help.

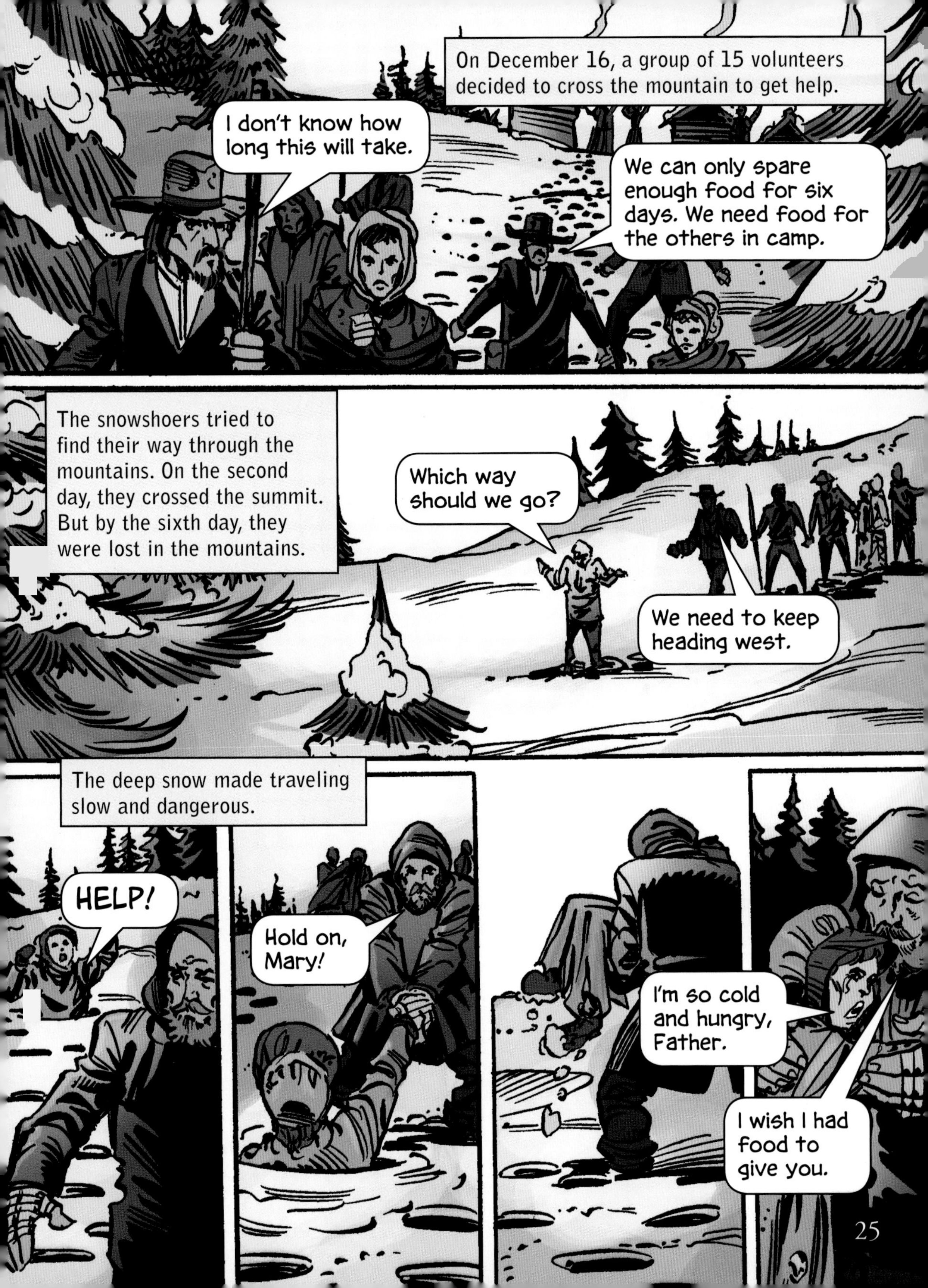
On December 16, a group of 15 volunteers decided to cross the mountain to get help.
I don't know how long this will take.
We can only spare enough food for six days. We need food for the others in camp.
The snowshoers tried to find their way through the mountains. On the second day, they crossed the summit. But by the sixth day, they were lost in the mountains.
Which way should we go?
We need to keep heading west.
The deep snow made traveling slow and dangerous.
HELP!
Hold on, Mary!
I'm so cold and hungry, Father.
I wish I had food to give you.

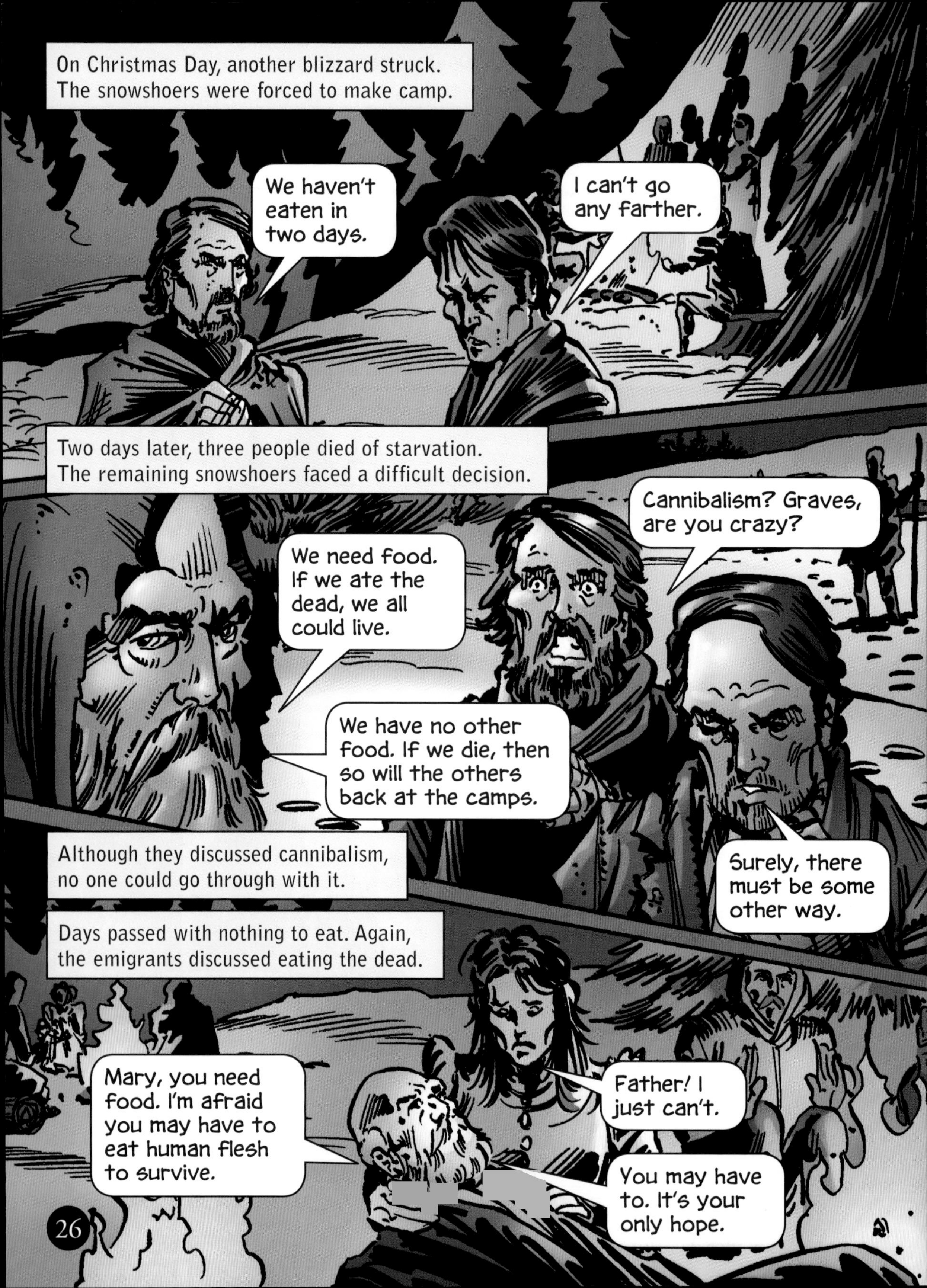

On Christmas Day, another blizzard struck. The snowshoers were forced to make camp.
We haven't eaten in two days.
I can't go any farther.
Two days later, three people died of starvation. The remaining snowshoers faced a difficult decision.
We need food. If we ate the dead, we all could live.
Cannibalism? Graves, are you crazy?
We have no other food. If we die, then so will the others back at the camps.
Surely, there must be some other way.
Although they discussed cannibalism, no one could go through with it.
Days passed with nothing to eat. Again, the emigrants discussed eating the dead.
Mary, you need food. I'm afraid you may have to eat human flesh to survive.
Father! I just can't.
You may have to. It's your only hope.

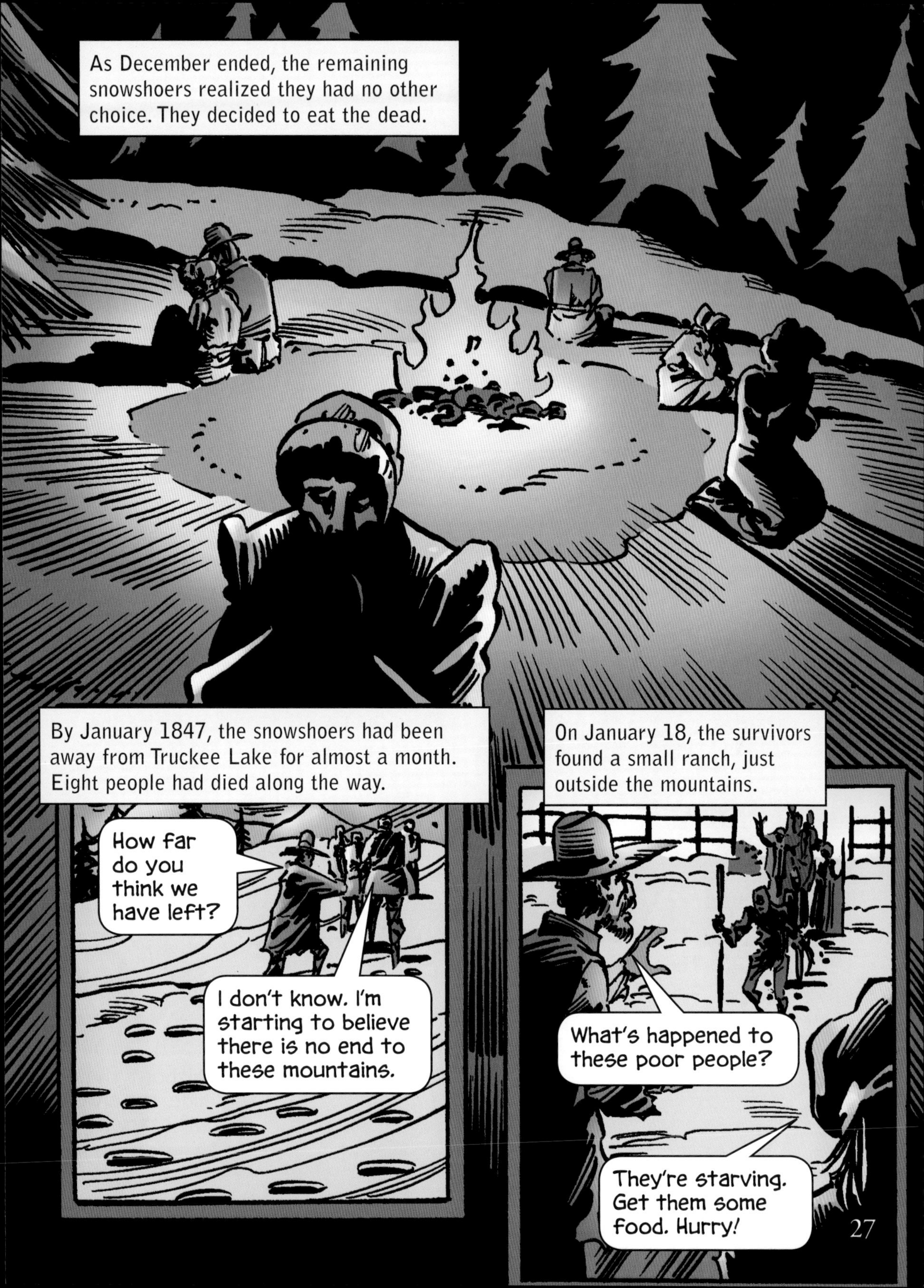

As December ended, the remaining snowshoers realized they had no other choice. They decided to eat the dead.
By January 1847, the snowshoers had been away from Truckee Lake for almost a month. Eight people had died along the way.
How far do you think we have left?
I don't know. I'm starting to believe there is no end to these mountains.
On January 18, the survivors found a small ranch, just outside the mountains.
What's happened to these poor people?
They're starving. Get them some food. Hurry!

CHAPTER 4
A LAST HOPE

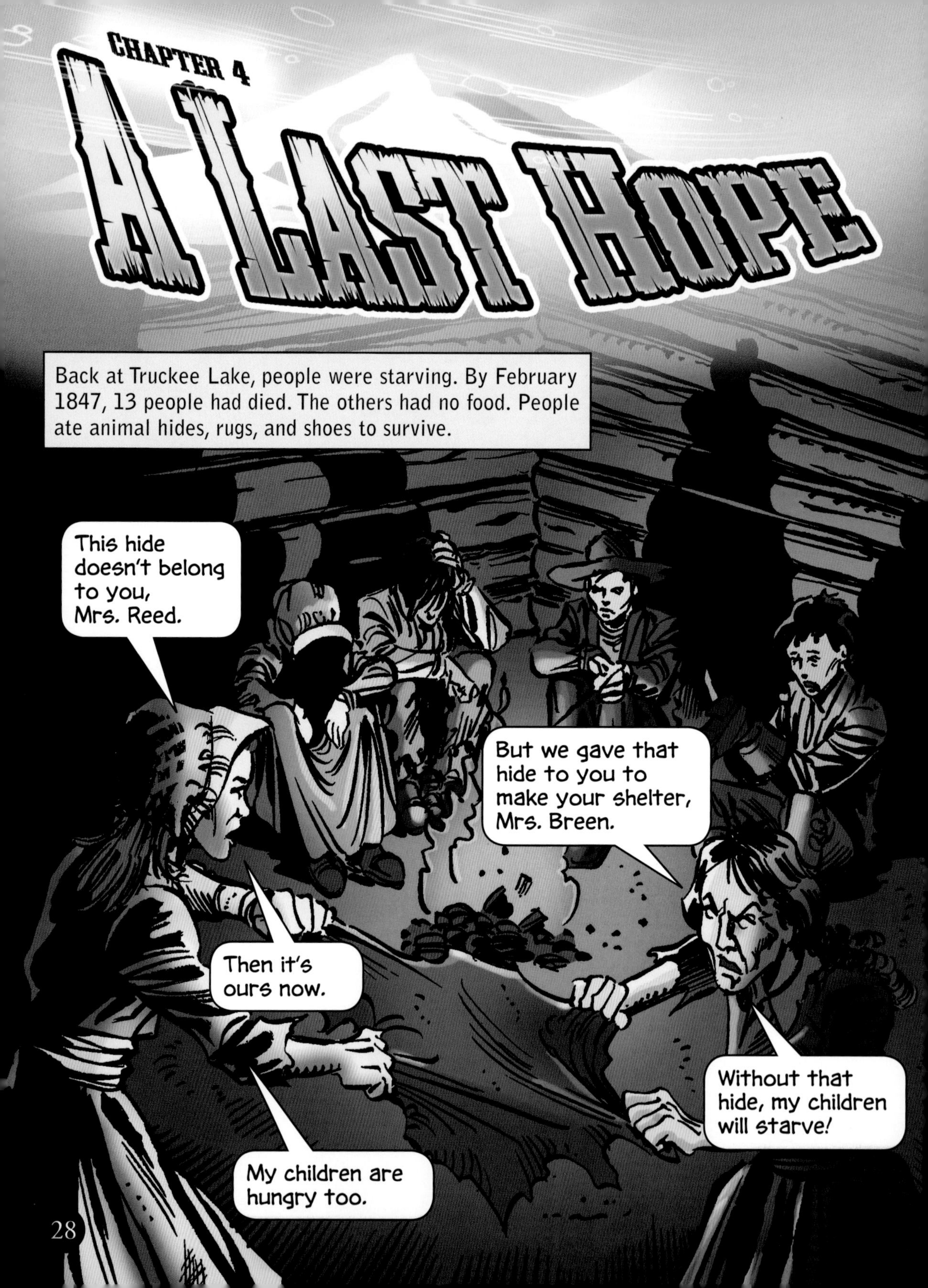

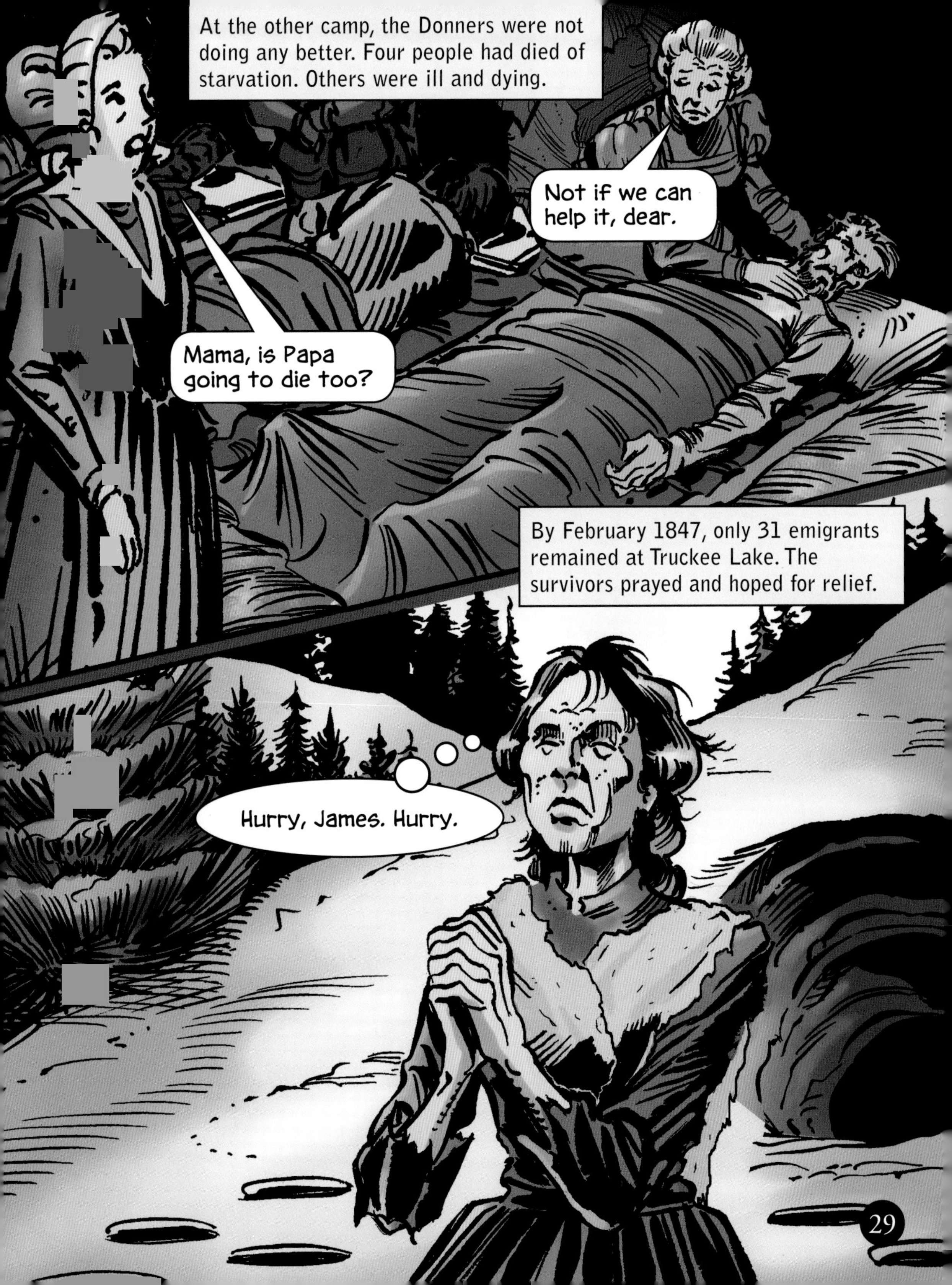
At the other camp, the Donners were not doing any better. Four people had died of starvation. Others were ill and dying.
Mama, is Papa going to die too?
Not if we can help it, dear.
By February 1847, only 31 emigrants remained at Truckee Lake. The survivors prayed and hoped for relief.
Hurry, James. Hurry.

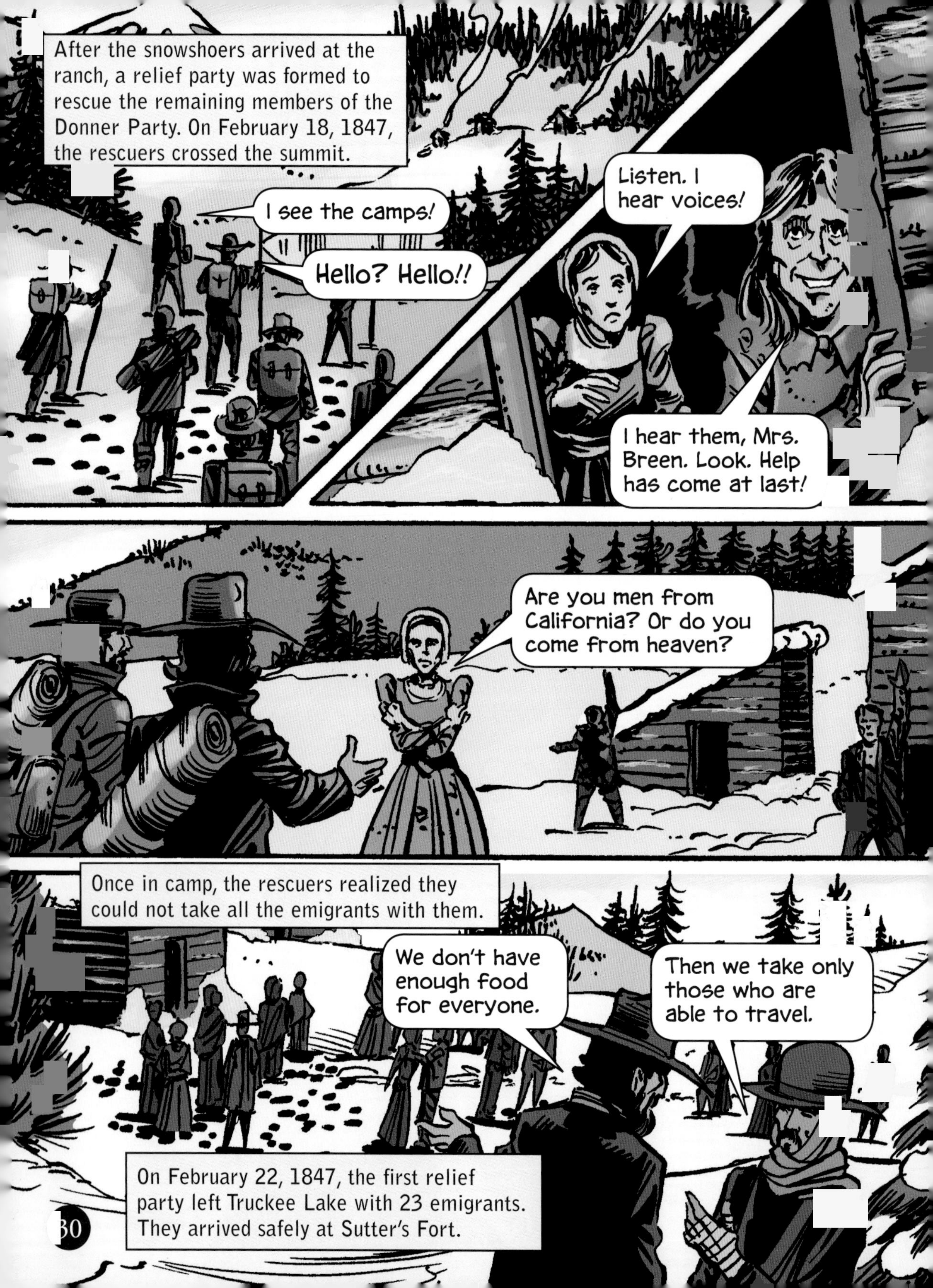
After the snowshoers arrived at the ranch, a relief party was formed to rescue the remaining members of the Donner Party. On February 18, 1847, the rescuers crossed the summit.
I see the camps!
Hello? Hello!!
Listen. I hear voices!
I hear them, Mrs. Breen. Look. Help has come at last!
Are you men from California? Or do you come from heaven?
Once in camp, the rescuers realized they could not take all the emigrants with them.
We don't have enough food for everyone.
Then we take only those who are able to travel.
On February 22, 1847, the first relief party left Truckee Lake with 23 emigrants. They arrived safely at Sutter's Fort.

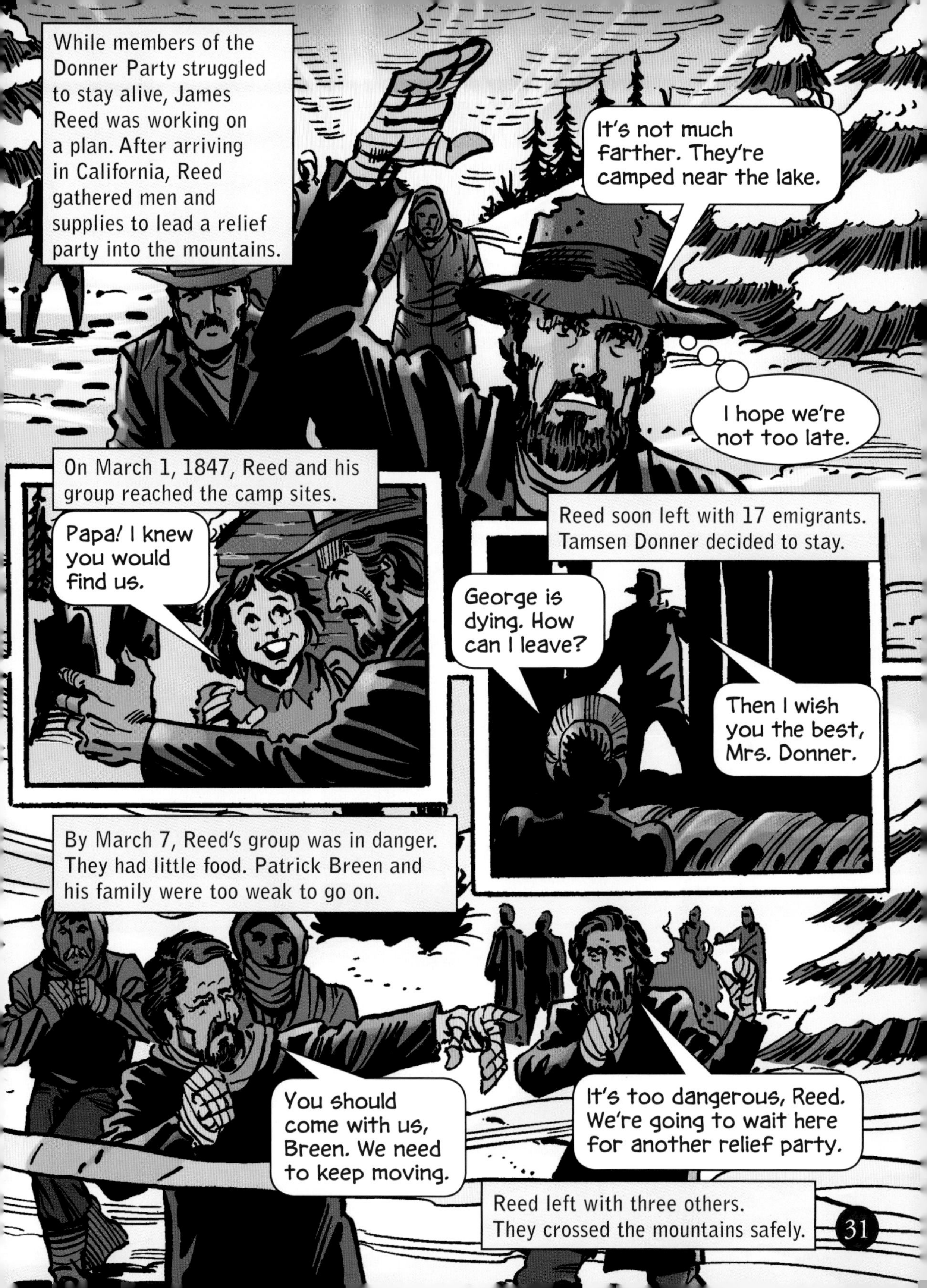
While members of the Donner Party struggled to stay alive, James Reed was working on a plan. After arriving in California, Reed gathered men and supplies to lead a relief party into the mountains.
It's not much farther. They're camped near the lake.
I hope we're not too late.
On March 1, 1847, Reed and his group reached the camp sites.
Papa! I knew you would find us.
Reed soon left with 17 emigrants. Tamsen Donner decided to stay.
George is dying. How can I leave?
Then I wish you the best, Mrs. Donner.
By March 7, Reed's group was in danger. They had little food. Patrick Breen and his family were too weak to go on.
You should come with us, Breen. We need to keep moving.
It's too dangerous, Reed. We're going to wait here for another relief party.
Reed left with three others. They crossed the mountains safely.

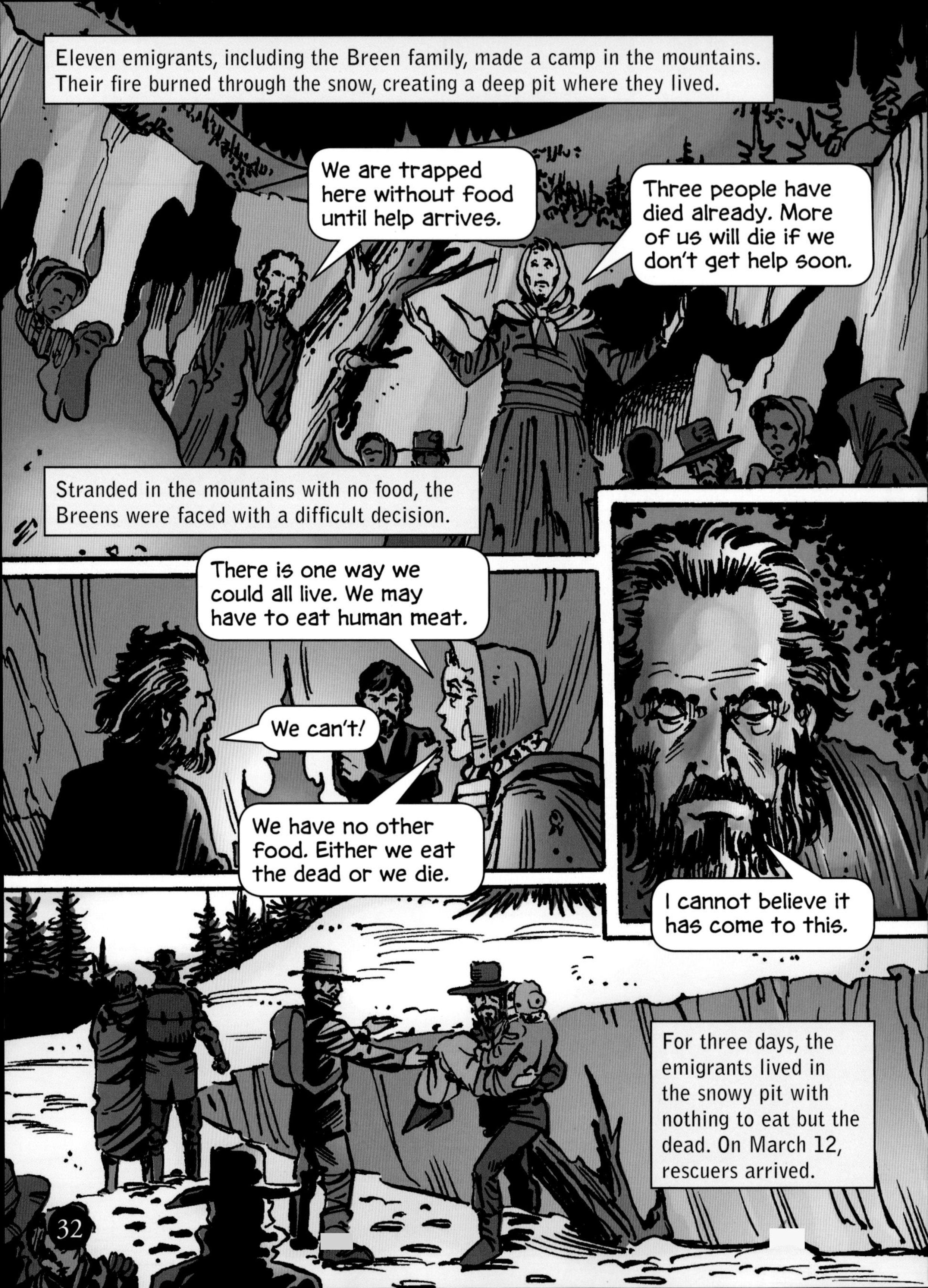
Eleven emigrants, including the Breen family, made a camp in the mountains. Their fire burned through the snow, creating a deep pit where they lived.
We are trapped here without food until help arrives.
Three people have died already. More of us will die if we don't get help soon.
Stranded in the mountains with no food, the Breens were faced with a difficult decision.
There is one way we could all live. We may have to eat human meat.
We can't!
We have no other food. Either we eat the dead or we die.
I cannot believe it has come to this.
For three days, the emigrants lived in the snowy pit with nothing to eat but the dead. On March 12, rescuers arrived.

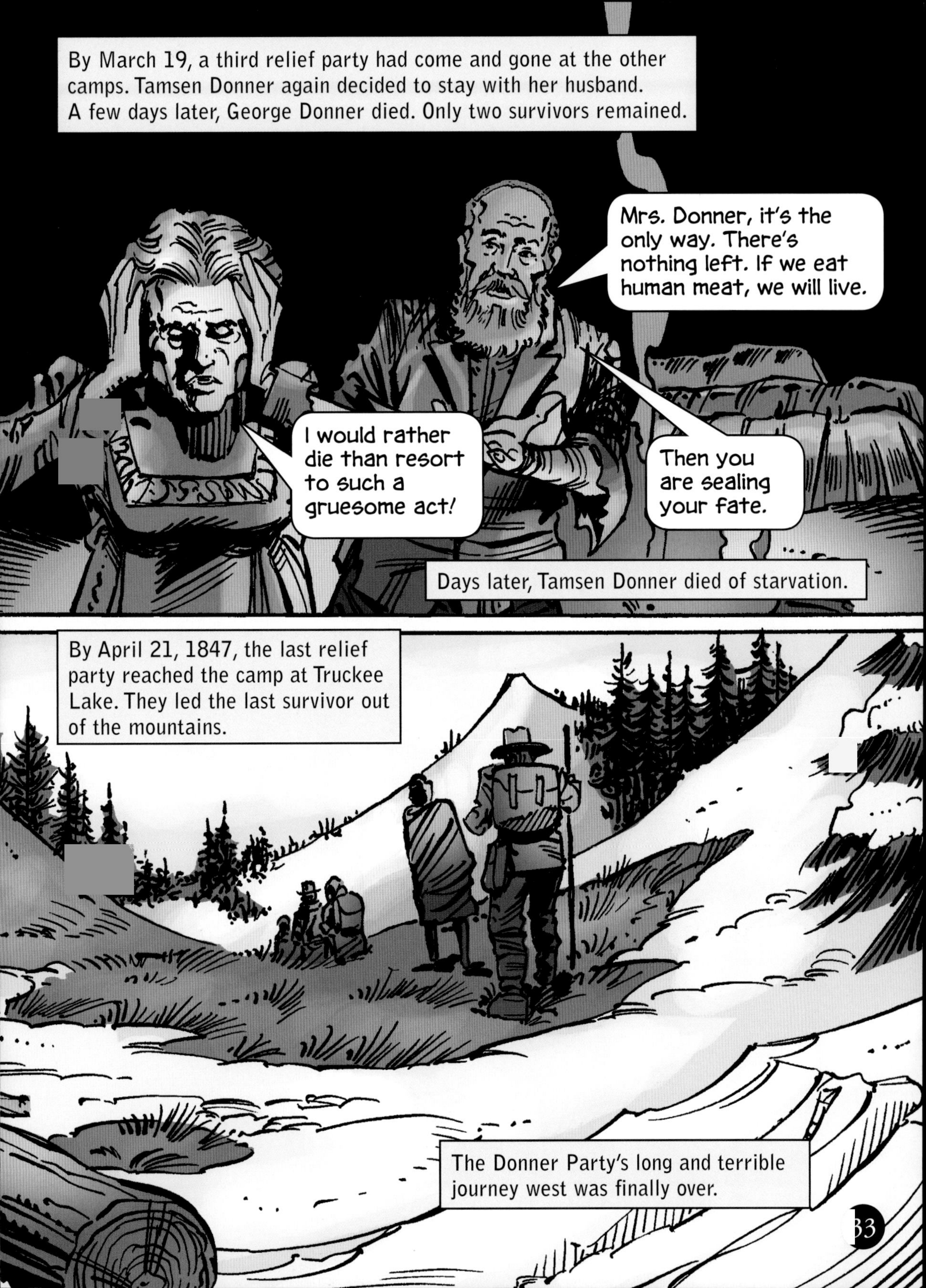
By March 19, a third relief party had come and gone at the other camps. Tamsen Donner again decided to stay with her husband. A few days later, George Donner died. Only two survivors remained.
Mrs. Donner, it's the only way. There's nothing left. If we eat human meat, we will live.
I would rather die than resort to such a gruesome act!
Then you are sealing your fate.
Days later, Tamsen Donner died of starvation.
By April 21, 1847, the last relief party reached the camp at Truckee Lake. They led the last survivor out of the mountains.
The Donner Party's long and terrible journey west was finally over.

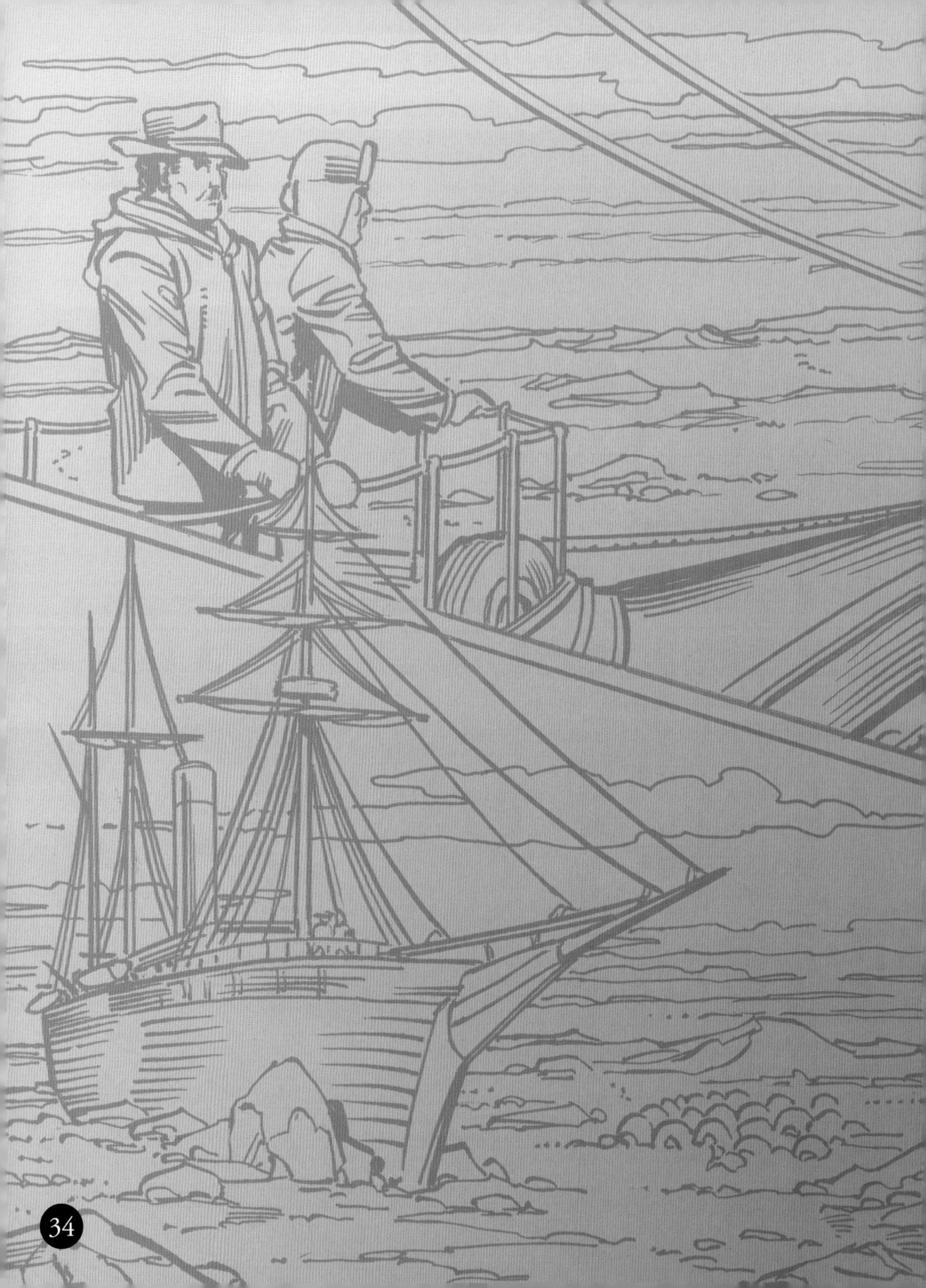

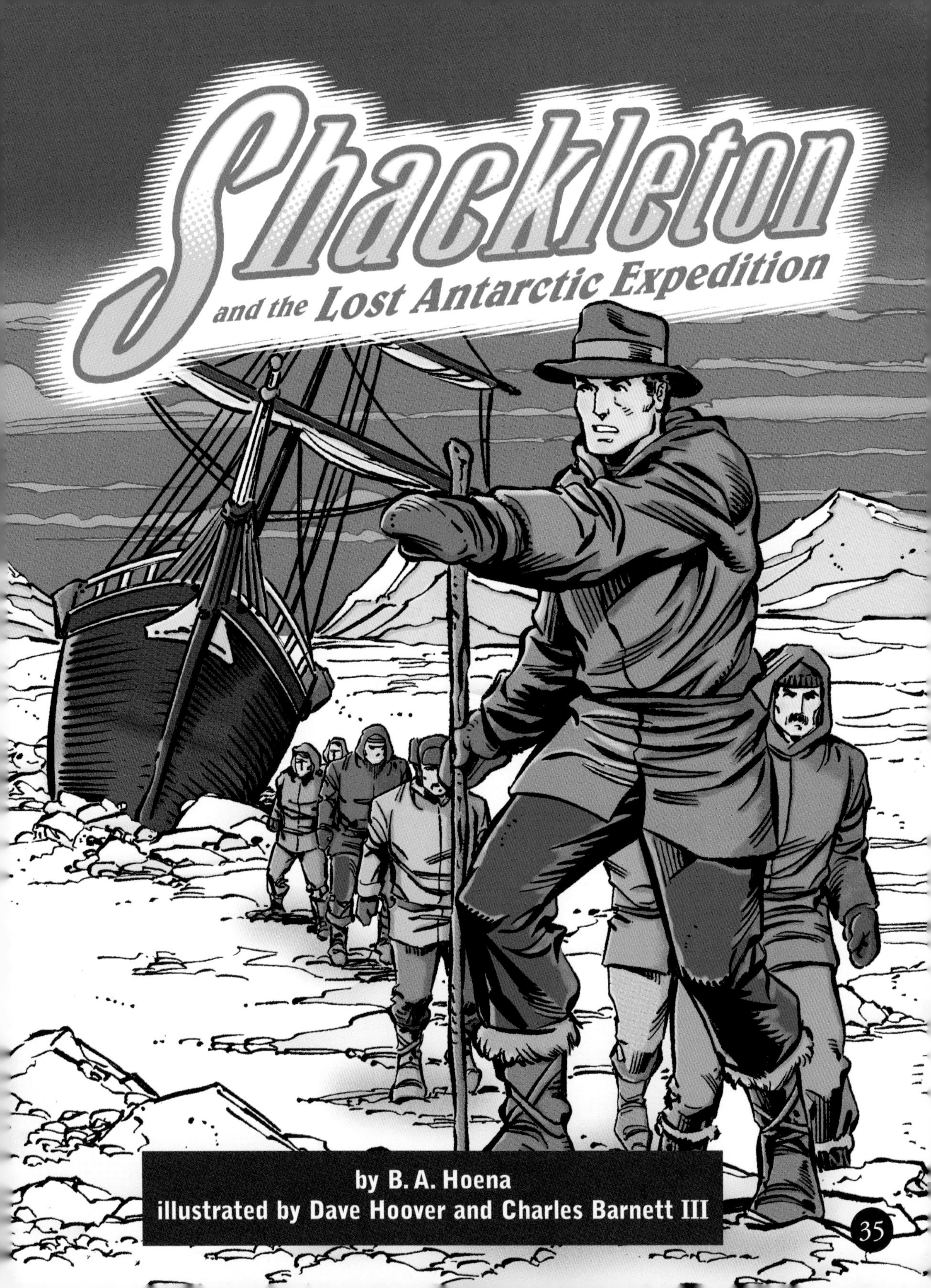
Shackleton
and the Lost Antarctic Expedition
by B. A. Hoena
illustrated by Dave Hoover and Charles Barnett III

Chapter 1
A Daring Expedition

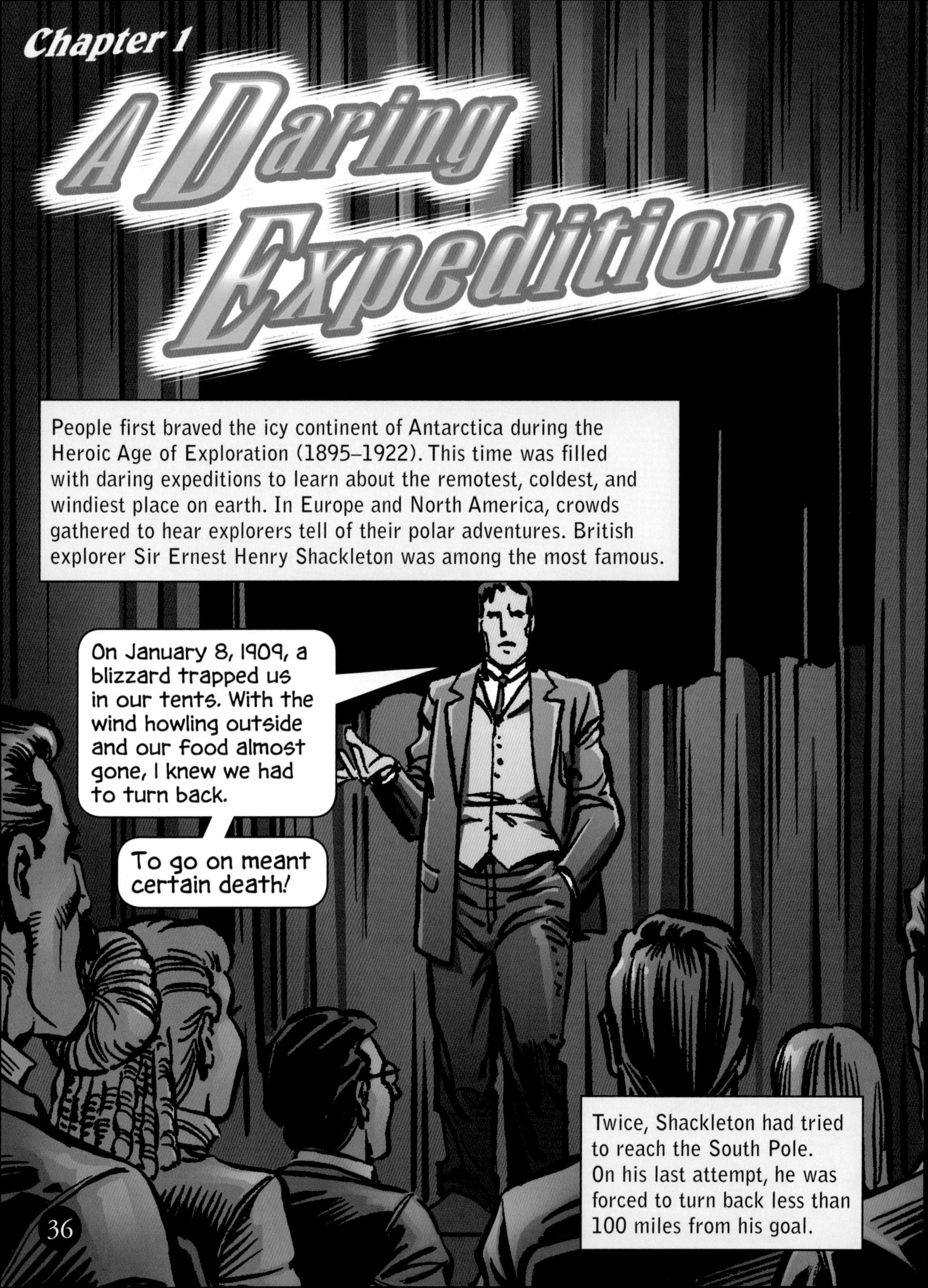
People first braved the icy continent of Antarctica during the Heroic Age of Exploration (1895–1922). This time was filled with daring expeditions to learn about the remotest, coldest, and windiest place on earth. In Europe and North America, crowds gathered to hear explorers tell of their polar adventures. British explorer Sir Ernest Henry Shackleton was among the most famous.
On January 8, 1909, a blizzard trapped us in our tents. With the wind howling outside and our food almost gone, I knew we had to turn back.
To go on meant certain death!
Twice, Shackleton had tried to reach the South Pole. On his last attempt, he was forced to turn back less than 100 miles from his goal.

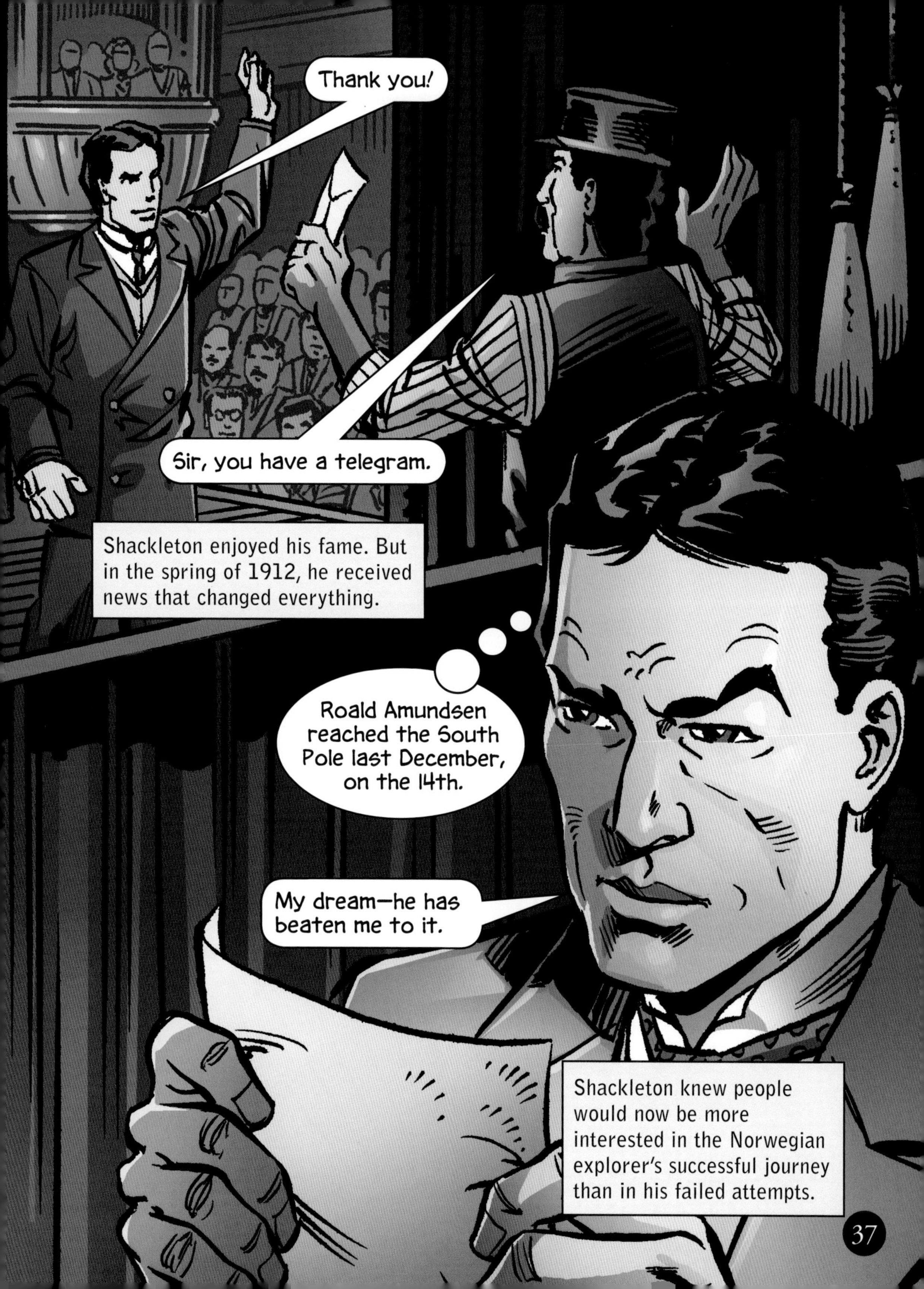

Thank you!
Sir, you have a telegram.
Shackleton enjoyed his fame. But in the spring of 1912, he received news that changed everything.
Roald Amundsen reached the South Pole last December, on the 14th.
My dream—he has beaten me to it.
Shackleton knew people would now be more interested in the Norwegian explorer's successful journey than in his failed attempts.

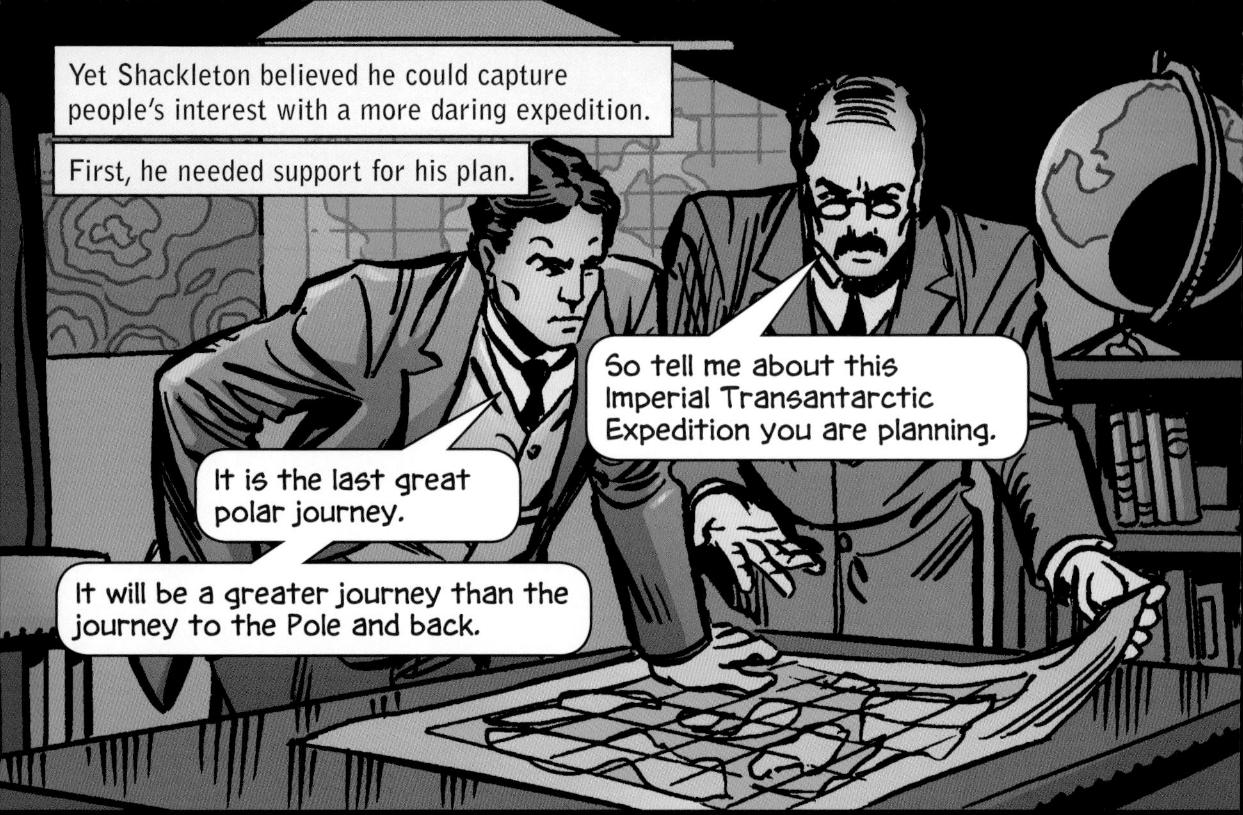
Yet Shackleton believed he could capture people's interest with a more daring expedition.
First, he needed support for his plan.
So tell me about this Imperial Transantarctic Expedition you are planning.
It is the last great polar journey.
It will be a greater journey than the journey to the Pole and back.

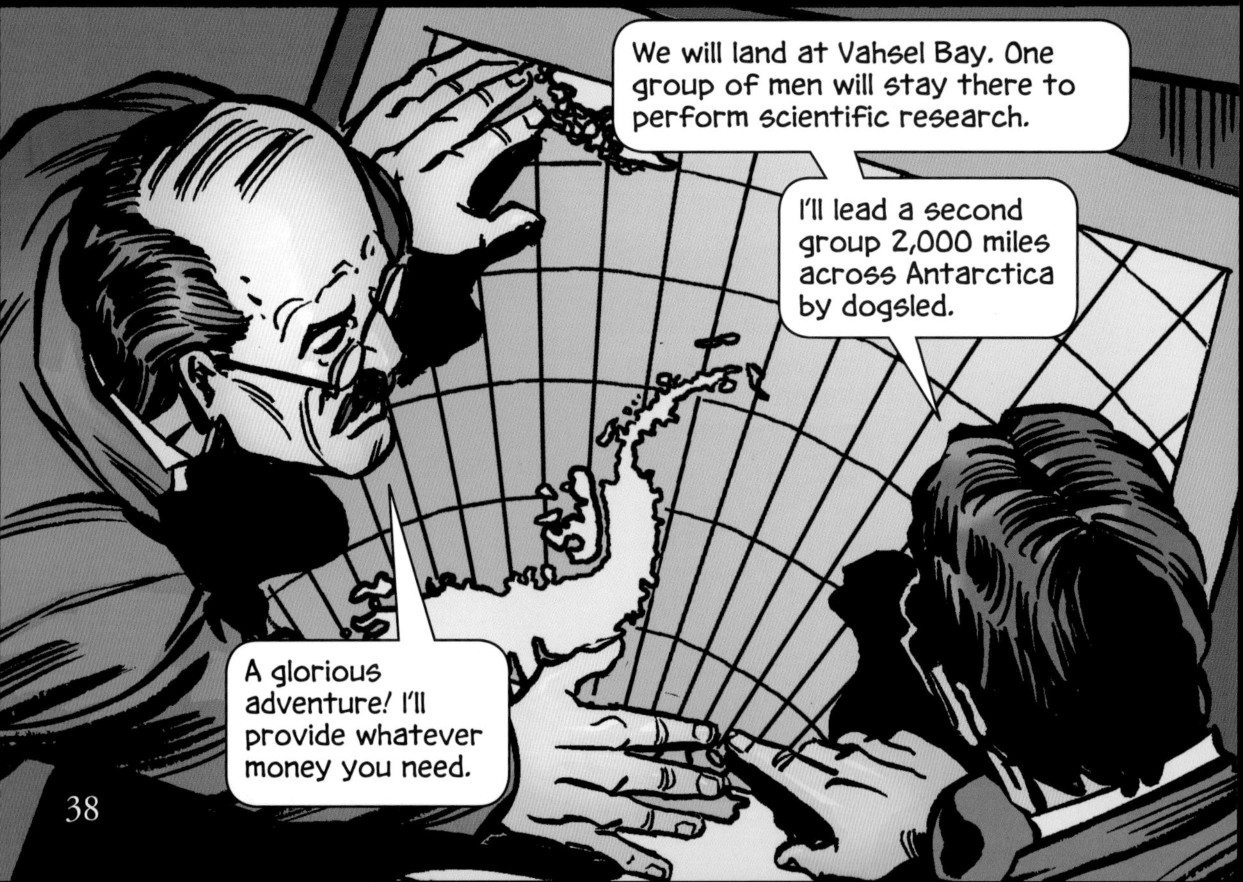
We will land at Vahsel Bay. One group of men will stay there to perform scientific research.
I'll lead a second group 2,000 miles across Antarctica by dogsled.
A glorious adventure! I'll provide whatever money you need.

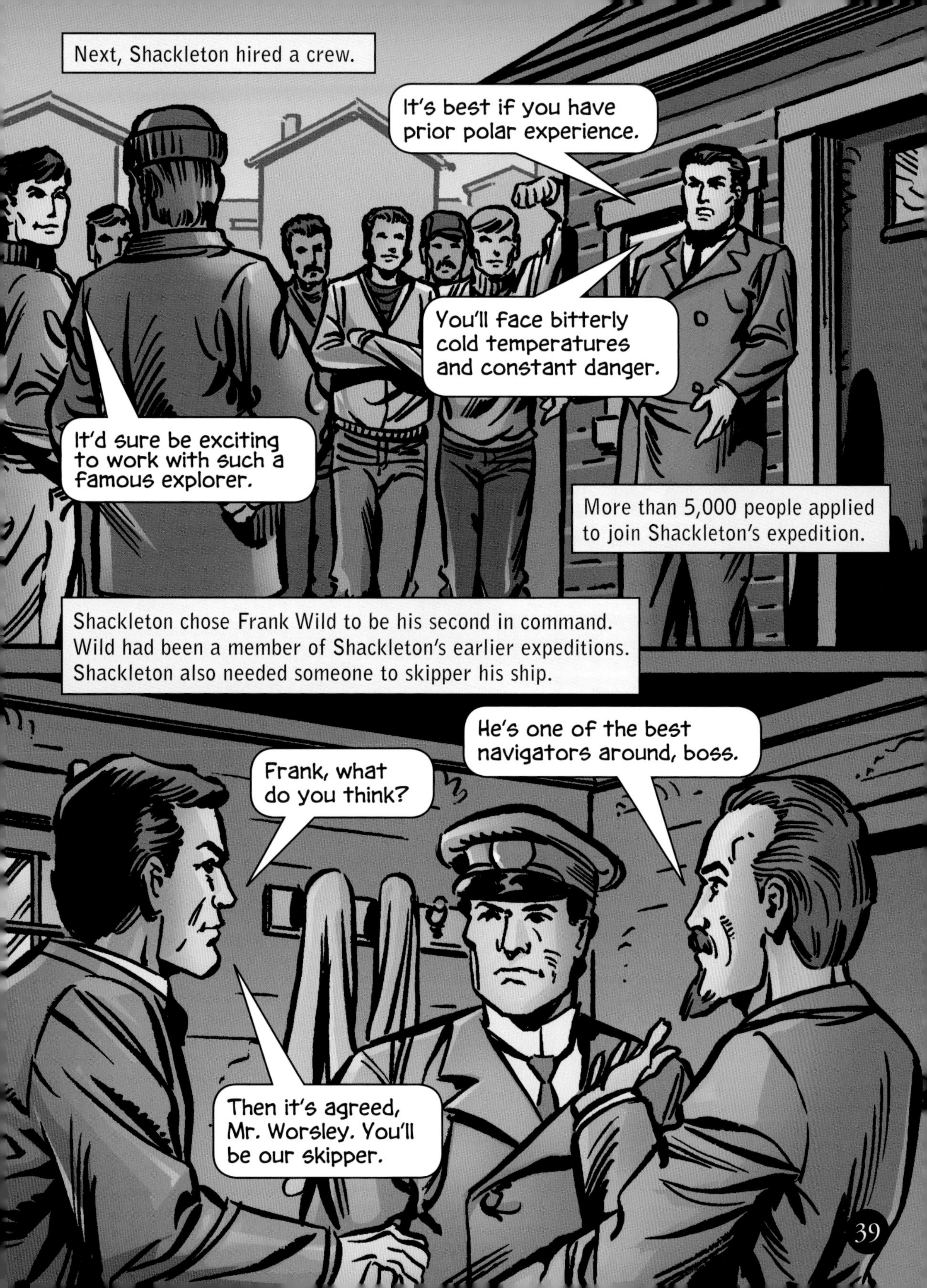
Next, Shackleton hired a crew.
It's best if you have prior polar experience.
You'll face bitterly cold temperatures and constant danger.
It'd sure be exciting to work with such a famous explorer.
More than 5,000 people applied to join Shackleton's expedition.
Shackleton chose Frank Wild to be his second in command. Wild had been a member of Shackleton's earlier expeditions. Shackleton also needed someone to skipper his ship.
Frank, what do you think?
He's one of the best navigators around, boss.
Then it's agreed, Mr. Worsley. You'll be our skipper.

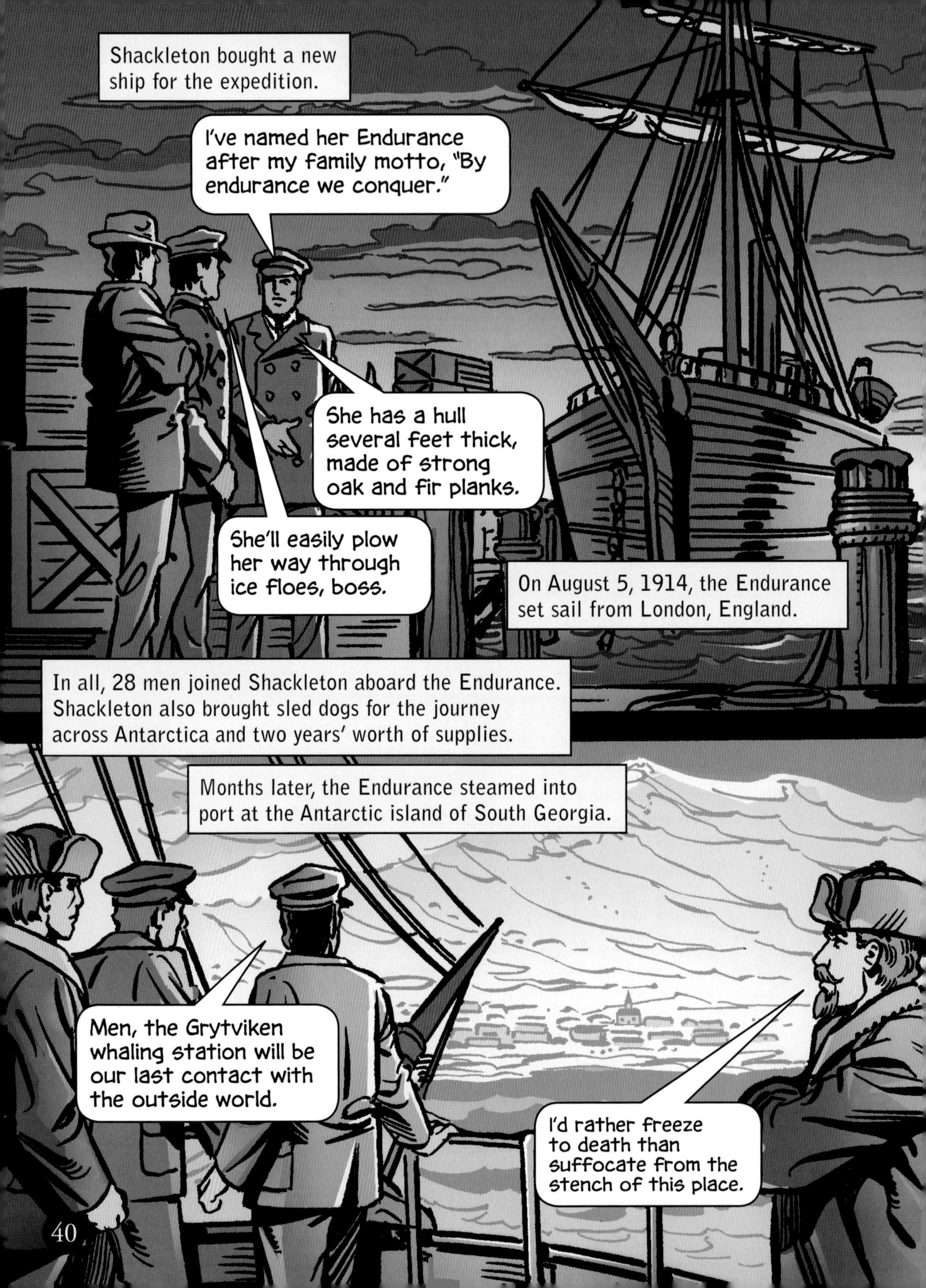
Shackleton bought a new ship for the expedition.
I've named her Endurance after my family motto, "By endurance we conquer."
She has a hull several feet thick, made of strong oak and fir planks.
She'll easily plow her way through ice floes, boss.
On August 5, 1914, the Endurance set sail from London, England.
In all, 28 men joined Shackleton aboard the Endurance. Shackleton also brought sled dogs for the journey across Antarctica and two years' worth of supplies.
Months later, the Endurance steamed into port at the Antarctic island of South Georgia.
Men, the Grytviken whaling station will be our last contact with the outside world.
I'd rather freeze to death than suffocate from the stench of this place.

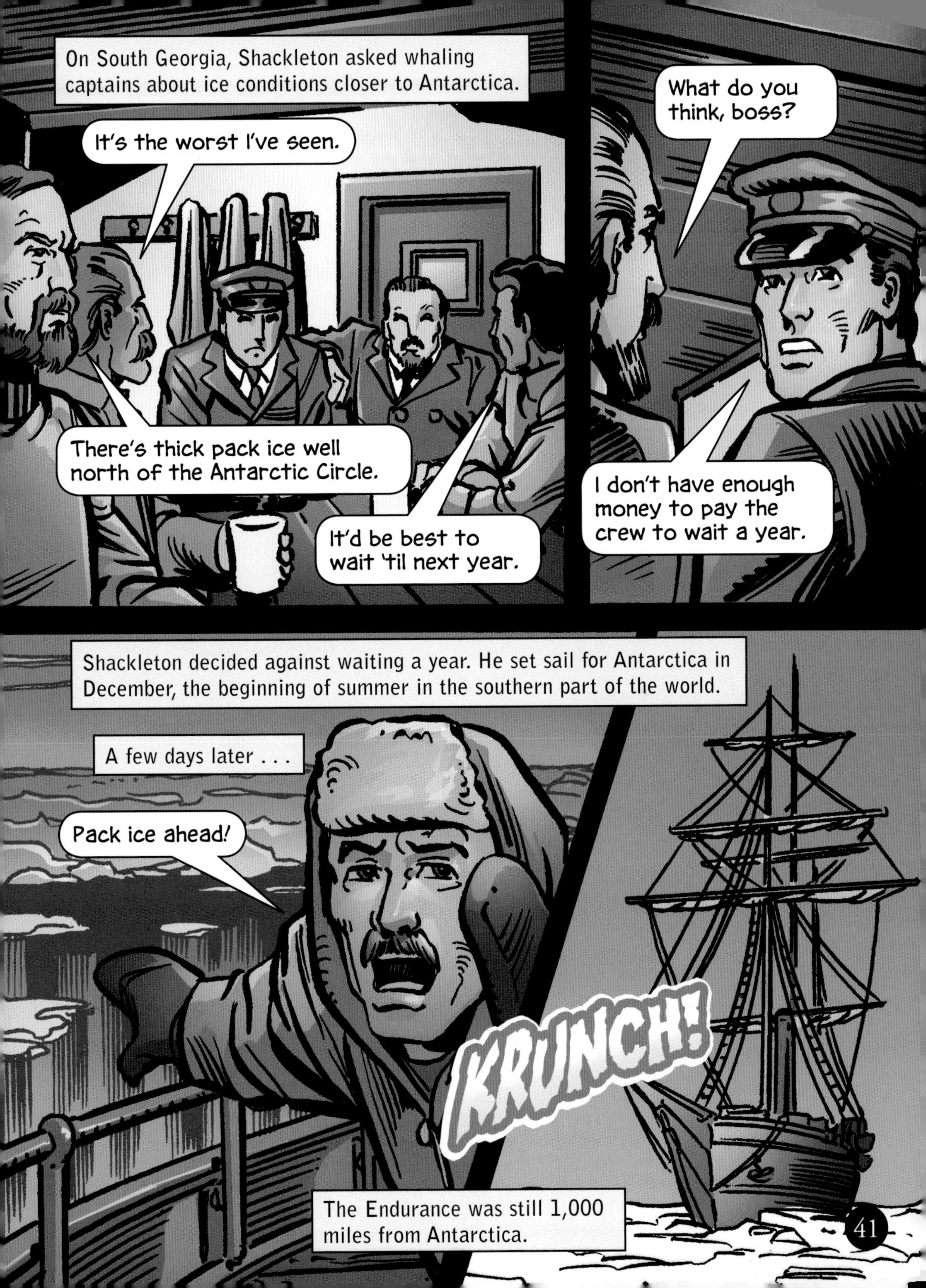

On South Georgia, Shackleton asked whaling captains about ice conditions closer to Antarctica.
It's the worst I've seen.
There's thick pack ice well north of the Antarctic Circle.
It'd be best to wait 'til next year.
What do you think, boss?
I don't have enough money to pay the crew to wait a year.
Shackleton decided against waiting a year. He set sail for Antarctica in December, the beginning of summer in the southern part of the world.
A few days later . . .
Pack ice ahead!
KRUNCH!
The Endurance was still 1,000 miles from Antarctica.

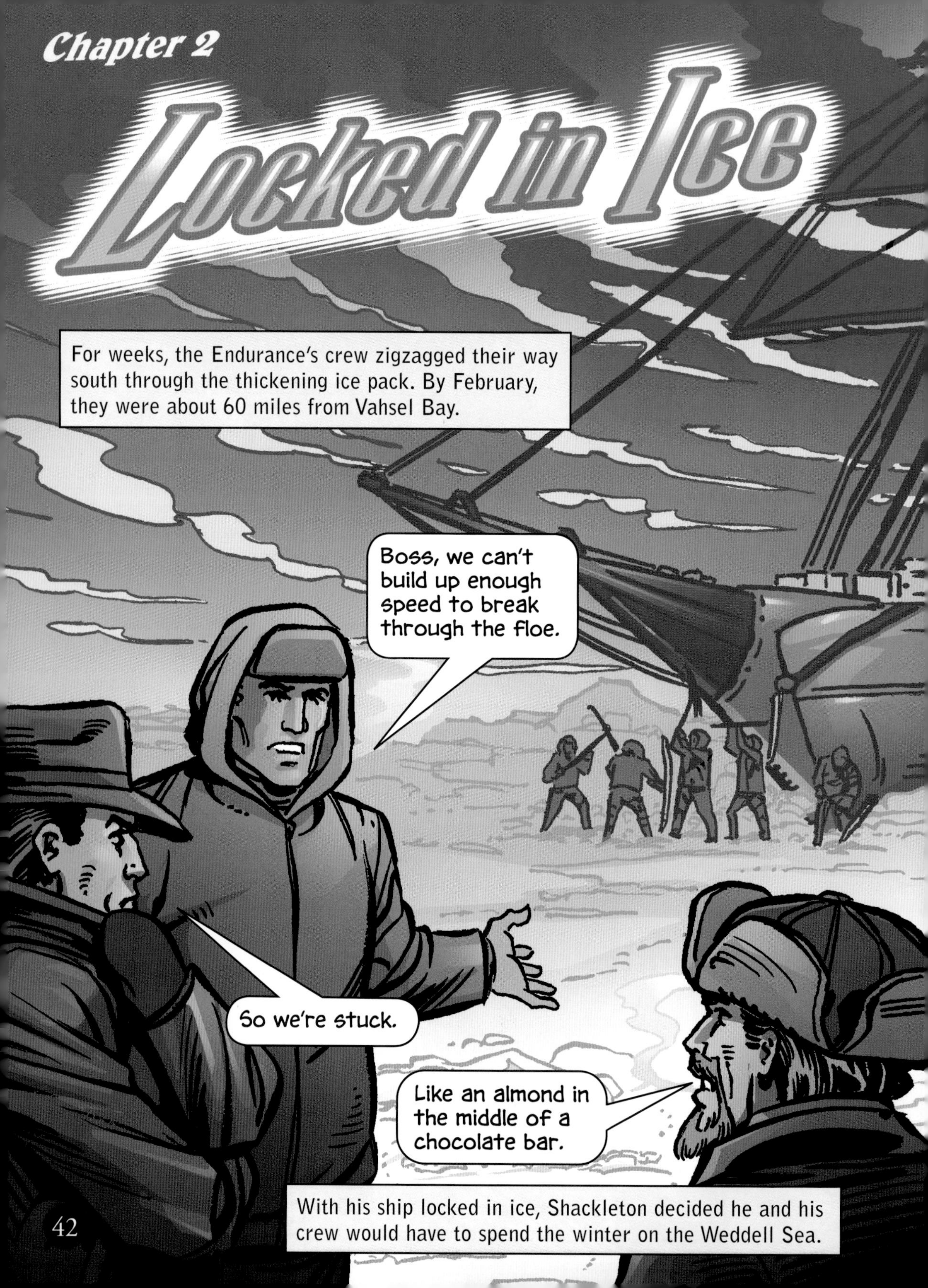
Chapter 2
Locked in Ice
For weeks, the Endurance's crew zigzagged their way south through the thickening ice pack. By February, they were about 60 miles from Vahsel Bay.
Boss, we can't build up enough speed to break through the floe.
So we're stuck.
Like an almond in the middle of a chocolate bar.
With his ship locked in ice, Shackleton decided he and his crew would have to spend the winter on the Weddell Sea.

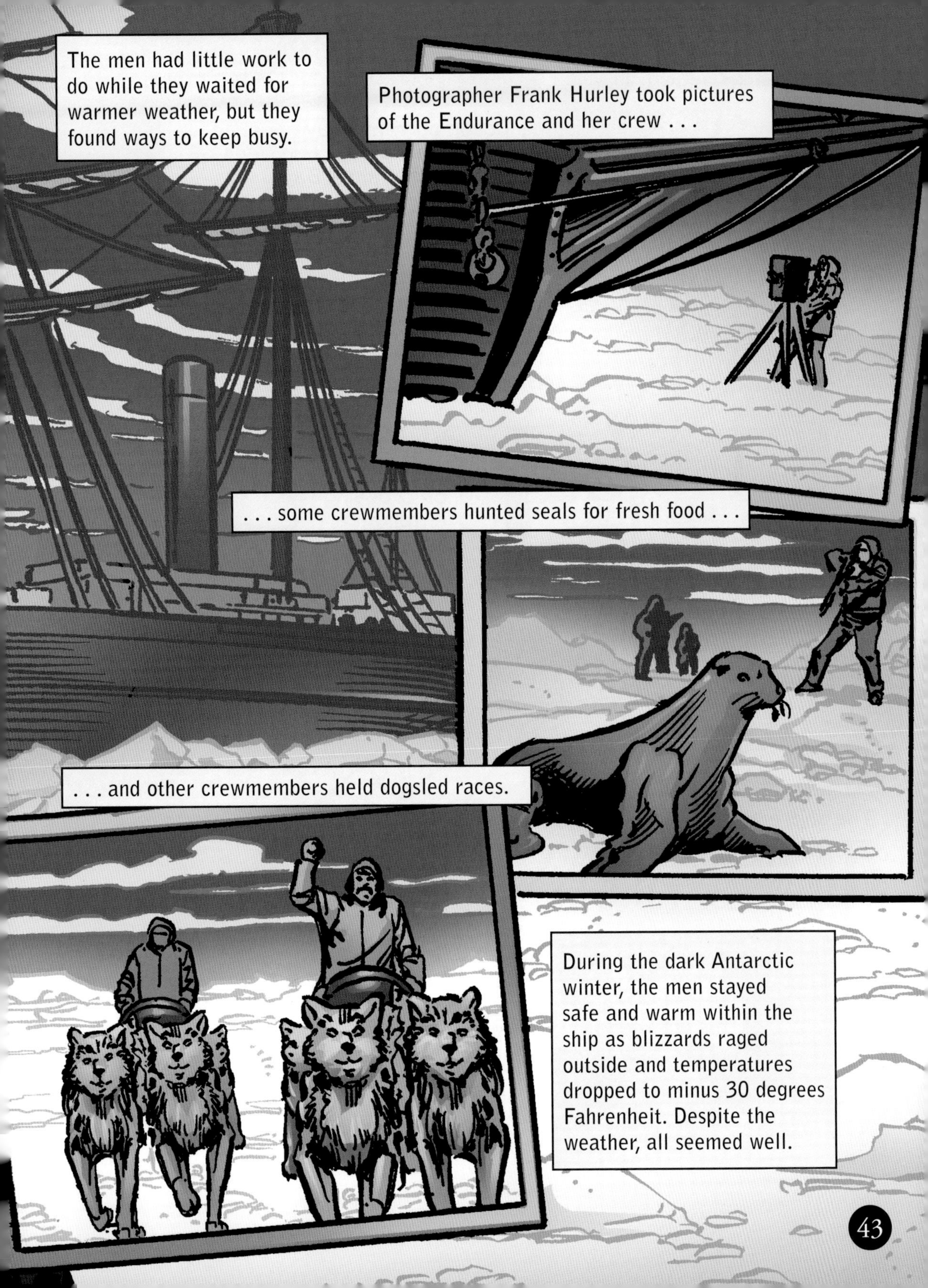

The men had little work to do while they waited for warmer weather, but they found ways to keep busy.
Photographer Frank Hurley took pictures of the Endurance and her crew . . .
. . . some crewmembers hunted seals for fresh food . . .
. . . and other crewmembers held dogsled races.
During the dark Antarctic winter, the men stayed safe and warm within the ship as blizzards raged outside and temperatures dropped to minus 30 degrees Fahrenheit. Despite the weather, all seemed well.

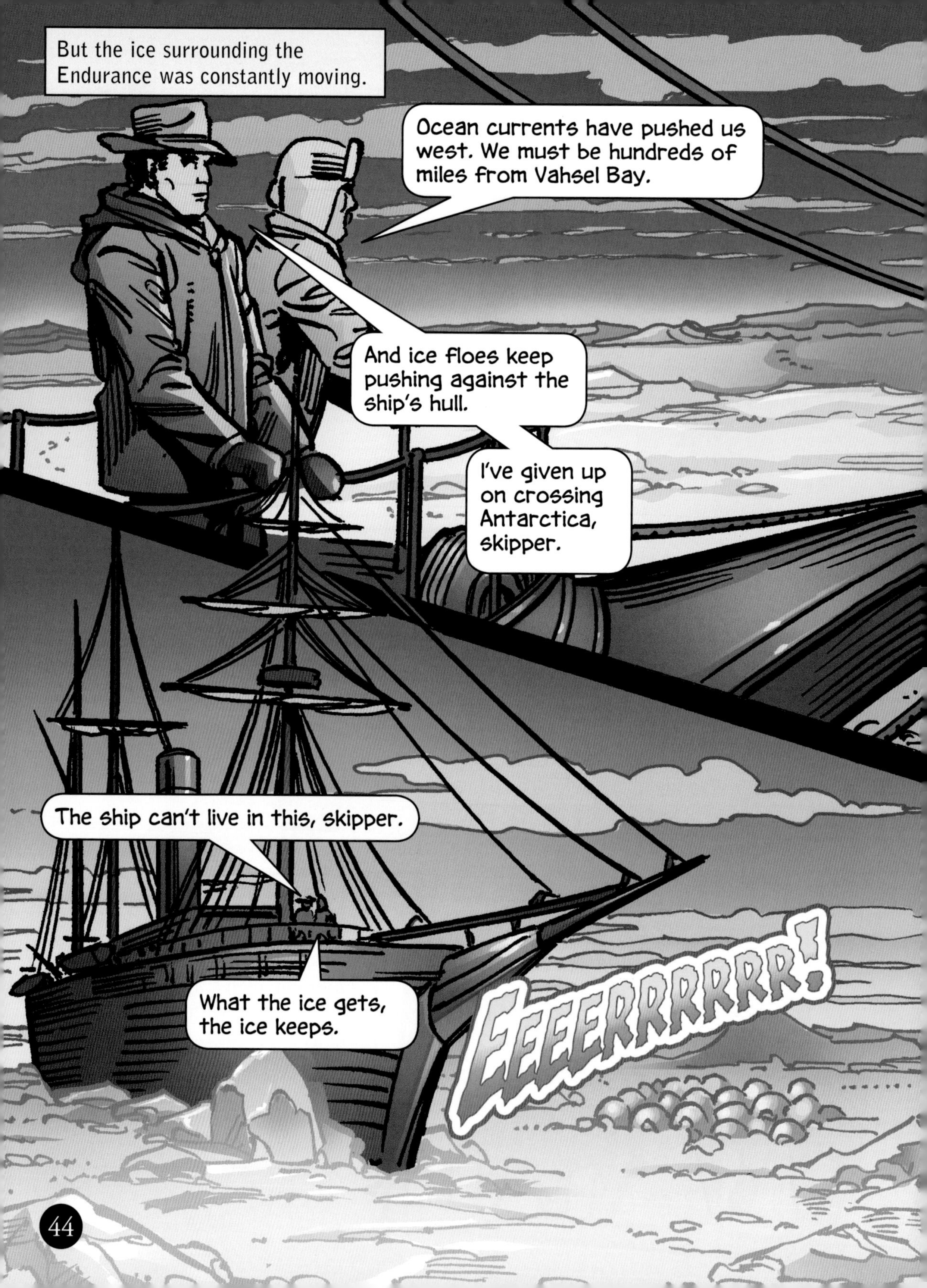
But the ice surrounding the Endurance was constantly moving.
Ocean currents have pushed us west. We must be hundreds of miles from Vahsel Bay.
And ice floes keep pushing against the ship's hull.
I've given up on crossing Antarctica, skipper.
The ship can't live in this, skipper.
What the ice gets, the ice keeps.
EEEERRRRRR!

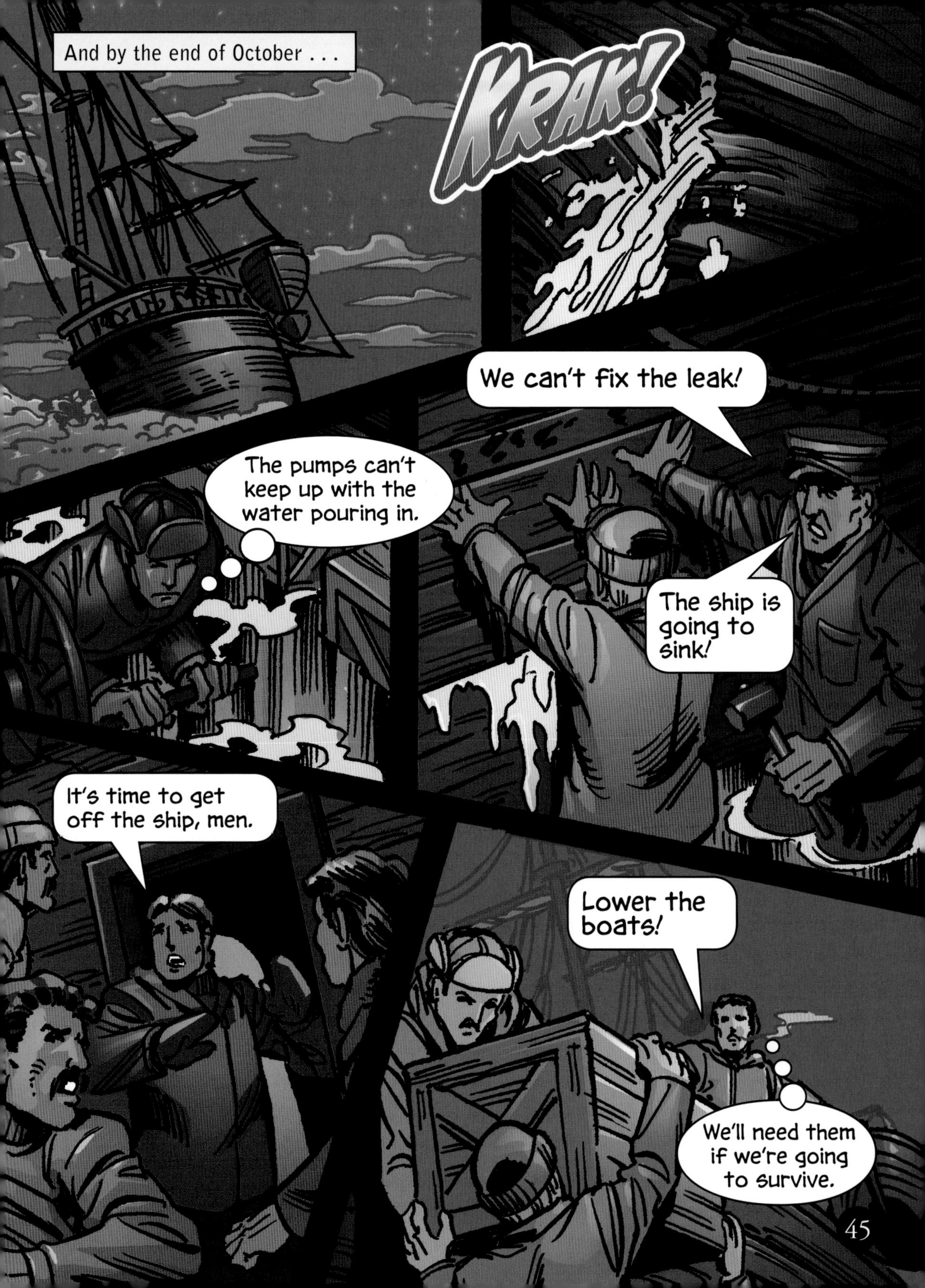

And by the end of October . . .
KRAK!
We can't fix the leak!
The pumps can't keep up with the water pouring in.
The ship is going to sink!
It's time to get off the ship, men.
Lower the boats!
We'll need them if we're going to survive.

Chapter 3
The Fight to Survive

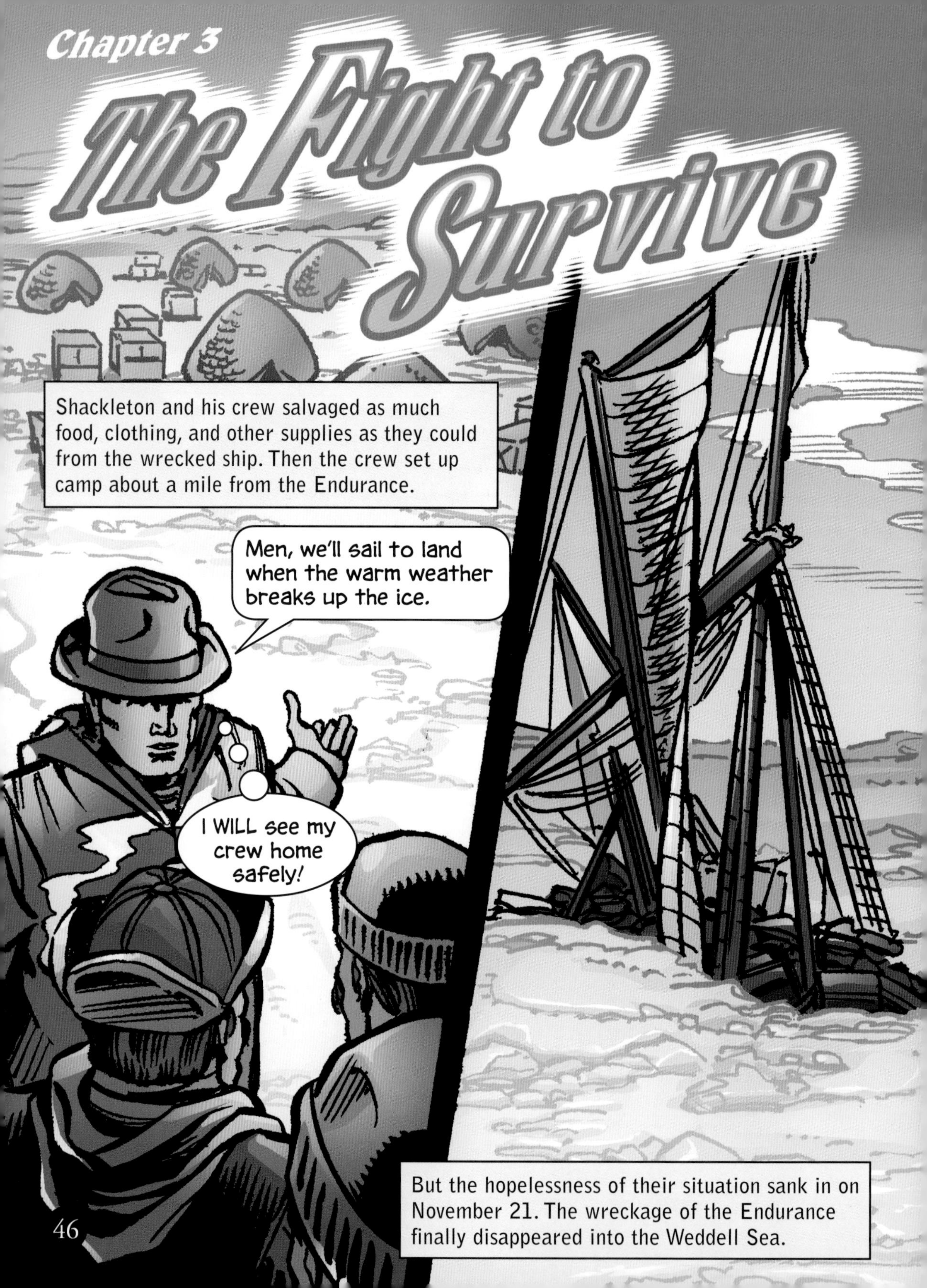

Shackleton and his crew salvaged as much food, clothing, and other supplies as they could from the wrecked ship. Then the crew set up camp about a mile from the Endurance.
Men, we'll sail to land when the warm weather breaks up the ice.
I WILL see my crew home safely!
But the hopelessness of their situation sank in on November 21. The wreckage of the Endurance finally disappeared into the Weddell Sea.

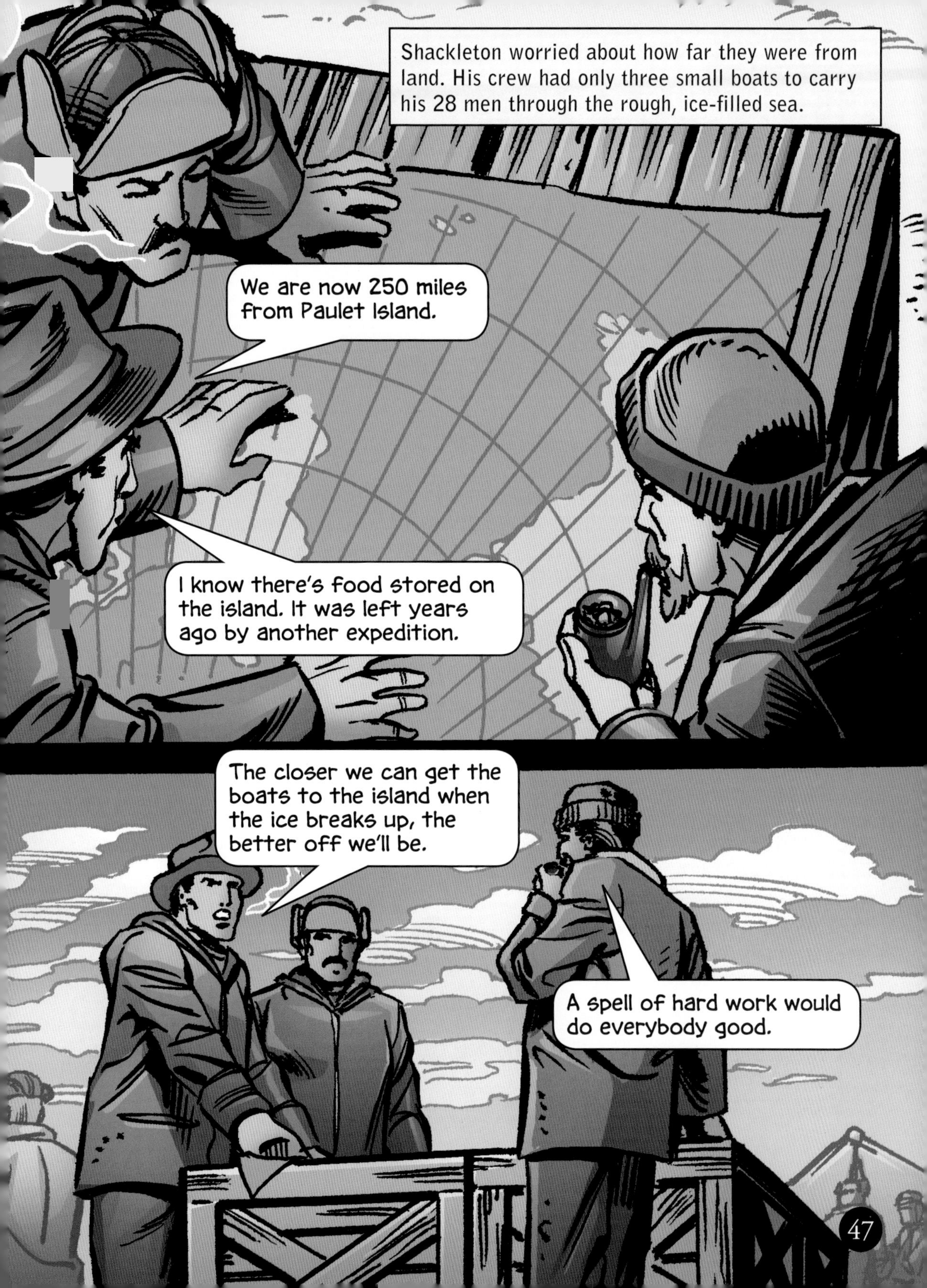
Shackleton worried about how far they were from land. His crew had only three small boats to carry his 28 men through the rough, ice-filled sea.
We are now 250 miles from Paulet Island.
I know there's food stored on the island. It was left years ago by another expedition.
The closer we can get the boats to the island when the ice breaks up, the better off we'll be.
A spell of hard work would do everybody good.

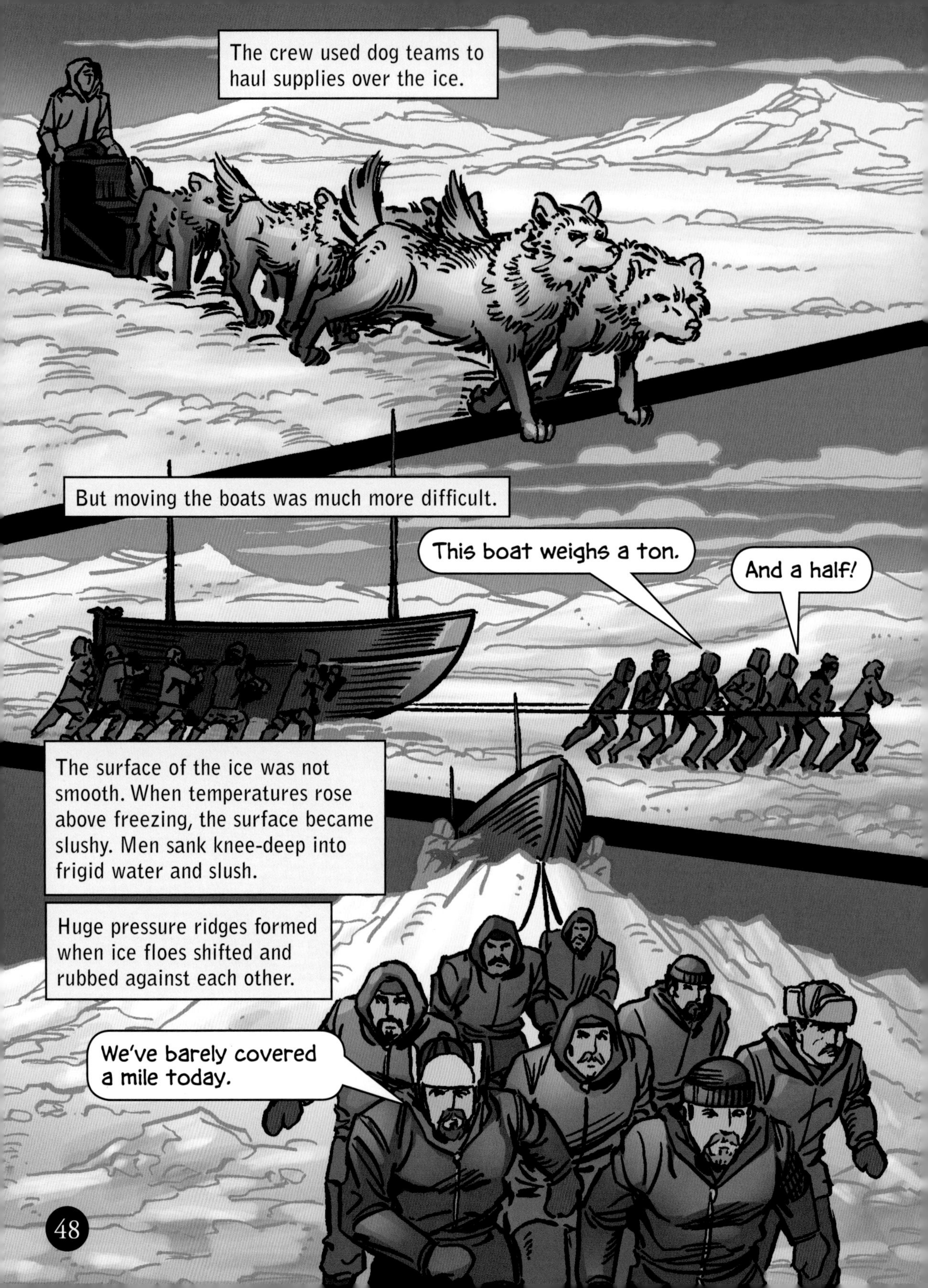
The crew used dog teams to haul supplies over the ice.
But moving the boats was much more difficult.
This boat weighs a ton.
And a half!
The surface of the ice was not smooth. When temperatures rose above freezing, the surface became slushy. Men sank knee-deep into frigid water and slush.
Huge pressure ridges formed when ice floes shifted and rubbed against each other.
We've barely covered a mile today.

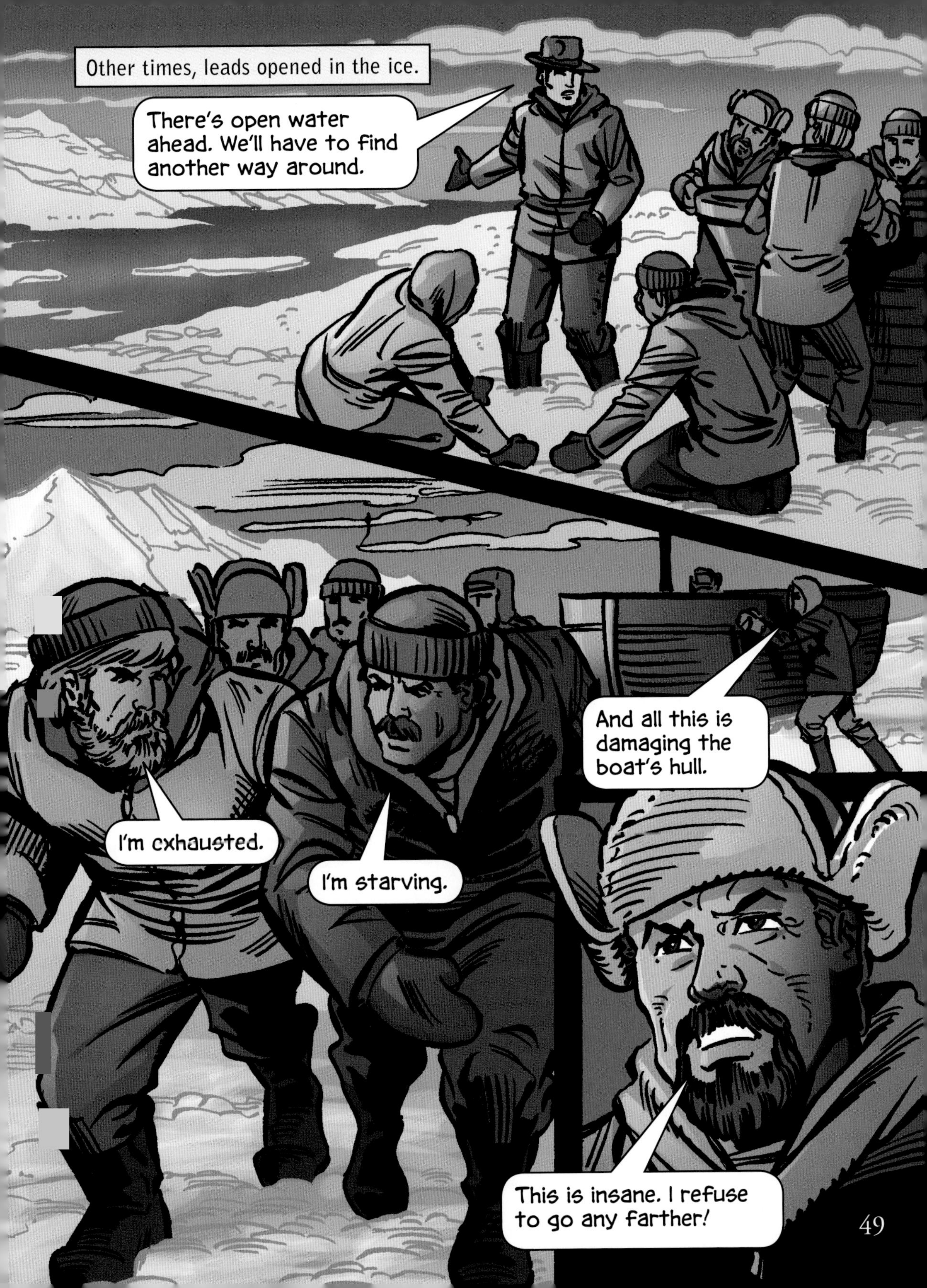
Other times, leads opened in the ice.
There's open water ahead. We'll have to find another way around.
I'm exhausted.
I'm starving.
And all this is damaging the boat's hull.
This is insane. I refuse to go any farther!

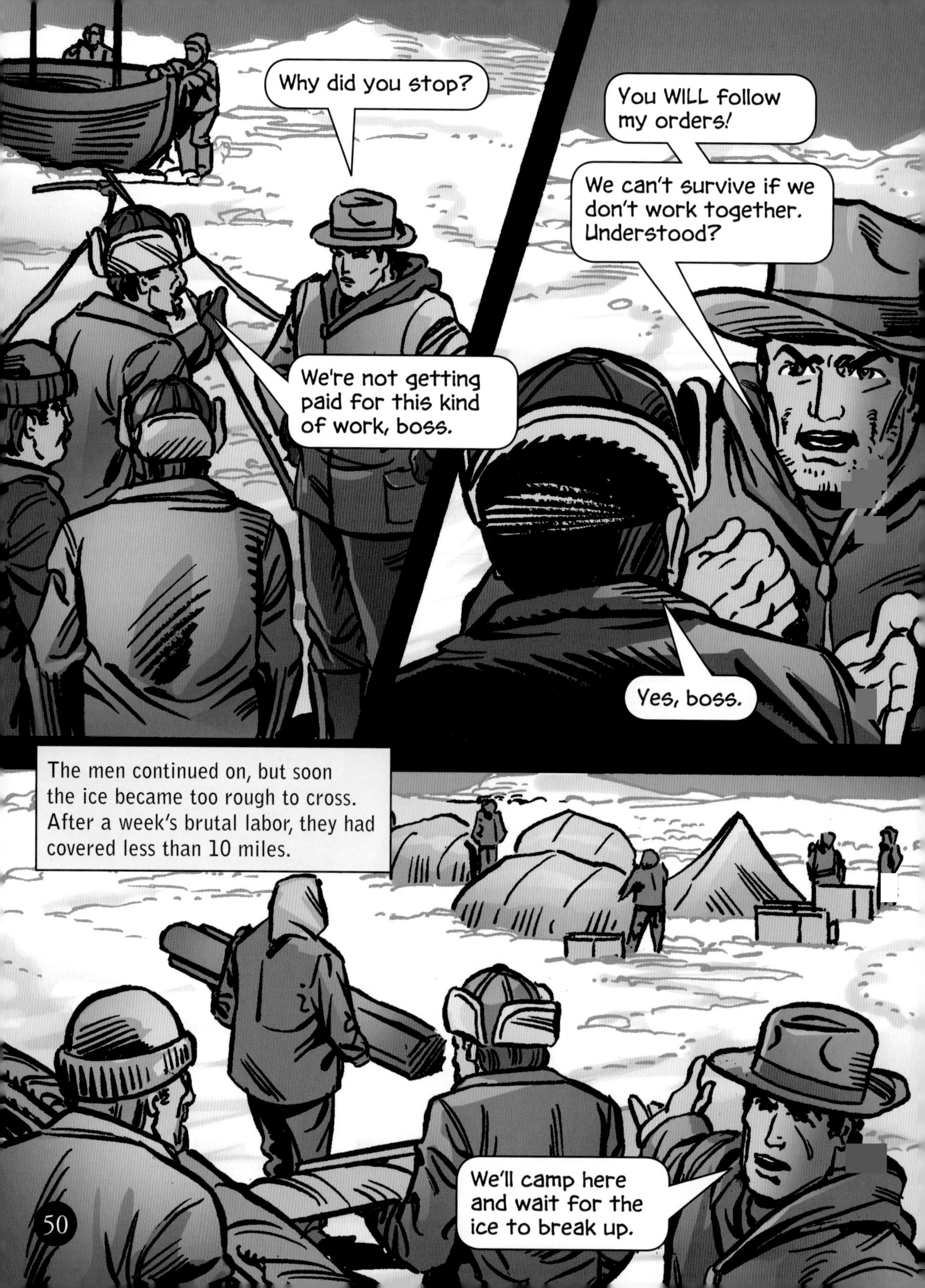
Why did you stop?
We're not getting paid for this kind of work, boss.
You WILL follow my orders!
We can't survive if we don't work together. Understood?
Yes, boss.
The men continued on, but soon the ice became too rough to cross. After a week's brutal labor, they had covered less than 10 miles.
We'll camp here and wait for the ice to break up.

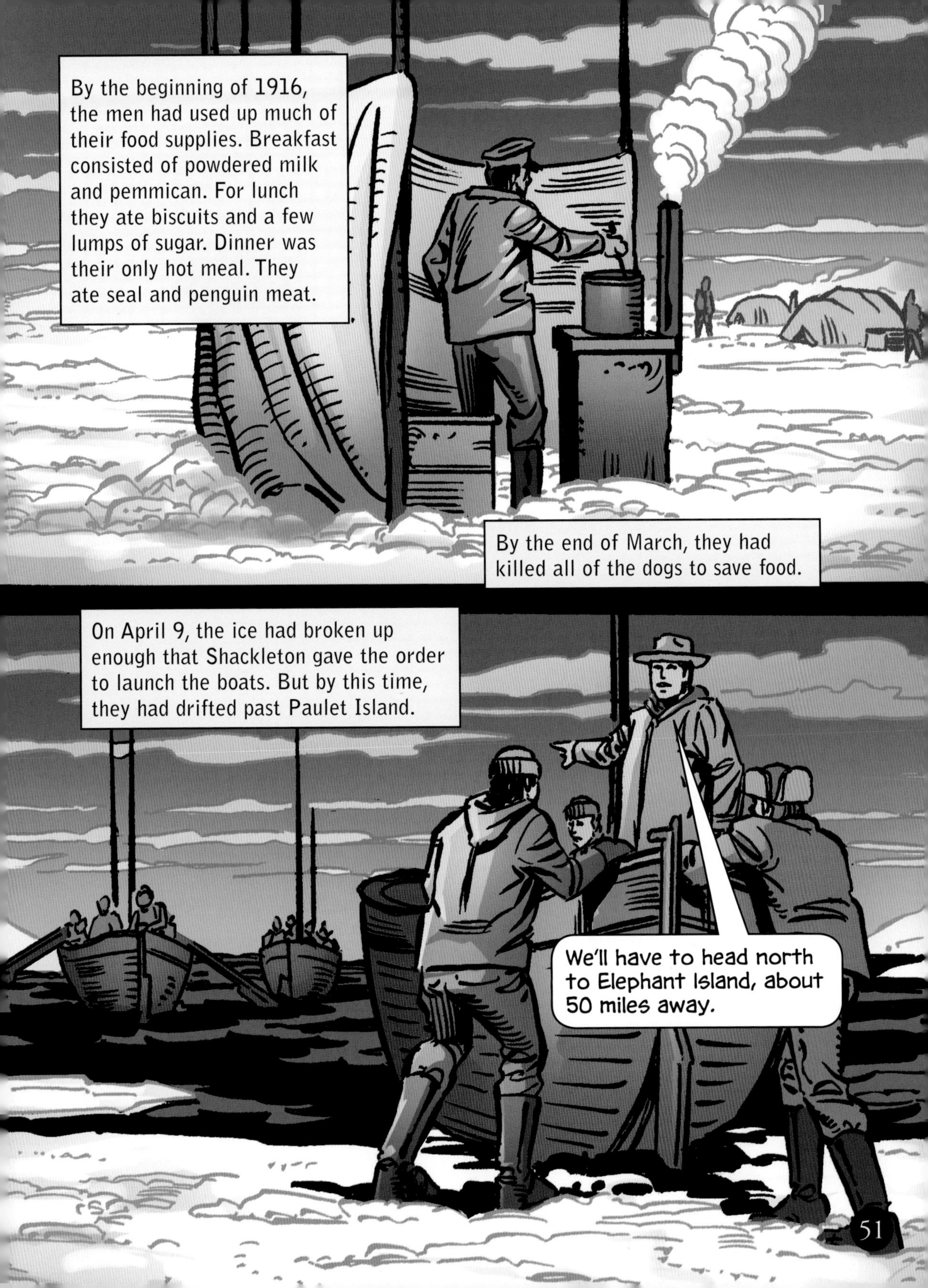
By the beginning of 1916, the men had used up much of their food supplies. Breakfast consisted of powdered milk and pemmican. For lunch they ate biscuits and a few lumps of sugar. Dinner was their only hot meal. They ate seal and penguin meat.
By the end of March, they had killed all of the dogs to save food.
On April 9, the ice had broken up enough that Shackleton gave the order to launch the boats. But by this time, they had drifted past Paulet Island.
We'll have to head north to Elephant Island, about 50 miles away.

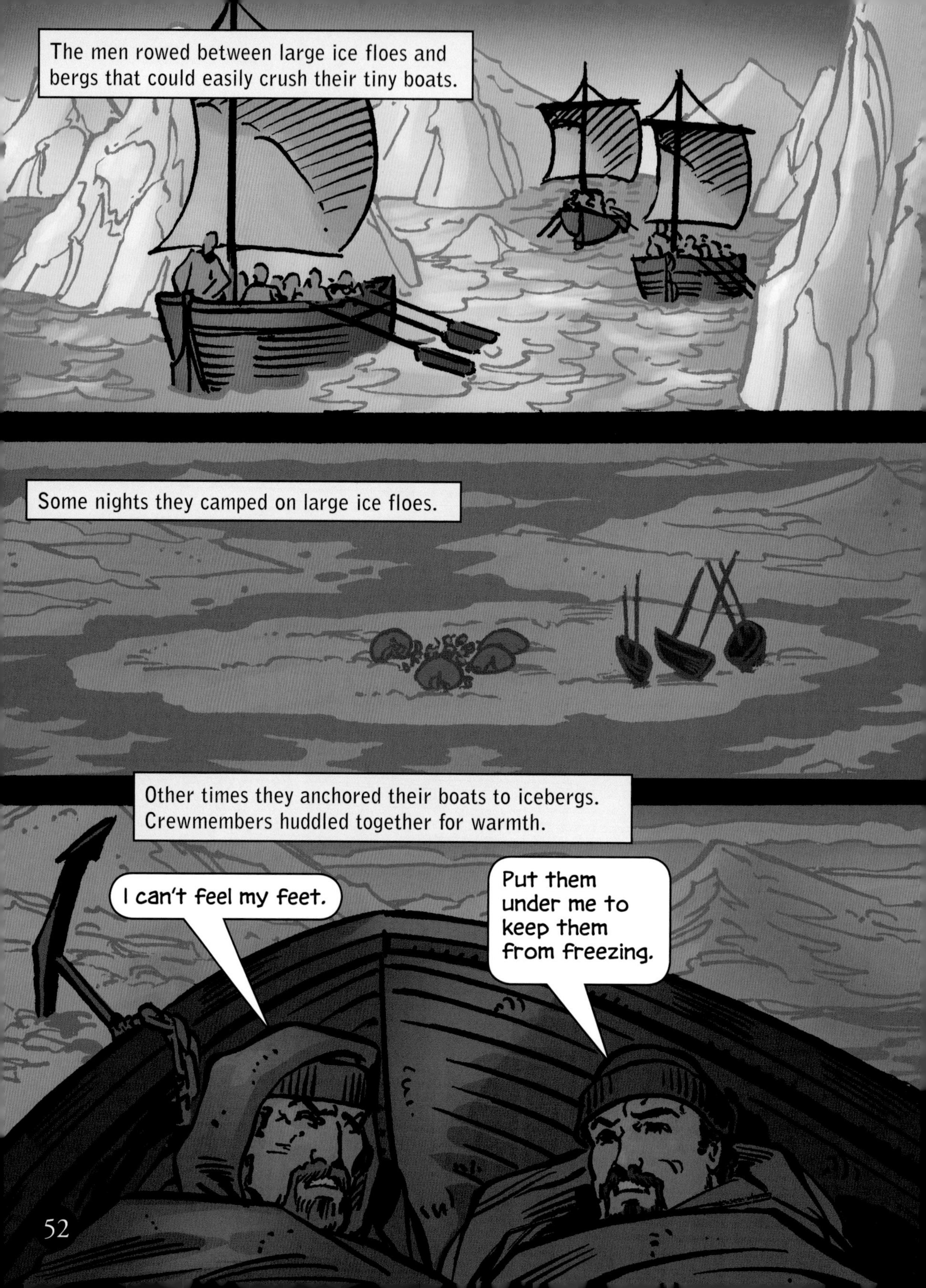
The men rowed between large ice floes and bergs that could easily crush their tiny boats.
Some nights they camped on large ice floes.
Other times they anchored their boats to icebergs. Crewmembers huddled together for warmth.
I can't feel my feet.
Put them under me to keep them from freezing.

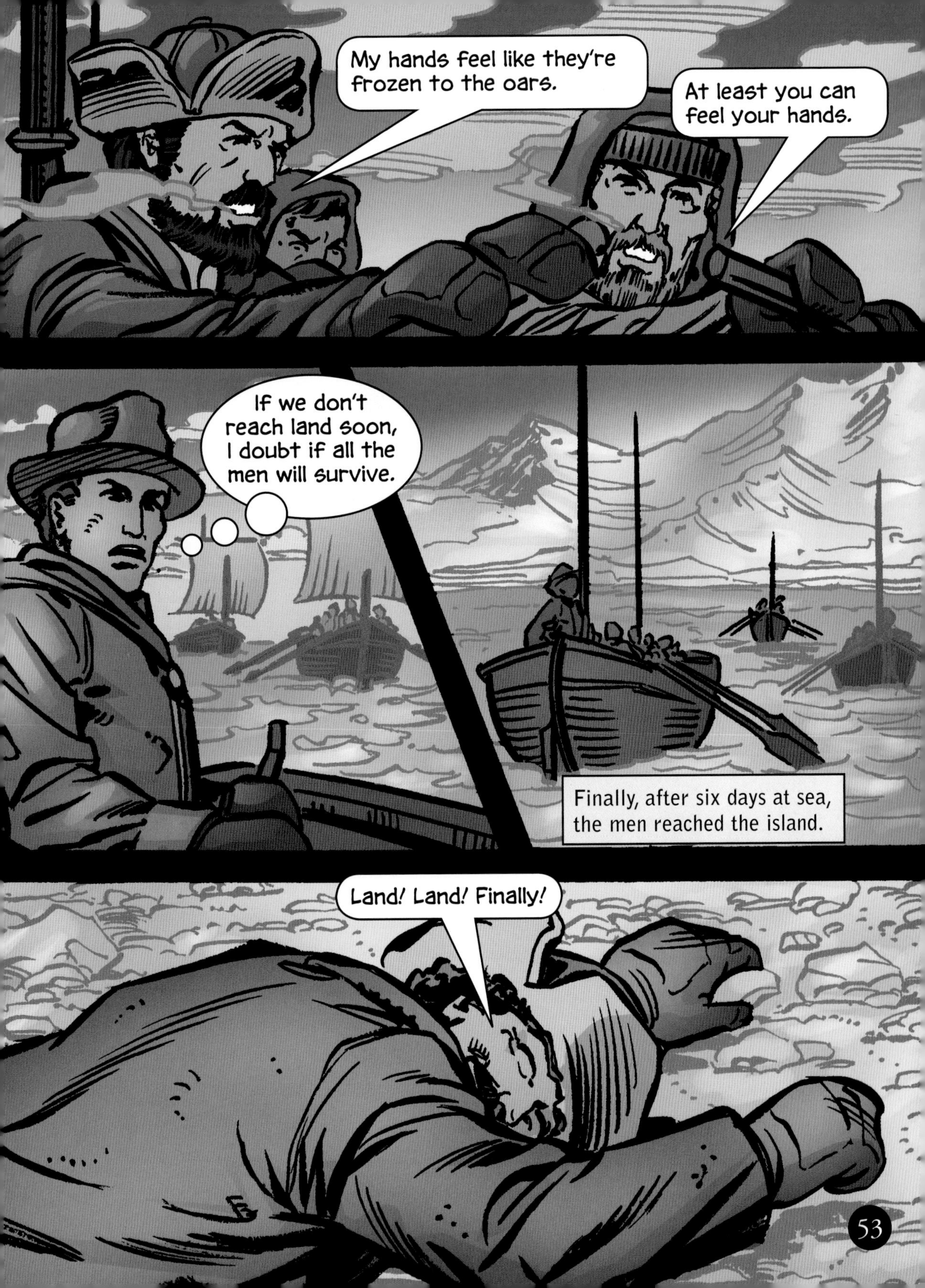
My hands feel like they're frozen to the oars.
At least you can feel your hands.
If we don't reach land soon, I doubt if all the men will survive.
Finally, after six days at sea, the men reached the island.
Land! Land! Finally!

Chapter 4 Rescue

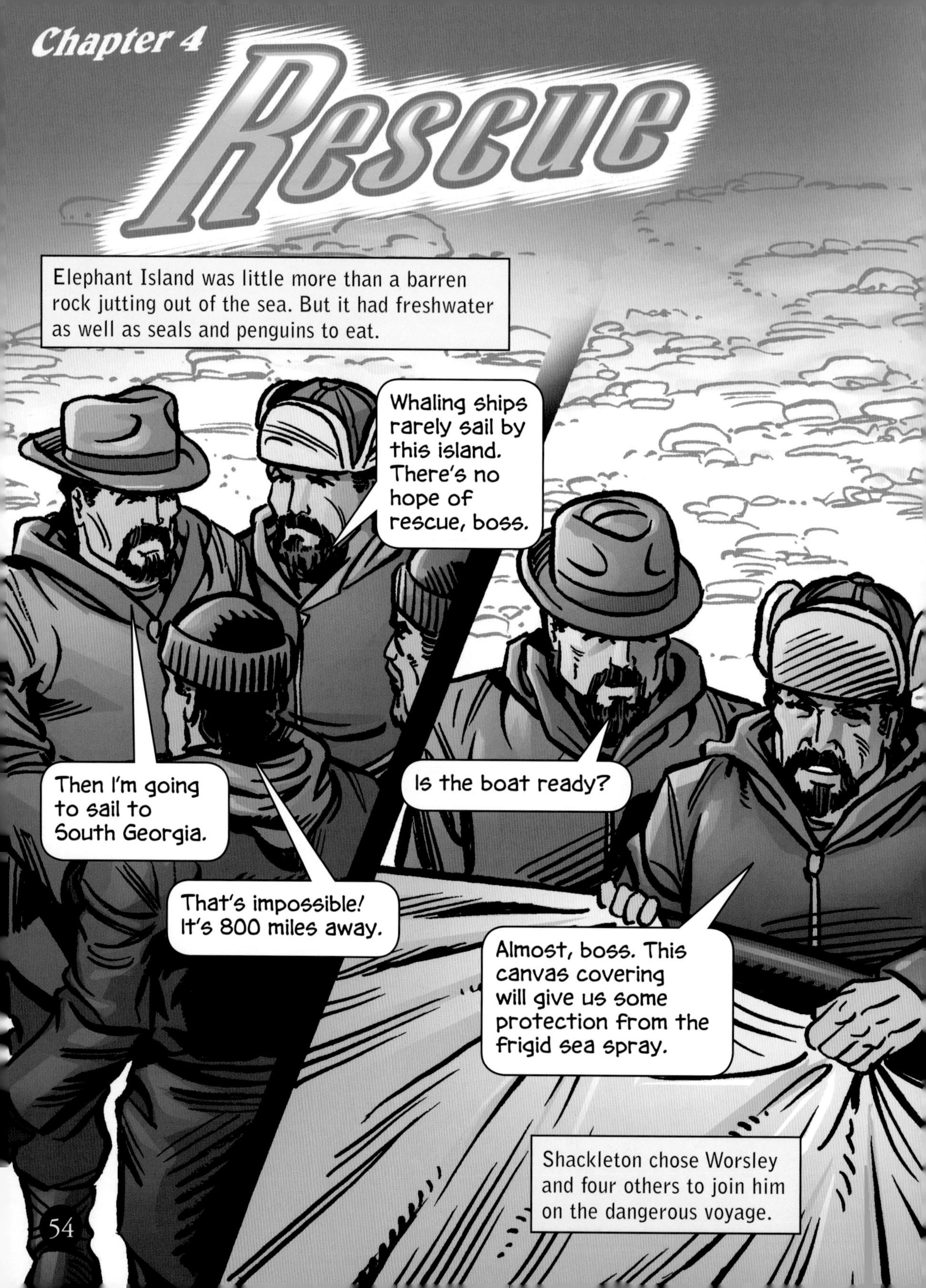
Elephant Island was little more than a barren rock jutting out of the sea. But it had freshwater as well as seals and penguins to eat.
Whaling ships rarely sail by this island. There's no hope of rescue, boss.
Then I'm going to sail to South Georgia.
That's impossible! It's 800 miles away.
Is the boat ready?
Almost, boss. This canvas covering will give us some protection from the frigid sea spray.
Shackleton chose Worsley and four others to join him on the dangerous voyage.

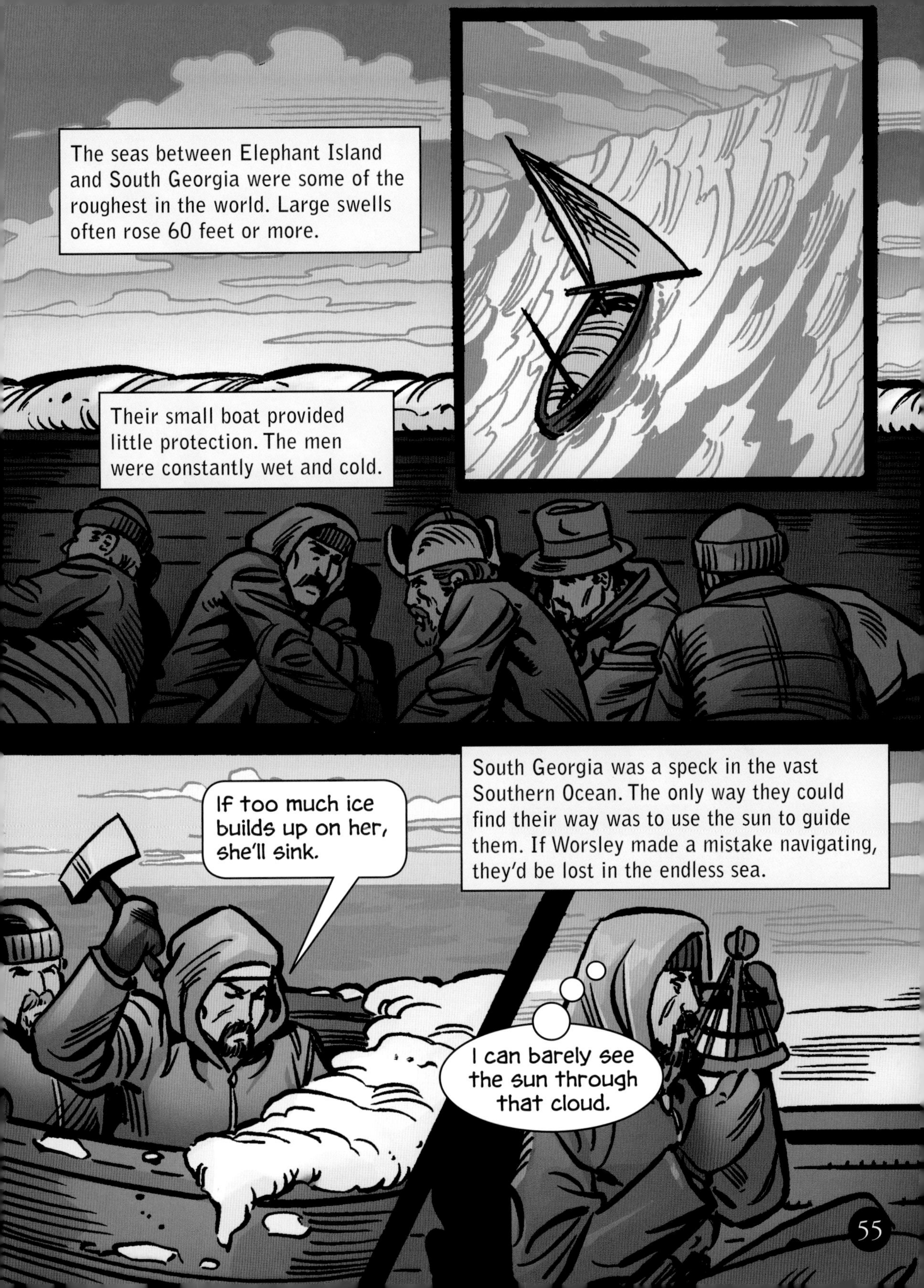

The seas between Elephant Island and South Georgia were some of the roughest in the world. Large swells often rose 60 feet or more.
Their small boat provided little protection. The men were constantly wet and cold.
If too much ice builds up on her, she'll sink.
South Georgia was a speck in the vast Southern Ocean. The only way they could find their way was to use the sun to guide them. If Worsley made a mistake navigating, they'd be lost in the endless sea.
I can barely see the sun through that cloud.

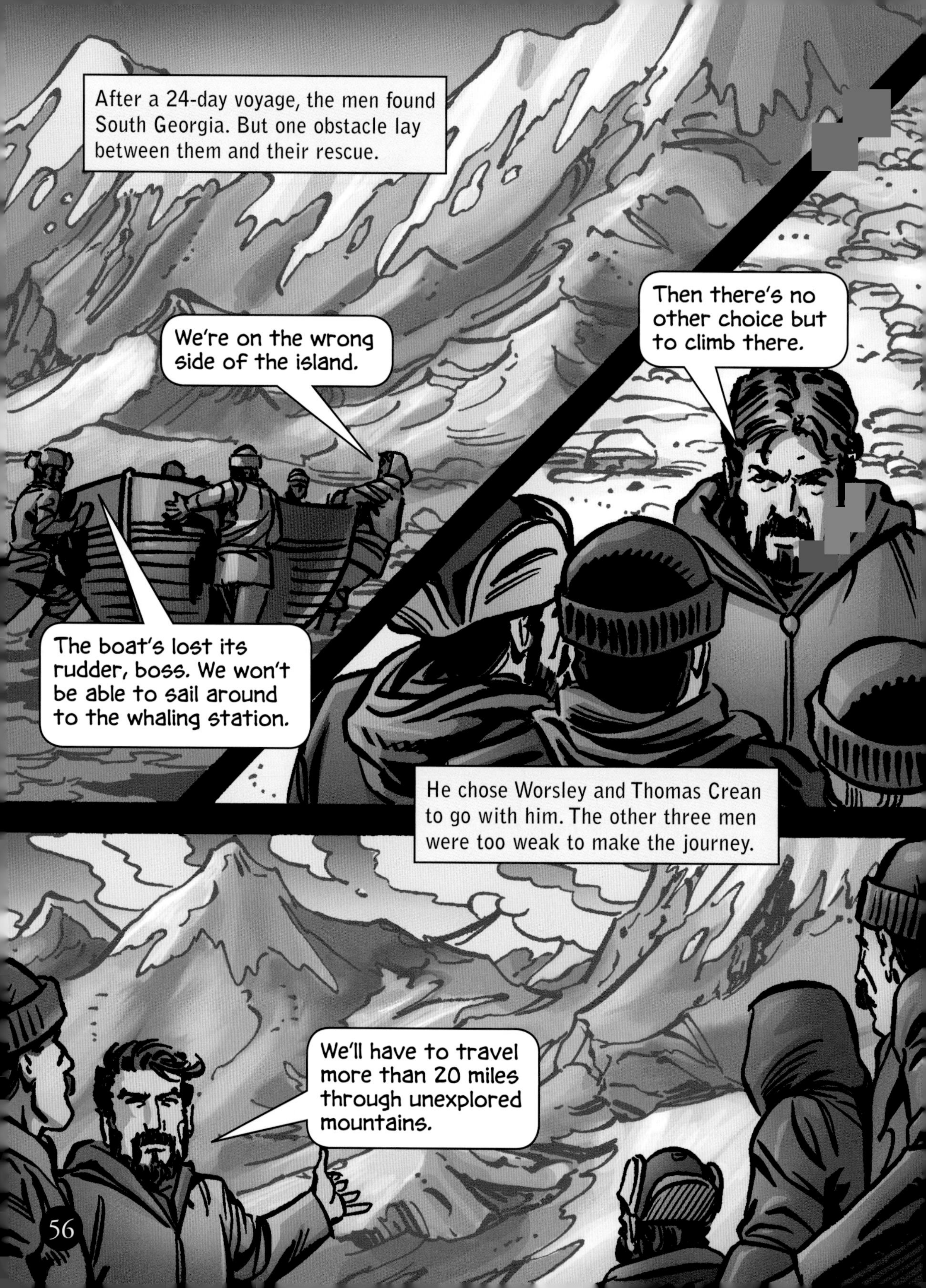
After a 24-day voyage, the men found South Georgia. But one obstacle lay between them and their rescue.
We're on the wrong side of the island.
The boat's lost its rudder, boss. We won't be able to sail around to the whaling station.
Then there's no other choice but to climb there.
He chose Worsley and Thomas Crean to go with him. The other three men were too weak to make the journey.
We'll have to travel more than 20 miles through unexplored mountains.

They continued for 36 straight hours, resting no longer than five minutes at a time.

The men climbed through passes between towering mountains and crossed jagged glaciers.

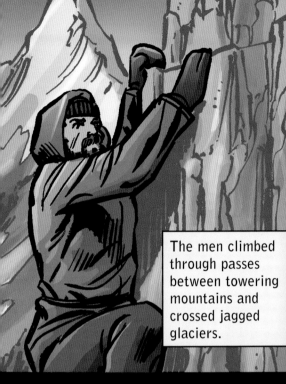

On the dawn of May 20, the three men lumbered into the whaling station. People were shocked to see them.

Who are you?

My name is Shackleton.

Where have you been for the past year and a half?

It's a long story, but first, my men need rescuing.

57

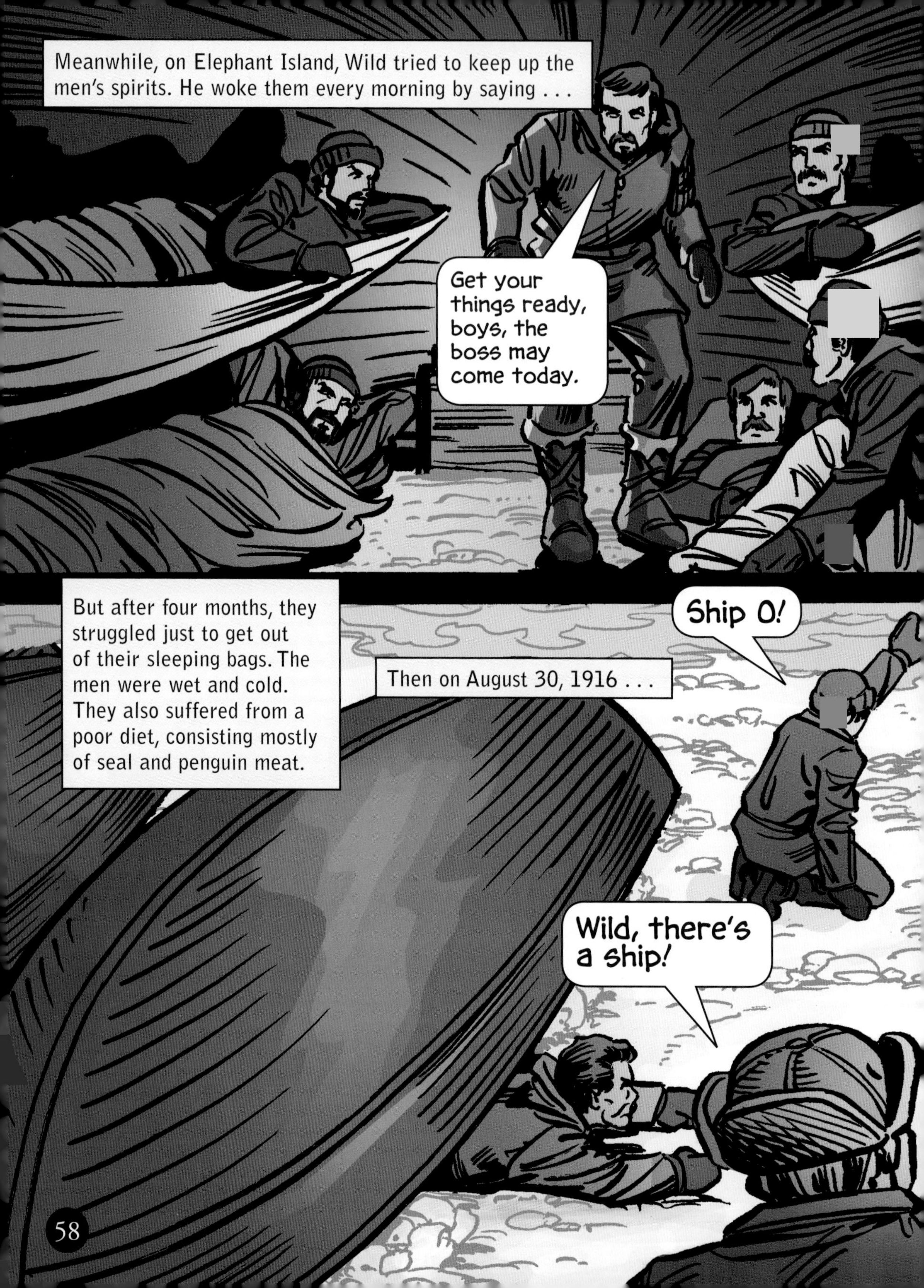
Meanwhile, on Elephant Island, Wild tried to keep up the men's spirits. He woke them every morning by saying . . .
Get your things ready, boys, the boss may come today.
But after four months, they struggled just to get out of their sleeping bags. The men were wet and cold. They also suffered from a poor diet, consisting mostly of seal and penguin meat.
Then on August 30, 1916 . . .
Ship O!
Wild, there's a ship!

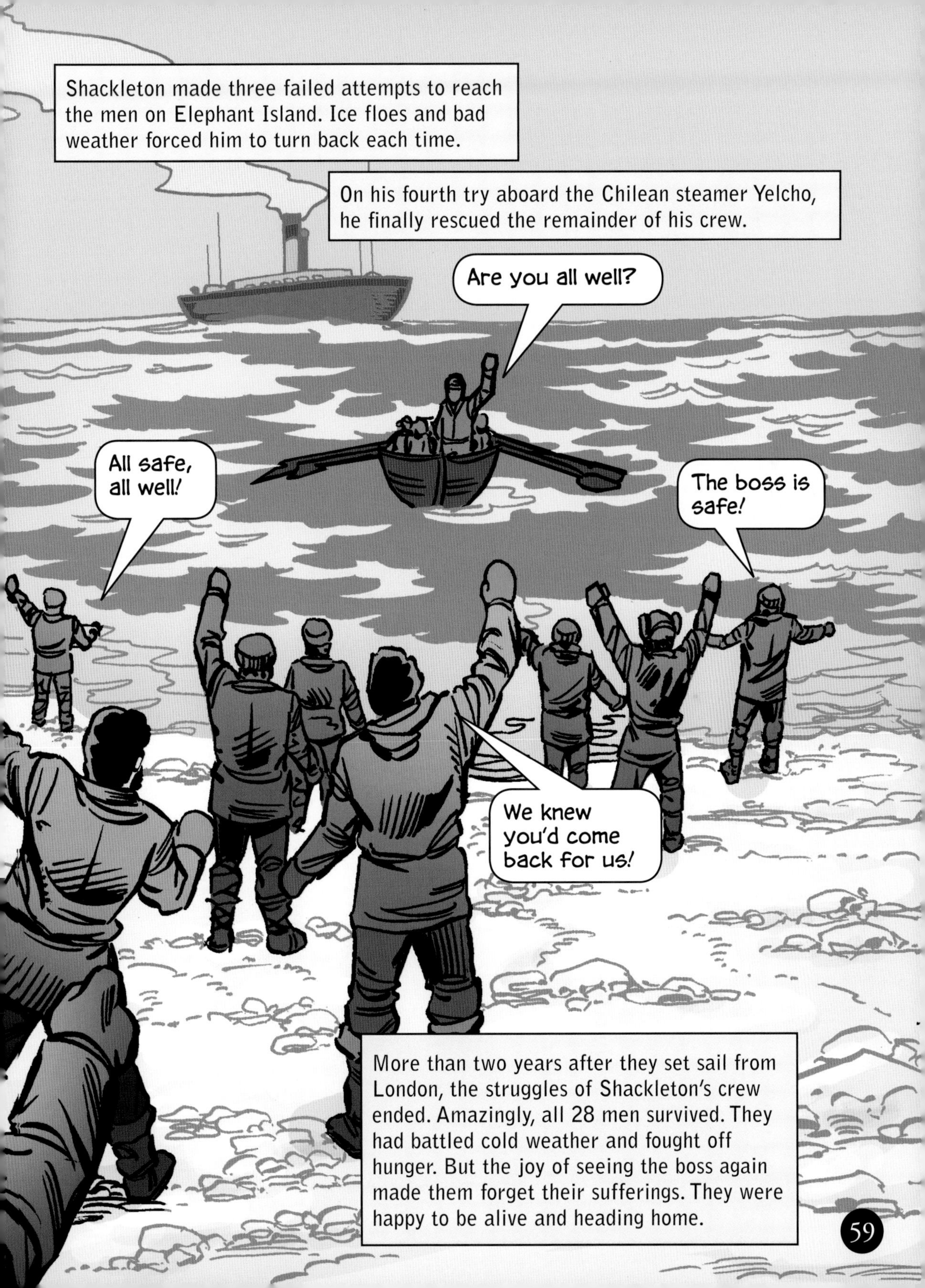
Shackleton made three failed attempts to reach the men on Elephant Island. Ice floes and bad weather forced him to turn back each time.
On his fourth try aboard the Chilean steamer Yelcho, he finally rescued the remainder of his crew.
Are you all well?
All safe, all well!
The boss is safe!
We knew you'd come back for us!
More than two years after they set sail from London, the struggles of Shackleton's crew ended. Amazingly, all 28 men survived. They had battled cold weather and fought off hunger. But the joy of seeing the boss again made them forget their sufferings. They were happy to be alive and heading home.

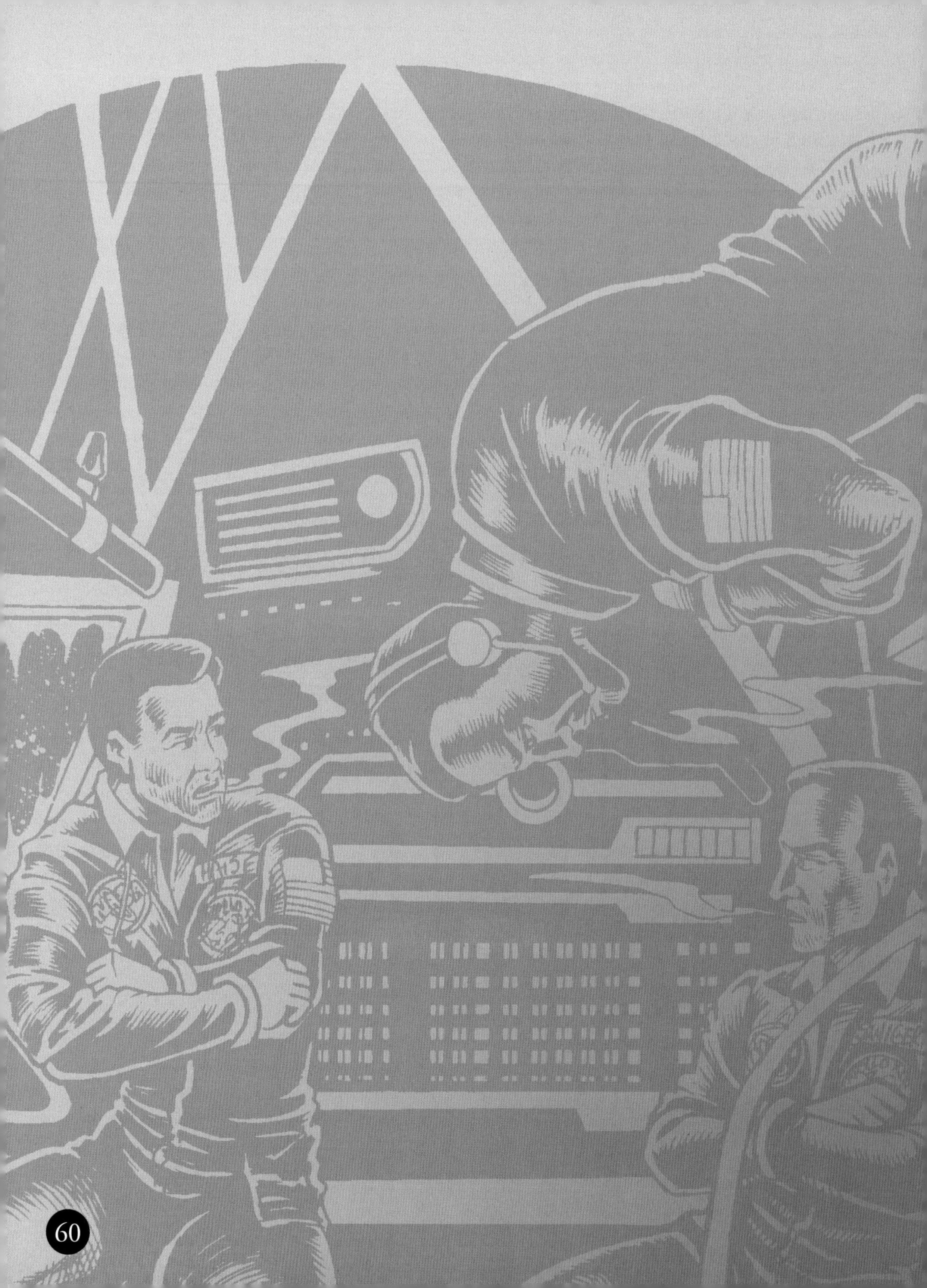

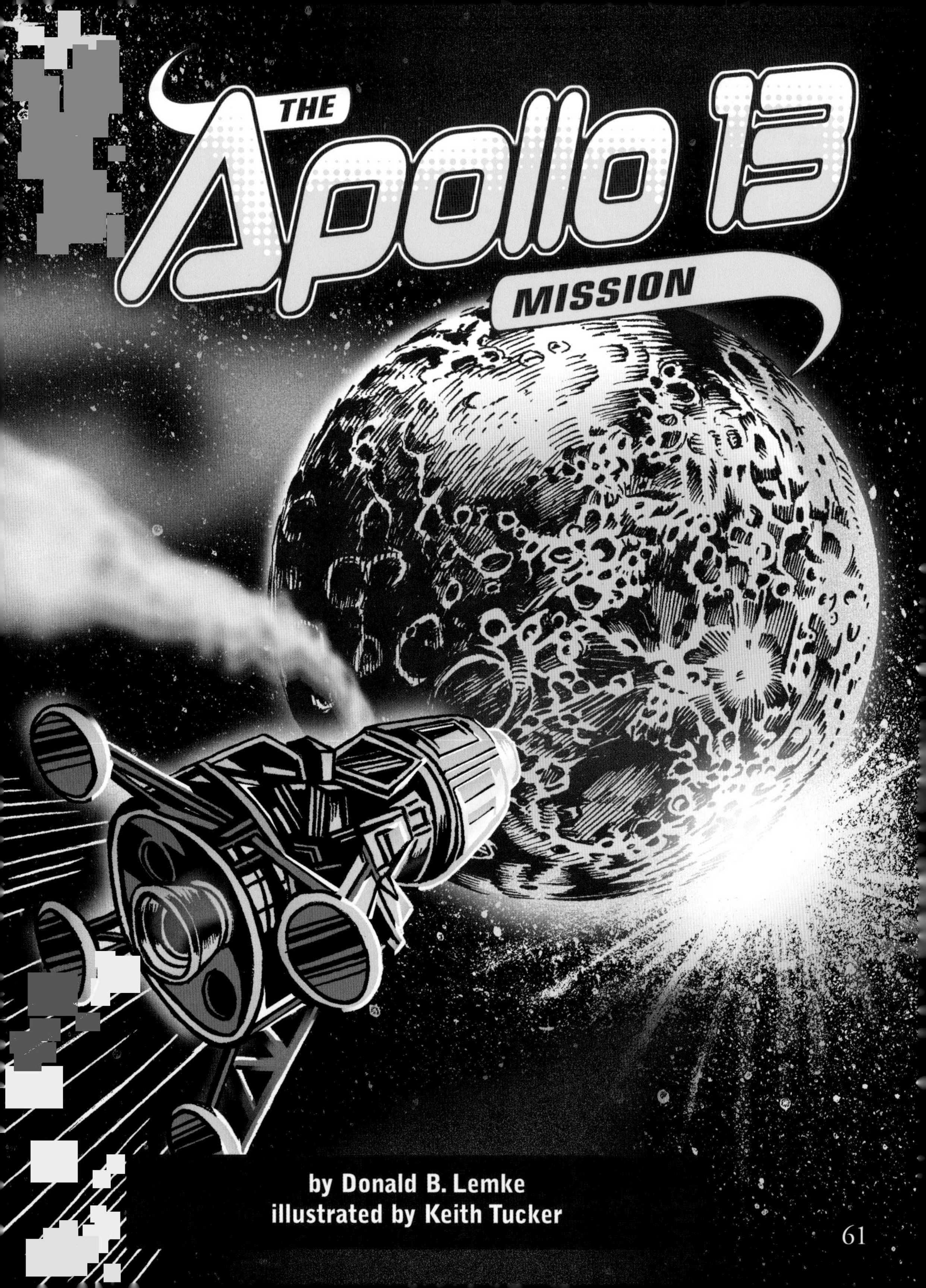

The Apollo 13 Mission

by Donald B. Lemke
illustrated by Keith Tucker

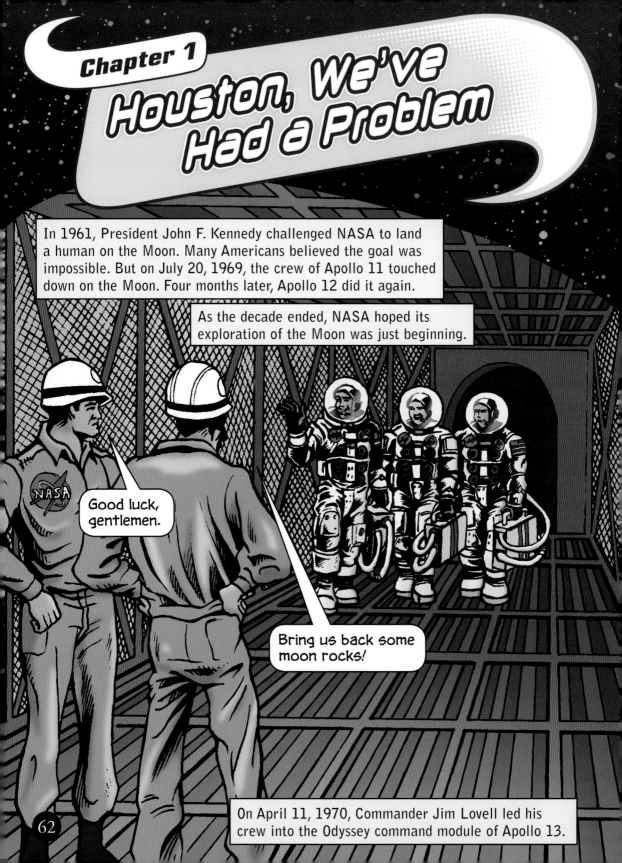

Chapter 1
Houston, We've Had a Problem

In 1961, President John F. Kennedy challenged NASA to land a human on the Moon. Many Americans believed the goal was impossible. But on July 20, 1969, the crew of Apollo 11 touched down on the Moon. Four months later, Apollo 12 did it again.

As the decade ended, NASA hoped its exploration of the Moon was just beginning.

Good luck, gentlemen.

Bring us back some moon rocks!

On April 11, 1970, Commander Jim Lovell led his crew into the Odyssey command module of Apollo 13.

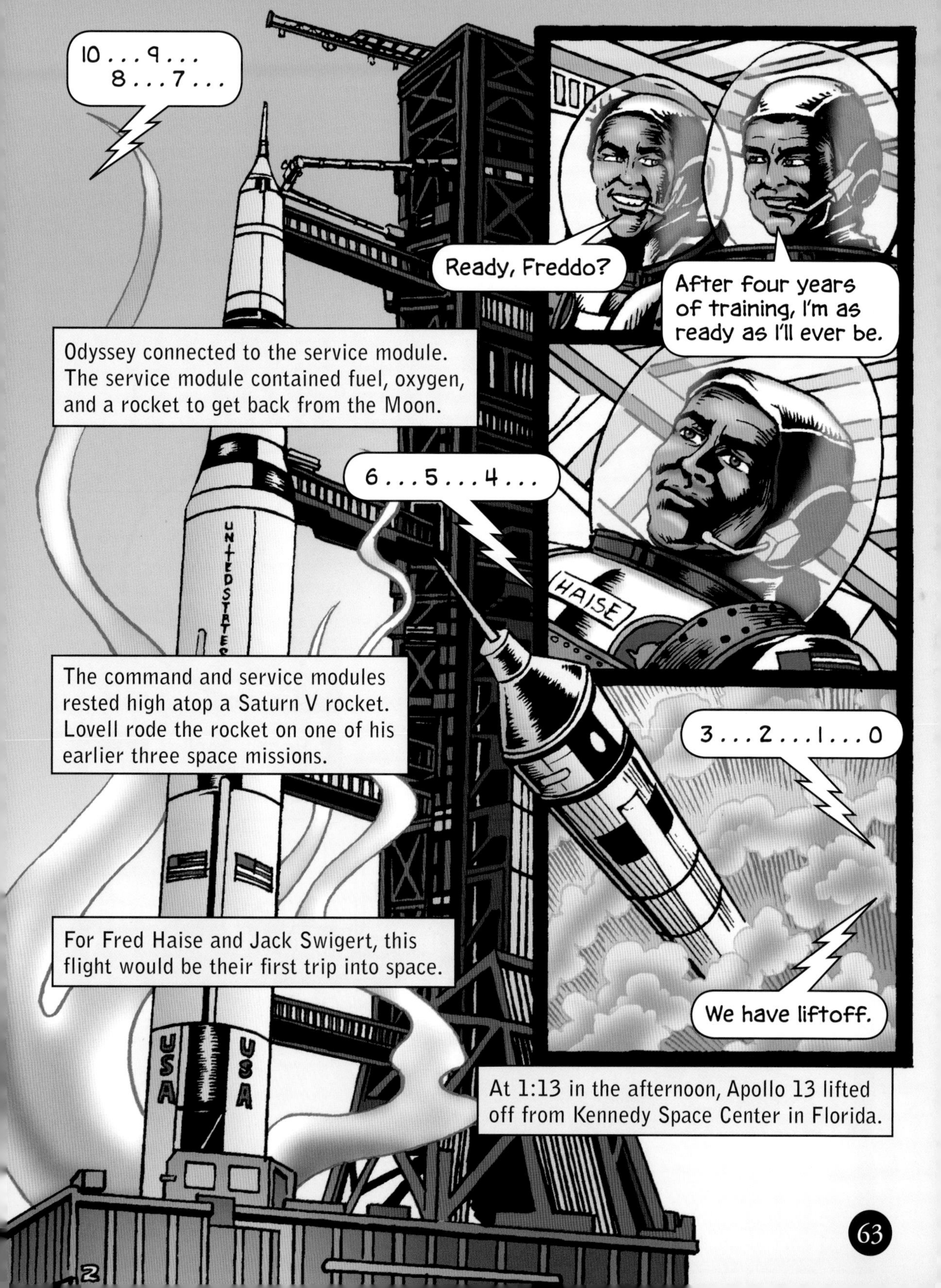
10 . . . 9 . . . 8 . . . 7 . . .
Ready, Freddo?
After four years of training, I'm as ready as I'll ever be.
Odyssey connected to the service module. The service module contained fuel, oxygen, and a rocket to get back from the Moon.
6 . . . 5 . . . 4 . . .
UNITED STATES
HAISE
The command and service modules rested high atop a Saturn V rocket. Lovell rode the rocket on one of his earlier three space missions.
3 . . . 2 . . . 1 . . . 0
For Fred Haise and Jack Swigert, this flight would be their first trip into space.
We have liftoff.
USA
USA
At 1:13 in the afternoon, Apollo 13 lifted off from Kennedy Space Center in Florida.

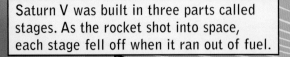

Saturn V was built in three parts called stages. As the rocket shot into space, each stage fell off when it ran out of fuel.

KKKKRRRR!

Houston, this is Apollo. We've separated from the second stage and we're firing the third.

Teams of flight controllers monitored the spacecraft from Mission Control in Houston, Texas. During the launch, Joe Kerwin was in charge of the Capcom team. Capcom radioed messages between the controllers and the crew.

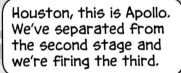

Roger, Apollo. Everything looks good.

Let's head for the hills!

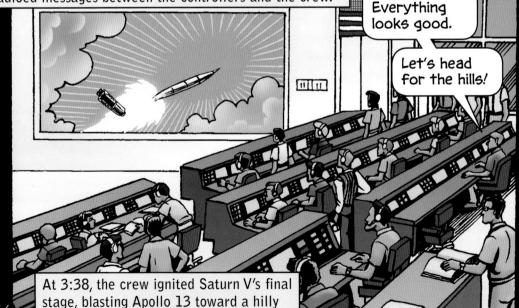

At 3:38, the crew ignited Saturn V's final stage, blasting Apollo 13 toward a hilly part of the Moon called Fra Mauro.

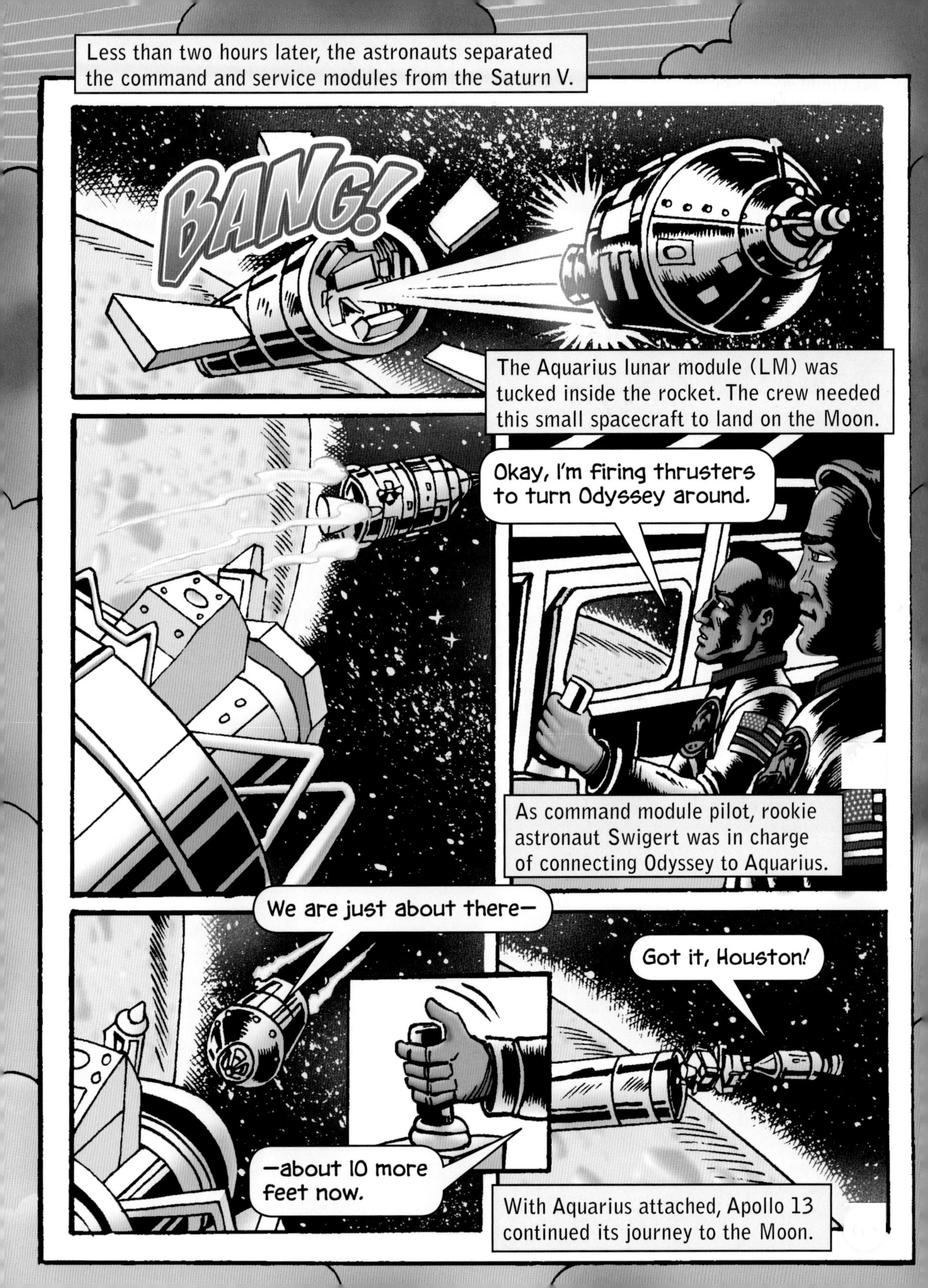

Less than two hours later, the astronauts separated the command and service modules from the Saturn V.
BANG!
The Aquarius lunar module (LM) was tucked inside the rocket. The crew needed this small spacecraft to land on the Moon.
Okay, I'm firing thrusters to turn Odyssey around.
As command module pilot, rookie astronaut Swigert was in charge of connecting Odyssey to Aquarius.
We are just about there—
—about 10 more feet now.
Got it, Houston!
With Aquarius attached, Apollo 13 continued its journey to the Moon.

On the evening of April 13, the astronauts made their first TV broadcast to Earth.

Fred and I are going to move from Odyssey, through the tunnel, and into Aquarius.

Aquarius is about the size of a small car. In less than two days, I'll land this tiny spacecraft on the Moon. A place only four people have walked before.

Let's see if Jim can get a good picture.

We can see some of the Moon's features pretty clearly now.

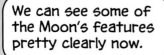

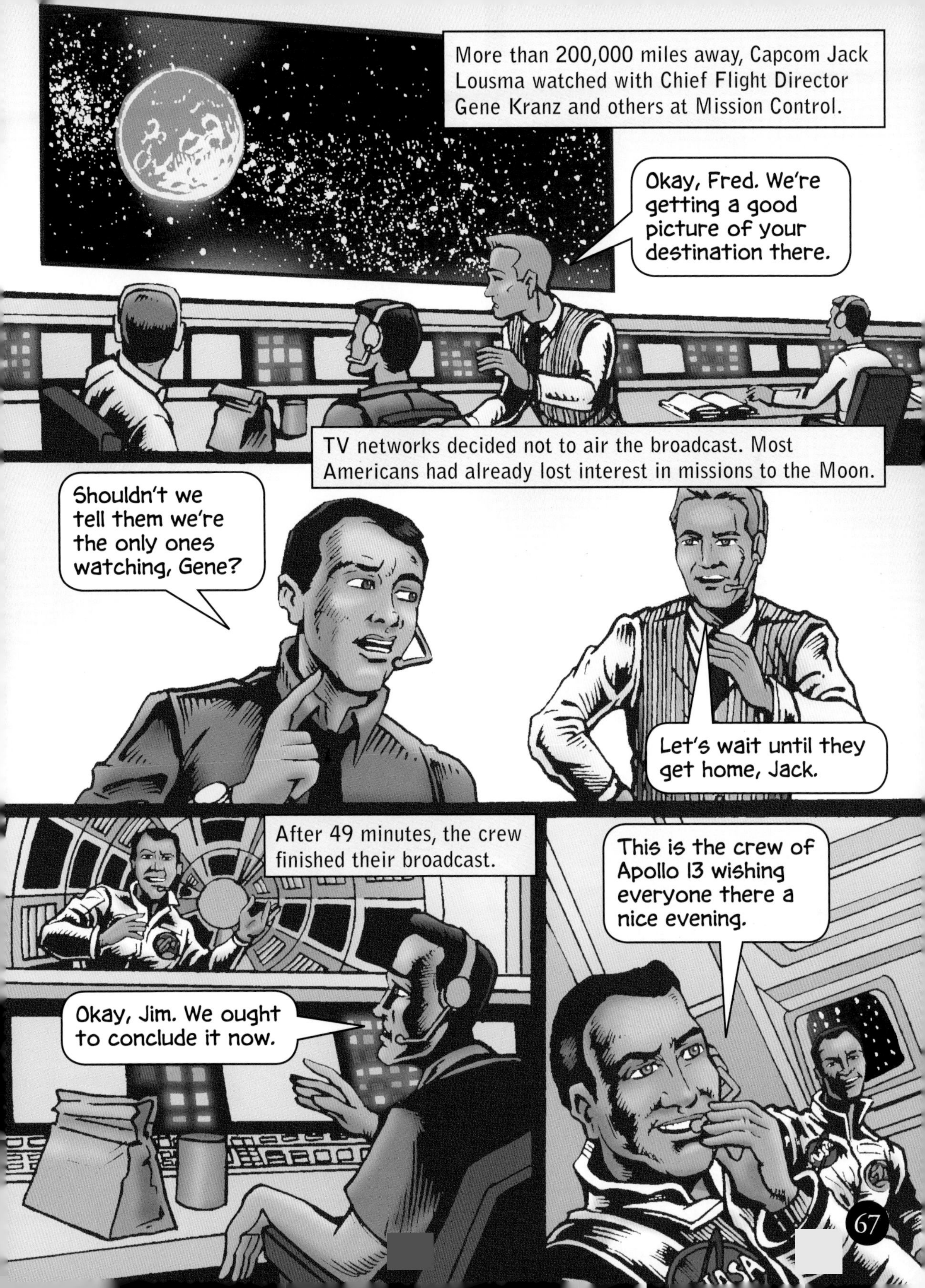
More than 200,000 miles away, Capcom Jack Lousma watched with Chief Flight Director Gene Kranz and others at Mission Control.
Okay, Fred. We're getting a good picture of your destination there.
TV networks decided not to air the broadcast. Most Americans had already lost interest in missions to the Moon.
Shouldn't we tell them we're the only ones watching, Gene?
Let's wait until they get home, Jack.
After 49 minutes, the crew finished their broadcast.
Okay, Jim. We ought to conclude it now.
This is the crew of Apollo 13 wishing everyone there a nice evening.

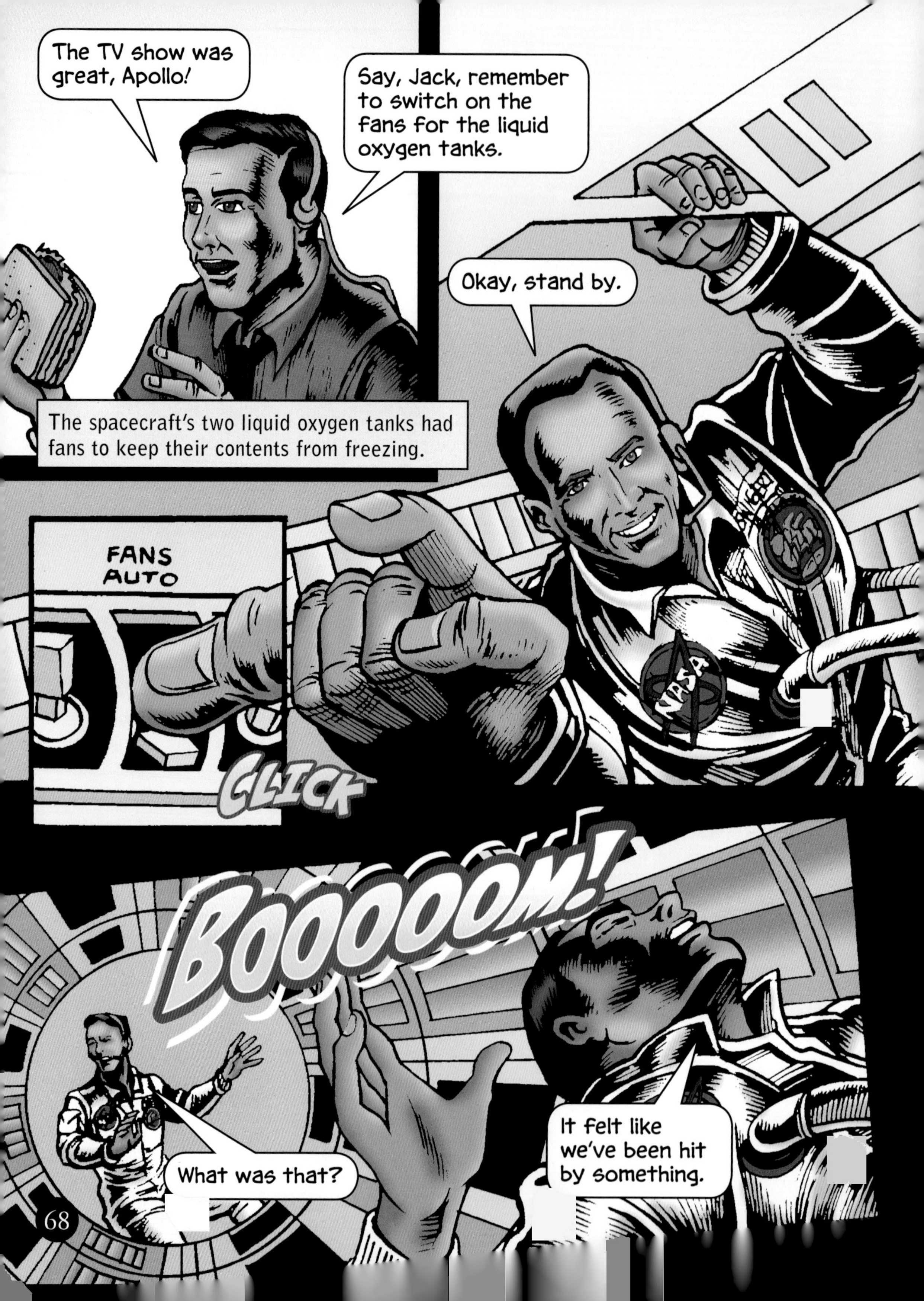

The TV show was great, Apollo!
Say, Jack, remember to switch on the fans for the liquid oxygen tanks.
Okay, stand by.
The spacecraft's two liquid oxygen tanks had fans to keep their contents from freezing.
FANS AUTO
CLICK
BOOOOOM!
What was that?
It felt like we've been hit by something.

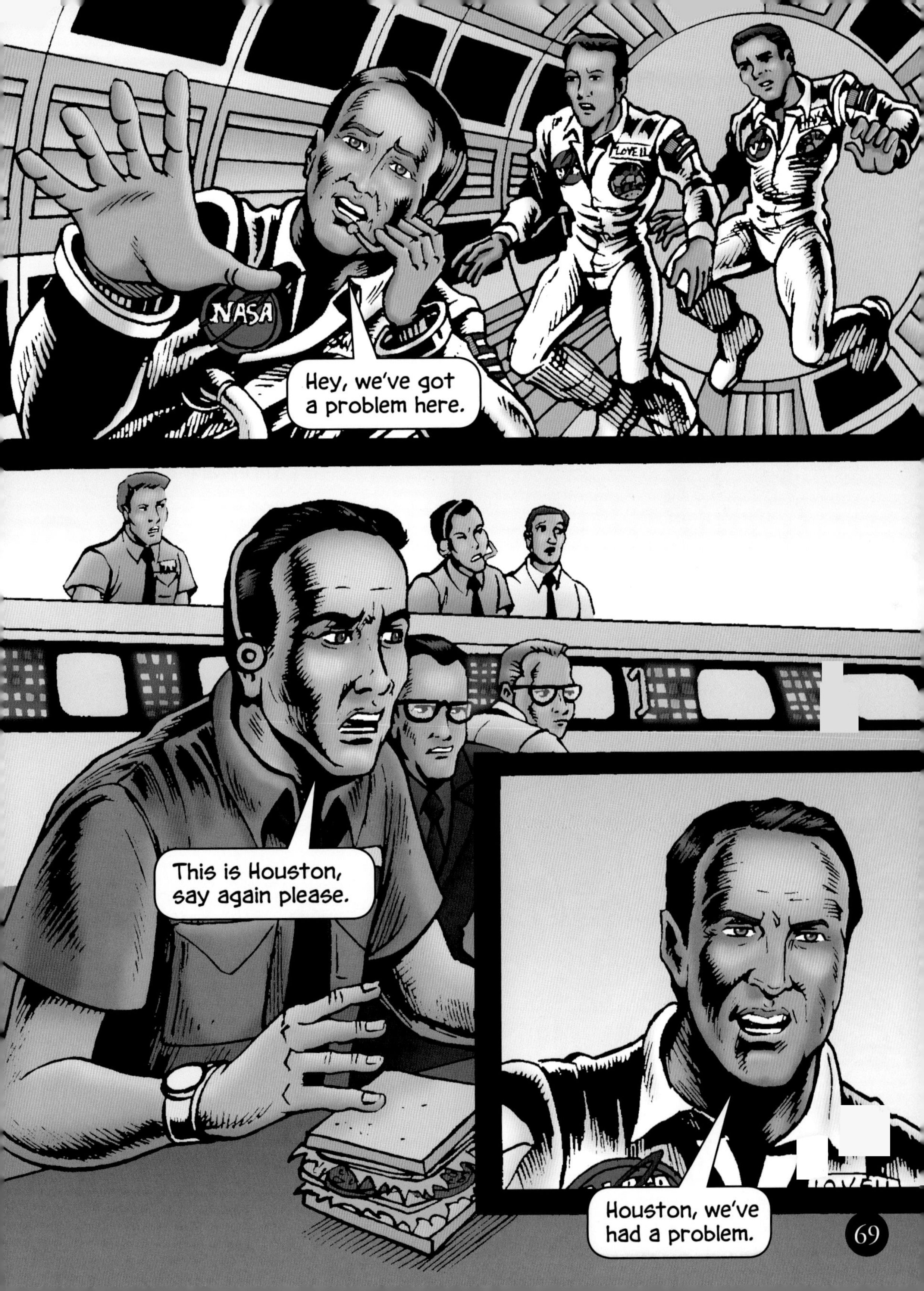
Hey, we've got a problem here.
This is Houston, say again please.
Houston, we've had a problem.

Chapter 2

Solving the Problem

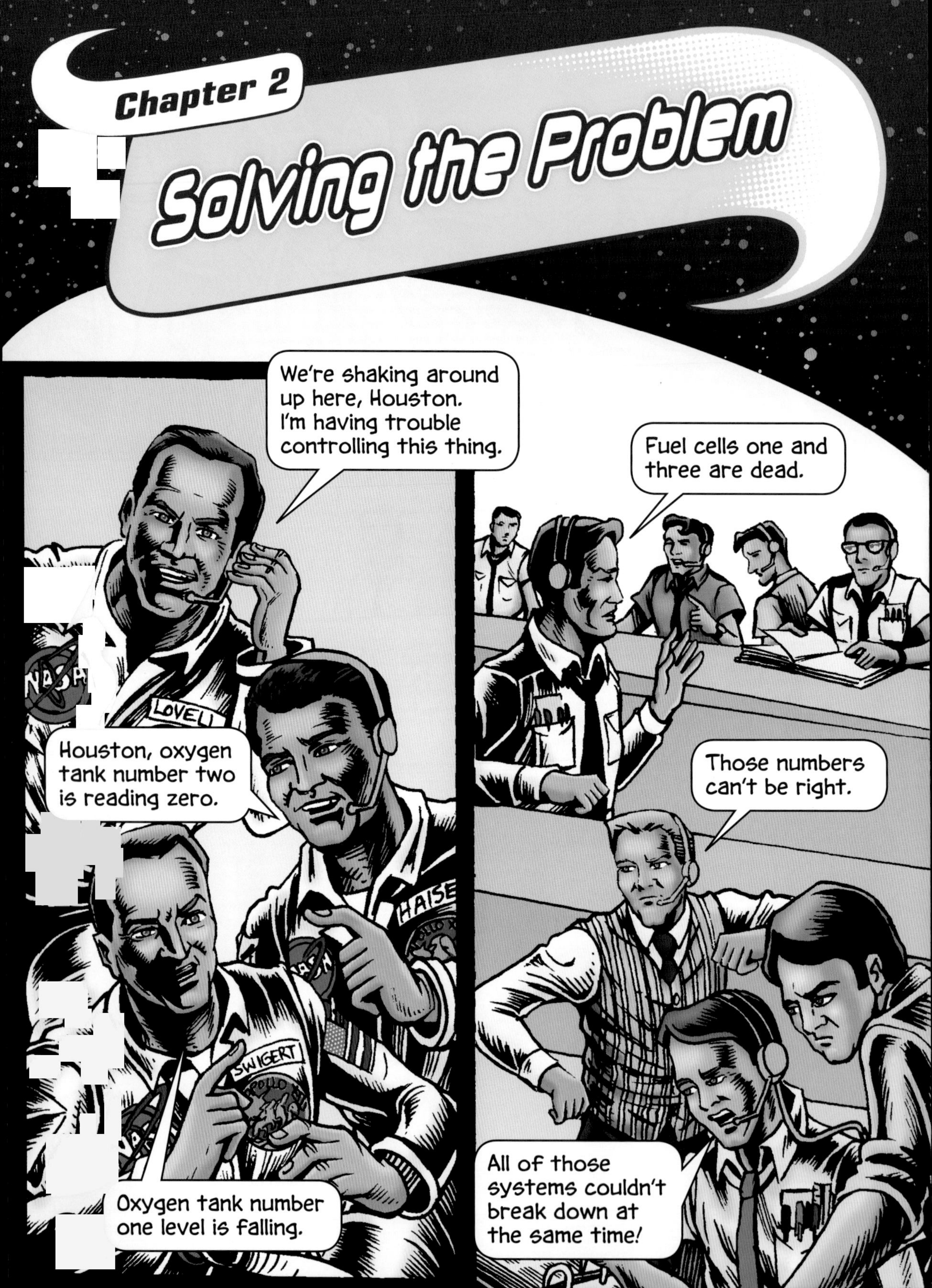

We're shaking around up here, Houston. I'm having trouble controlling this thing.
LOVELL
Houston, oxygen tank number two is reading zero.
HAISE
SWIGERT
Oxygen tank number one level is falling.
Fuel cells one and three are dead.
Those numbers can't be right.
All of those systems couldn't break down at the same time!

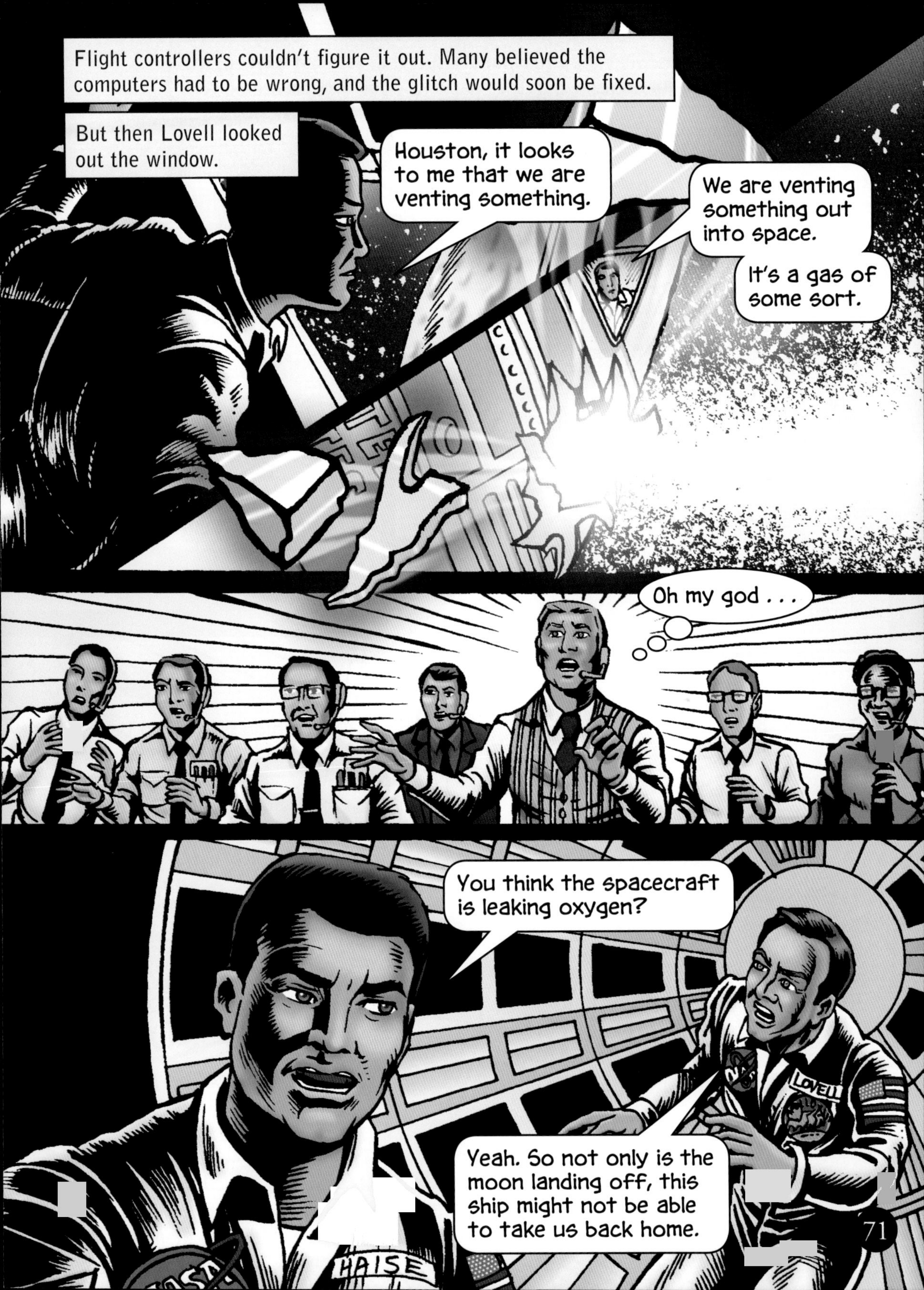

Flight controllers couldn't figure it out. Many believed the computers had to be wrong, and the glitch would soon be fixed.
But then Lovell looked out the window.
Houston, it looks to me that we are venting something.
We are venting something out into space.
It's a gas of some sort.
Oh my god . . .
You think the spacecraft is leaking oxygen?
Yeah. So not only is the moon landing off, this ship might not be able to take us back home.
LOVELL
HAISE

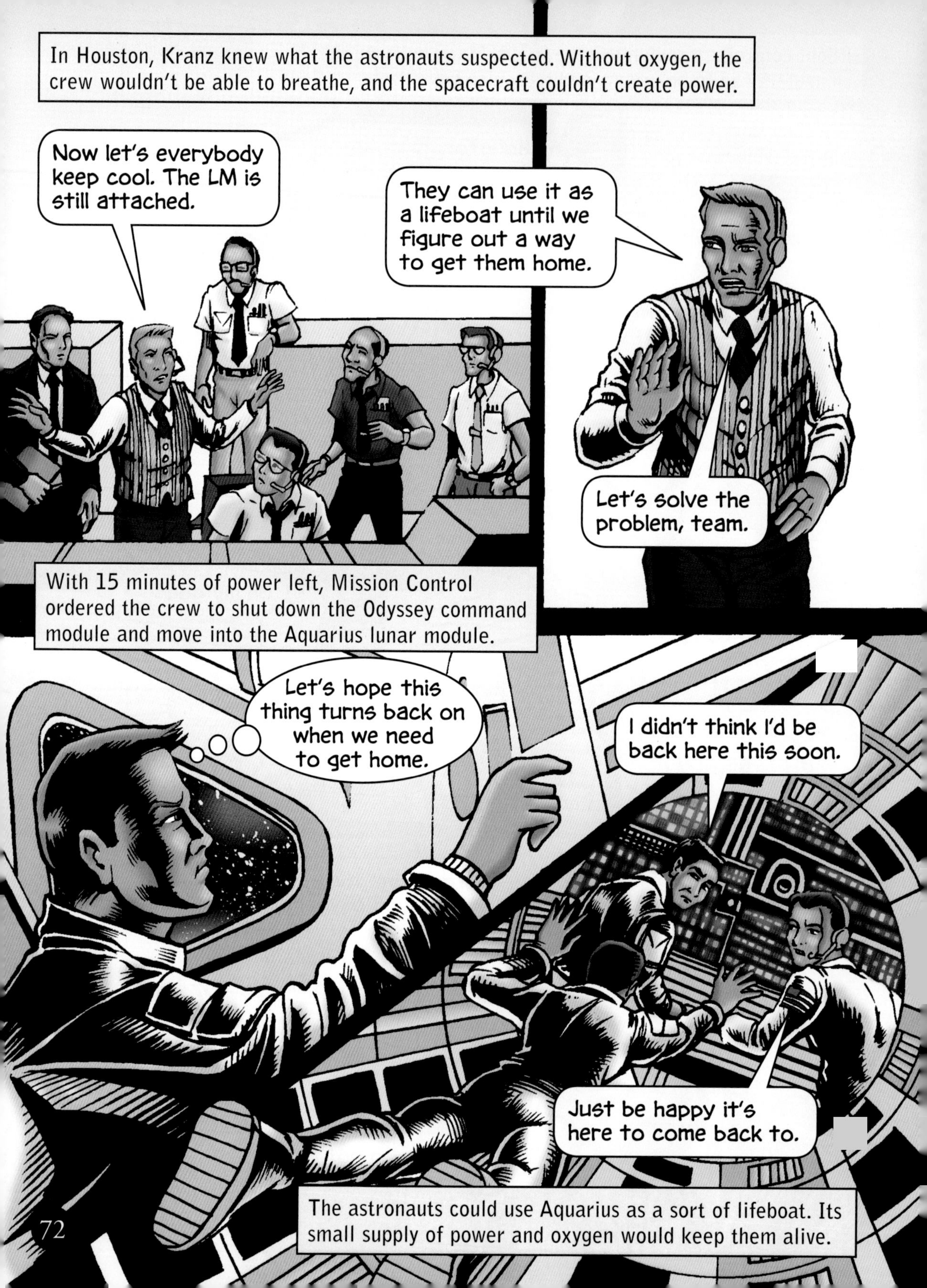
In Houston, Kranz knew what the astronauts suspected. Without oxygen, the crew wouldn't be able to breathe, and the spacecraft couldn't create power.
Now let's everybody keep cool. The LM is still attached.
They can use it as a lifeboat until we figure out a way to get them home.
Let's solve the problem, team.
With 15 minutes of power left, Mission Control ordered the crew to shut down the Odyssey command module and move into the Aquarius lunar module.
Let's hope this thing turns back on when we need to get home.
I didn't think I'd be back here this soon.
Just be happy it's here to come back to.
The astronauts could use Aquarius as a sort of lifeboat. Its small supply of power and oxygen would keep them alive.

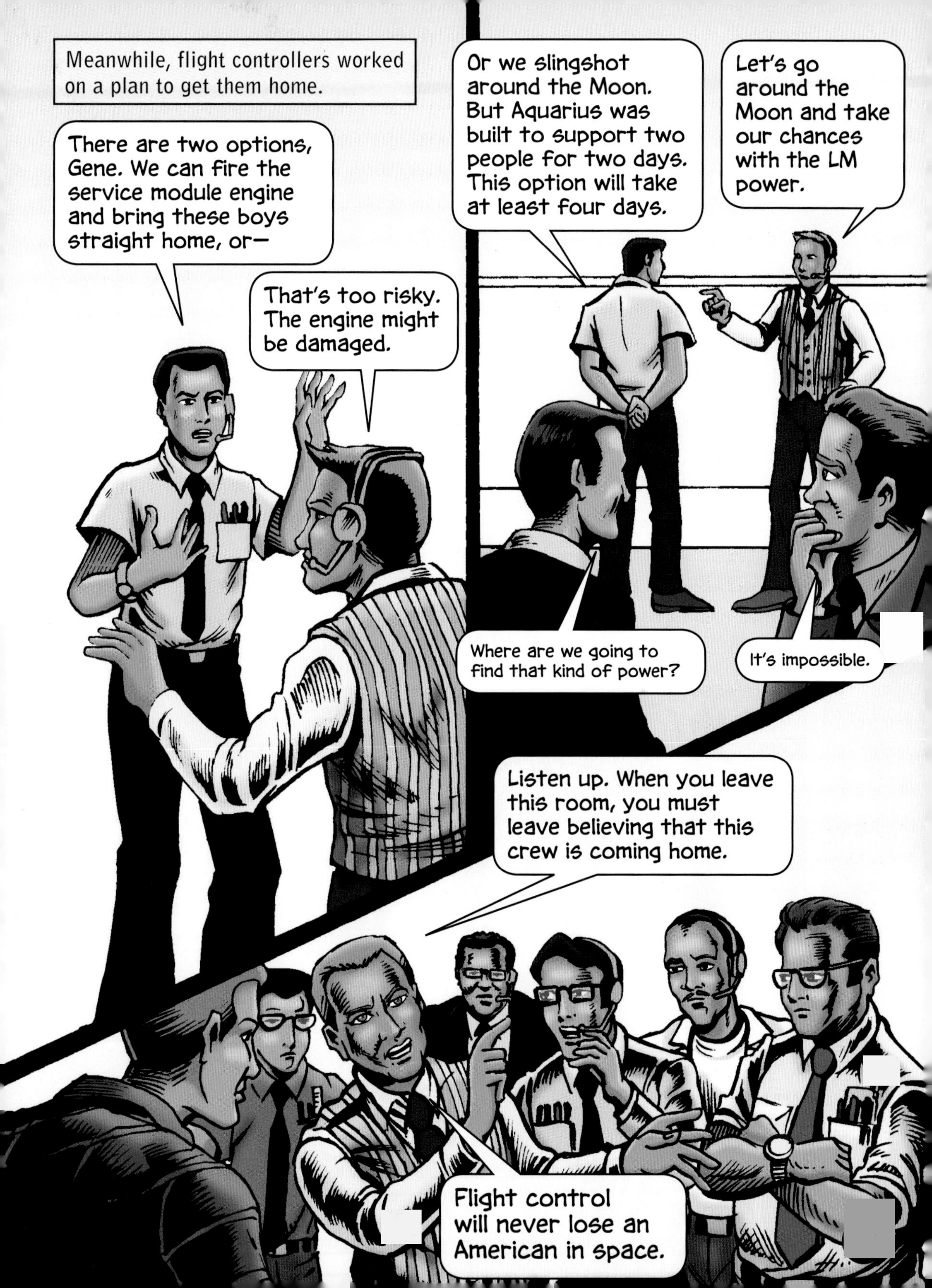

Meanwhile, flight controllers worked on a plan to get them home.
There are two options, Gene. We can fire the service module engine and bring these boys straight home, or—
That's too risky. The engine might be damaged.
Or we slingshot around the Moon. But Aquarius was built to support two people for two days. This option will take at least four days.
Let's go around the Moon and take our chances with the LM power.
Where are we going to find that kind of power?
It's impossible.
Listen up. When you leave this room, you must leave believing that this crew is coming home.
Flight control will never lose an American in space.

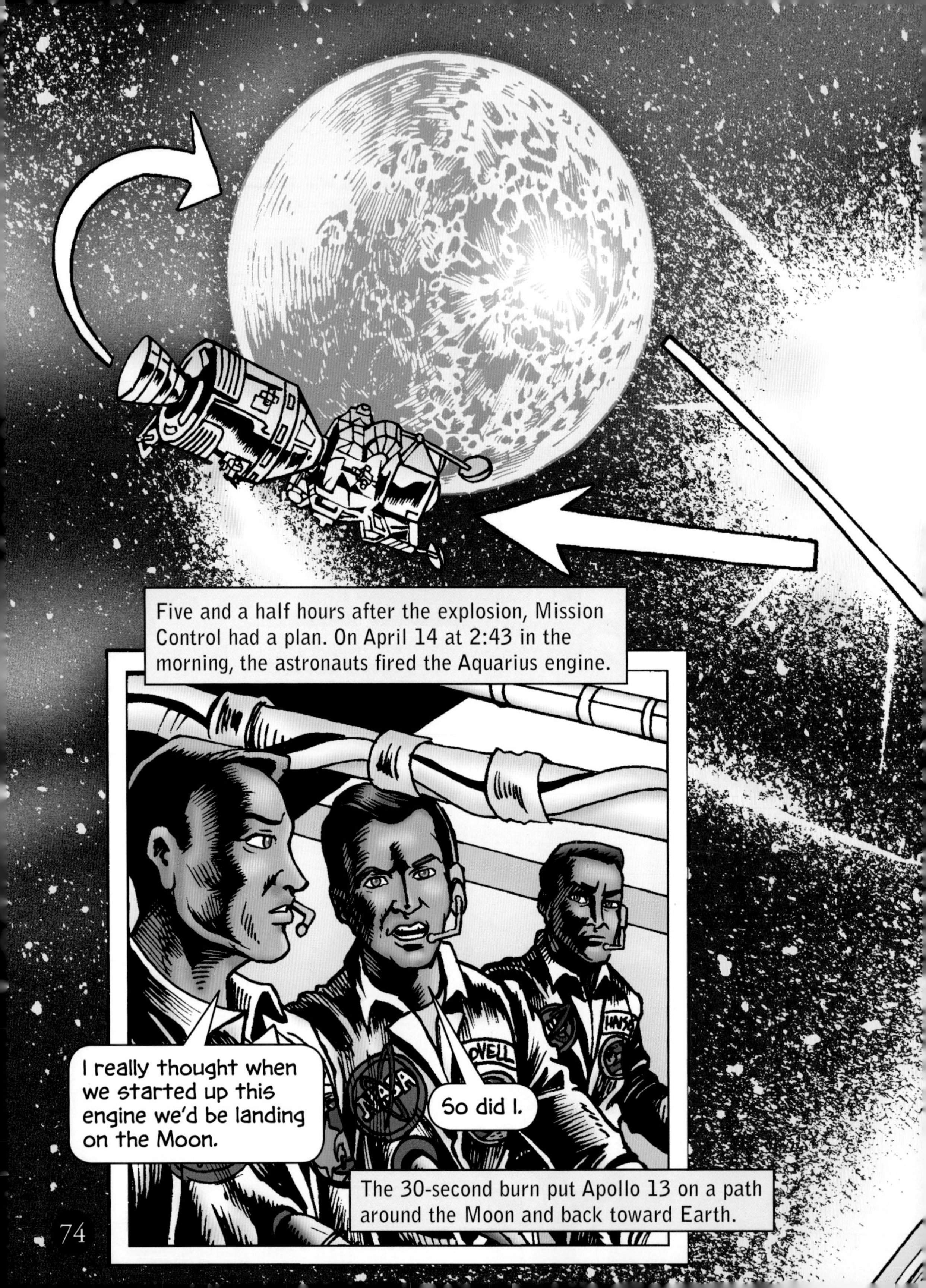
Five and a half hours after the explosion, Mission Control had a plan. On April 14 at 2:43 in the morning, the astronauts fired the Aquarius engine.
I really thought when we started up this engine we'd be landing on the Moon.
So did I.
The 30-second burn put Apollo 13 on a path around the Moon and back toward Earth.

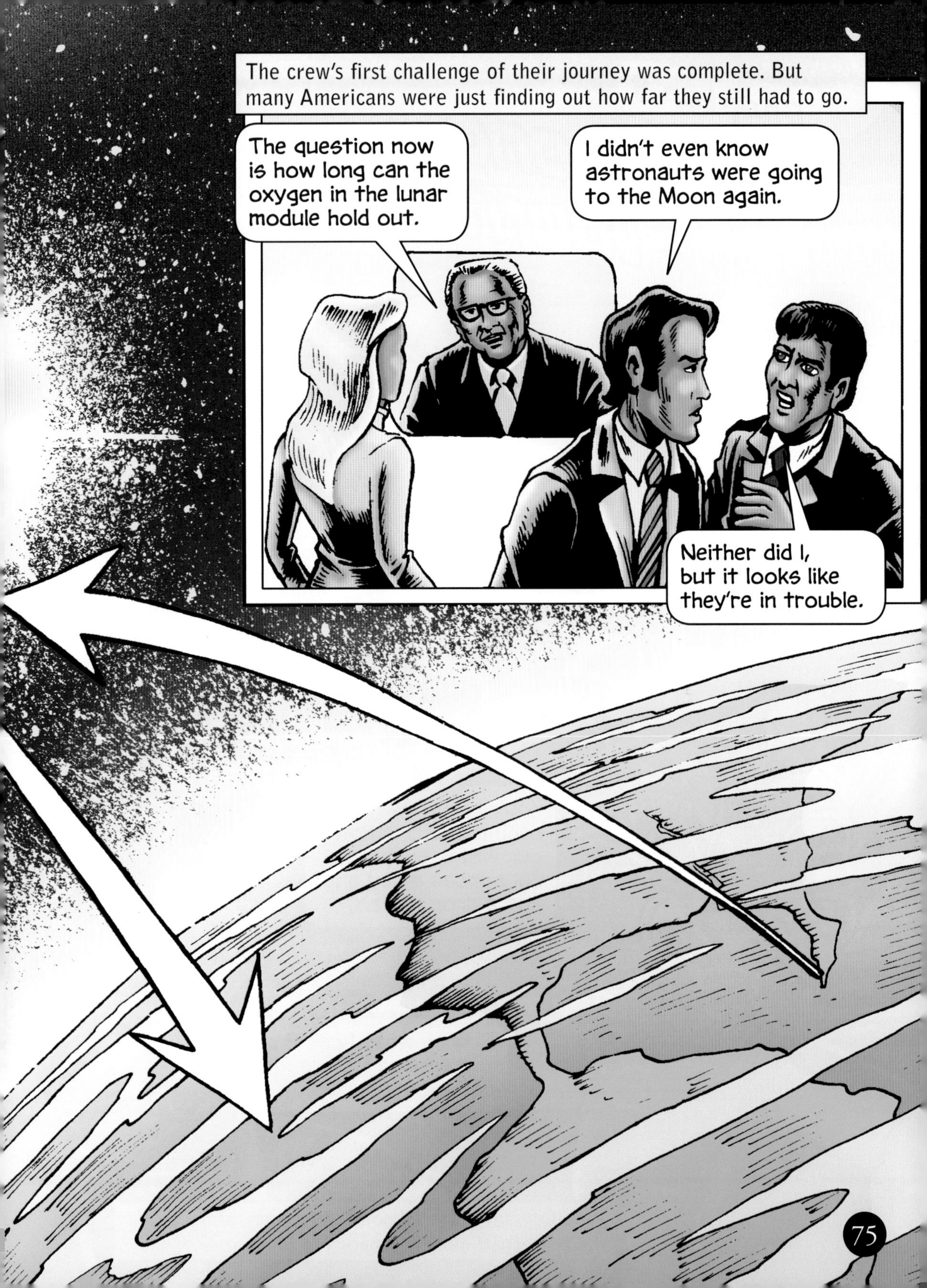
The crew's first challenge of their journey was complete. But many Americans were just finding out how far they still had to go.
The question now is how long can the oxygen in the lunar module hold out.
I didn't even know astronauts were going to the Moon again.
Neither did I, but it looks like they're in trouble.

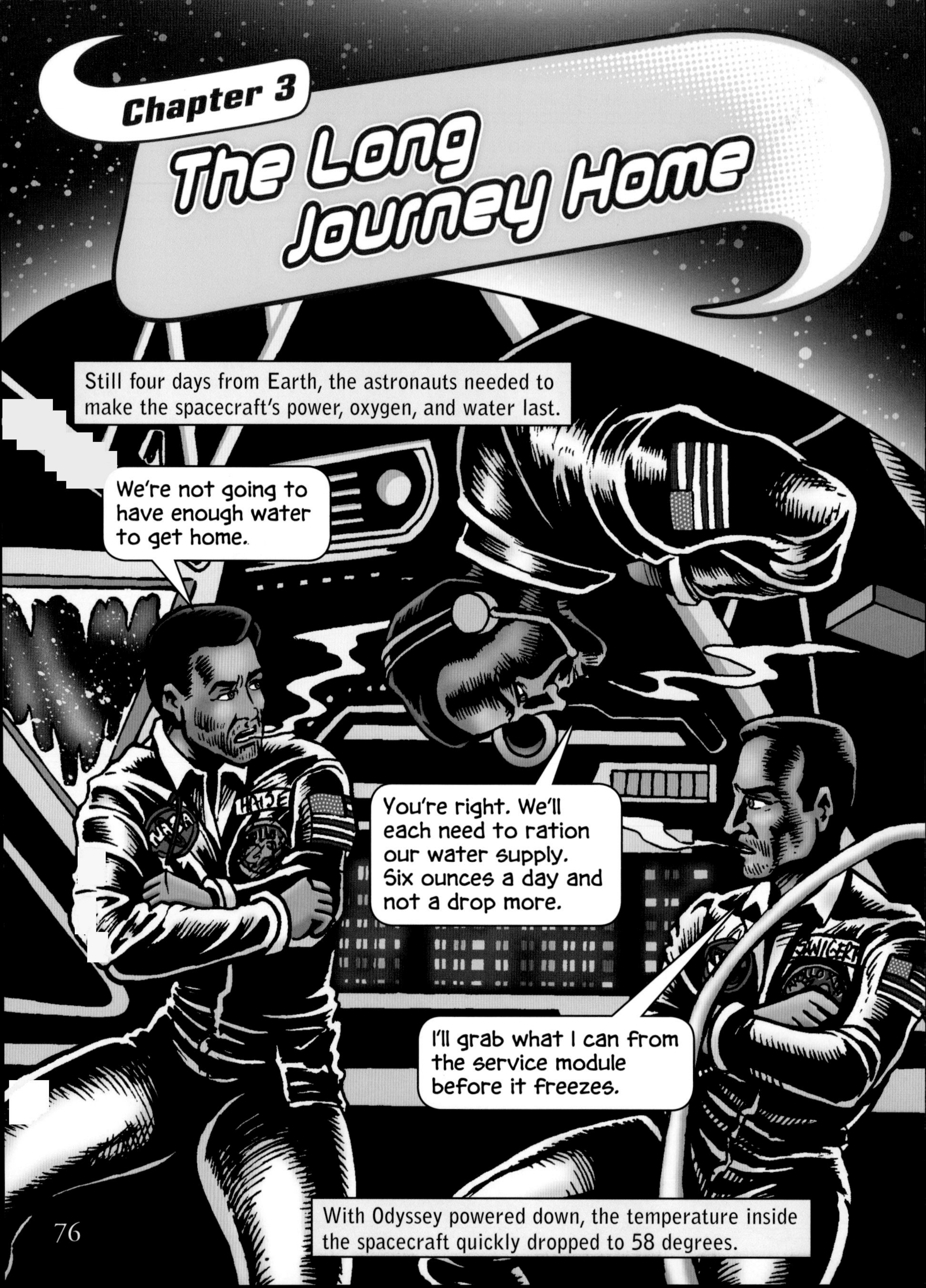
Chapter 3
The Long Journey Home
Still four days from Earth, the astronauts needed to make the spacecraft's power, oxygen, and water last.
We're not going to have enough water to get home.
You're right. We'll each need to ration our water supply. Six ounces a day and not a drop more.
I'll grab what I can from the service module before it freezes.
With Odyssey powered down, the temperature inside the spacecraft quickly dropped to 58 degrees.

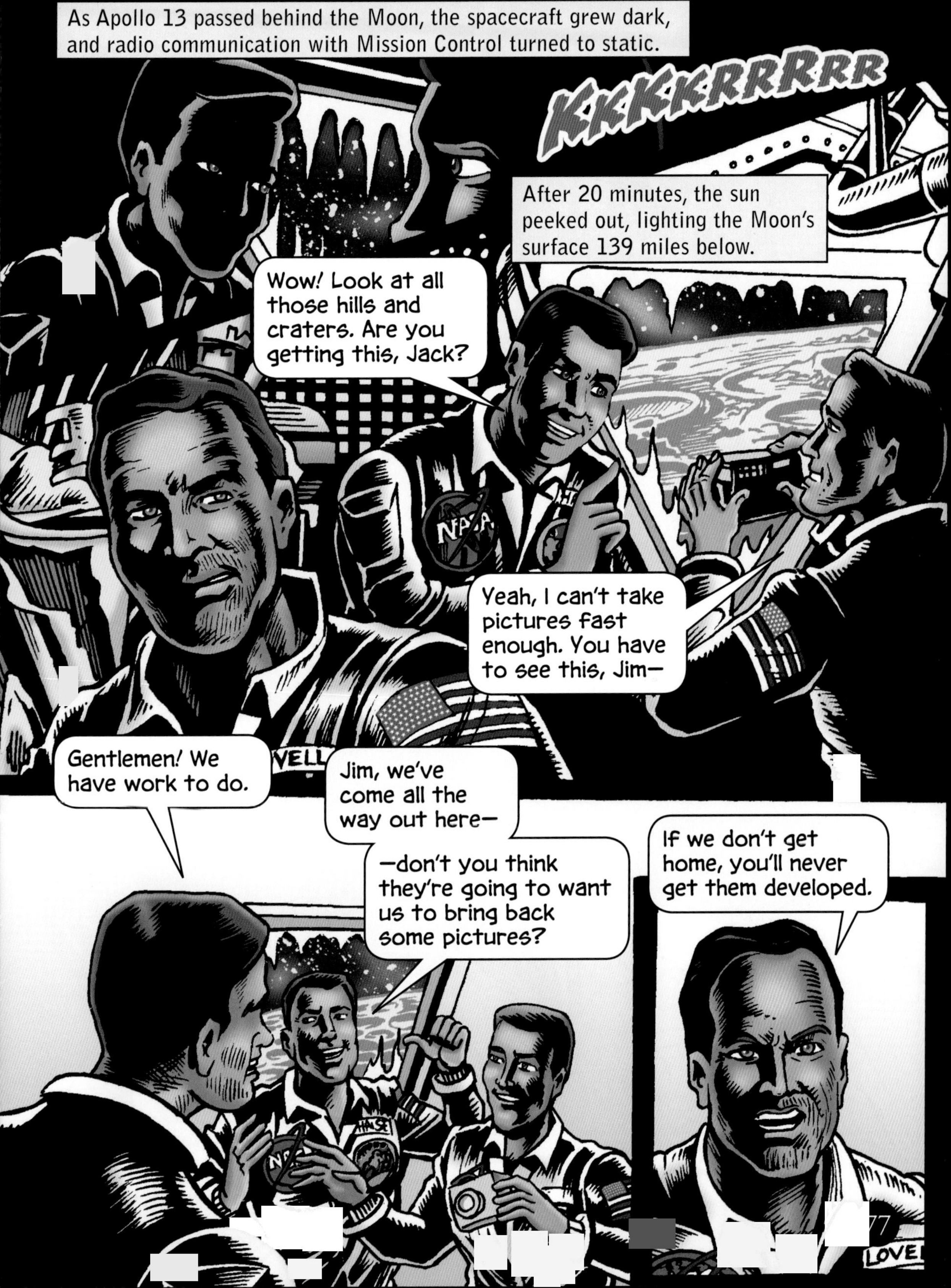
As Apollo 13 passed behind the Moon, the spacecraft grew dark, and radio communication with Mission Control turned to static.
KKKKRRRRR
After 20 minutes, the sun peeked out, lighting the Moon's surface 139 miles below.
Wow! Look at all those hills and craters. Are you getting this, Jack?
Yeah, I can't take pictures fast enough. You have to see this, Jim—
Gentlemen! We have work to do.
Jim, we've come all the way out here—
—don't you think they're going to want us to bring back some pictures?
If we don't get home, you'll never get them developed.

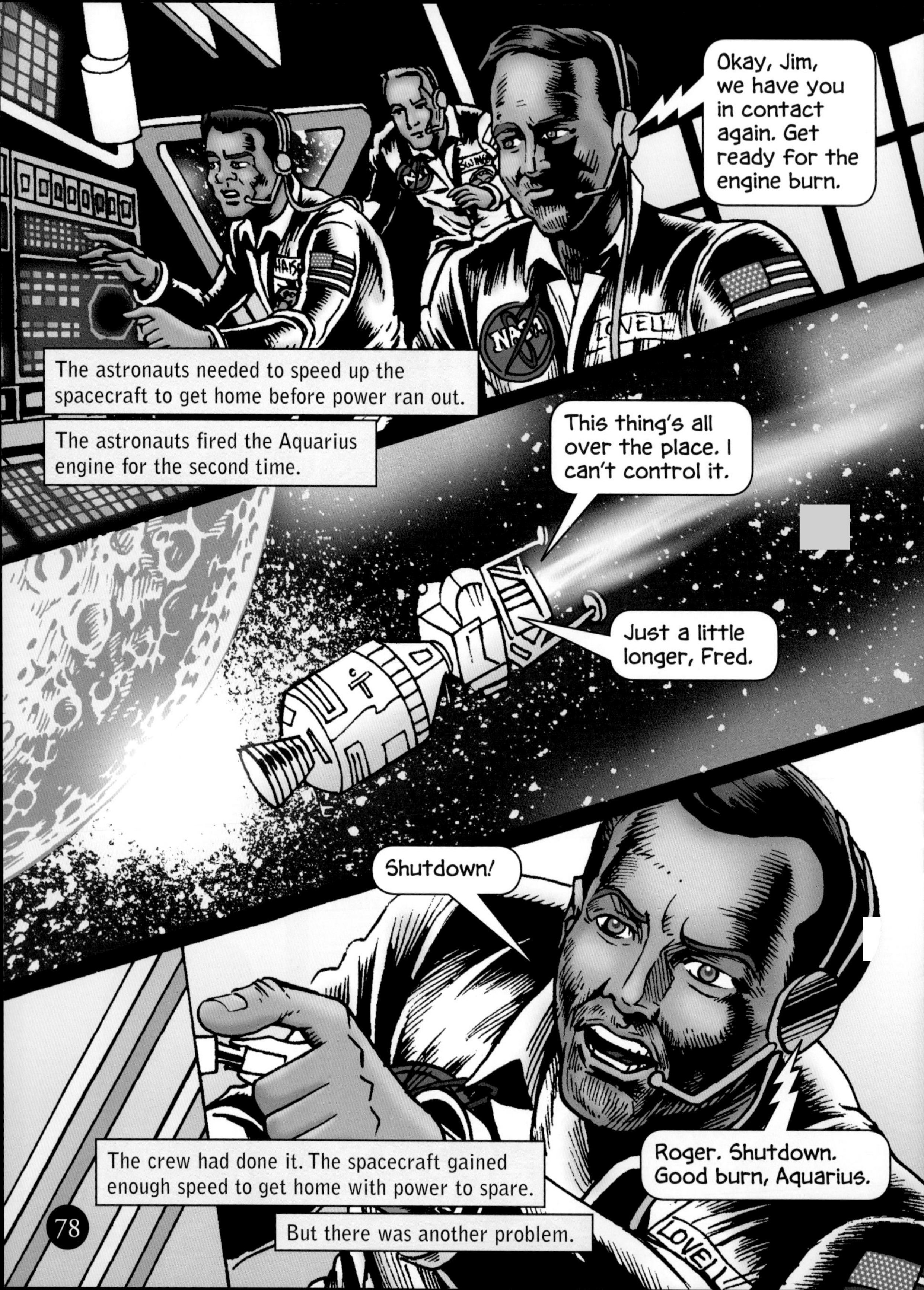
Okay, Jim, we have you in contact again. Get ready for the engine burn.
The astronauts needed to speed up the spacecraft to get home before power ran out.
The astronauts fired the Aquarius engine for the second time.
This thing's all over the place. I can't control it.
Just a little longer, Fred.
Shutdown!
Roger. Shutdown. Good burn, Aquarius.
The crew had done it. The spacecraft gained enough speed to get home with power to spare.
But there was another problem.

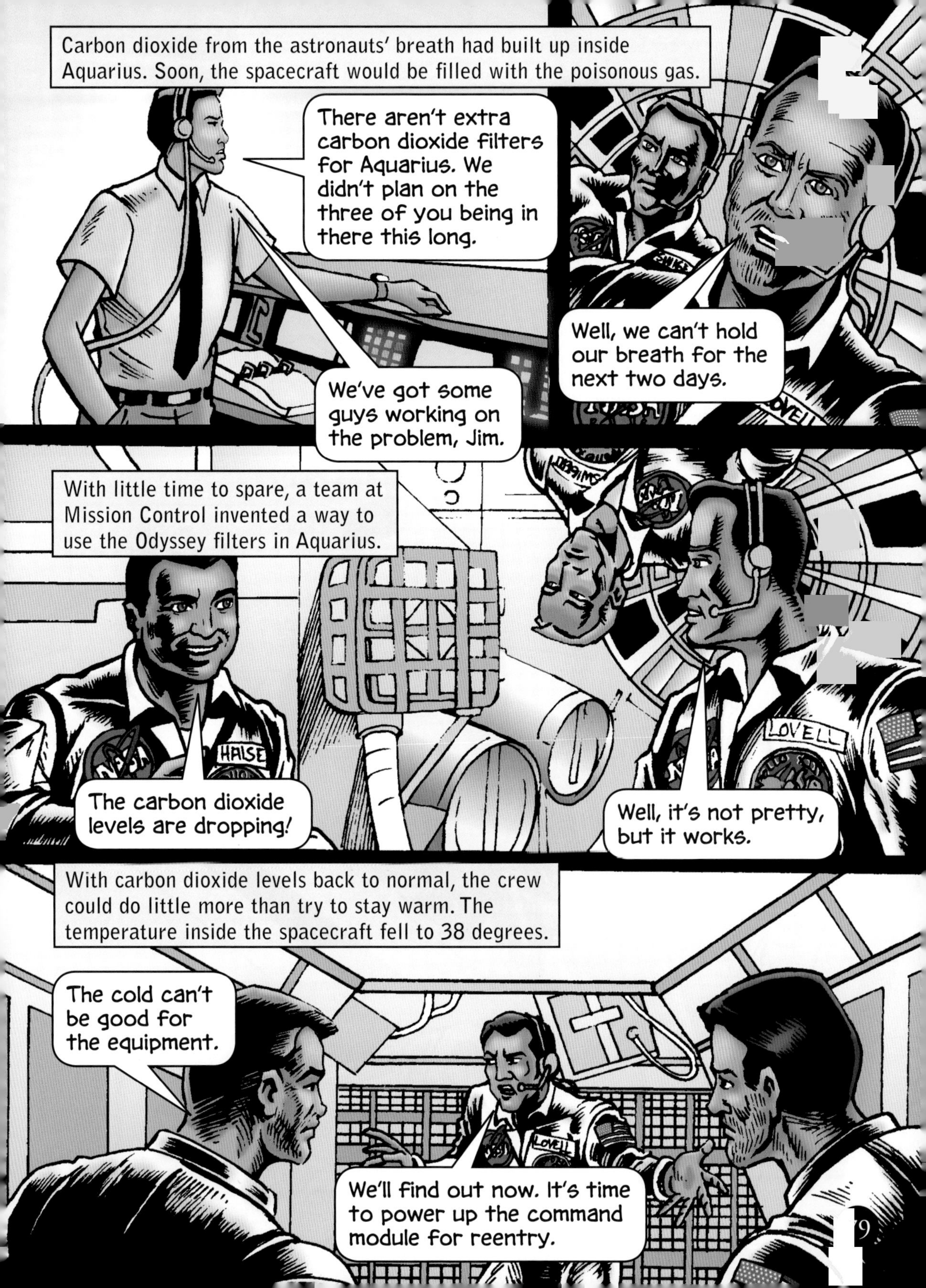
Carbon dioxide from the astronauts' breath had built up inside Aquarius. Soon, the spacecraft would be filled with the poisonous gas.
There aren't extra carbon dioxide filters for Aquarius. We didn't plan on the three of you being in there this long.
We've got some guys working on the problem, Jim.
Well, we can't hold our breath for the next two days.
With little time to spare, a team at Mission Control invented a way to use the Odyssey filters in Aquarius.
The carbon dioxide levels are dropping!
Well, it's not pretty, but it works.
With carbon dioxide levels back to normal, the crew could do little more than try to stay warm. The temperature inside the spacecraft fell to 38 degrees.
The cold can't be good for the equipment.
We'll find out now. It's time to power up the command module for reentry.

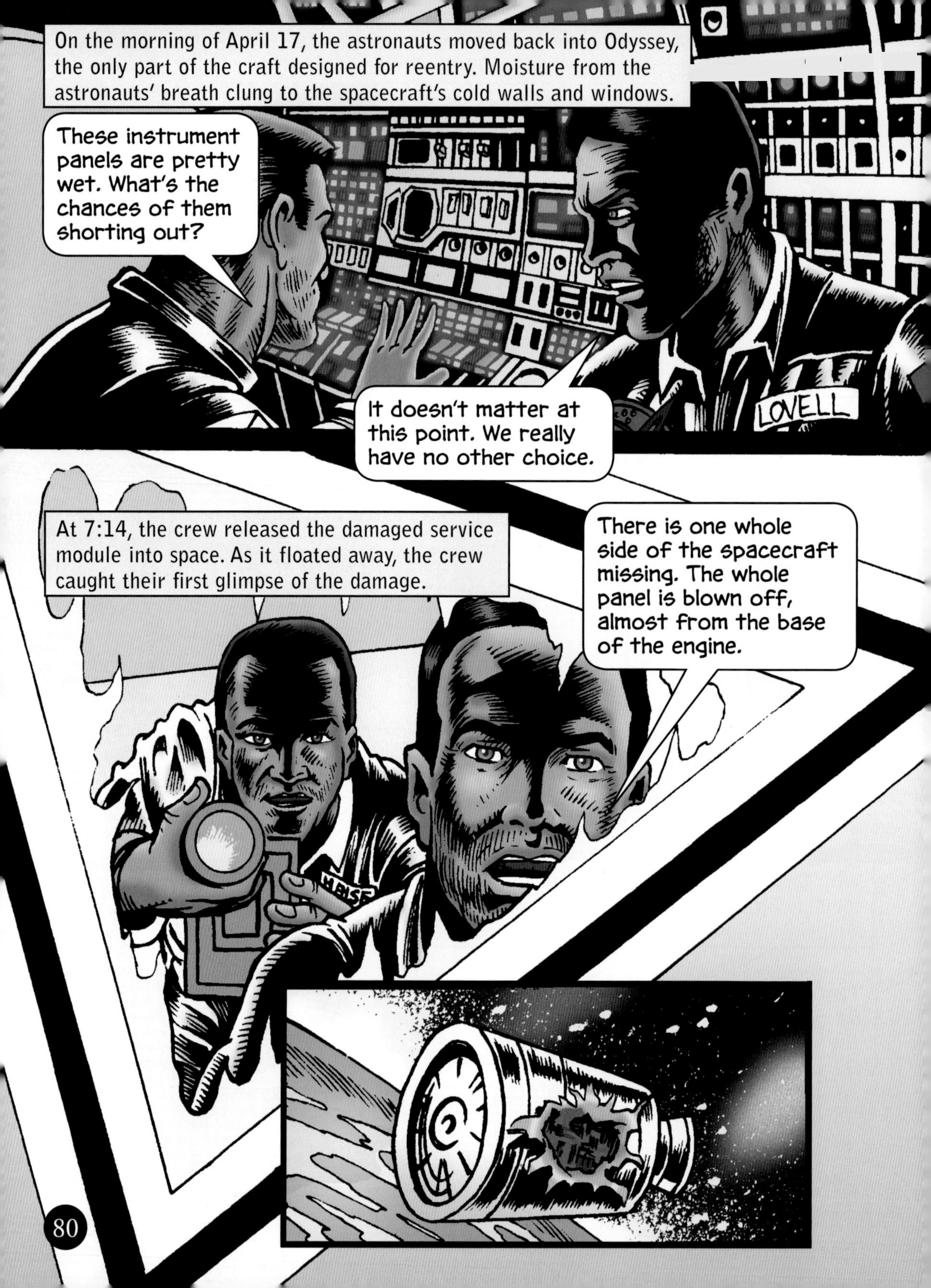
On the morning of April 17, the astronauts moved back into Odyssey, the only part of the craft designed for reentry. Moisture from the astronauts' breath clung to the spacecraft's cold walls and windows.
These instrument panels are pretty wet. What's the chances of them shorting out?
It doesn't matter at this point. We really have no other choice.
LOVELL
At 7:14, the crew released the damaged service module into space. As it floated away, the crew caught their first glimpse of the damage.
There is one whole side of the spacecraft missing. The whole panel is blown off, almost from the base of the engine.

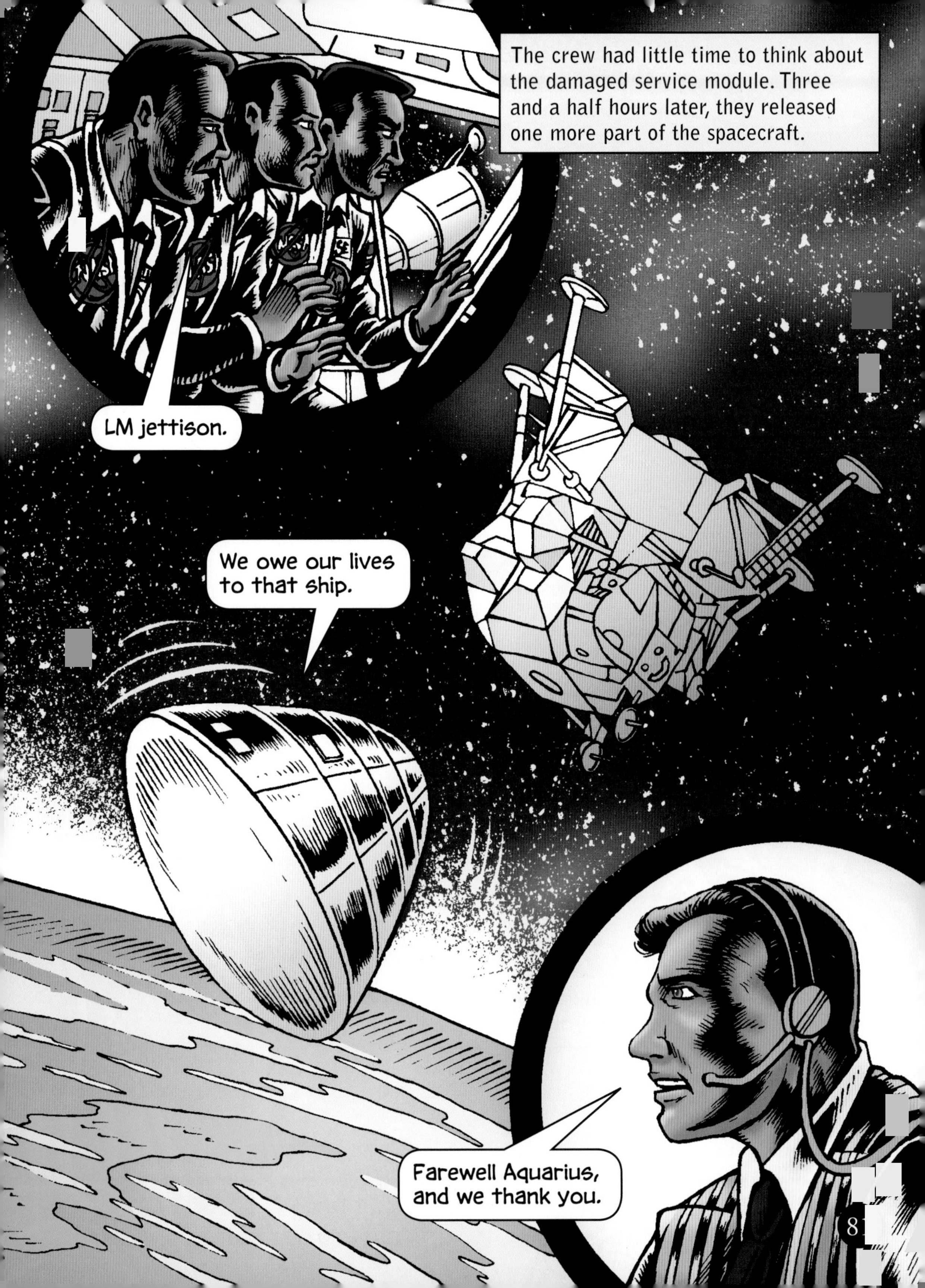
The crew had little time to think about the damaged service module. Three and a half hours later, they released one more part of the spacecraft.
LM jettison.
We owe our lives to that ship.
Farewell Aquarius, and we thank you.

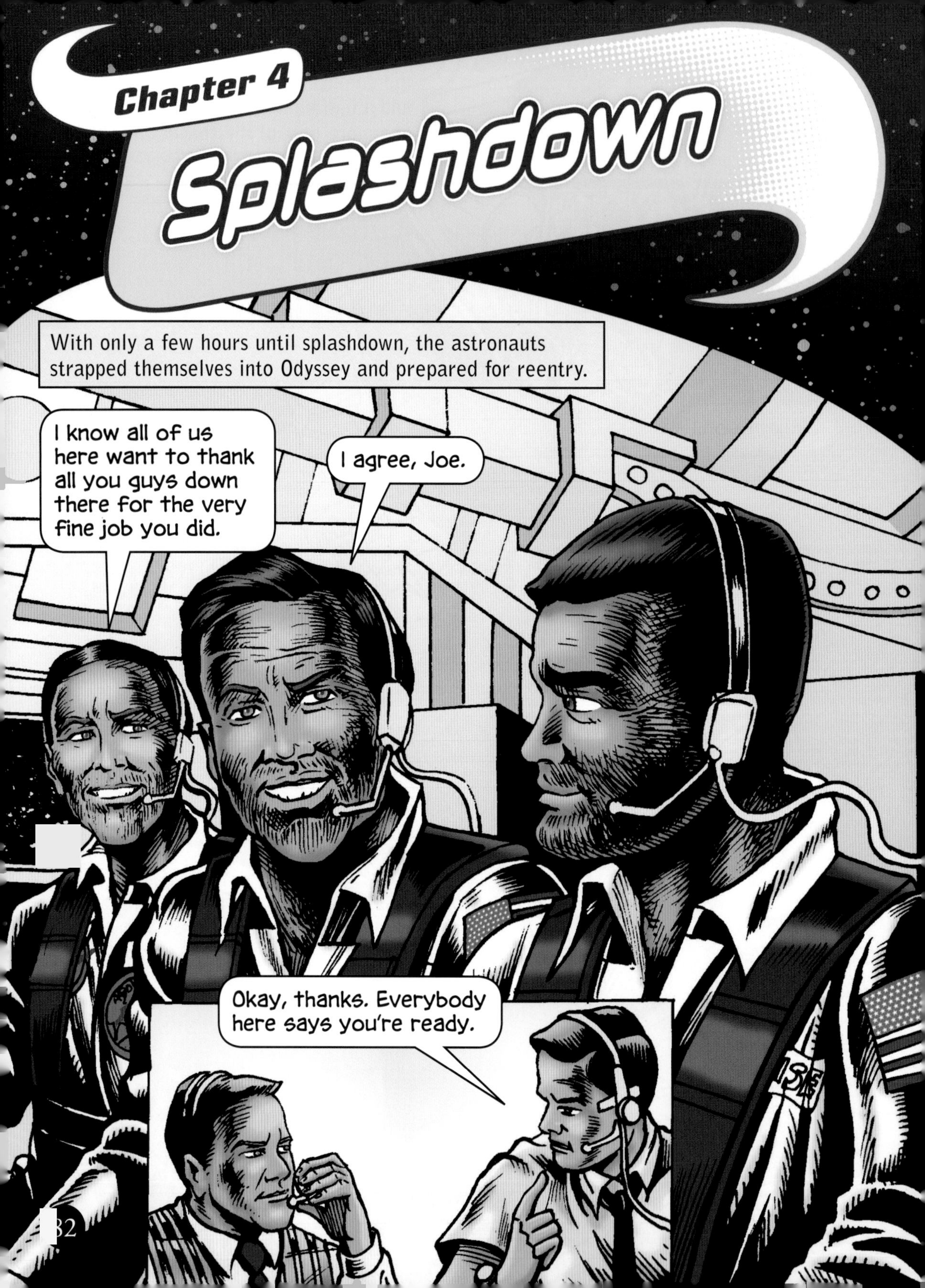
Chapter 4
Splashdown
With only a few hours until splashdown, the astronauts strapped themselves into Odyssey and prepared for reentry.
I know all of us here want to thank all you guys down there for the very fine job you did.
I agree, Joe.
Okay, thanks. Everybody here says you're ready.

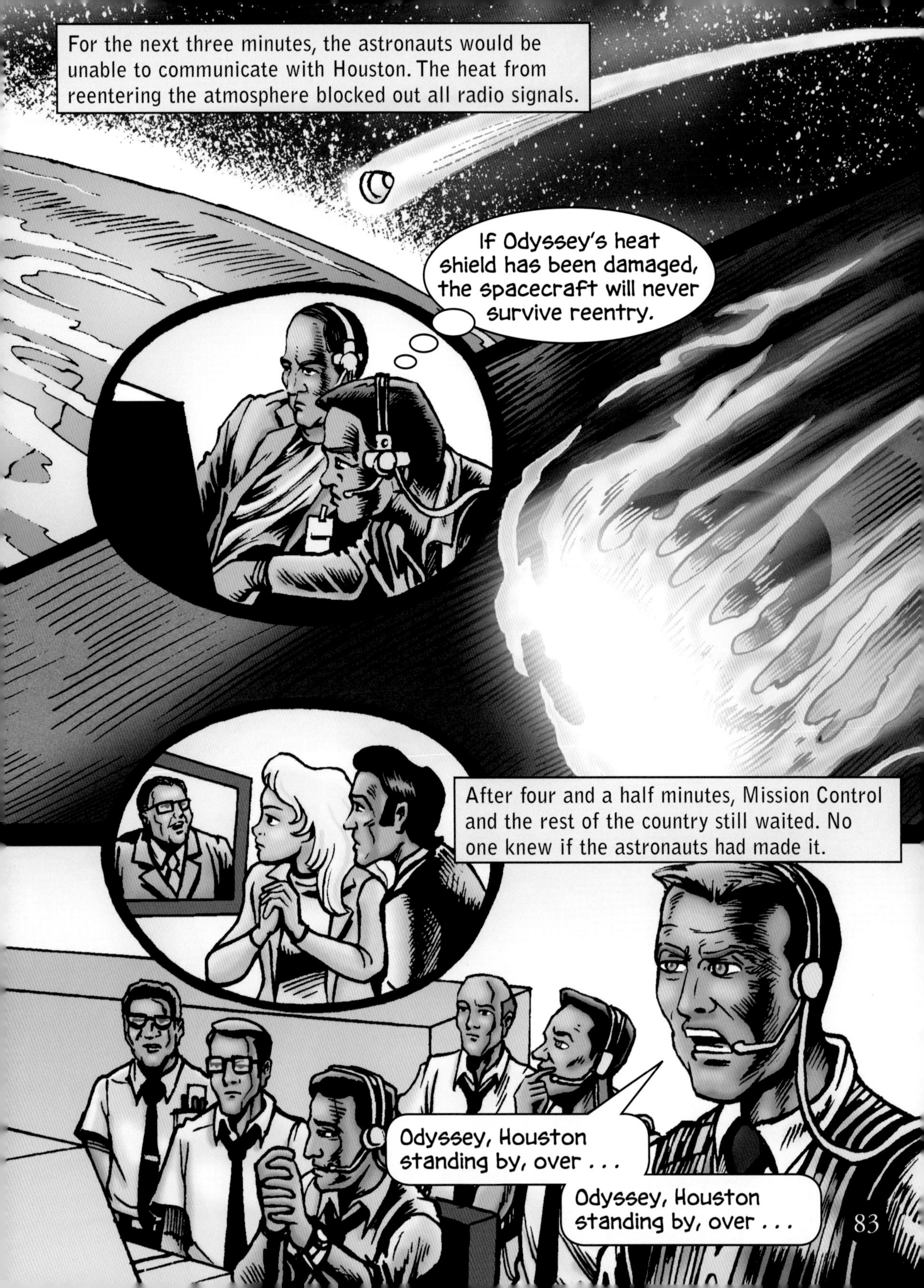
For the next three minutes, the astronauts would be unable to communicate with Houston. The heat from reentering the atmosphere blocked out all radio signals.
If Odyssey's heat shield has been damaged, the spacecraft will never survive reentry.
After four and a half minutes, Mission Control and the rest of the country still waited. No one knew if the astronauts had made it.
Odyssey, Houston standing by, over . . .
Odyssey, Houston standing by, over . . .

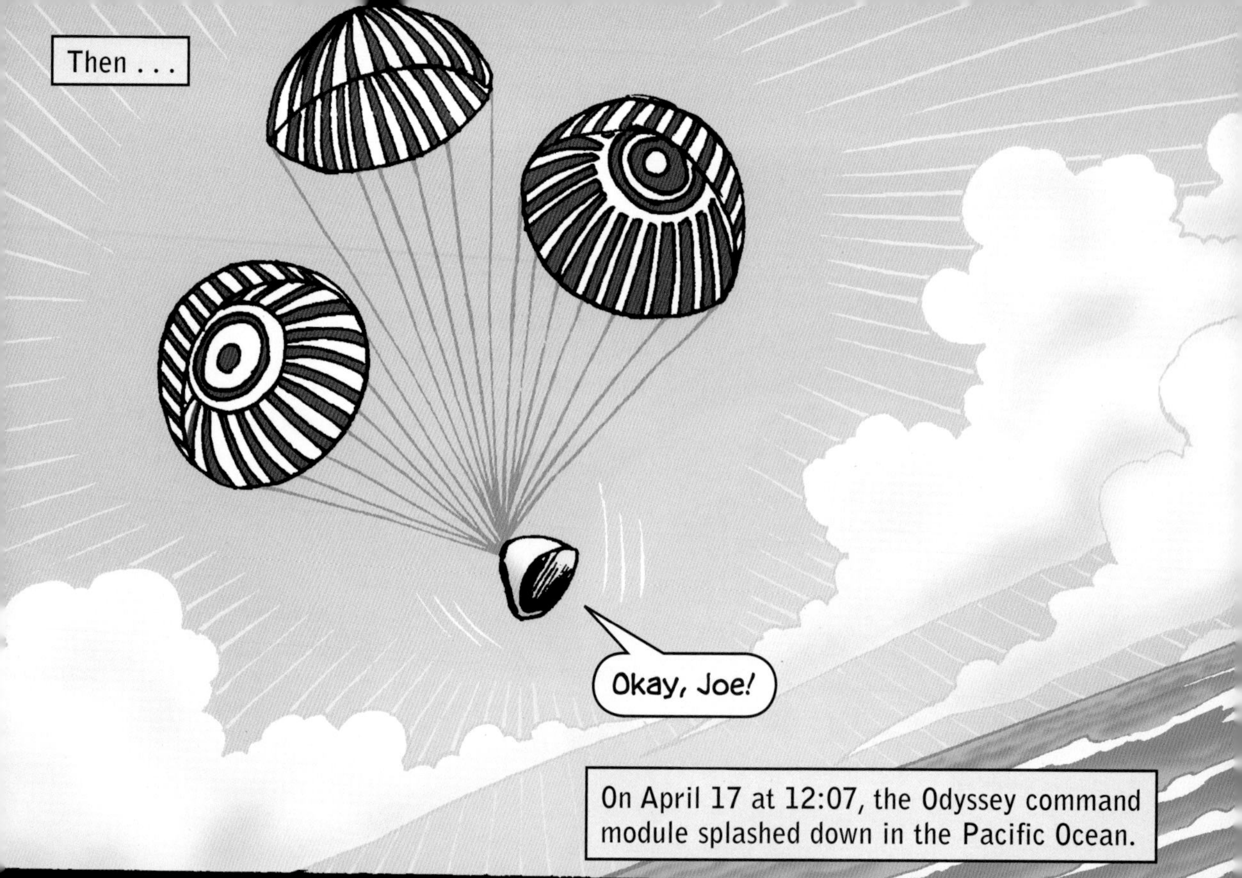
Then . . .
Okay, Joe!
On April 17 at 12:07, the Odyssey command module splashed down in the Pacific Ocean.

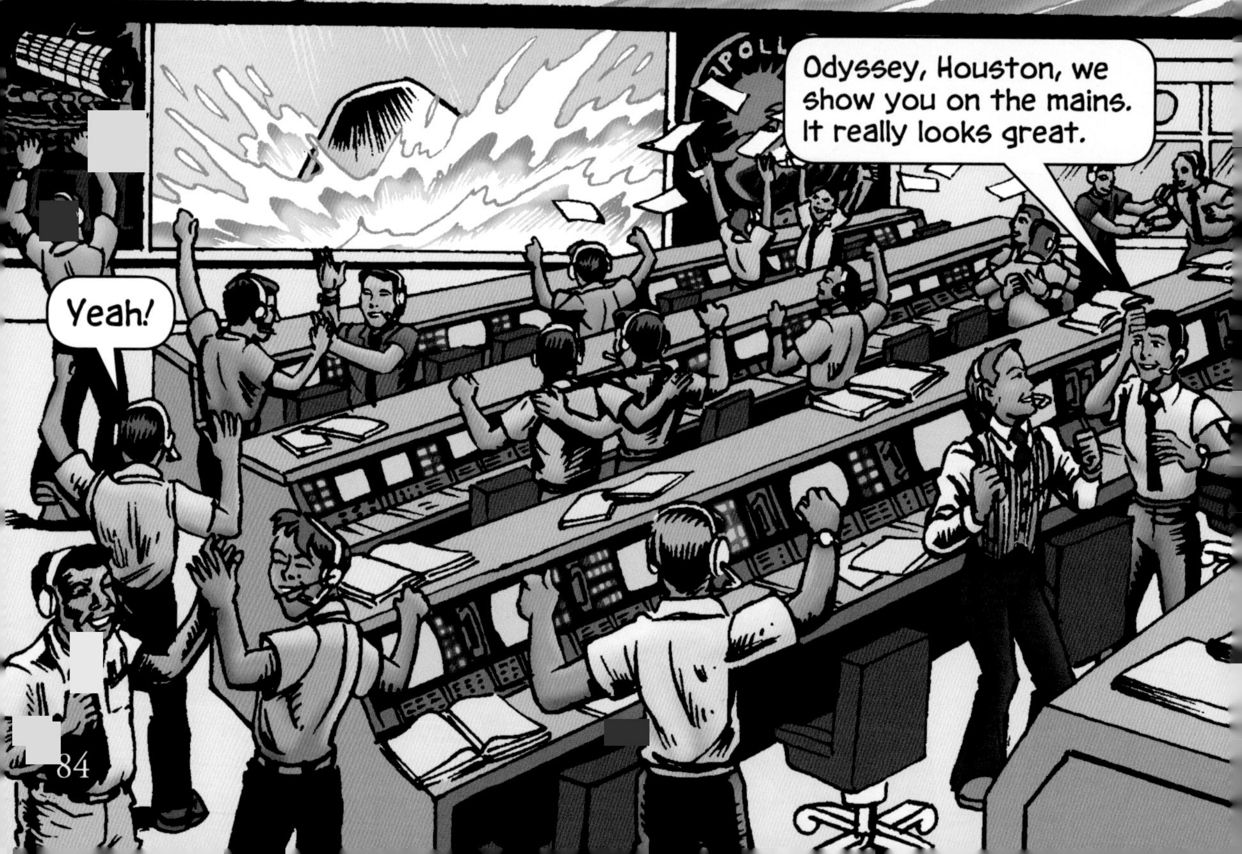
Yeah!
Odyssey, Houston, we show you on the mains. It really looks great.

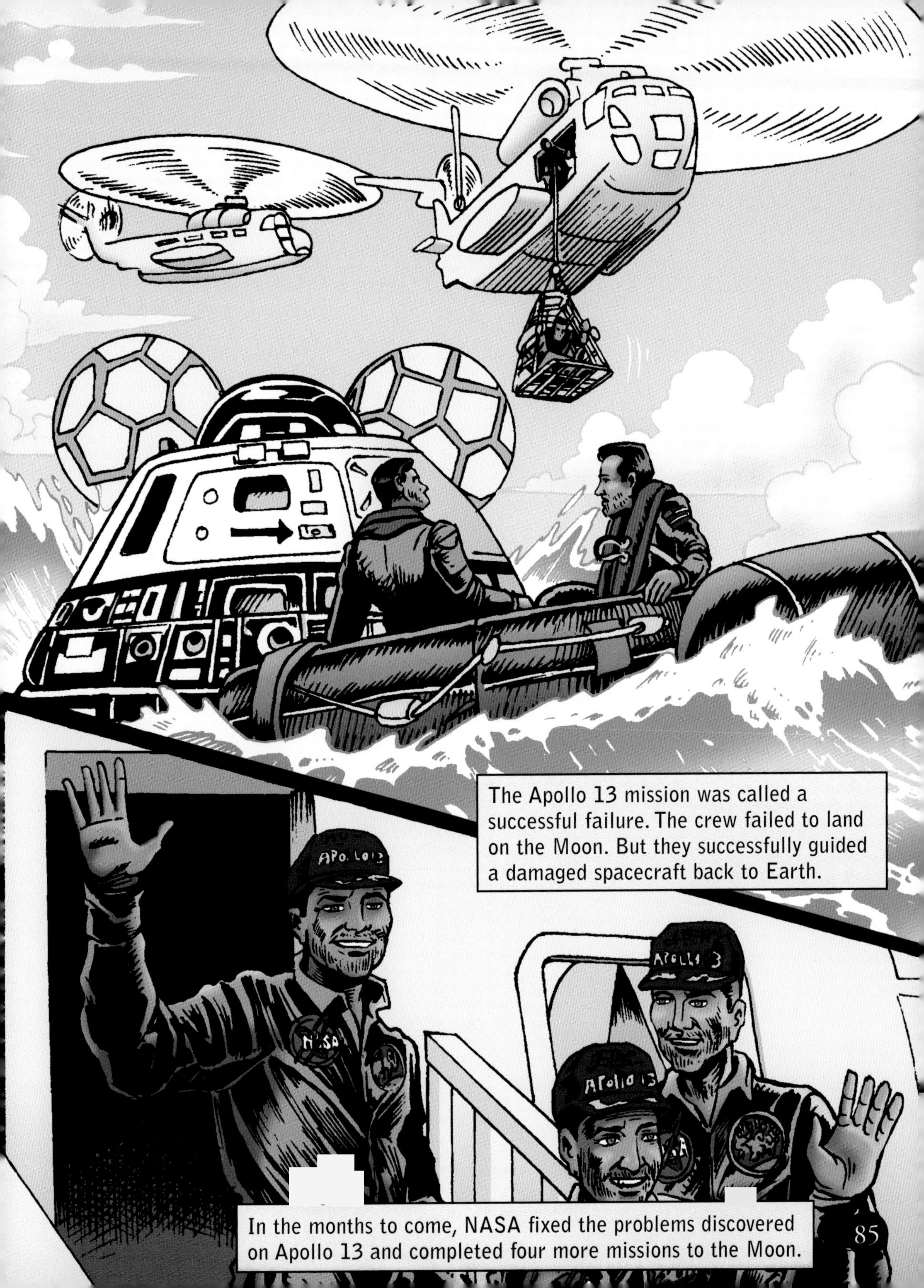
The Apollo 13 mission was called a successful failure. The crew failed to land on the Moon. But they successfully guided a damaged spacecraft back to Earth.
In the months to come, NASA fixed the problems discovered on Apollo 13 and completed four more missions to the Moon.

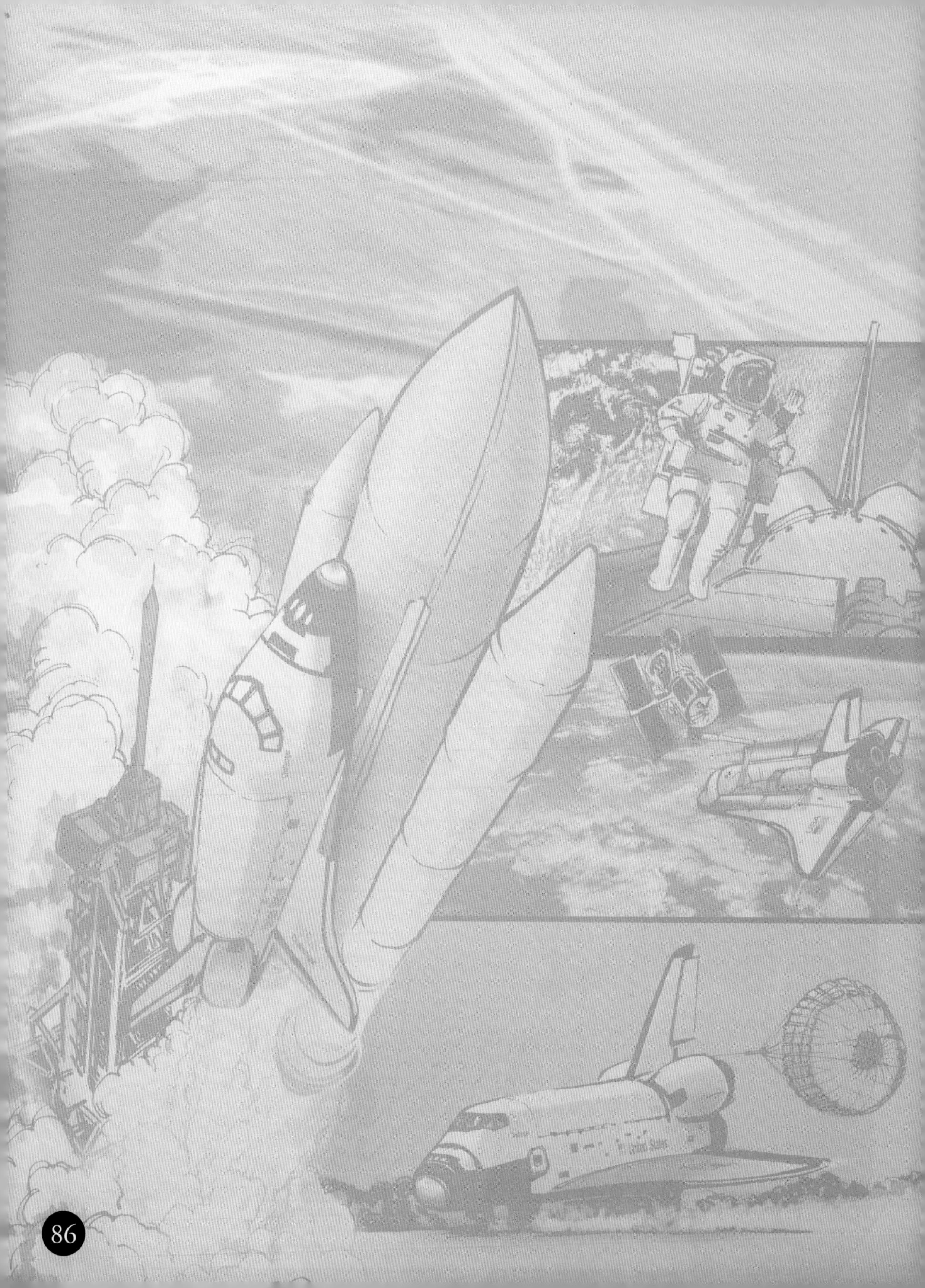

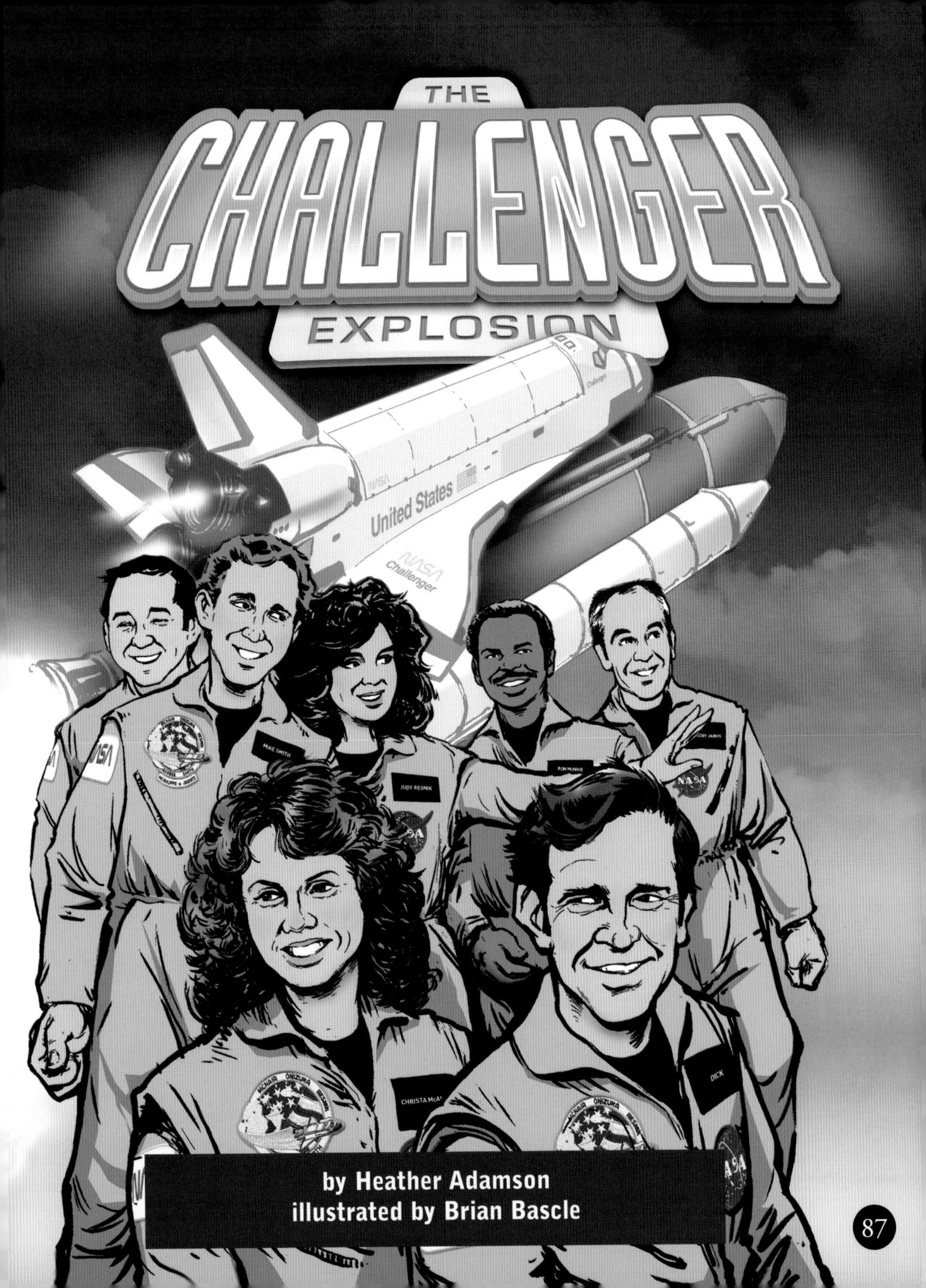
THE
CHALLENGER
EXPLOSION
United States
NASA
Challenger
MIKE SMITH
JUDY RESNIK
RON McNAIR
by Heather Adamson
illustrated by Brian Bascle

CHAPTER 1

A TEACHER IN SPACE

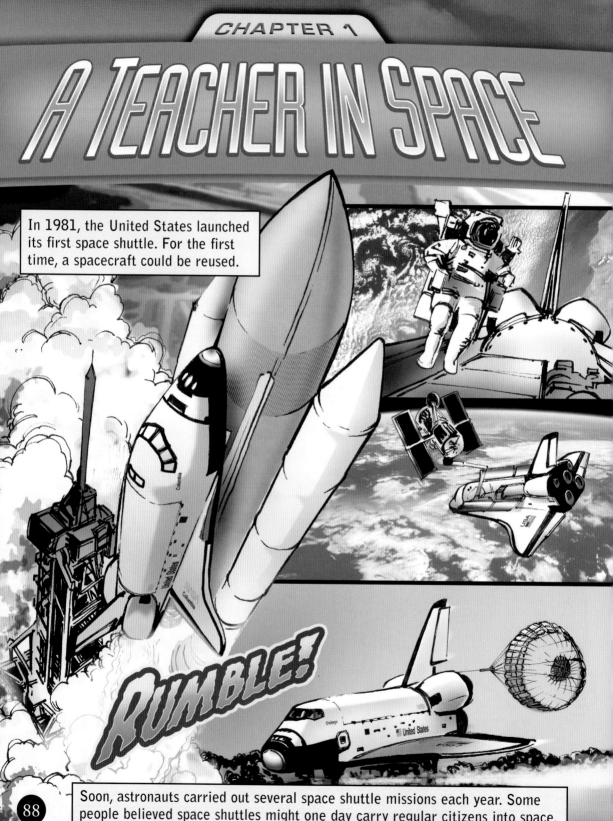

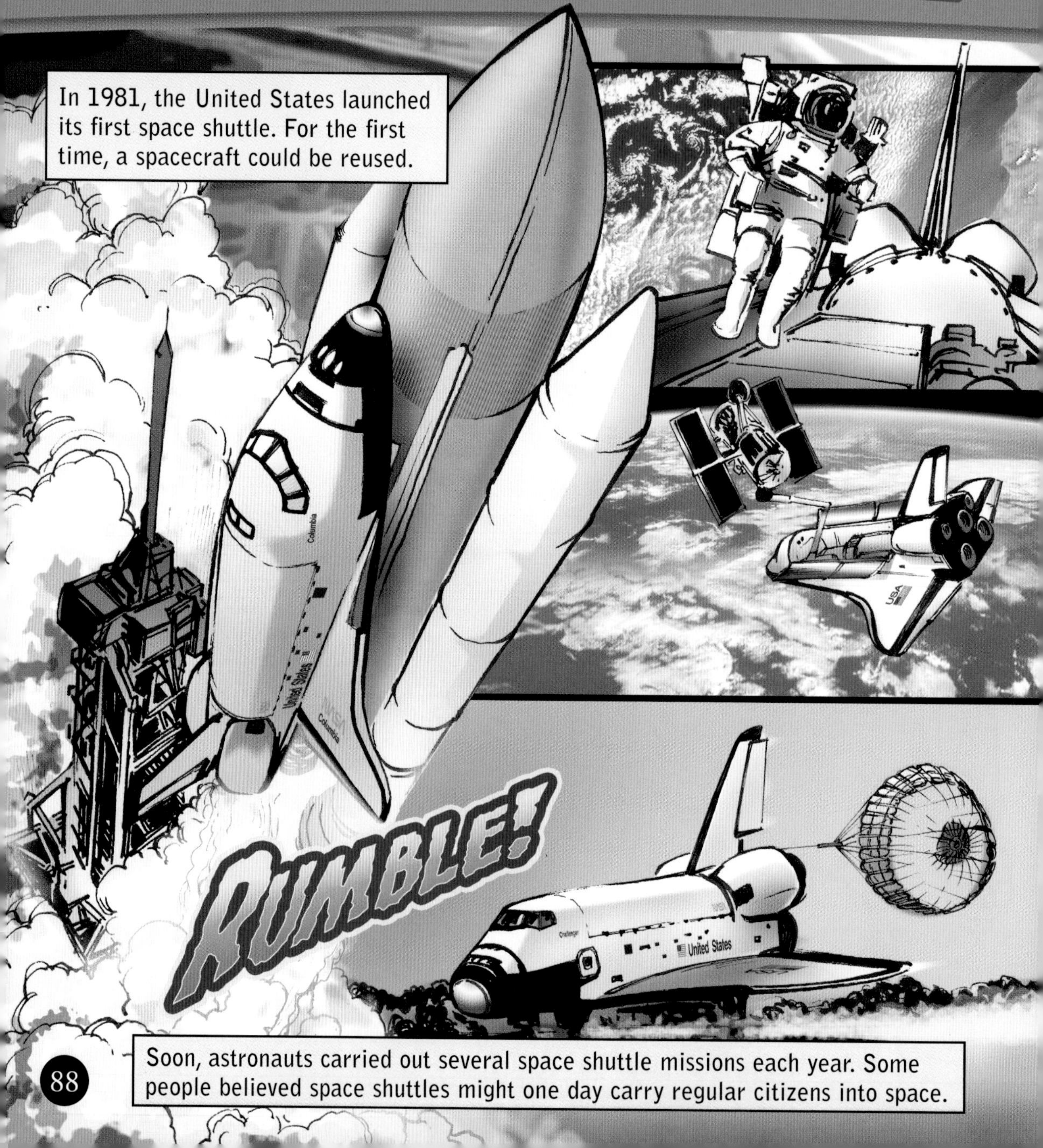
In 1981, the United States launched its first space shuttle. For the first time, a spacecraft could be reused.
Columbia
United States
NASA
Columbia
USA
RUMBLE!
United States
Soon, astronauts carried out several space shuttle missions each year. Some people believed space shuttles might one day carry regular citizens into space.

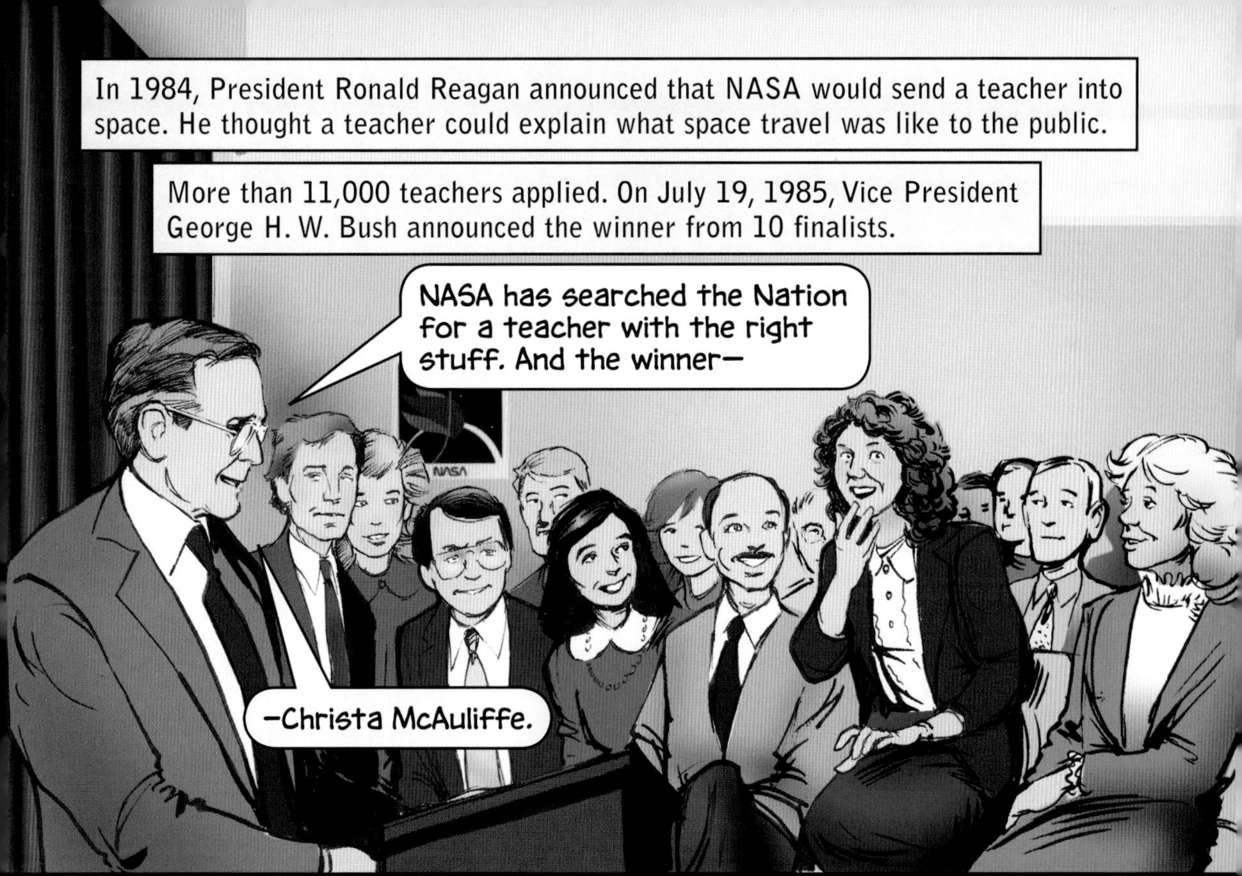
In 1984, President Ronald Reagan announced that NASA would send a teacher into space. He thought a teacher could explain what space travel was like to the public.
More than 11,000 teachers applied. On July 19, 1985, Vice President George H. W. Bush announced the winner from 10 finalists.
NASA has searched the Nation for a teacher with the right stuff. And the winner—
NASA
—Christa McAuliffe.

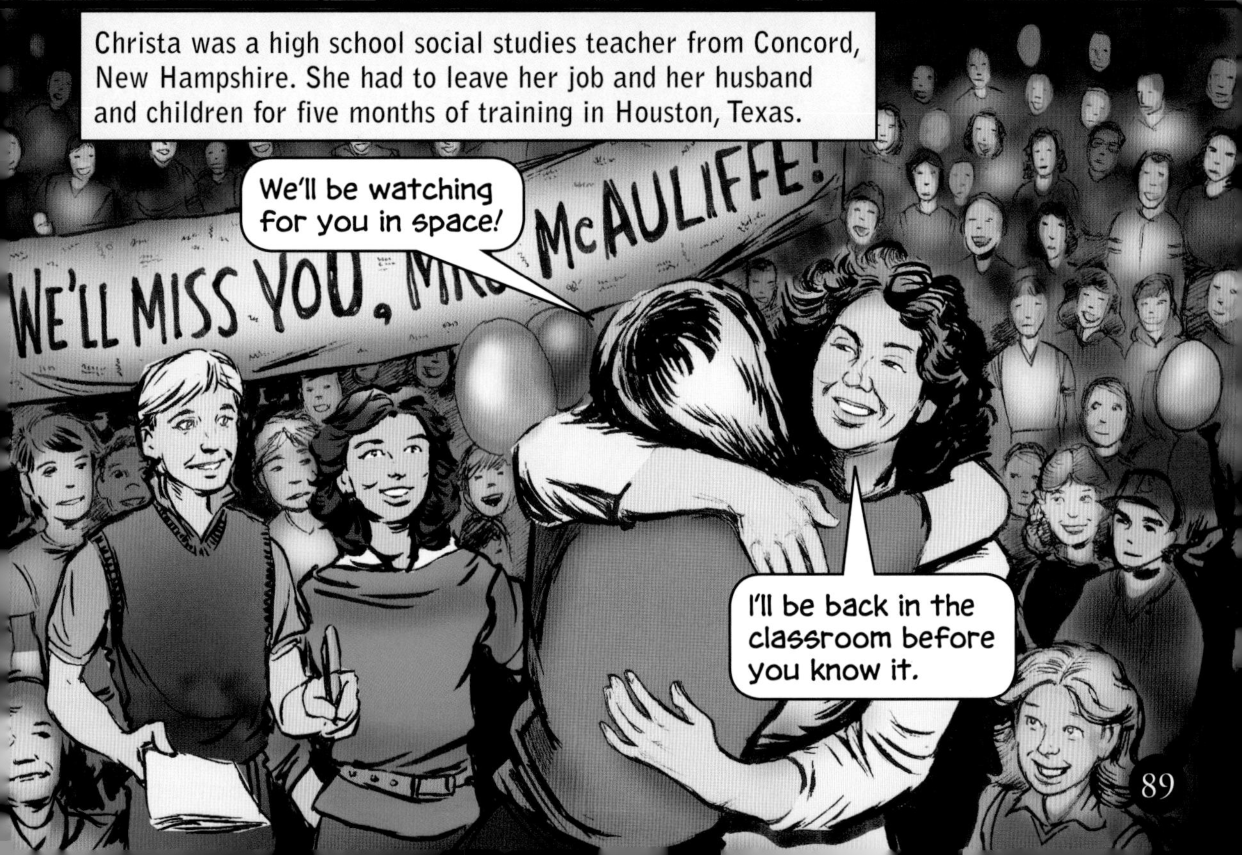
Christa was a high school social studies teacher from Concord, New Hampshire. She had to leave her job and her husband and children for five months of training in Houston, Texas.
WE'LL MISS YOU,
McAULIFFE!
We'll be watching for you in space!
I'll be back in the classroom before you know it.

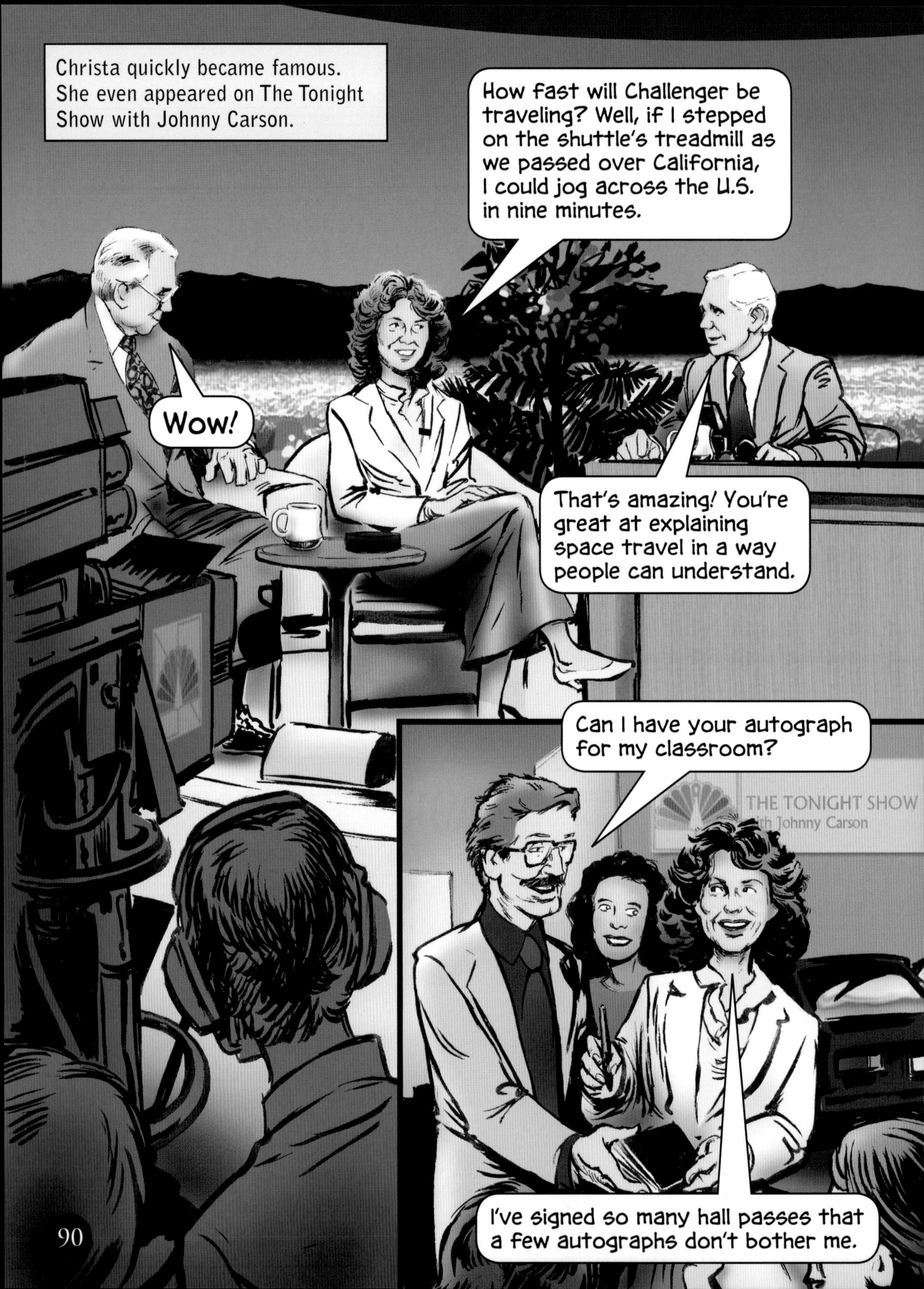
Christa quickly became famous. She even appeared on The Tonight Show with Johnny Carson.
How fast will Challenger be traveling? Well, if I stepped on the shuttle's treadmill as we passed over California, I could jog across the U.S. in nine minutes.
Wow!
That's amazing! You're great at explaining space travel in a way people can understand.
Can I have your autograph for my classroom?
THE TONIGHT SHOW
I've signed so many hall passes that a few autographs don't bother me.

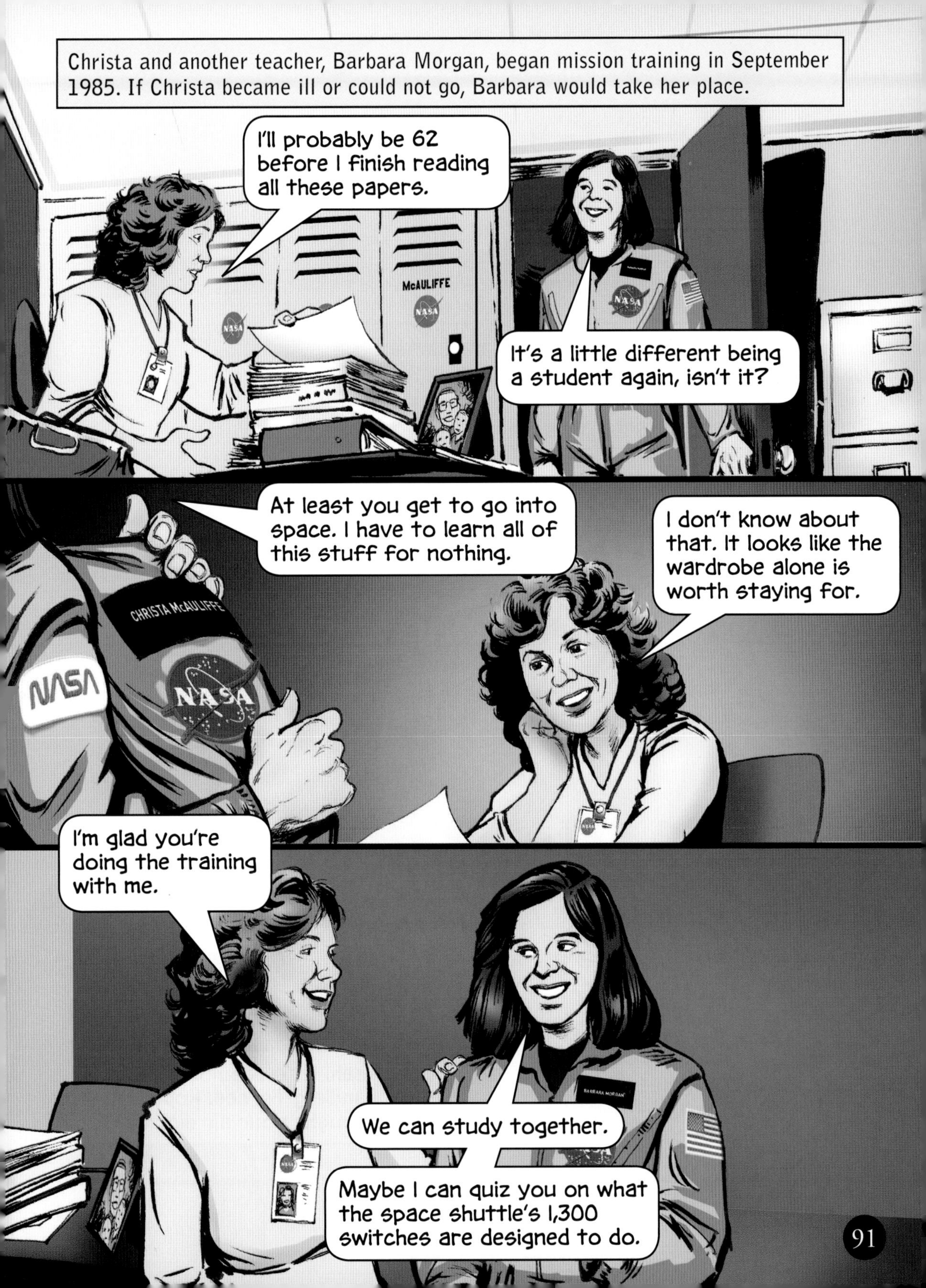
Christa and another teacher, Barbara Morgan, began mission training in September 1985. If Christa became ill or could not go, Barbara would take her place.
I'll probably be 62 before I finish reading all these papers.
McAULIFFE
It's a little different being a student again, isn't it?
At least you get to go into space. I have to learn all of this stuff for nothing.
I don't know about that. It looks like the wardrobe alone is worth staying for.
CHRISTA McAULIFFE
NASA
I'm glad you're doing the training with me.
BARBARA MORGAN
We can study together.
Maybe I can quiz you on what the space shuttle's 1,300 switches are designed to do.

CHAPTER 2

MISSION 51L

Six other astronauts trained with Christa and Barbara for the shuttle mission. Mission commander Dick Scobee and shuttle pilot Michael Smith introduced Christa and Barbara to high speed flight in their T-38 jets.

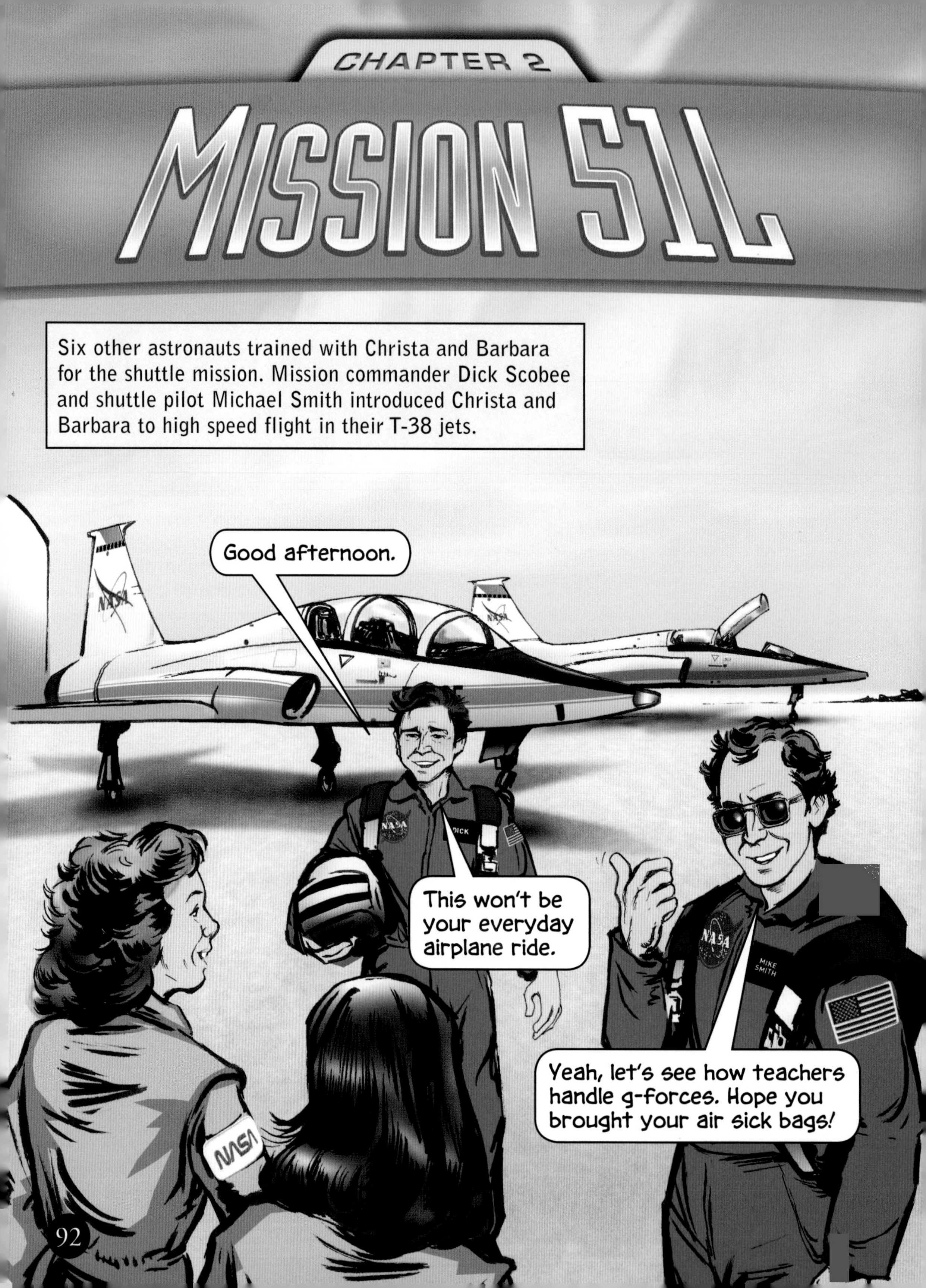
Good afternoon.
This won't be your everyday airplane ride.
Yeah, let's see how teachers handle g-forces. Hope you brought your air sick bags!
DICK
MIKE SMITH

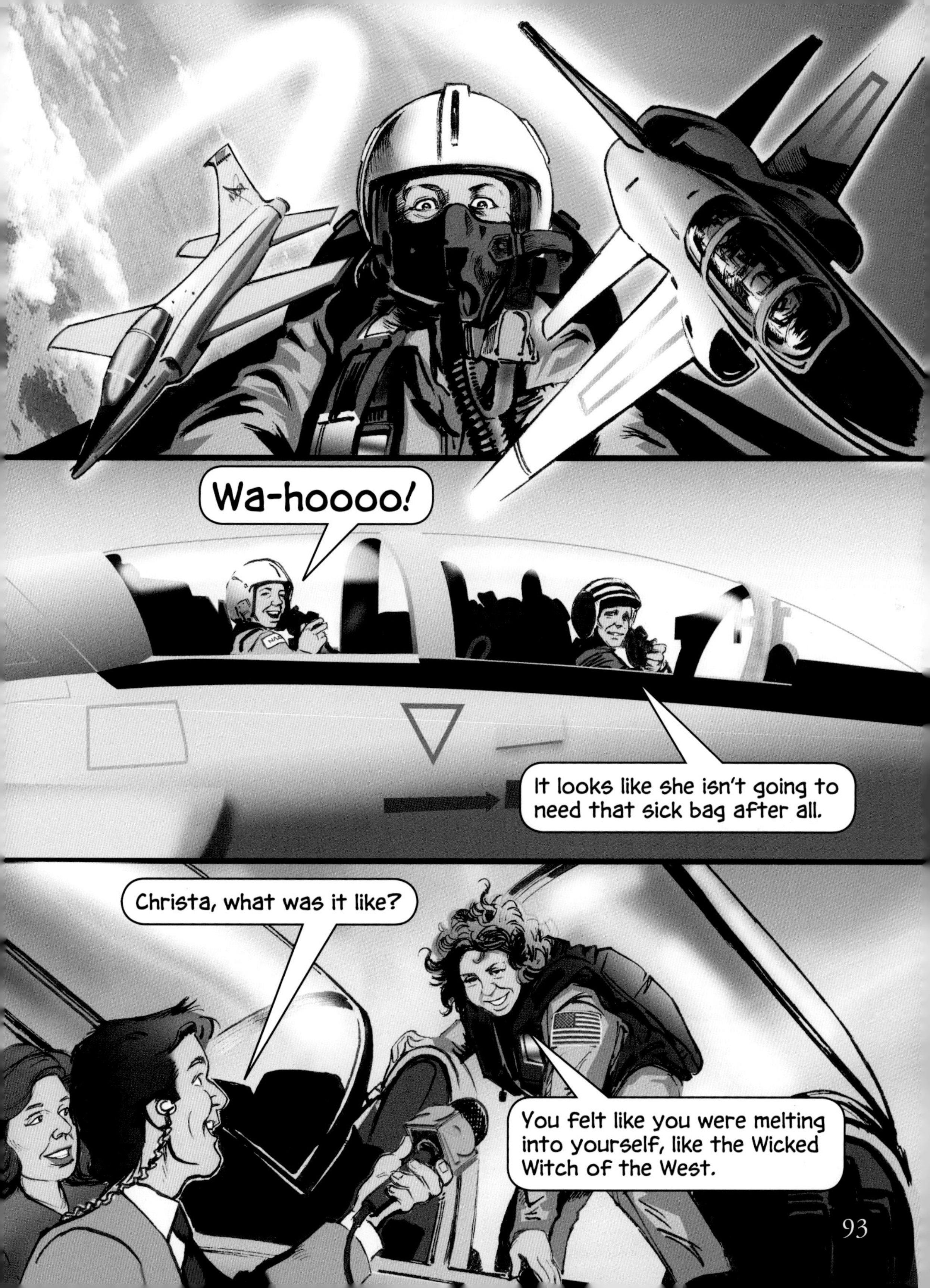

Wa-hoooo!
It looks like she isn't going to need that sick bag after all.
Christa, what was it like?
You felt like you were melting into yourself, like the Wicked Witch of the West.

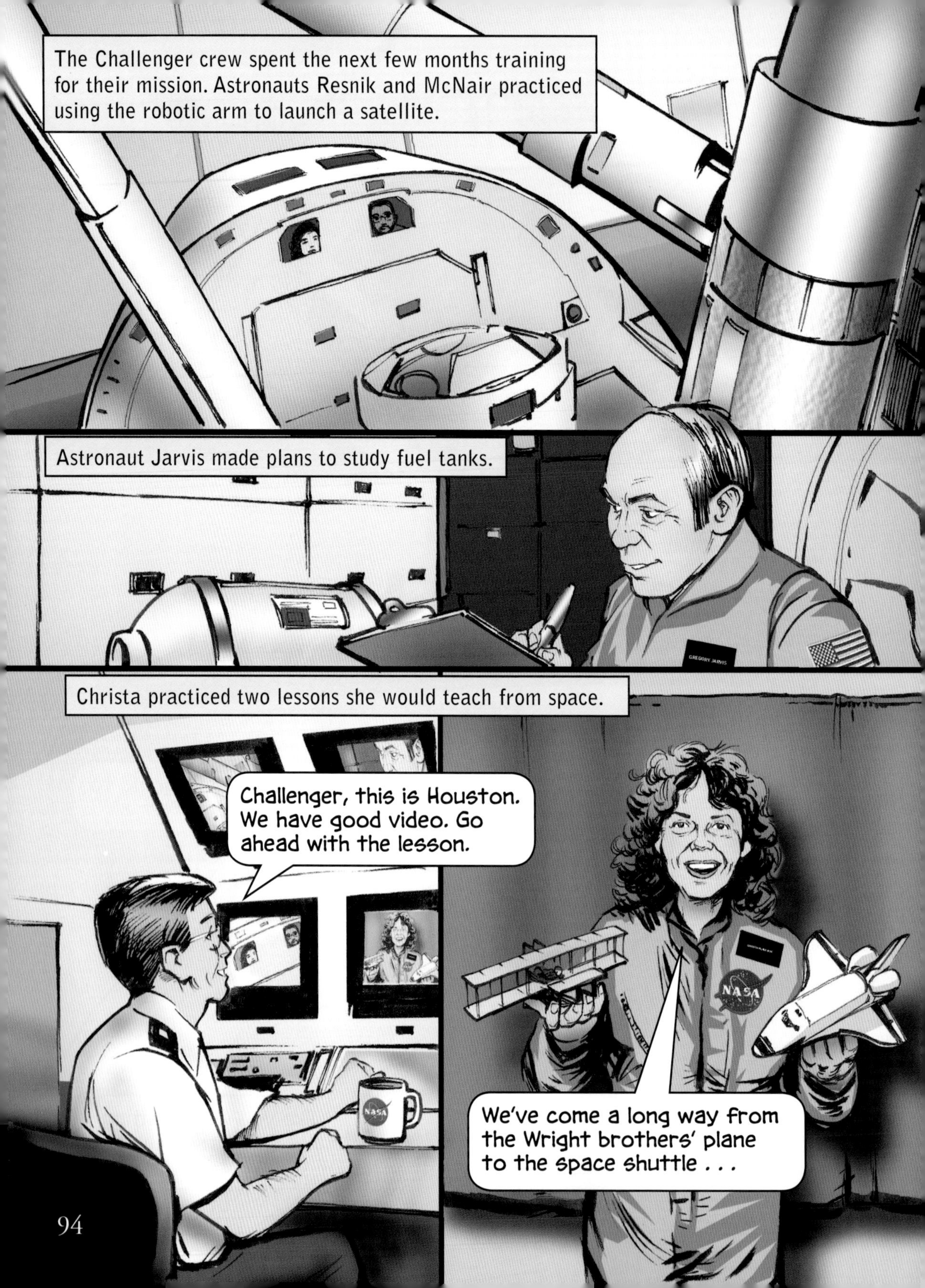
The Challenger crew spent the next few months training for their mission. Astronauts Resnik and McNair practiced using the robotic arm to launch a satellite.
Astronaut Jarvis made plans to study fuel tanks.
GREGORY JARVIS
Christa practiced two lessons she would teach from space.
Challenger, this is Houston. We have good video. Go ahead with the lesson.
NASA
NASA
We've come a long way from the Wright brothers' plane to the space shuttle . . .

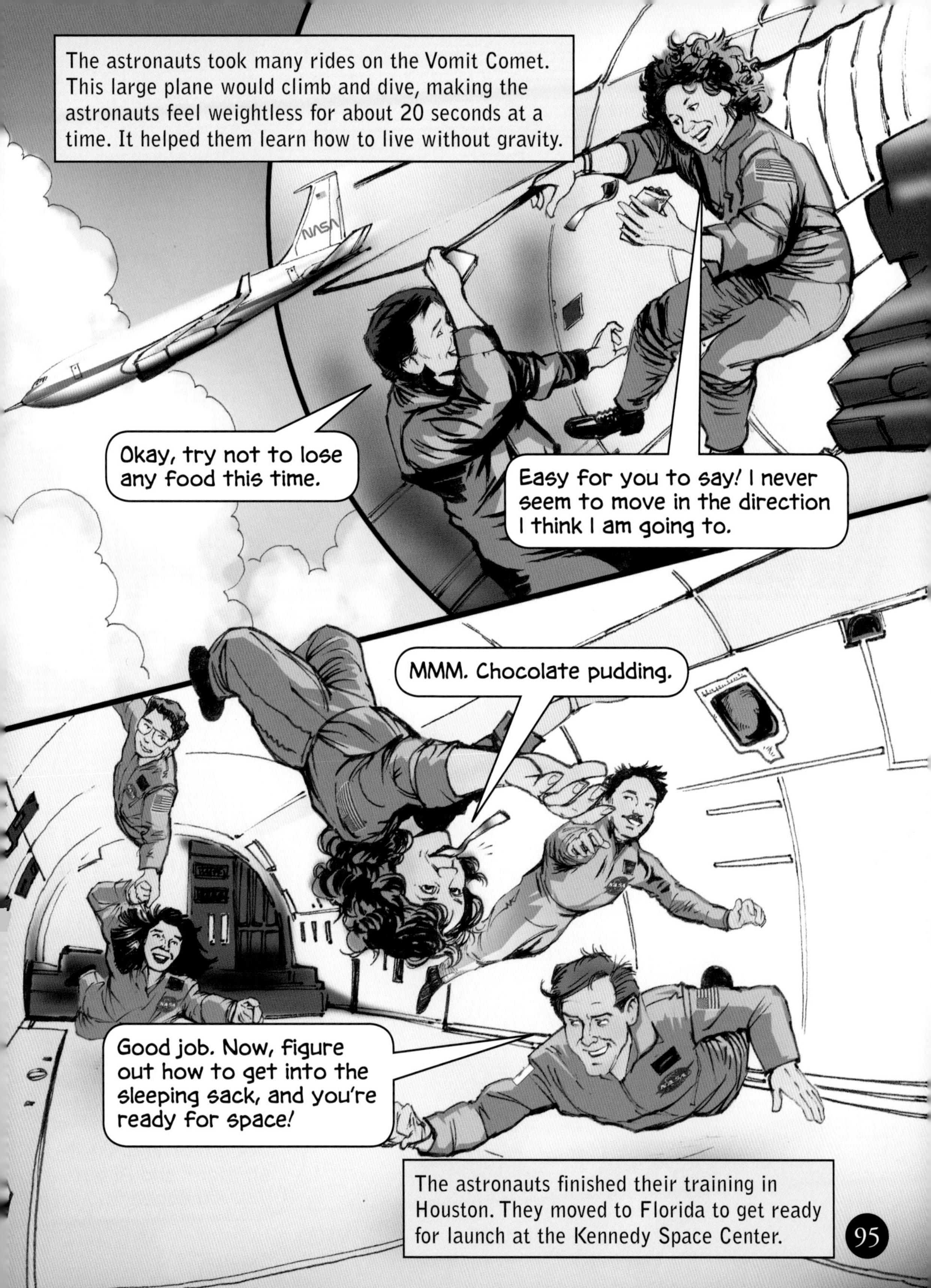
The astronauts took many rides on the Vomit Comet. This large plane would climb and dive, making the astronauts feel weightless for about 20 seconds at a time. It helped them learn how to live without gravity.
NASA
Okay, try not to lose any food this time.
Easy for you to say! I never seem to move in the direction I think I am going to.
MMM. Chocolate pudding.
Good job. Now, figure out how to get into the sleeping sack, and you're ready for space!
The astronauts finished their training in Houston. They moved to Florida to get ready for launch at the Kennedy Space Center.

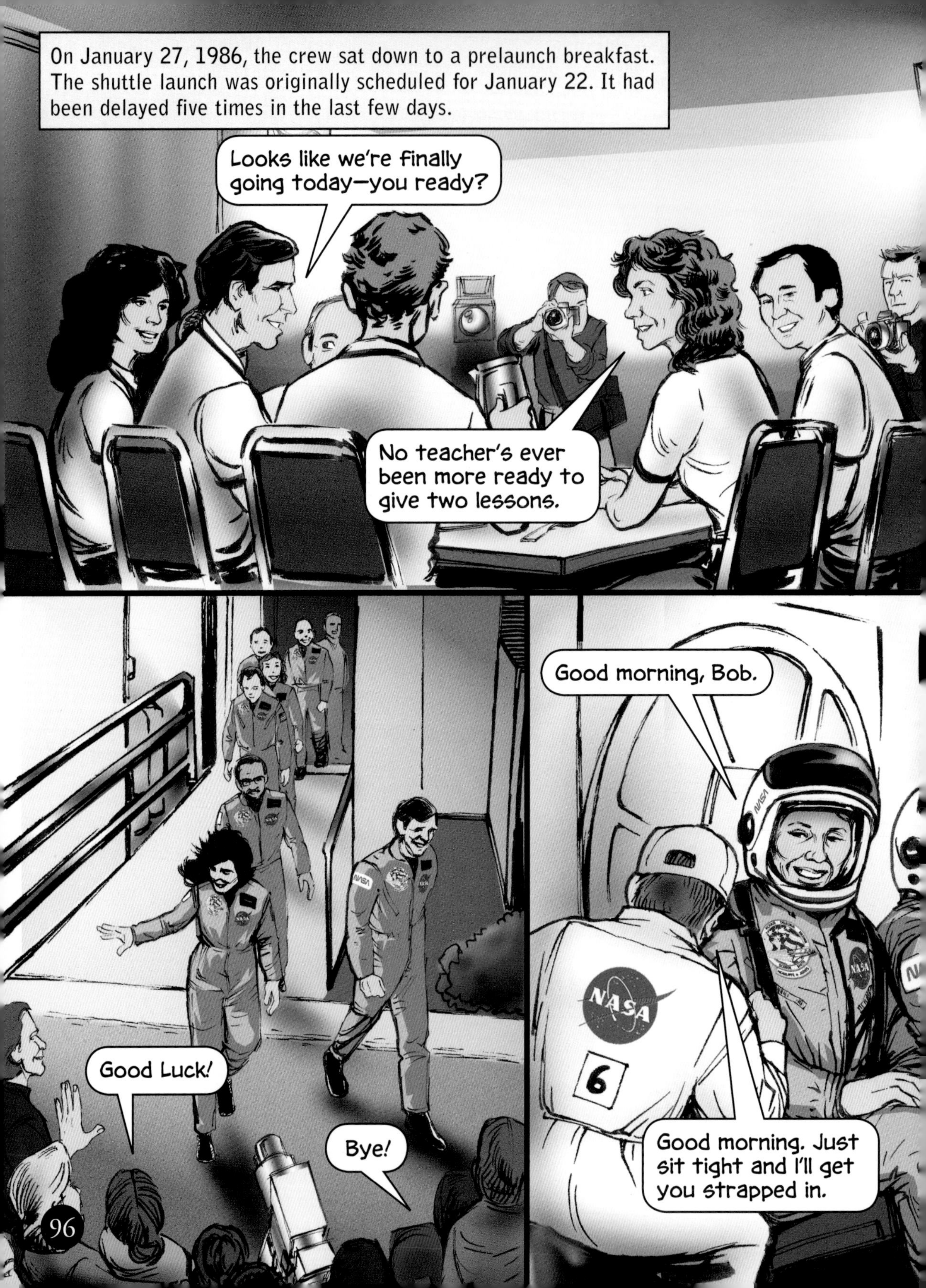
On January 27, 1986, the crew sat down to a prelaunch breakfast. The shuttle launch was originally scheduled for January 22. It had been delayed five times in the last few days.
Looks like we're finally going today—you ready?
No teacher's ever been more ready to give two lessons.
Good Luck!
Bye!
Good morning, Bob.
Good morning. Just sit tight and I'll get you strapped in.

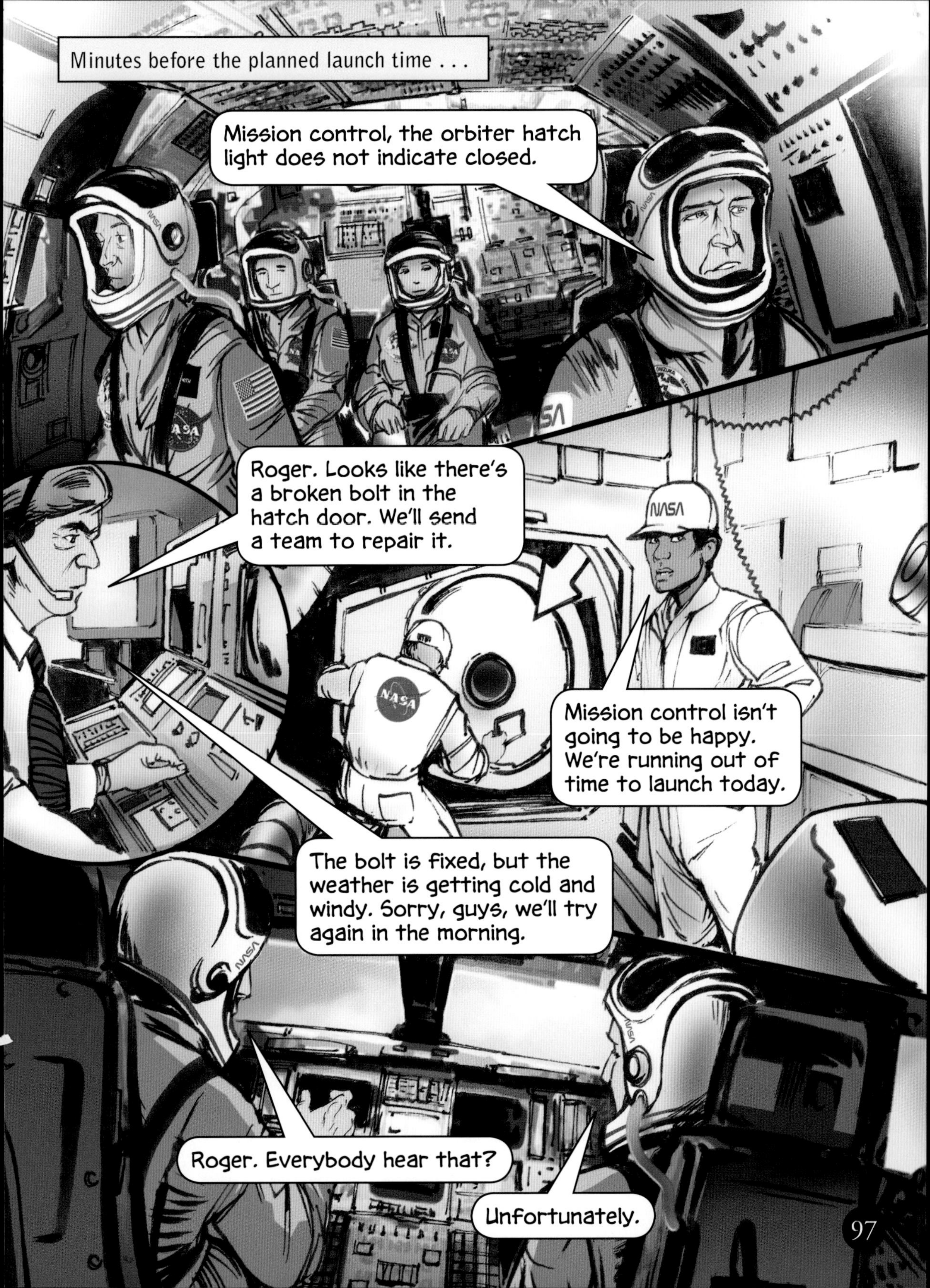
Minutes before the planned launch time . . .
Mission control, the orbiter hatch light does not indicate closed.
Roger. Looks like there's a broken bolt in the hatch door. We'll send a team to repair it.
Mission control isn't going to be happy. We're running out of time to launch today.
The bolt is fixed, but the weather is getting cold and windy. Sorry, guys, we'll try again in the morning.
Roger. Everybody hear that?
Unfortunately.

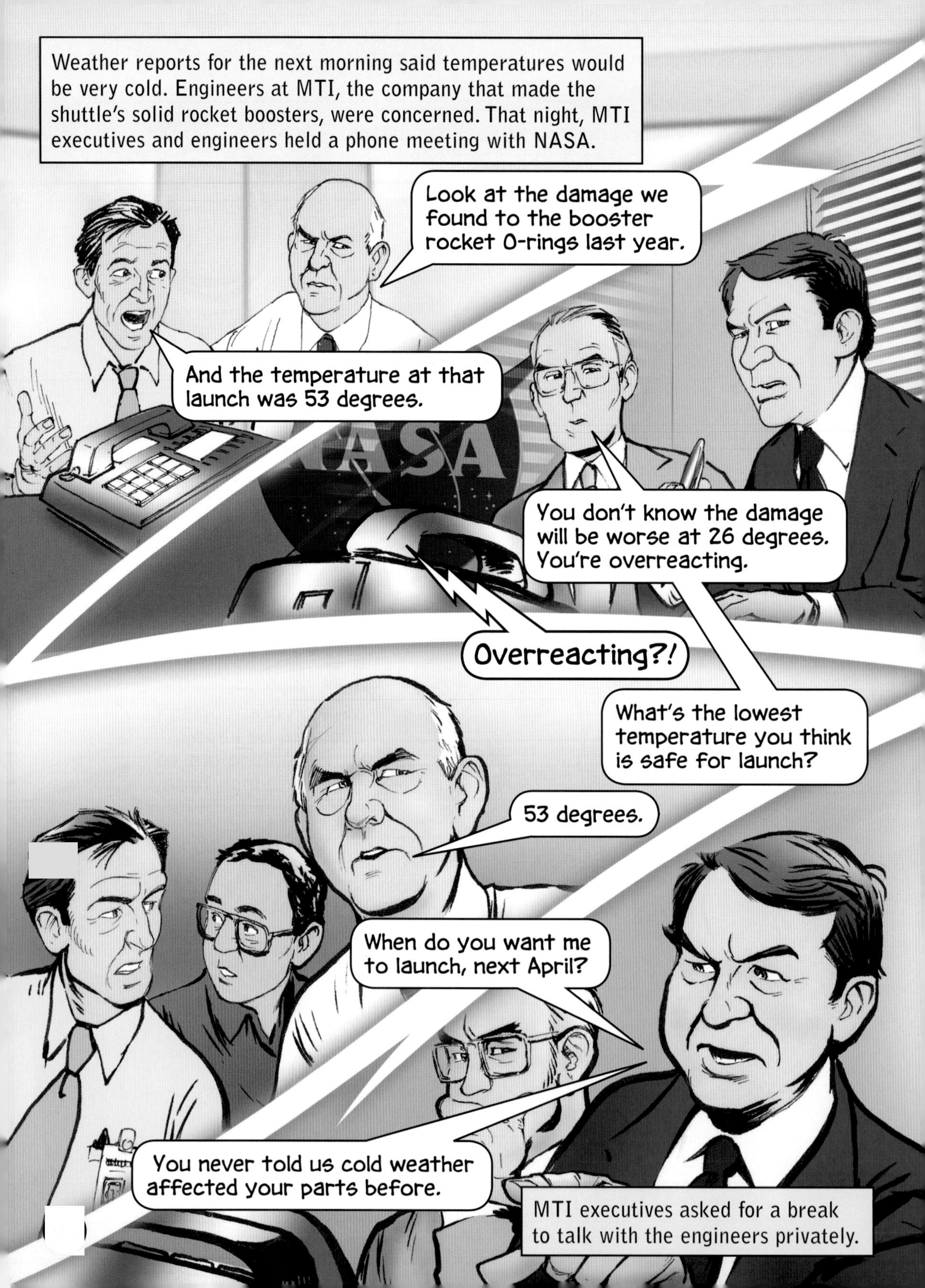
Weather reports for the next morning said temperatures would be very cold. Engineers at MTI, the company that made the shuttle's solid rocket boosters, were concerned. That night, MTI executives and engineers held a phone meeting with NASA.
Look at the damage we found to the booster rocket O-rings last year.
And the temperature at that launch was 53 degrees.
NASA
You don't know the damage will be worse at 26 degrees. You're overreacting.
Overreacting?!
What's the lowest temperature you think is safe for launch?
53 degrees.
When do you want me to launch, next April?
You never told us cold weather affected your parts before.
MTI executives asked for a break to talk with the engineers privately.

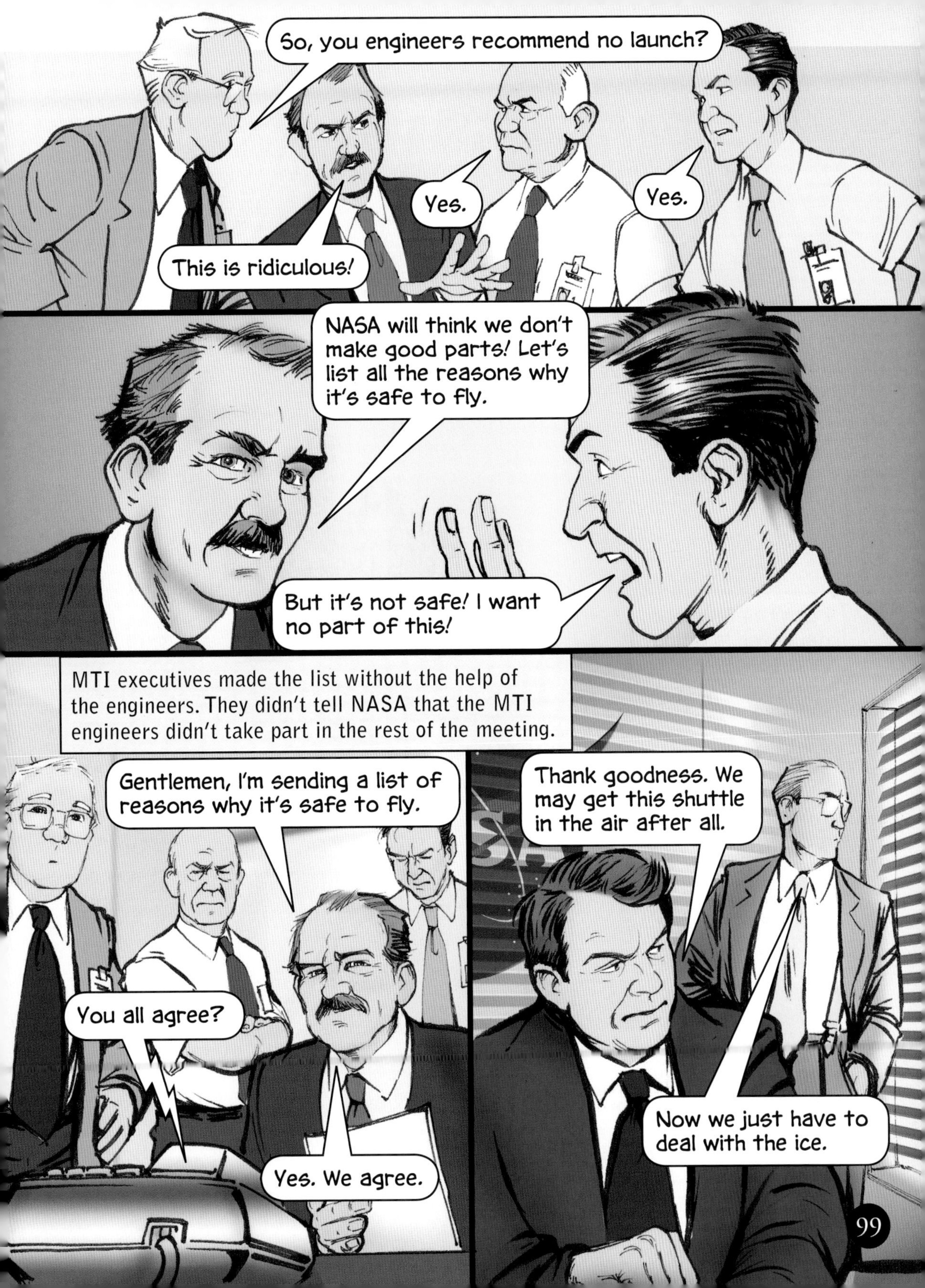

So, you engineers recommend no launch?
This is ridiculous!
Yes.
Yes.
NASA will think we don't make good parts! Let's list all the reasons why it's safe to fly.
But it's not safe! I want no part of this!
MTI executives made the list without the help of the engineers. They didn't tell NASA that the MTI engineers didn't take part in the rest of the meeting.
Gentlemen, I'm sending a list of reasons why it's safe to fly.
You all agree?
Yes. We agree.
Thank goodness. We may get this shuttle in the air after all.
Now we just have to deal with the ice.

CHAPTER 3

LIFT OFF TO DISASTER

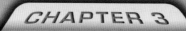

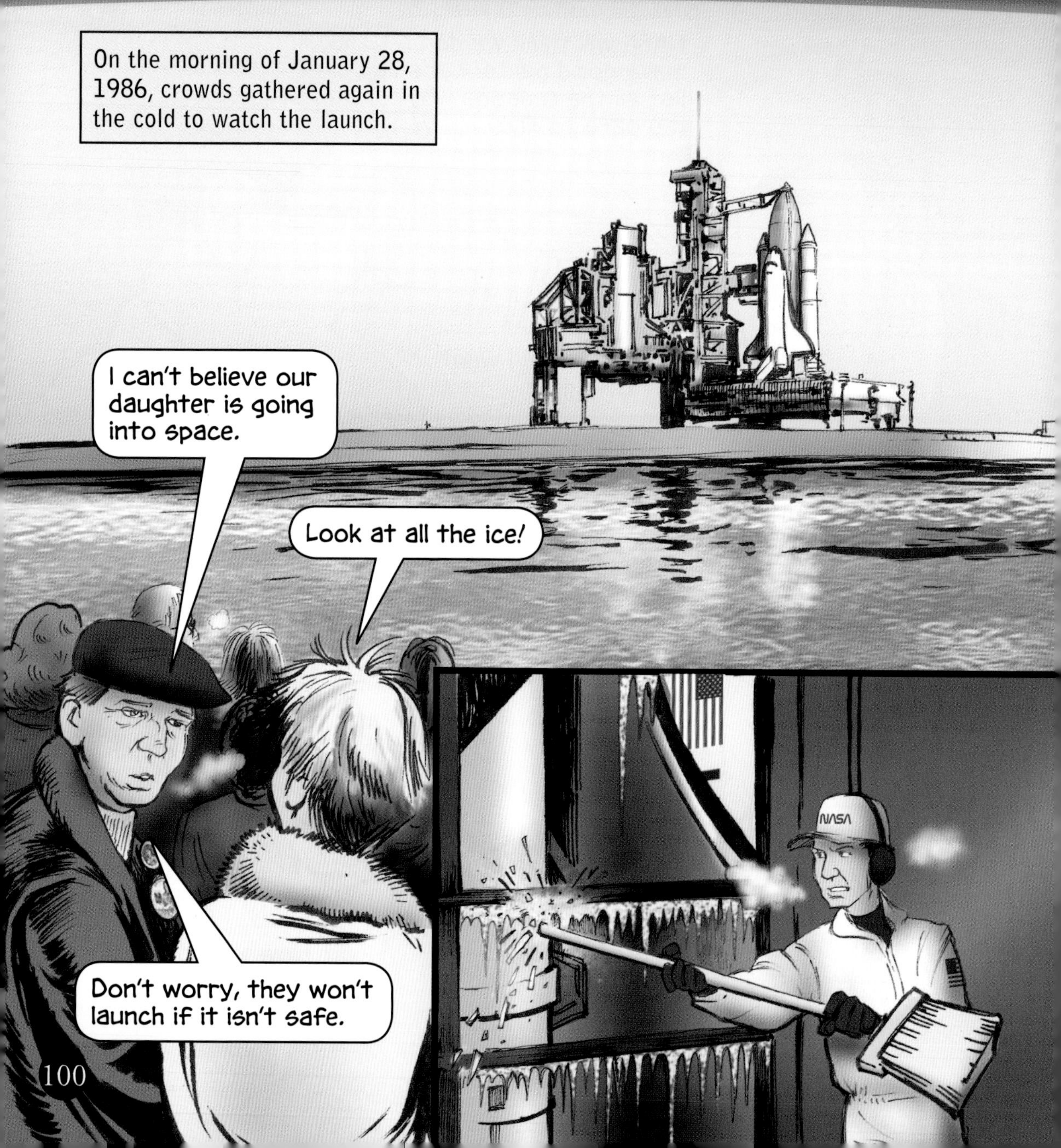
On the morning of January 28, 1986, crowds gathered again in the cold to watch the launch.
I can't believe our daughter is going into space.
Look at all the ice!
Don't worry, they won't launch if it isn't safe.
NASA

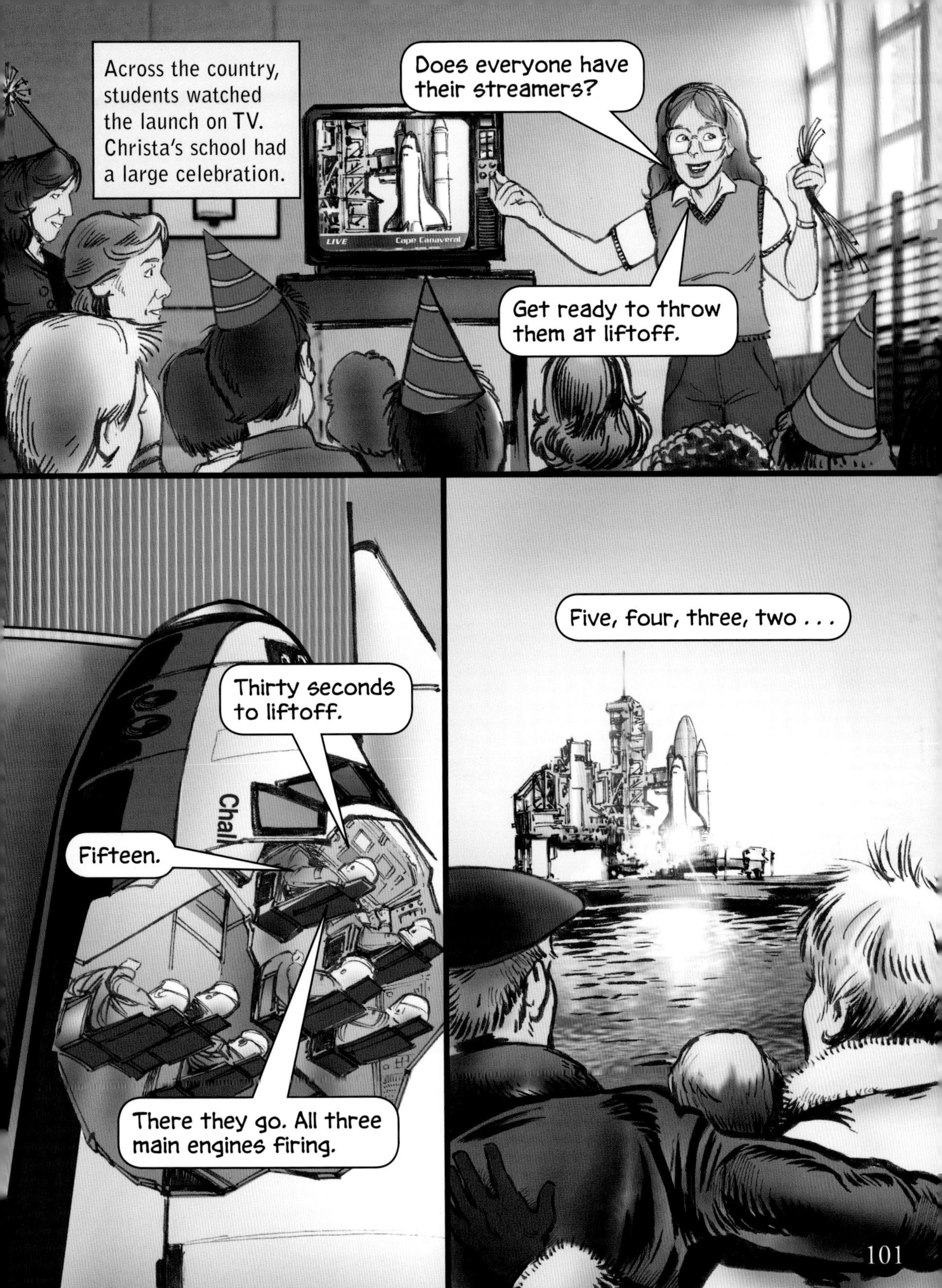

Across the country, students watched the launch on TV. Christa's school had a large celebration.
LIVE
Cape Canaveral
Does everyone have their streamers?
Get ready to throw them at liftoff.
Thirty seconds to liftoff.
Fifteen.
There they go. All three main engines firing.
Five, four, three, two . . .

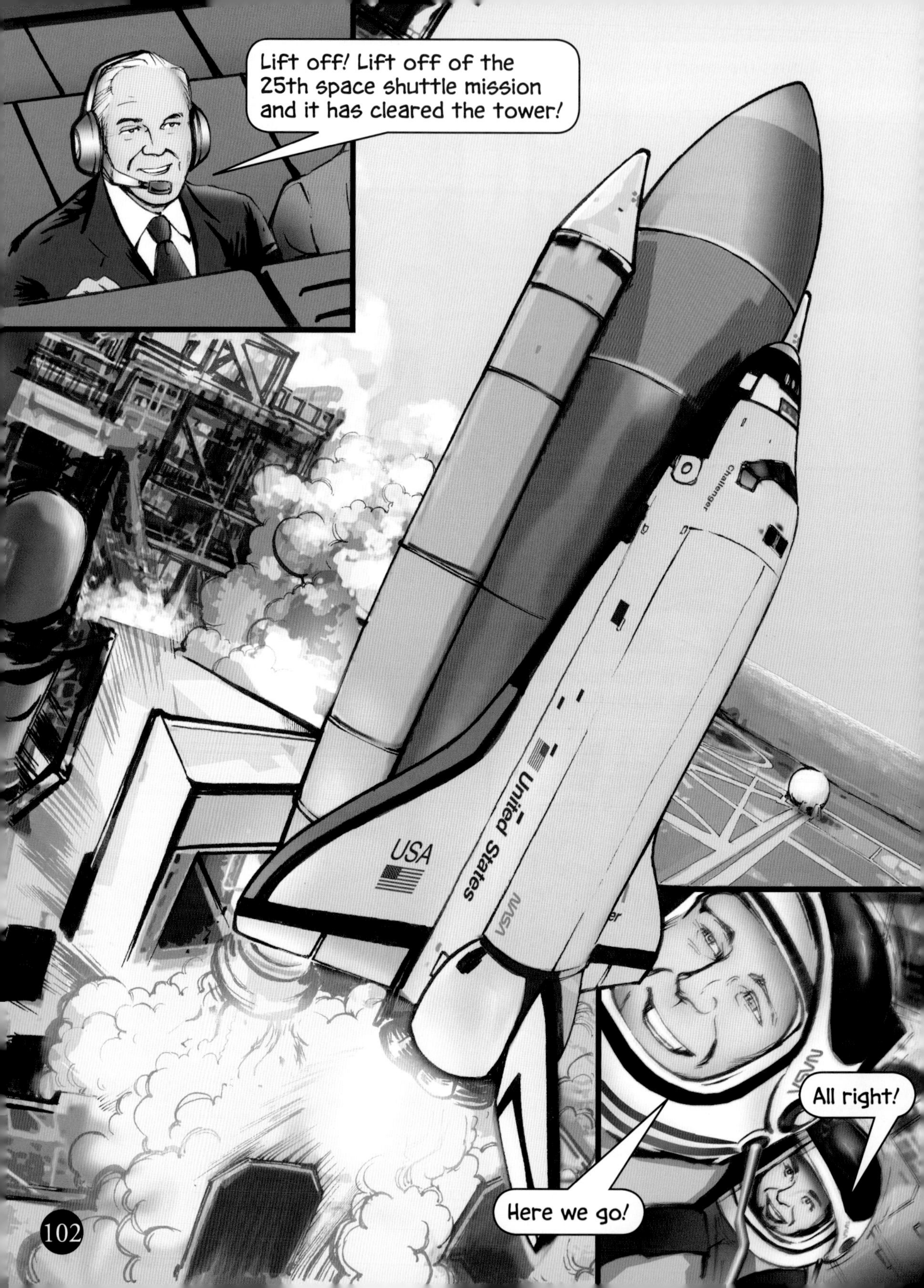
Lift off! Lift off of the 25th space shuttle mission and it has cleared the tower!
Challenger
United States
USA
NASA
Here we go!
All right!

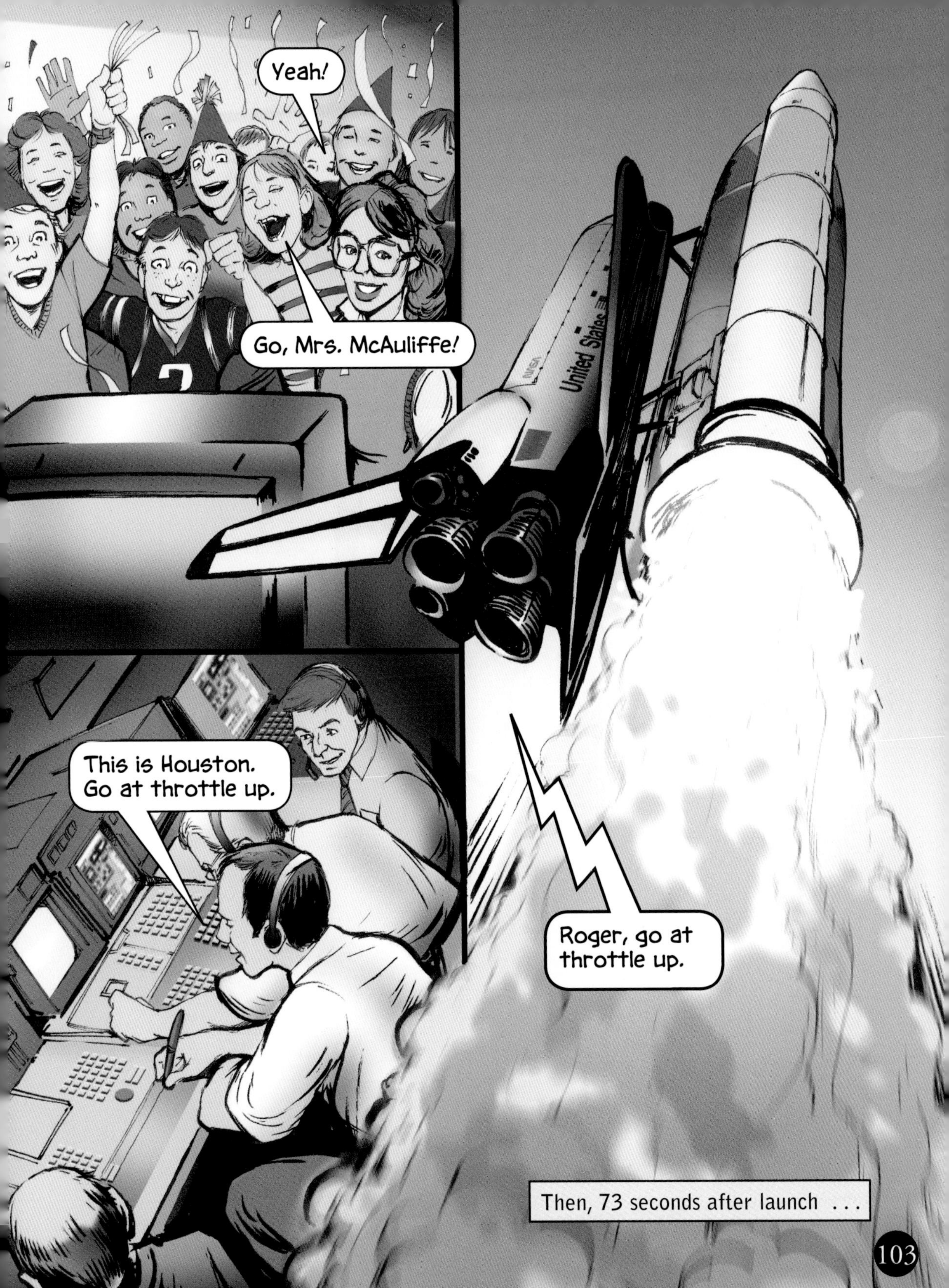
Yeah!
Go, Mrs. McAuliffe!
United States
This is Houston. Go at throttle up.
Roger, go at throttle up.
Then, 73 seconds after launch ...

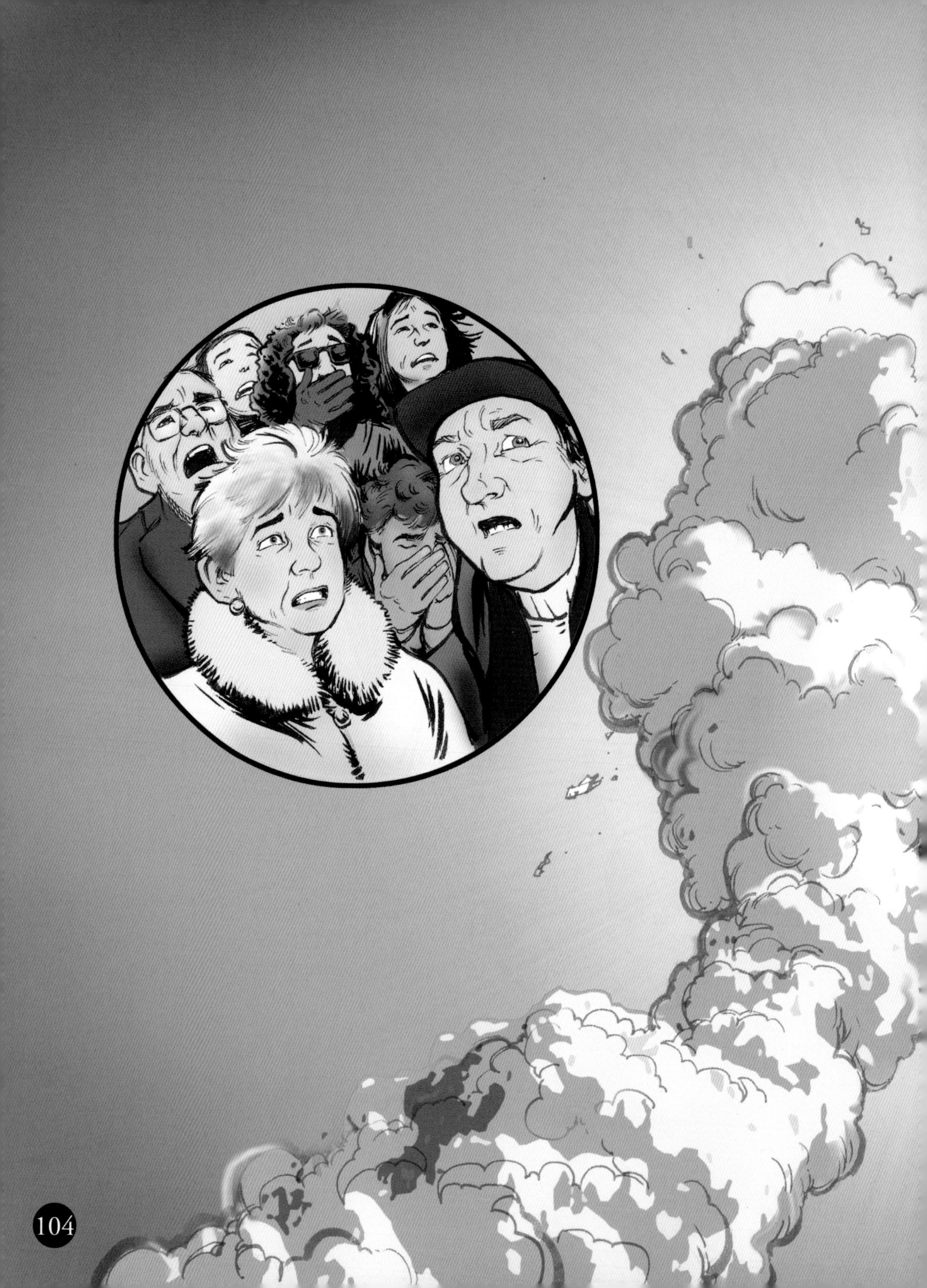

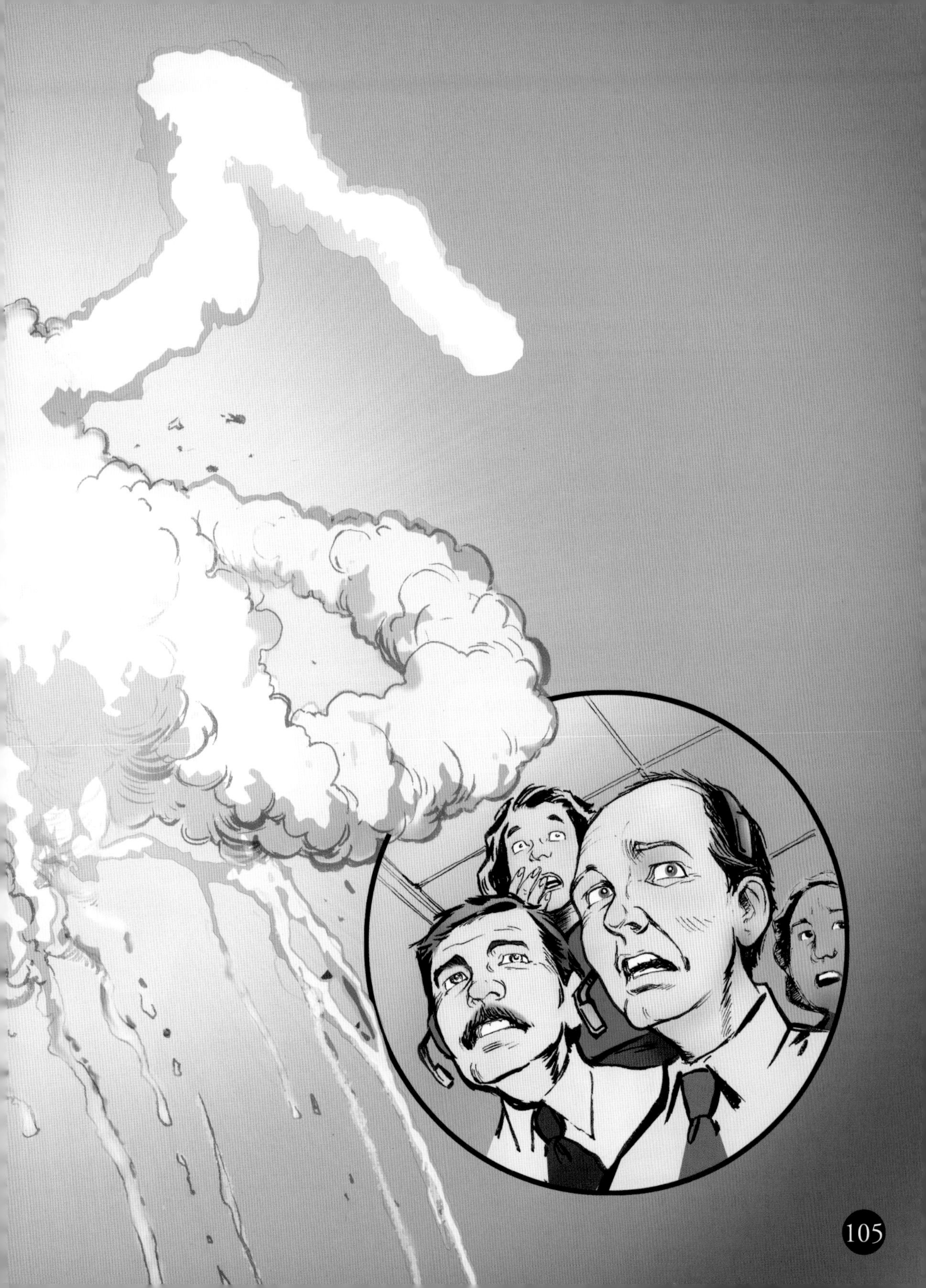

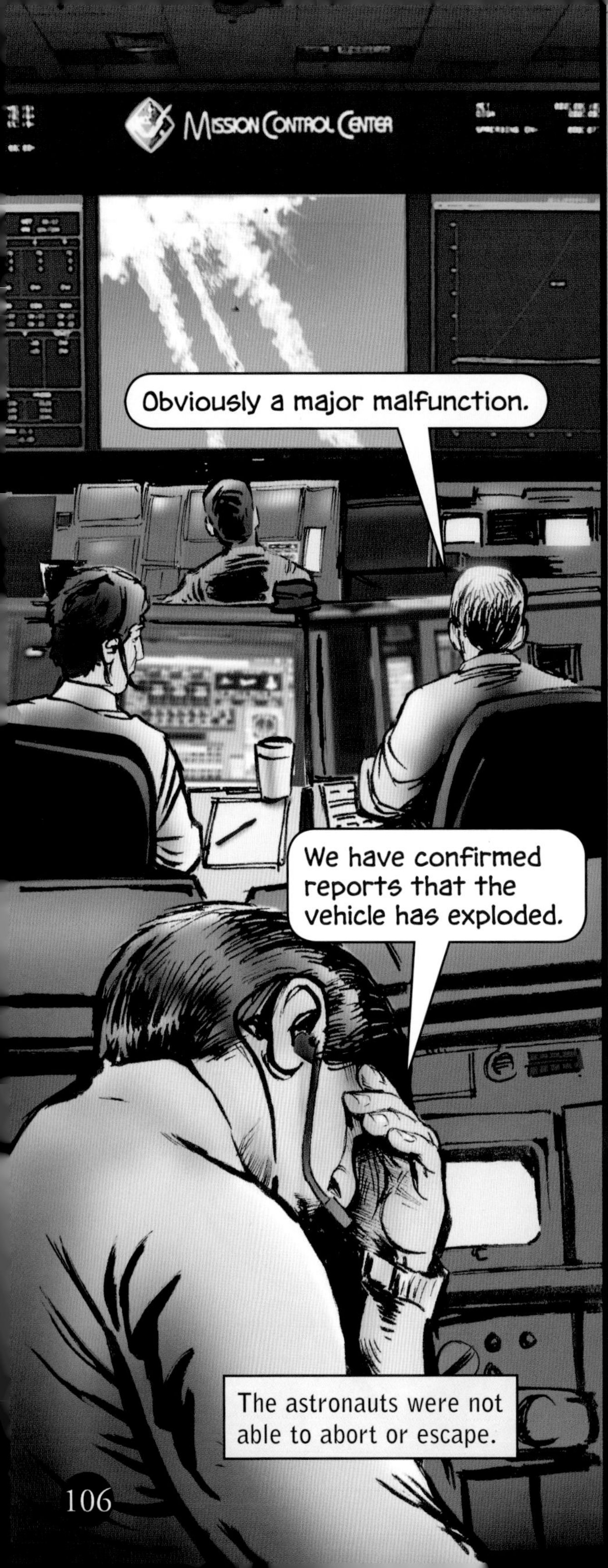
MISSION CONTROL CENTER
Obviously a major malfunction.
We have confirmed reports that the vehicle has exploded.
The astronauts were not able to abort or escape.

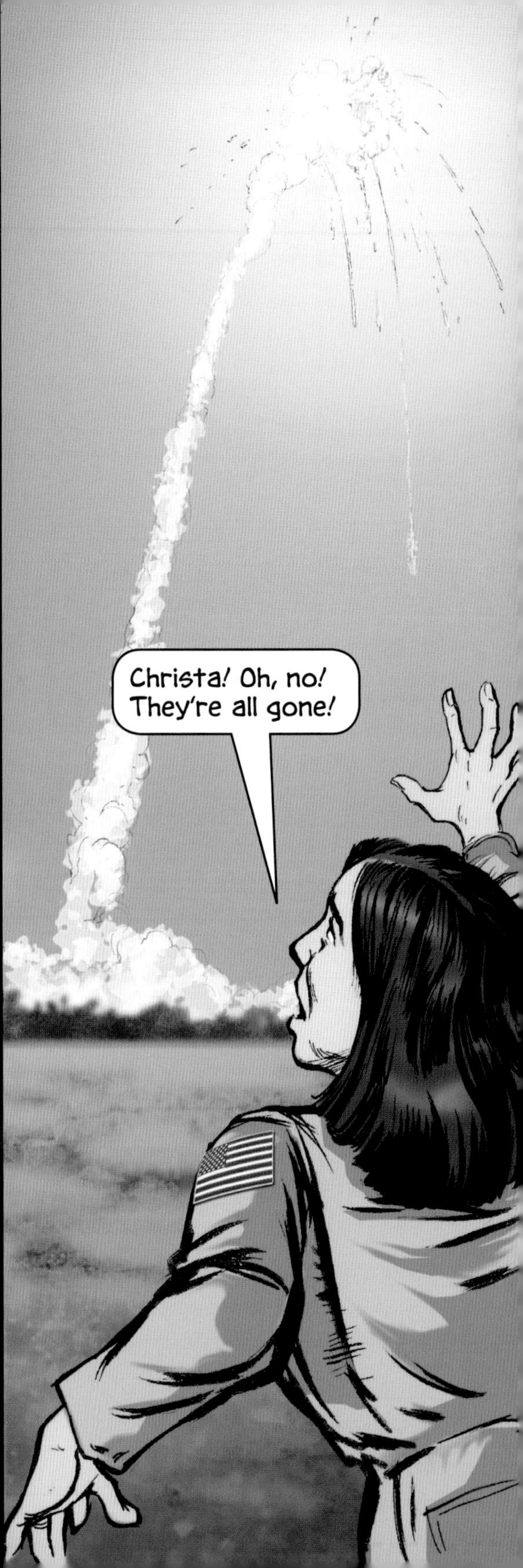
Christa! Oh, no! They're all gone!

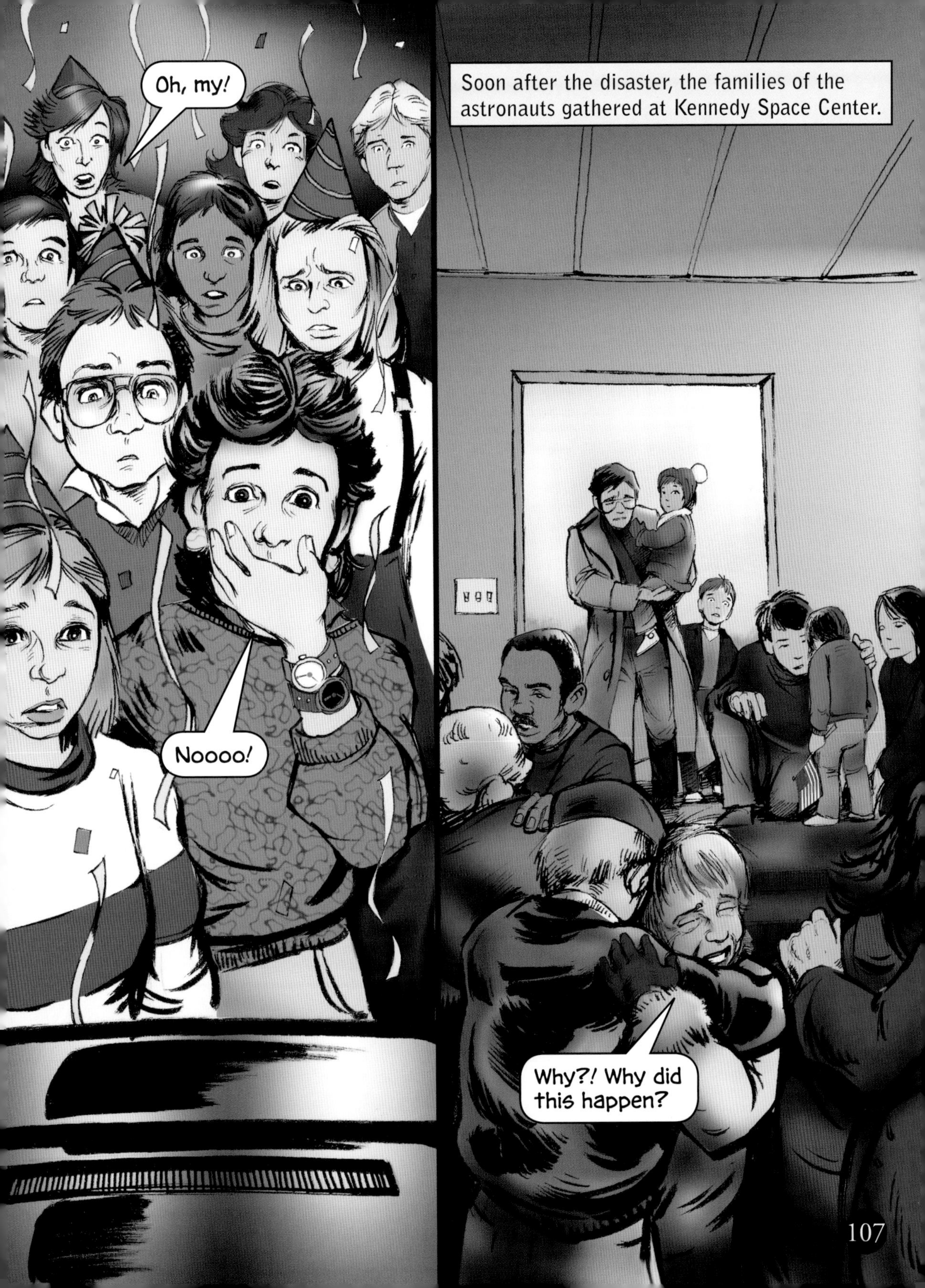
Oh, my!
Noooo!
Soon after the disaster, the families of the astronauts gathered at Kennedy Space Center.
Why?! Why did this happen?

CHAPTER 4

THE WORLD MOURNS

People across the country had been watching this flight. They were saddened when the Challenger astronauts were lost.

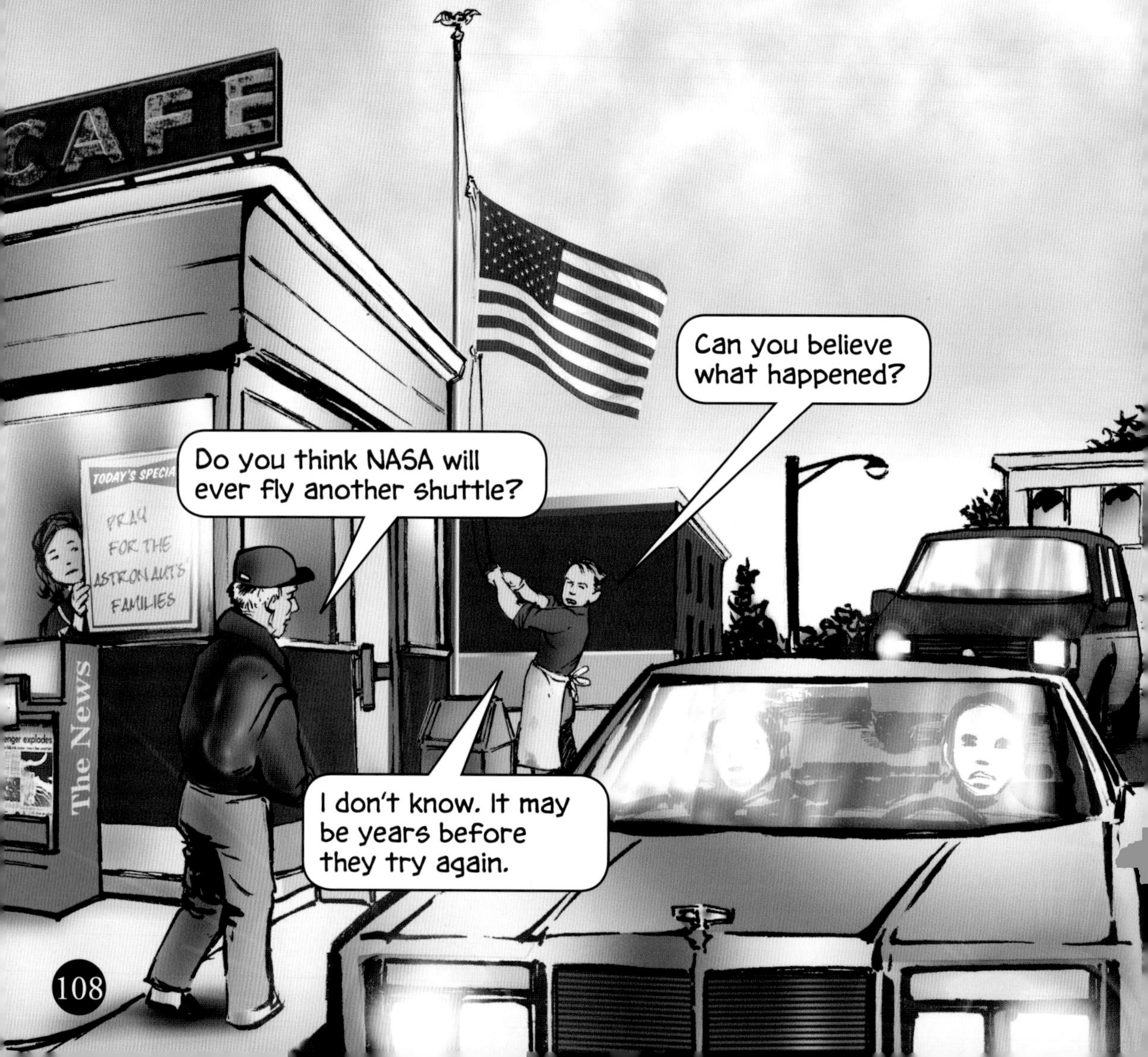
CAFE
PRAY FOR THE ASTRONAUTS' FAMILIES
The News
Can you believe what happened?
Do you think NASA will ever fly another shuttle?
I don't know. It may be years before they try again.

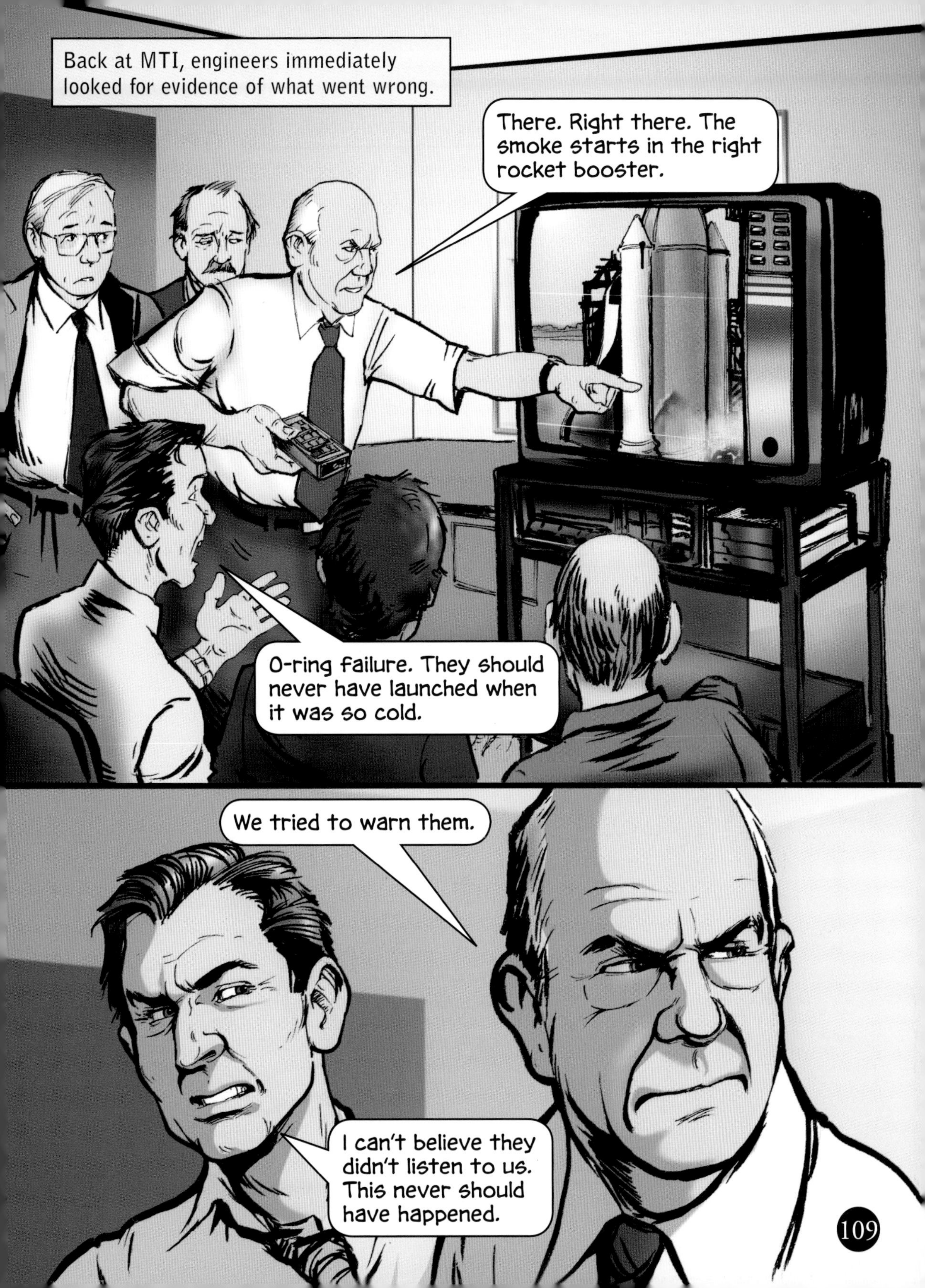
Back at MTI, engineers immediately looked for evidence of what went wrong.
There. Right there. The smoke starts in the right rocket booster.
O-ring failure. They should never have launched when it was so cold.
We tried to warn them.
I can't believe they didn't listen to us. This never should have happened.

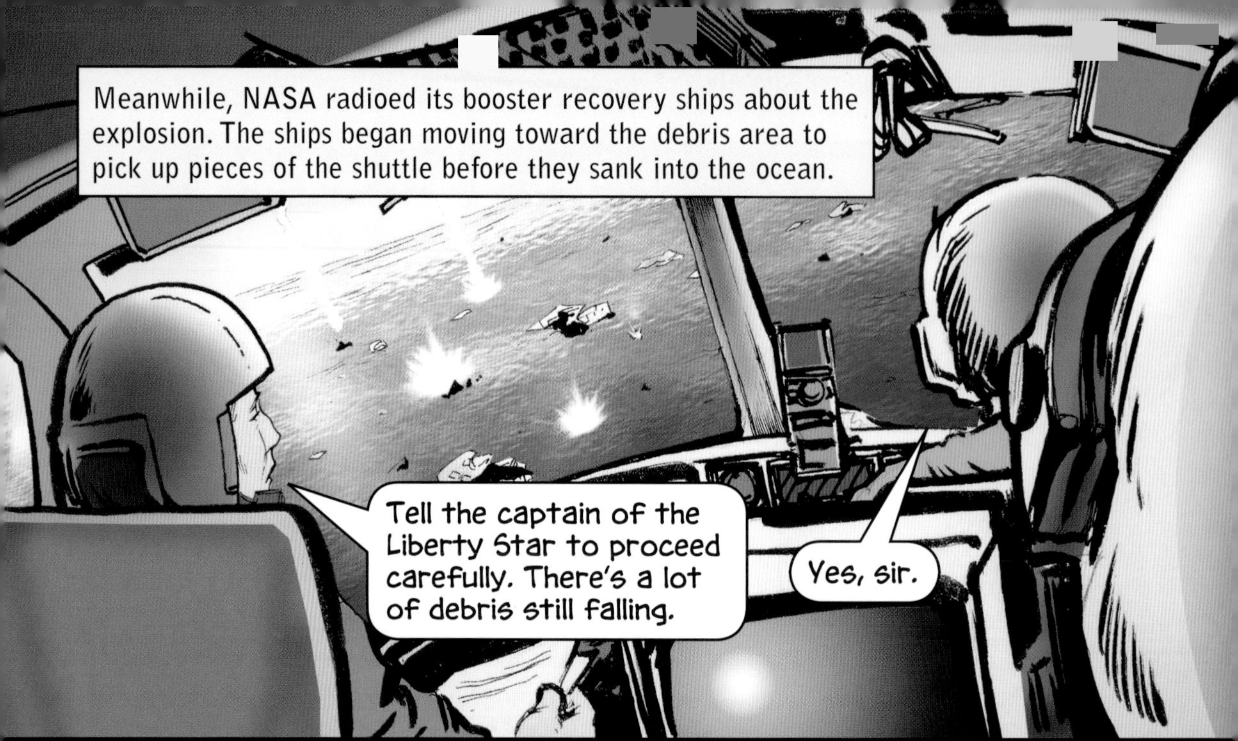
Meanwhile, NASA radioed its booster recovery ships about the explosion. The ships began moving toward the debris area to pick up pieces of the shuttle before they sank into the ocean.
Tell the captain of the Liberty Star to proceed carefully. There's a lot of debris still falling.
Yes, sir.

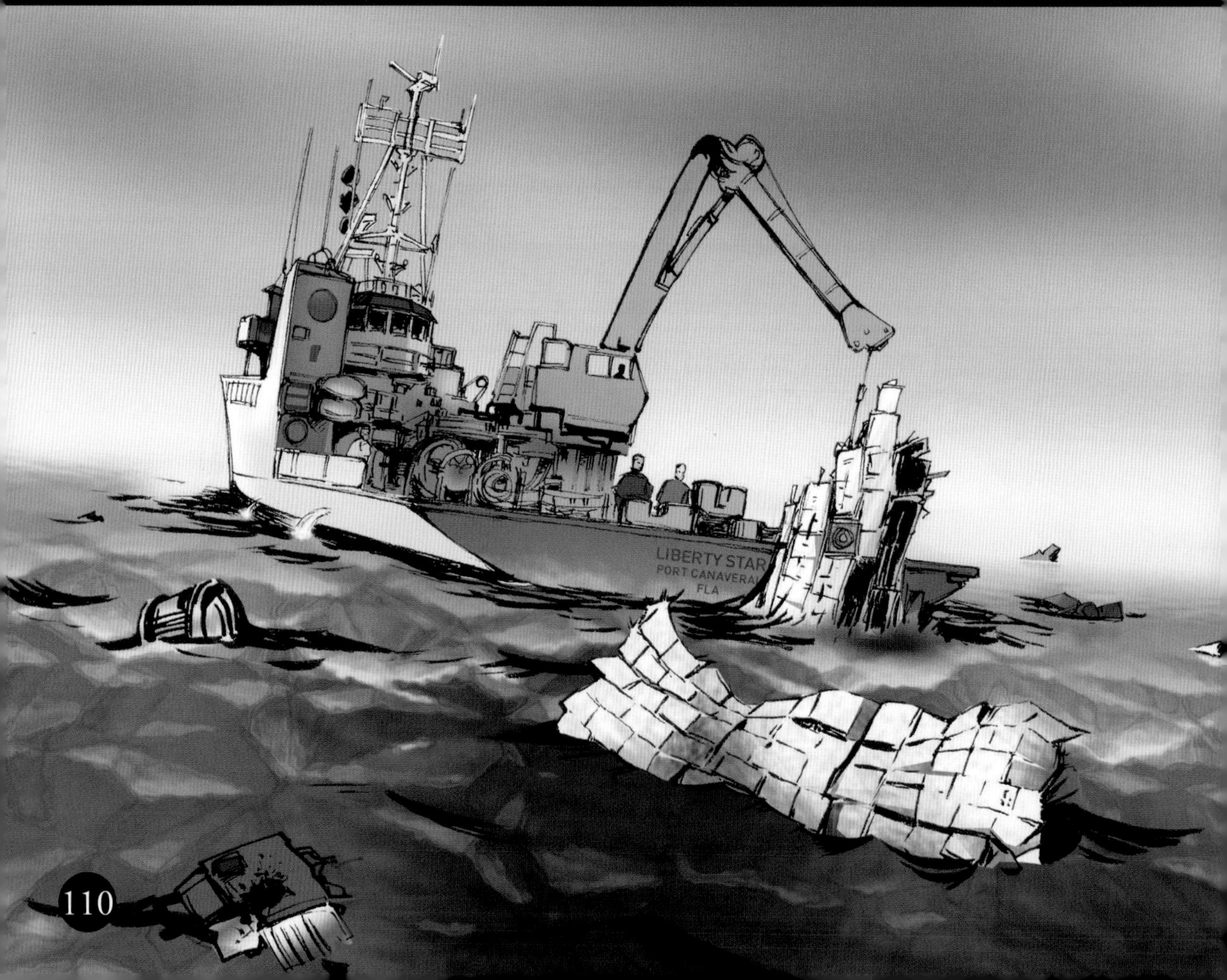
LIBERTY STAR
PORT CANAVERAL
FLA

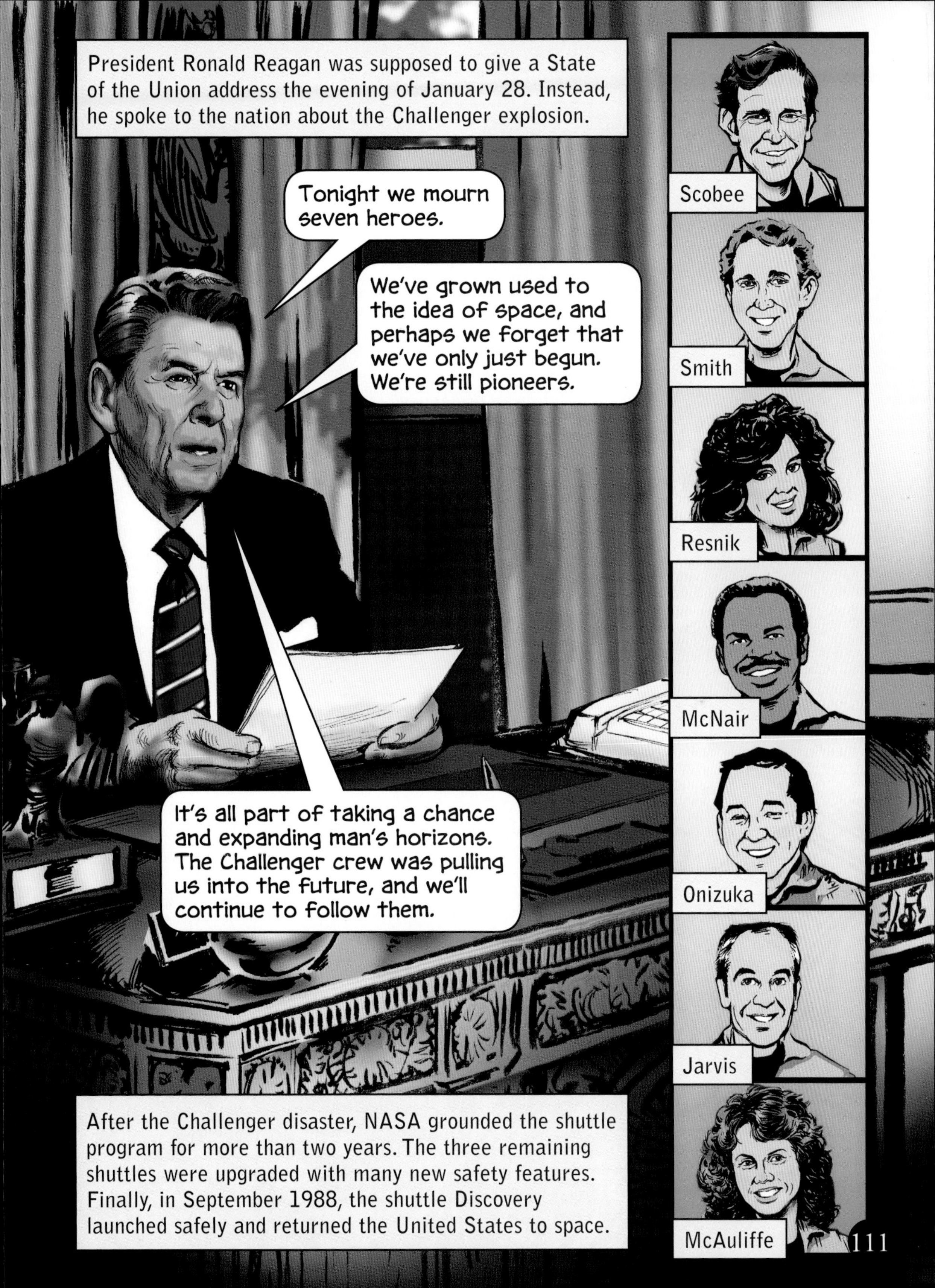
President Ronald Reagan was supposed to give a State of the Union address the evening of January 28. Instead, he spoke to the nation about the Challenger explosion.
Tonight we mourn seven heroes.
We've grown used to the idea of space, and perhaps we forget that we've only just begun. We're still pioneers.
It's all part of taking a chance and expanding man's horizons. The Challenger crew was pulling us into the future, and we'll continue to follow them.
Scobee
Smith
Resnik
McNair
Onizuka
Jarvis
McAuliffe
After the Challenger disaster, NASA grounded the shuttle program for more than two years. The three remaining shuttles were upgraded with many new safety features. Finally, in September 1988, the shuttle Discovery launched safely and returned the United States to space.

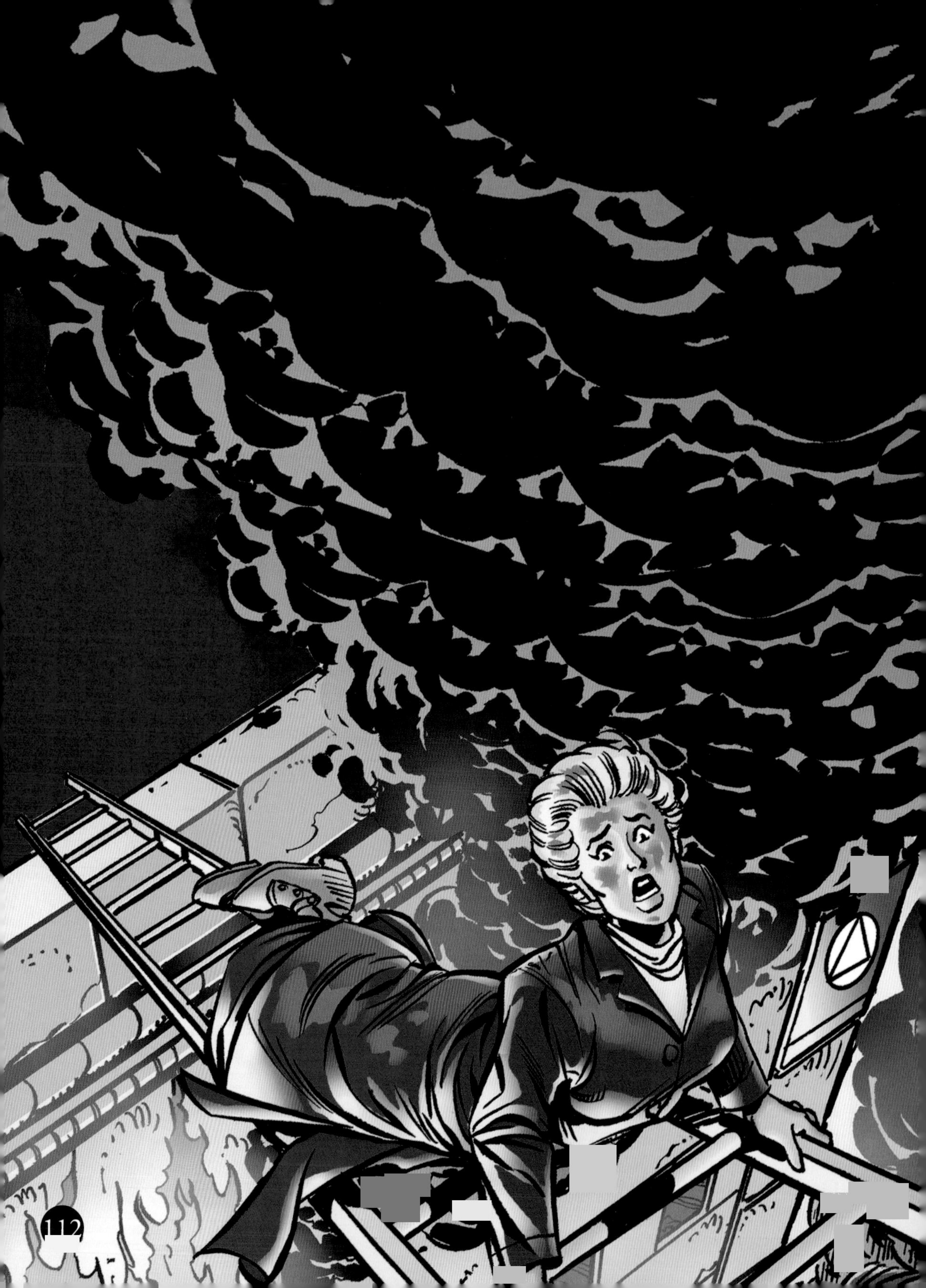

PART 2

FIRE & WARTIME DISASTERS

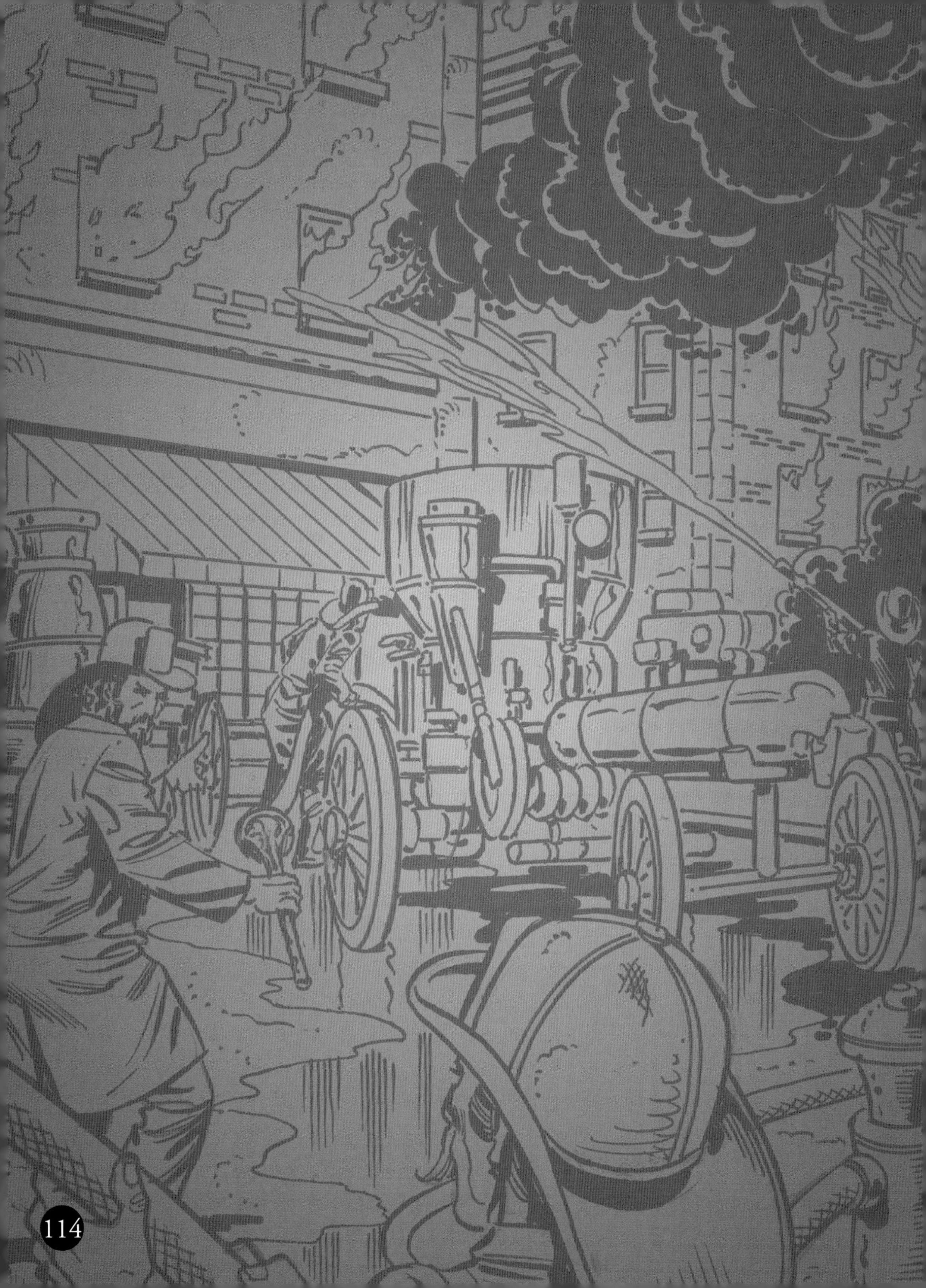

The Great Chicago Fire of 1871

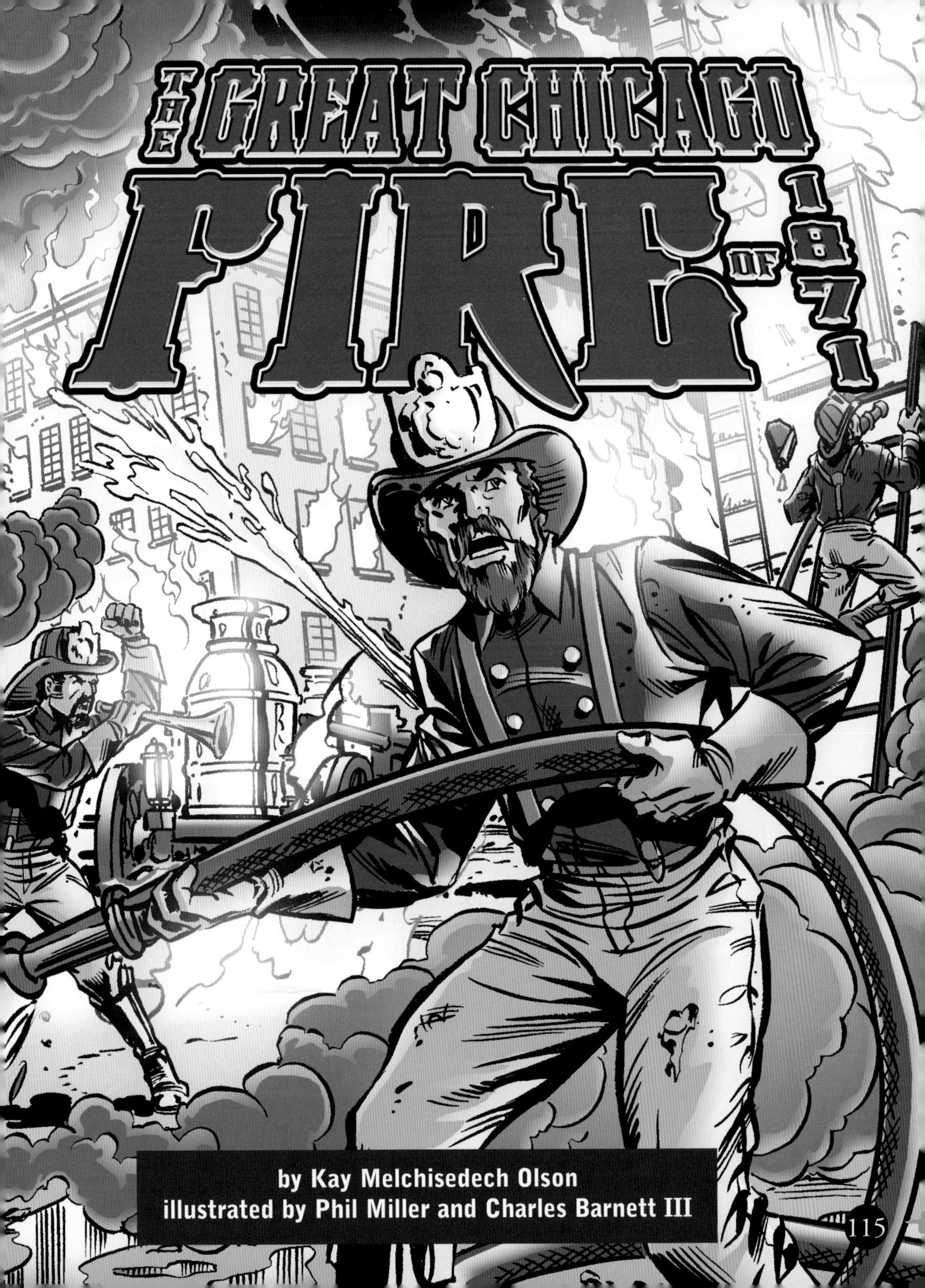

by Kay Melchisedech Olson
illustrated by Phil Miller and Charles Barnett III

CHAPTER 1
FIRST FLAMES

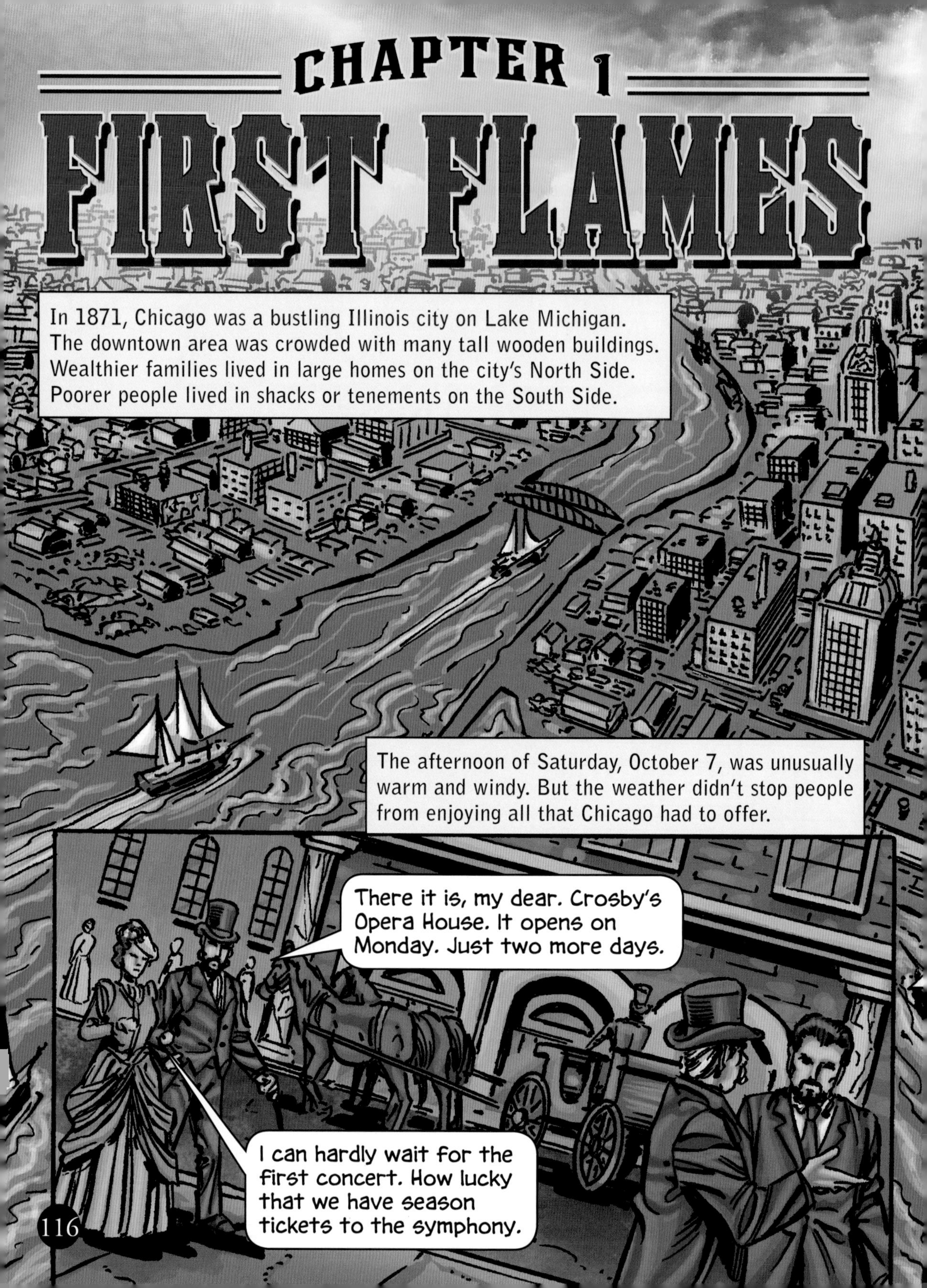
In 1871, Chicago was a bustling Illinois city on Lake Michigan. The downtown area was crowded with many tall wooden buildings. Wealthier families lived in large homes on the city's North Side. Poorer people lived in shacks or tenements on the South Side.
The afternoon of Saturday, October 7, was unusually warm and windy. But the weather didn't stop people from enjoying all that Chicago had to offer.
There it is, my dear. Crosby's Opera House. It opens on Monday. Just two more days.
I can hardly wait for the first concert. How lucky that we have season tickets to the symphony.

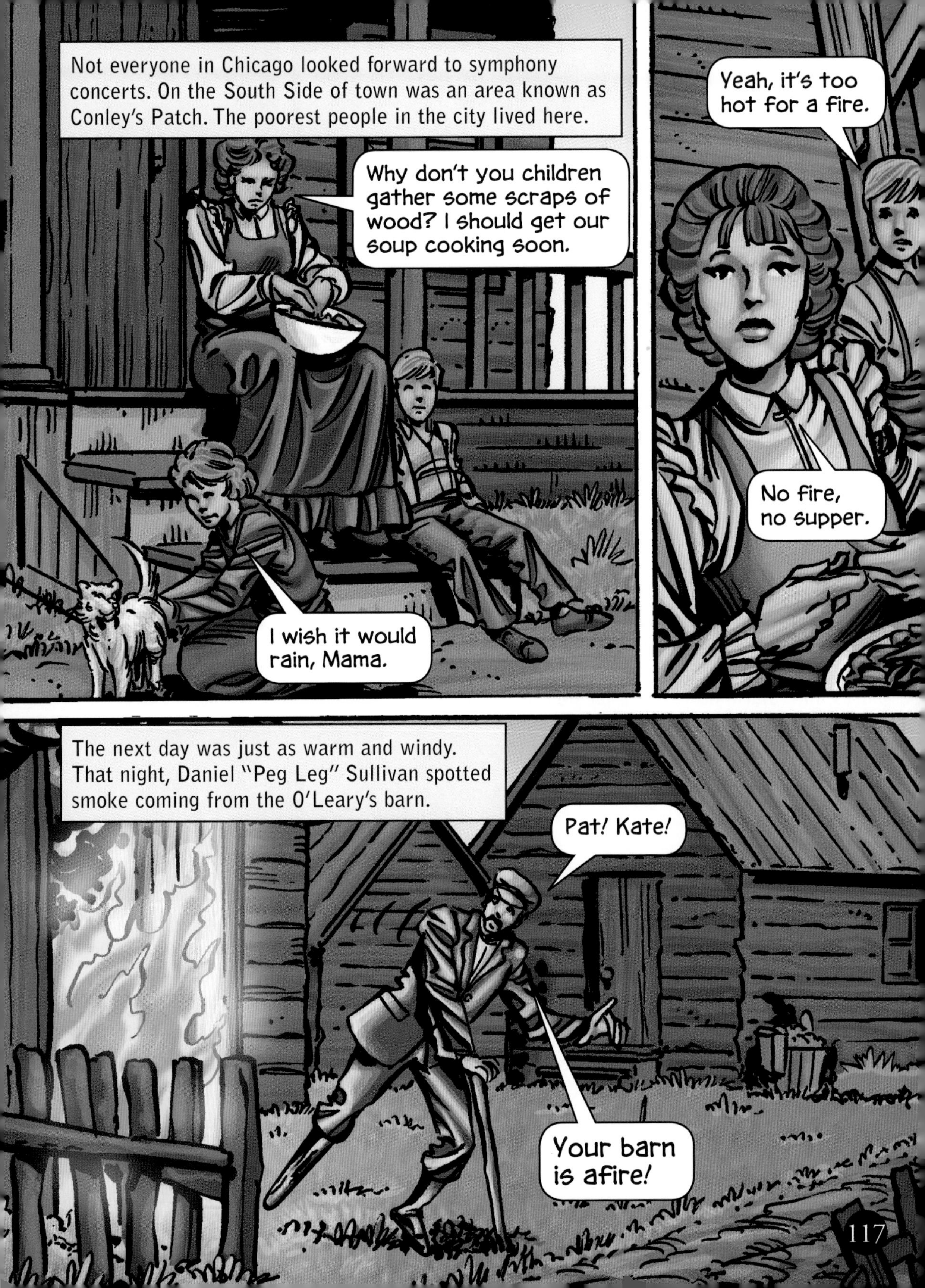

Not everyone in Chicago looked forward to symphony concerts. On the South Side of town was an area known as Conley's Patch. The poorest people in the city lived here.
Why don't you children gather some scraps of wood? I should get our soup cooking soon.
I wish it would rain, Mama.
Yeah, it's too hot for a fire.
No fire, no supper.
The next day was just as warm and windy. That night, Daniel "Peg Leg" Sullivan spotted smoke coming from the O'Leary's barn.
Pat! Kate!
Your barn is afire!

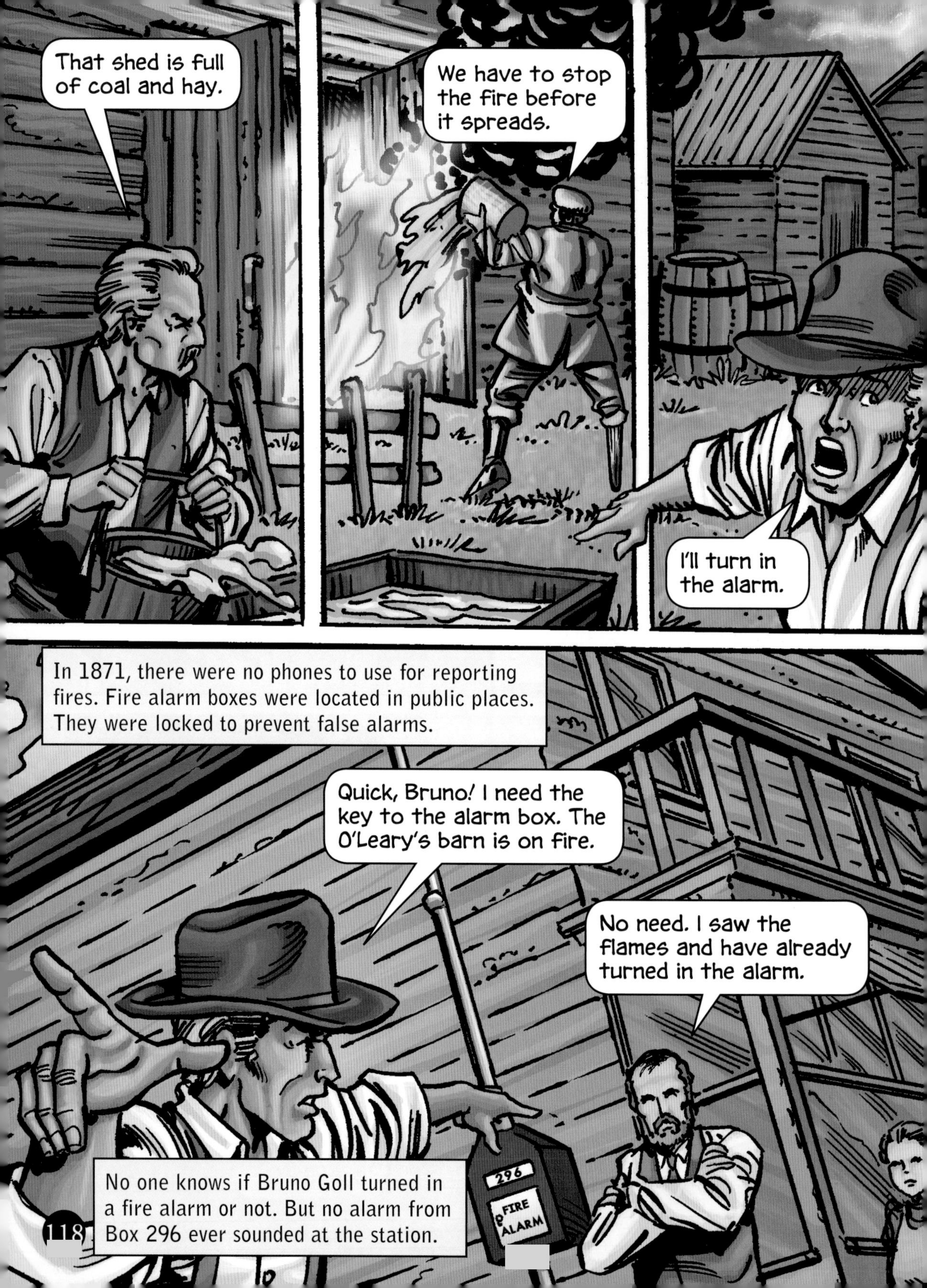
That shed is full of coal and hay.
We have to stop the fire before it spreads.
I'll turn in the alarm.
In 1871, there were no phones to use for reporting fires. Fire alarm boxes were located in public places. They were locked to prevent false alarms.
Quick, Bruno! I need the key to the alarm box. The O'Leary's barn is on fire.
No need. I saw the flames and have already turned in the alarm.
296
FIRE ALARM
No one knows if Bruno Goll turned in a fire alarm or not. But no alarm from Box 296 ever sounded at the station.

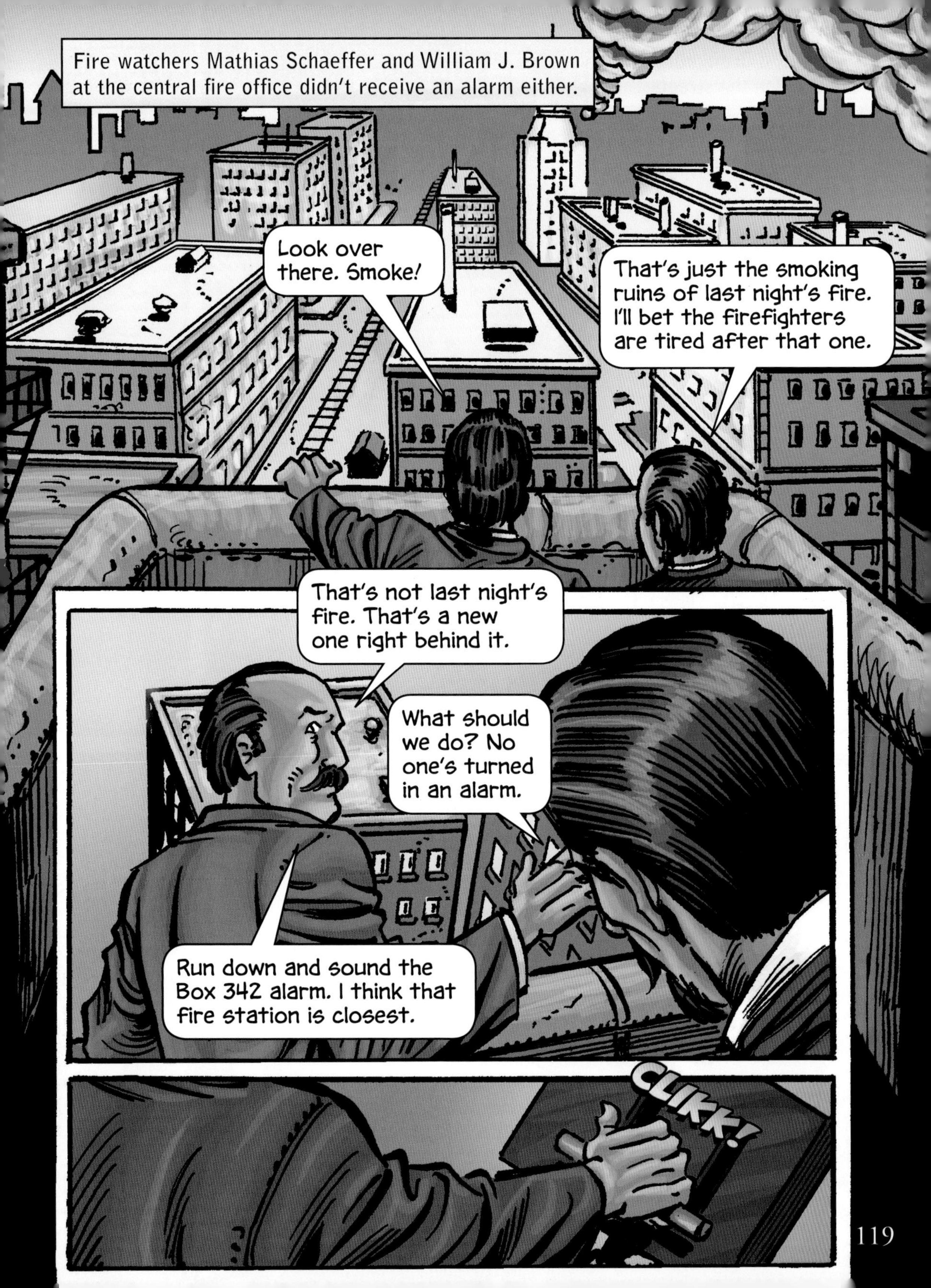
Fire watchers Mathias Schaeffer and William J. Brown at the central fire office didn't receive an alarm either.
Look over there. Smoke!
That's just the smoking ruins of last night's fire. I'll bet the firefighters are tired after that one.
That's not last night's fire. That's a new one right behind it.
What should we do? No one's turned in an alarm.
Run down and sound the Box 342 alarm. I think that fire station is closest.
CLIKK!

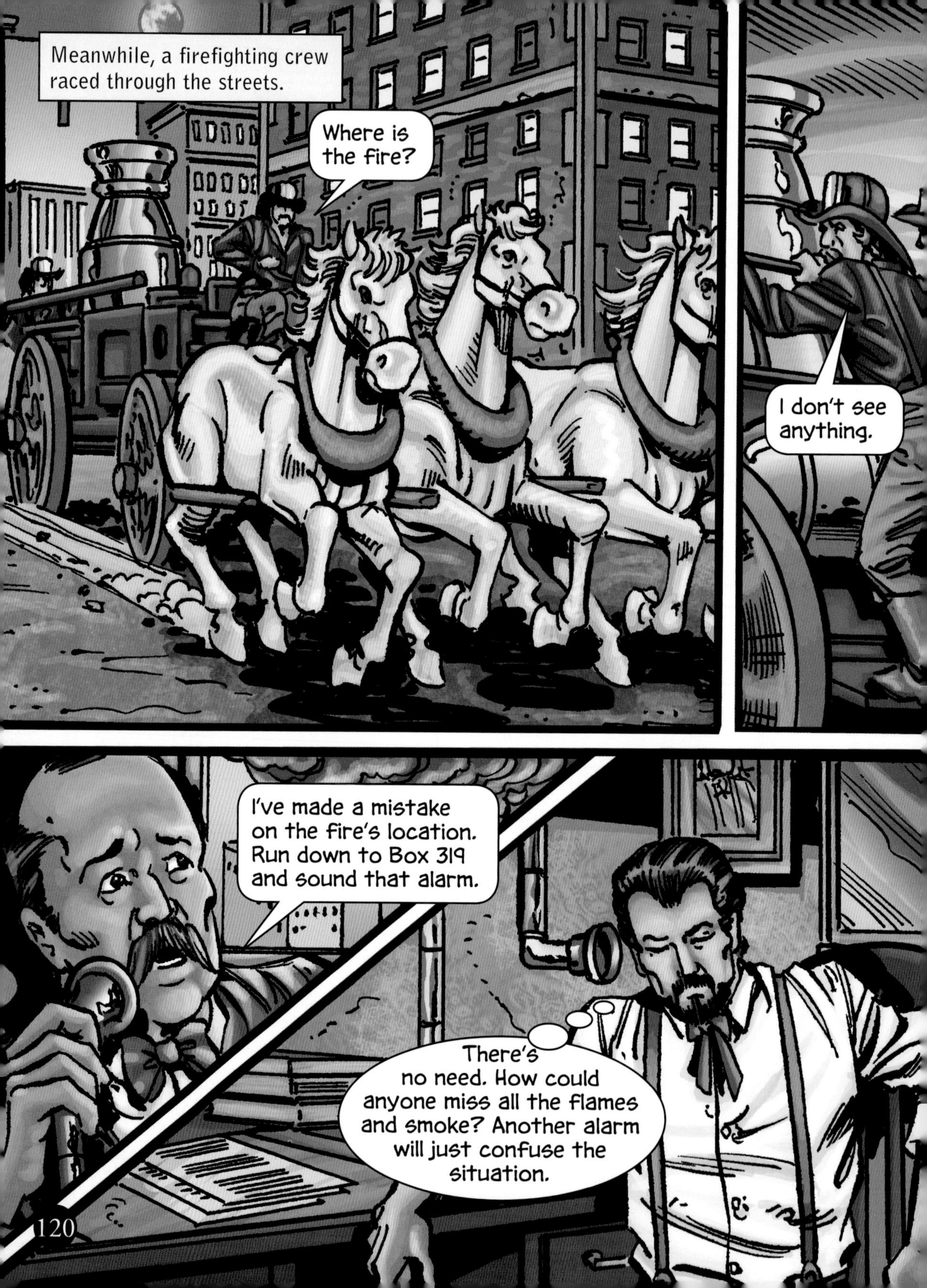
Meanwhile, a firefighting crew raced through the streets.
Where is the fire?
I don't see anything.
I've made a mistake on the fire's location. Run down to Box 319 and sound that alarm.
There's no need. How could anyone miss all the flames and smoke? Another alarm will just confuse the situation.

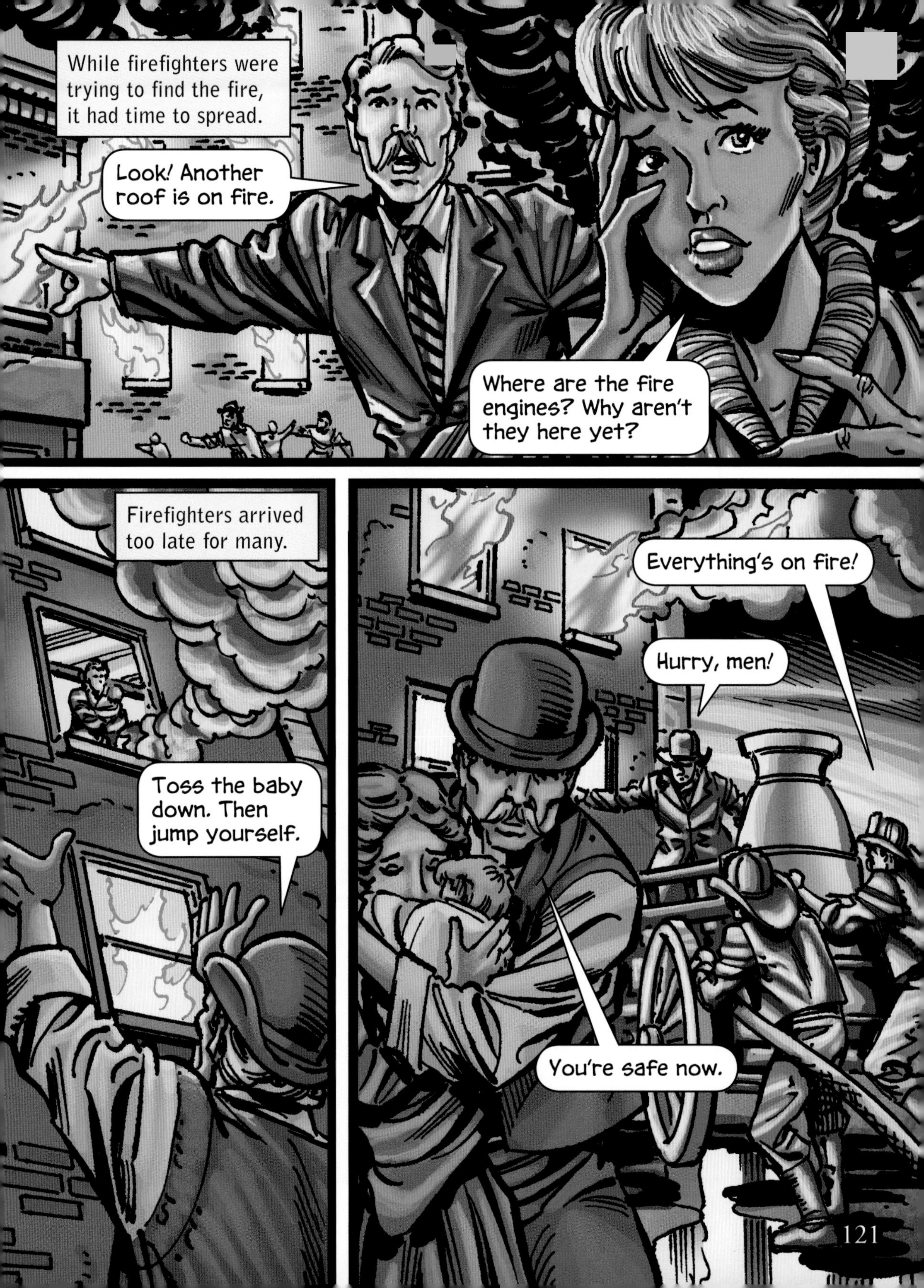
While firefighters were trying to find the fire, it had time to spread.
Look! Another roof is on fire.
Where are the fire engines? Why aren't they here yet?
Firefighters arrived too late for many.
Toss the baby down. Then jump yourself.
Everything's on fire!
Hurry, men!
You're safe now.

CHAPTER 2
GROWING PANIC

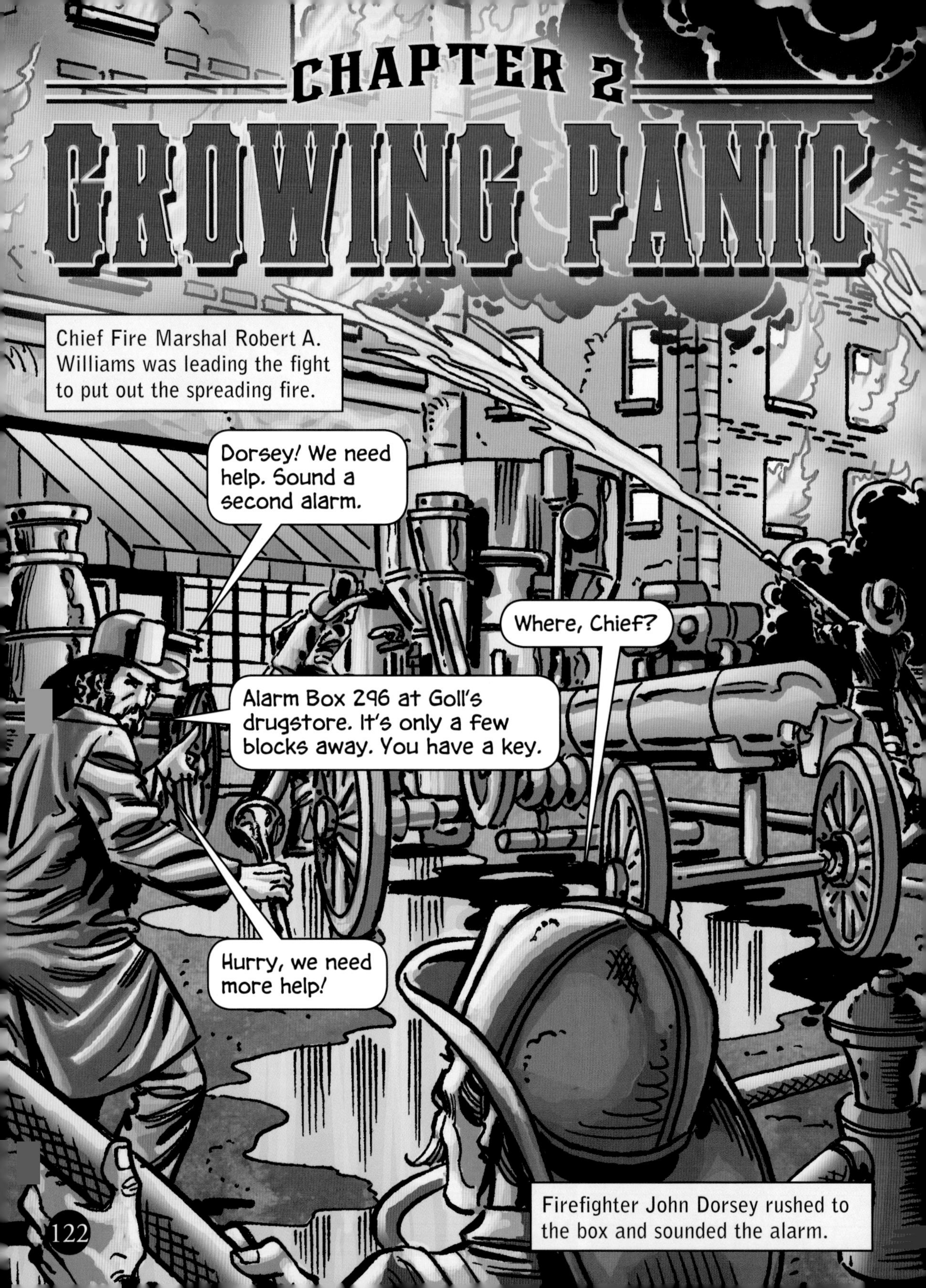
Chief Fire Marshal Robert A. Williams was leading the fight to put out the spreading fire.
Dorsey! We need help. Sound a second alarm.
Where, Chief?
Alarm Box 296 at Goll's drugstore. It's only a few blocks away. You have a key.
Hurry, we need more help!
Firefighter John Dorsey rushed to the box and sounded the alarm.

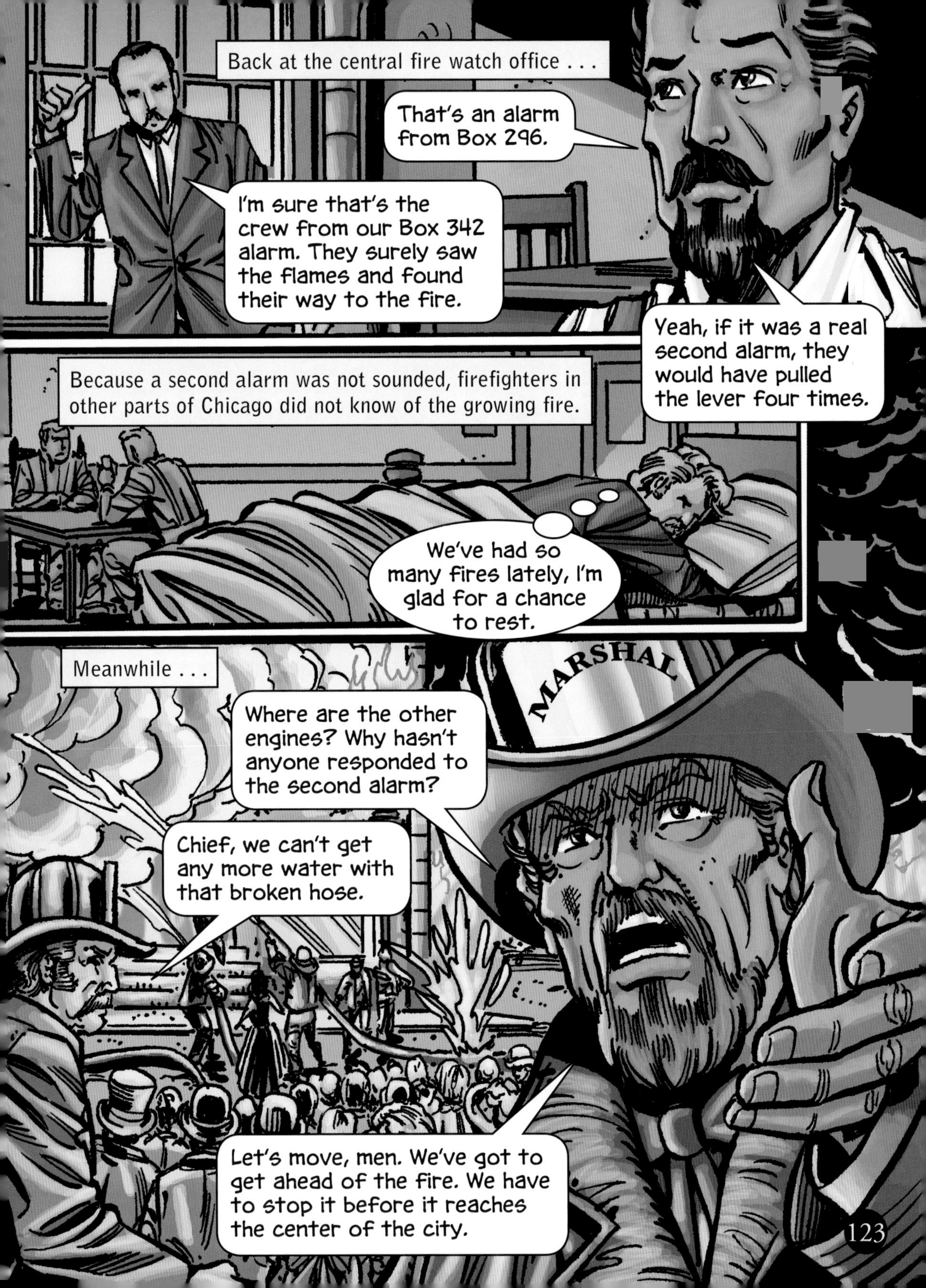

Back at the central fire watch office . . .
That's an alarm from Box 296.
I'm sure that's the crew from our Box 342 alarm. They surely saw the flames and found their way to the fire.
Yeah, if it was a real second alarm, they would have pulled the lever four times.
Because a second alarm was not sounded, firefighters in other parts of Chicago did not know of the growing fire.
We've had so many fires lately, I'm glad for a chance to rest.
Meanwhile . . .
MARSHAL
Where are the other engines? Why hasn't anyone responded to the second alarm?
Chief, we can't get any more water with that broken hose.
Let's move, men. We've got to get ahead of the fire. We have to stop it before it reaches the center of the city.

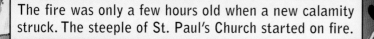

The fire was only a few hours old when a new calamity struck. The steeple of St. Paul's Church started on fire.

Send more men and engines to the church. If the wind blows embers from the steeple, the fire will jump across the river.

There's a shingle mill, box factory, and a furniture factory right across from the church.

Hurry! If those buildings burn, the fire will spread to the South Side. Nothing will stop it then.

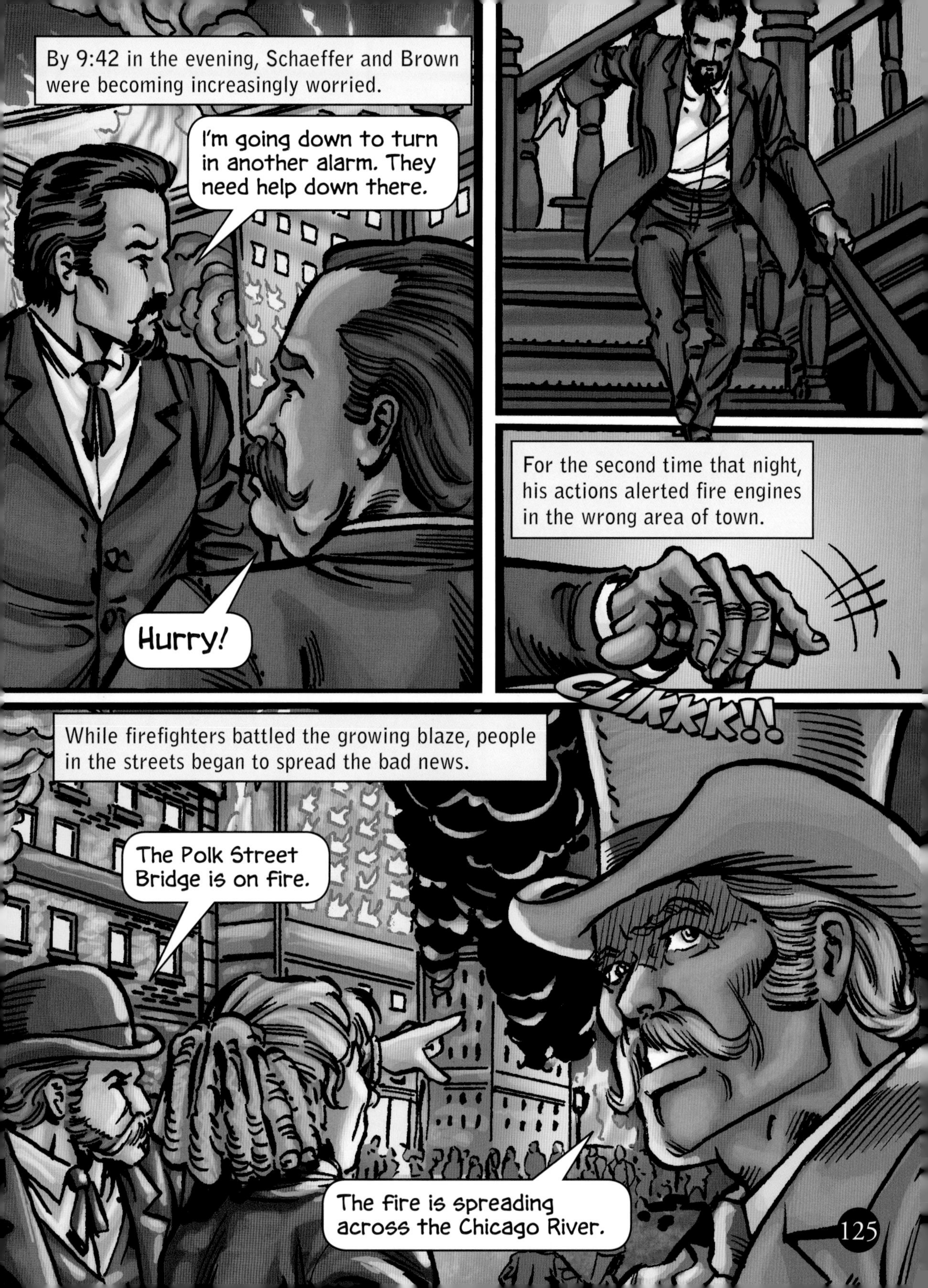

By 9:42 in the evening, Schaeffer and Brown were becoming increasingly worried.
I'm going down to turn in another alarm. They need help down there.
Hurry!
For the second time that night, his actions alerted fire engines in the wrong area of town.
CLIKKK!!
While firefighters battled the growing blaze, people in the streets began to spread the bad news.
The Polk Street Bridge is on fire.
The fire is spreading across the Chicago River.

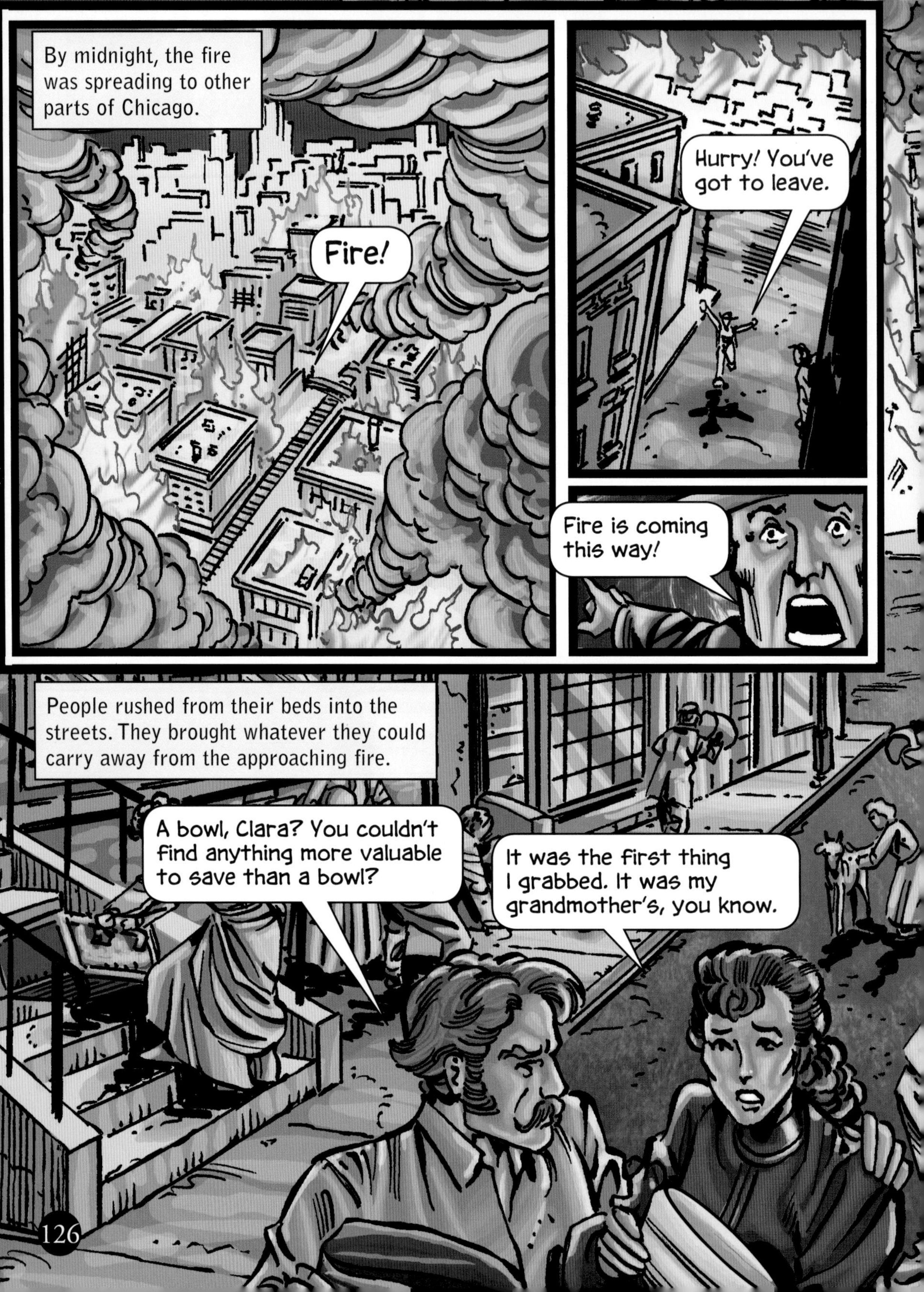
By midnight, the fire was spreading to other parts of Chicago.
Fire!
Hurry! You've got to leave.
Fire is coming this way!
People rushed from their beds into the streets. They brought whatever they could carry away from the approaching fire.
A bowl, Clara? You couldn't find anything more valuable to save than a bowl?
It was the first thing I grabbed. It was my grandmother's, you know.

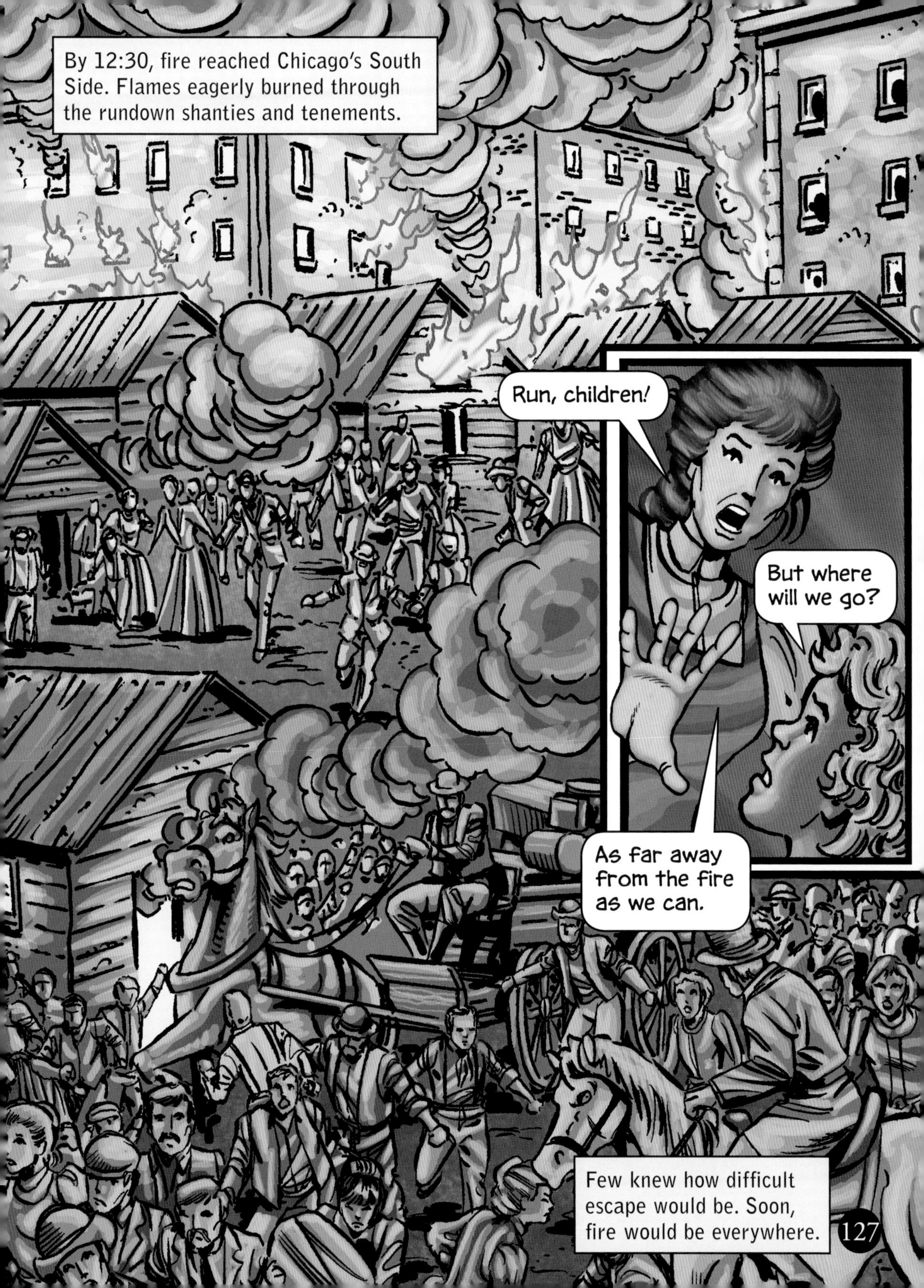
By 12:30, fire reached Chicago's South Side. Flames eagerly burned through the rundown shanties and tenements.
Run, children!
But where will we go?
As far away from the fire as we can.
Few knew how difficult escape would be. Soon, fire would be everywhere.

CHAPTER 3
TOTAL DISASTER

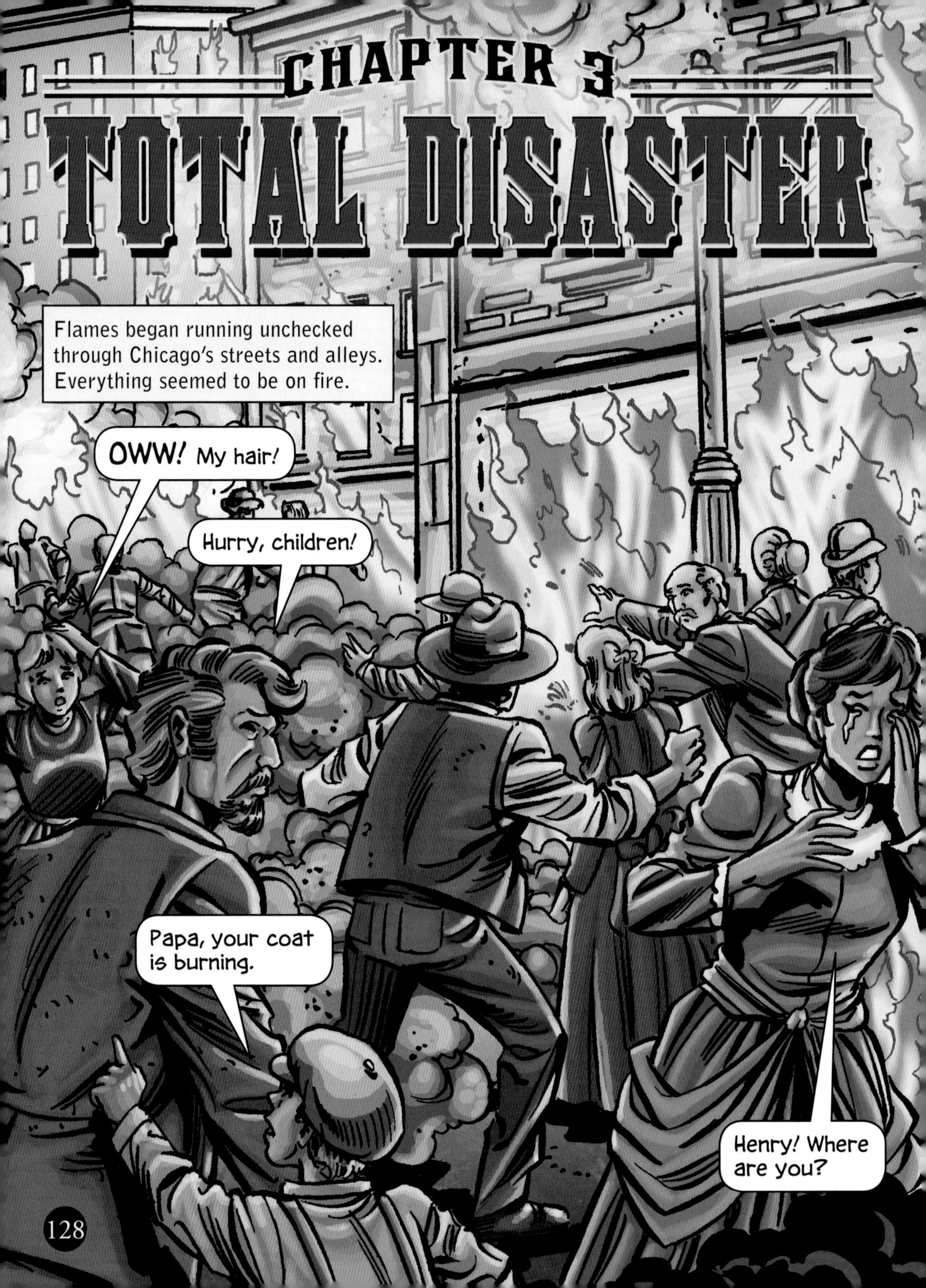
Flames began running unchecked through Chicago's streets and alleys. Everything seemed to be on fire.
OWW! My hair!
Hurry, children!
Papa, your coat is burning.
Henry! Where are you?

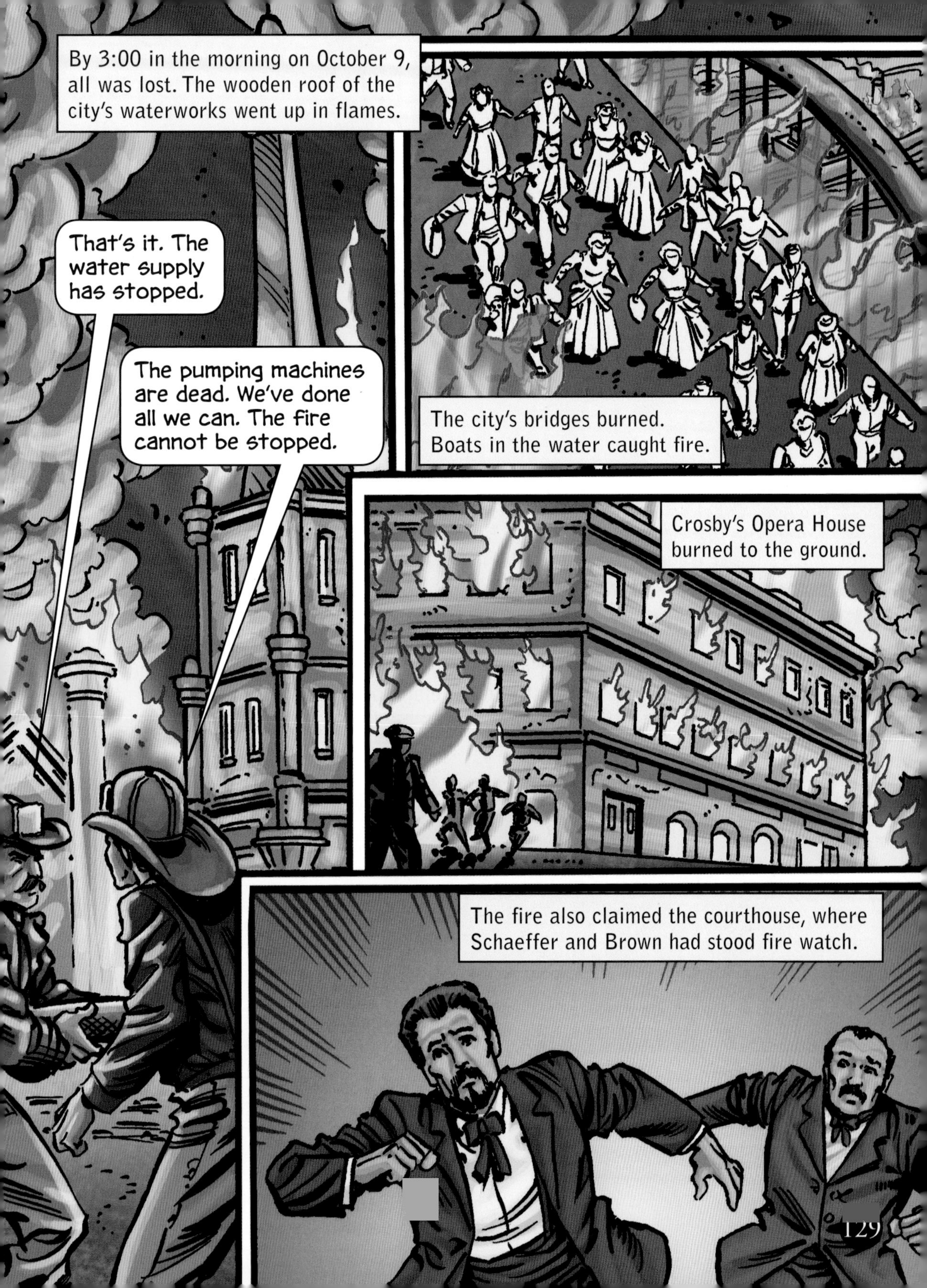

By 3:00 in the morning on October 9, all was lost. The wooden roof of the city's waterworks went up in flames.
That's it. The water supply has stopped.
The pumping machines are dead. We've done all we can. The fire cannot be stopped.
The city's bridges burned. Boats in the water caught fire.
Crosby's Opera House burned to the ground.
The fire also claimed the courthouse, where Schaeffer and Brown had stood fire watch.

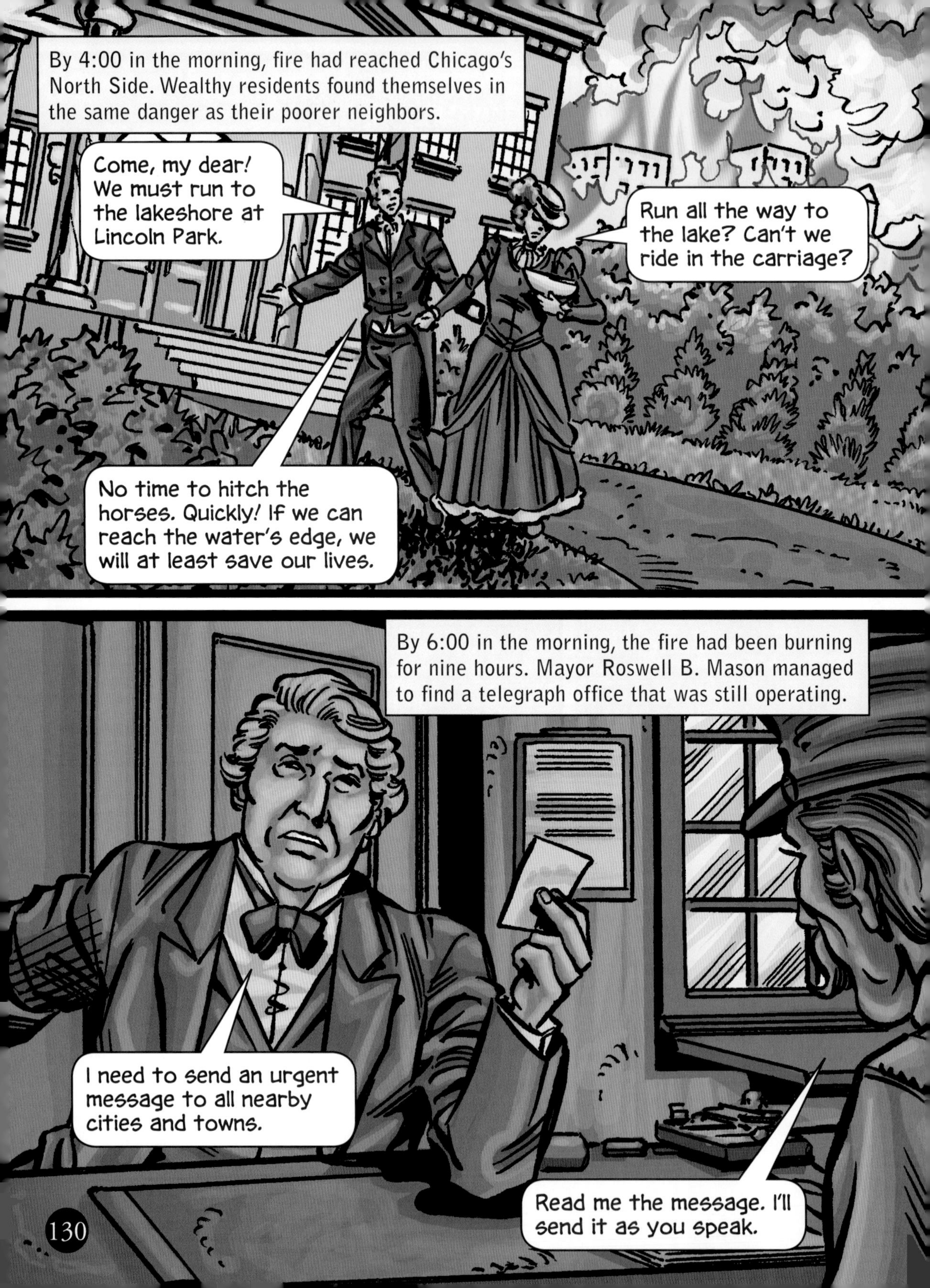
By 4:00 in the morning, fire had reached Chicago's North Side. Wealthy residents found themselves in the same danger as their poorer neighbors.
Come, my dear! We must run to the lakeshore at Lincoln Park.
Run all the way to the lake? Can't we ride in the carriage?
No time to hitch the horses. Quickly! If we can reach the water's edge, we will at least save our lives.
By 6:00 in the morning, the fire had been burning for nine hours. Mayor Roswell B. Mason managed to find a telegraph office that was still operating.
I need to send an urgent message to all nearby cities and towns.
Read me the message. I'll send it as you speak.

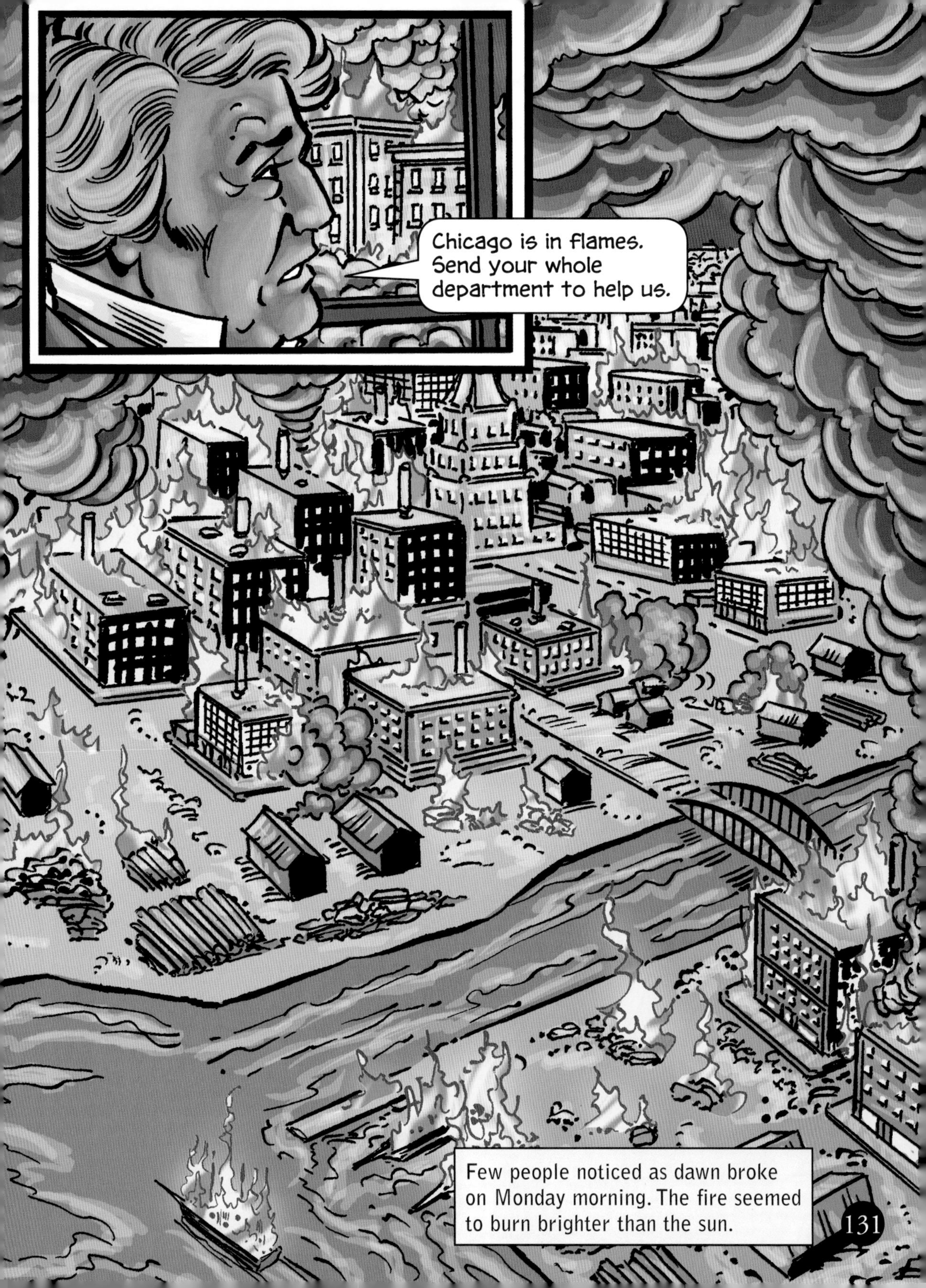
Chicago is in flames. Send your whole department to help us.
Few people noticed as dawn broke on Monday morning. The fire seemed to burn brighter than the sun.

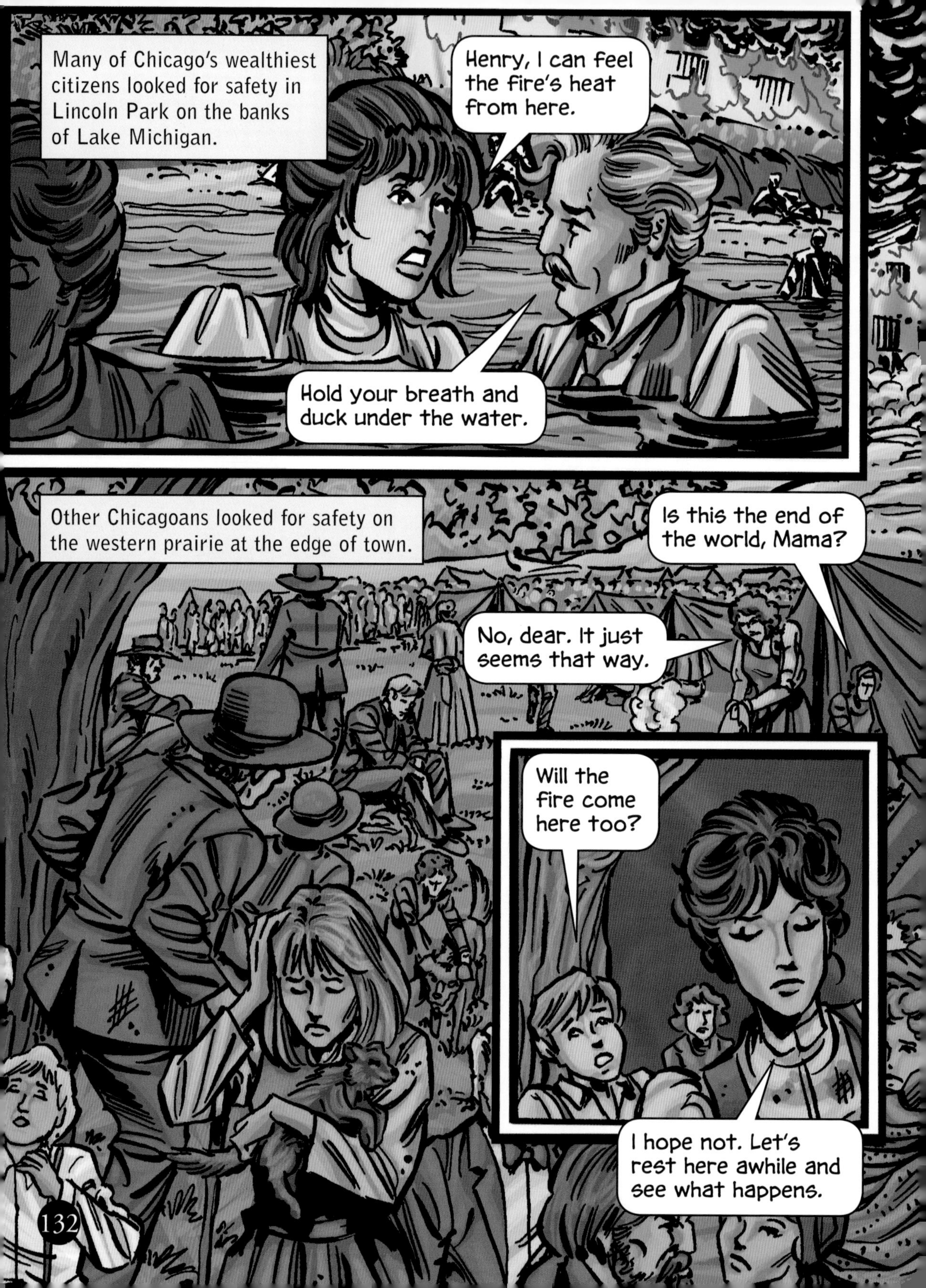
Many of Chicago's wealthiest citizens looked for safety in Lincoln Park on the banks of Lake Michigan.
Henry, I can feel the fire's heat from here.
Hold your breath and duck under the water.
Other Chicagoans looked for safety on the western prairie at the edge of town.
Is this the end of the world, Mama?
No, dear. It just seems that way.
Will the fire come here too?
I hope not. Let's rest here awhile and see what happens.

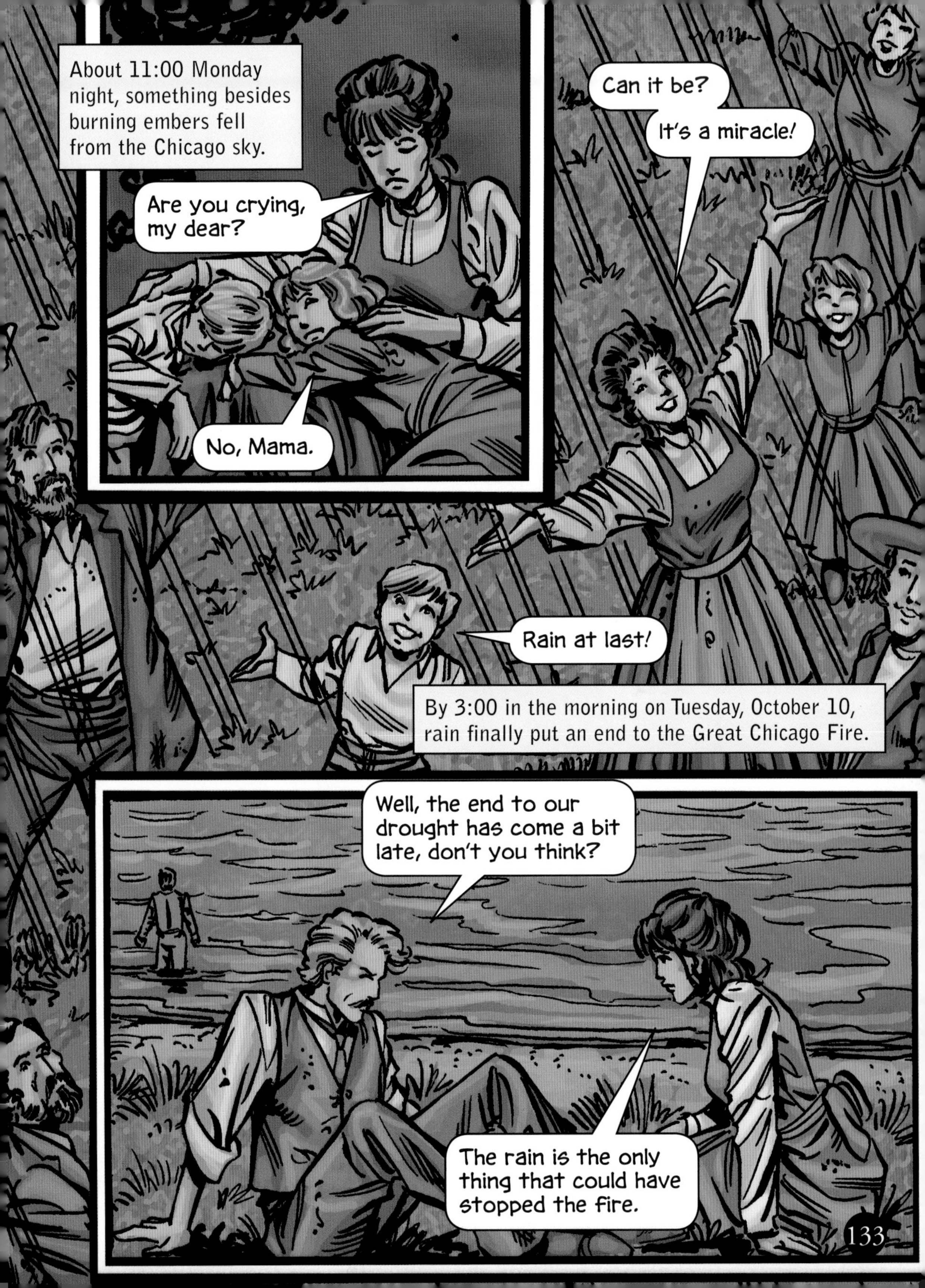
About 11:00 Monday night, something besides burning embers fell from the Chicago sky.
Are you crying, my dear?
No, Mama.
Can it be?
It's a miracle!
Rain at last!
By 3:00 in the morning on Tuesday, October 10, rain finally put an end to the Great Chicago Fire.
Well, the end to our drought has come a bit late, don't you think?
The rain is the only thing that could have stopped the fire.

CHAPTER 4
AFTER THE ASHES

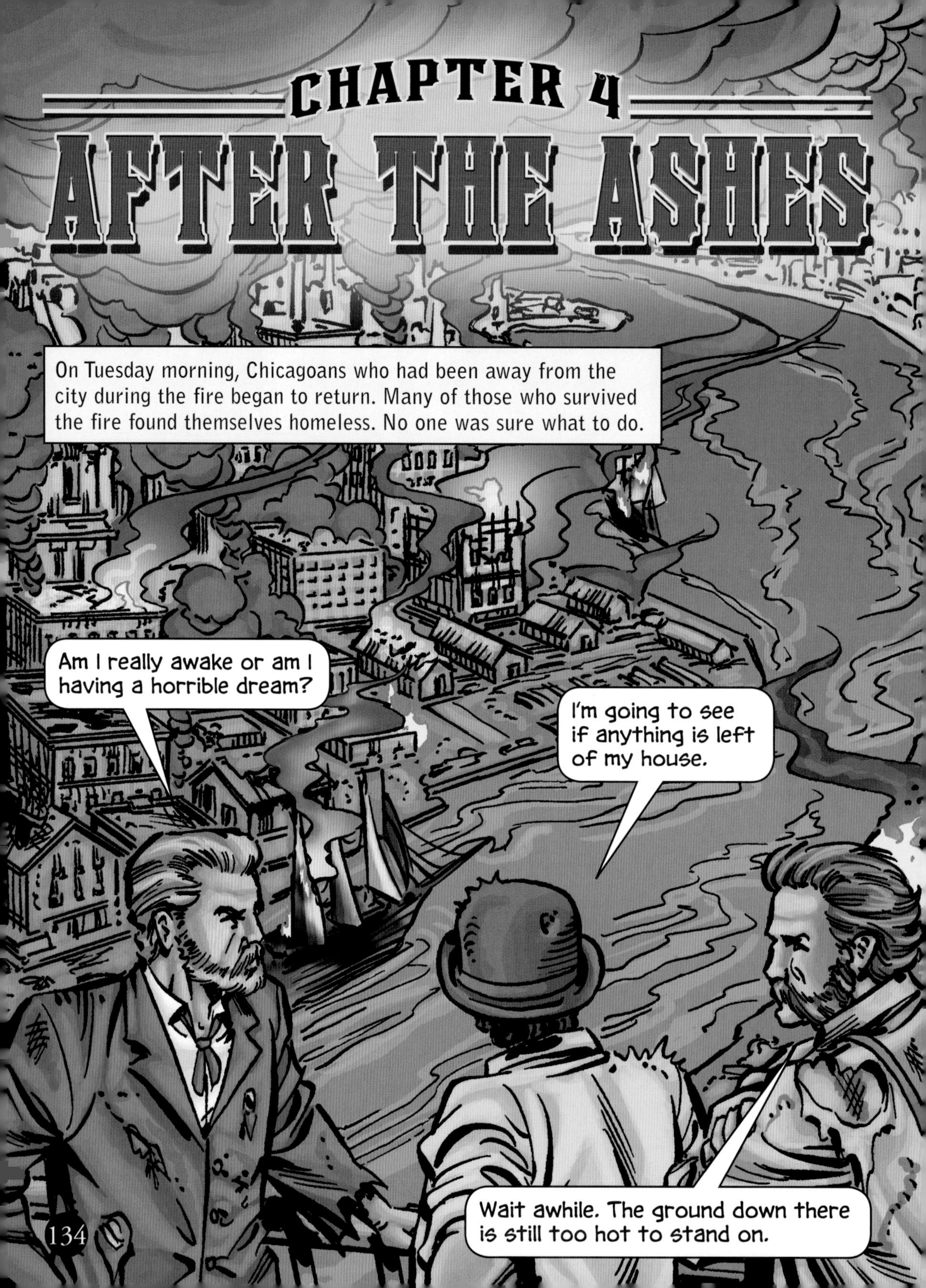
On Tuesday morning, Chicagoans who had been away from the city during the fire began to return. Many of those who survived the fire found themselves homeless. No one was sure what to do.
Am I really awake or am I having a horrible dream?
I'm going to see if anything is left of my house.
Wait awhile. The ground down there is still too hot to stand on.

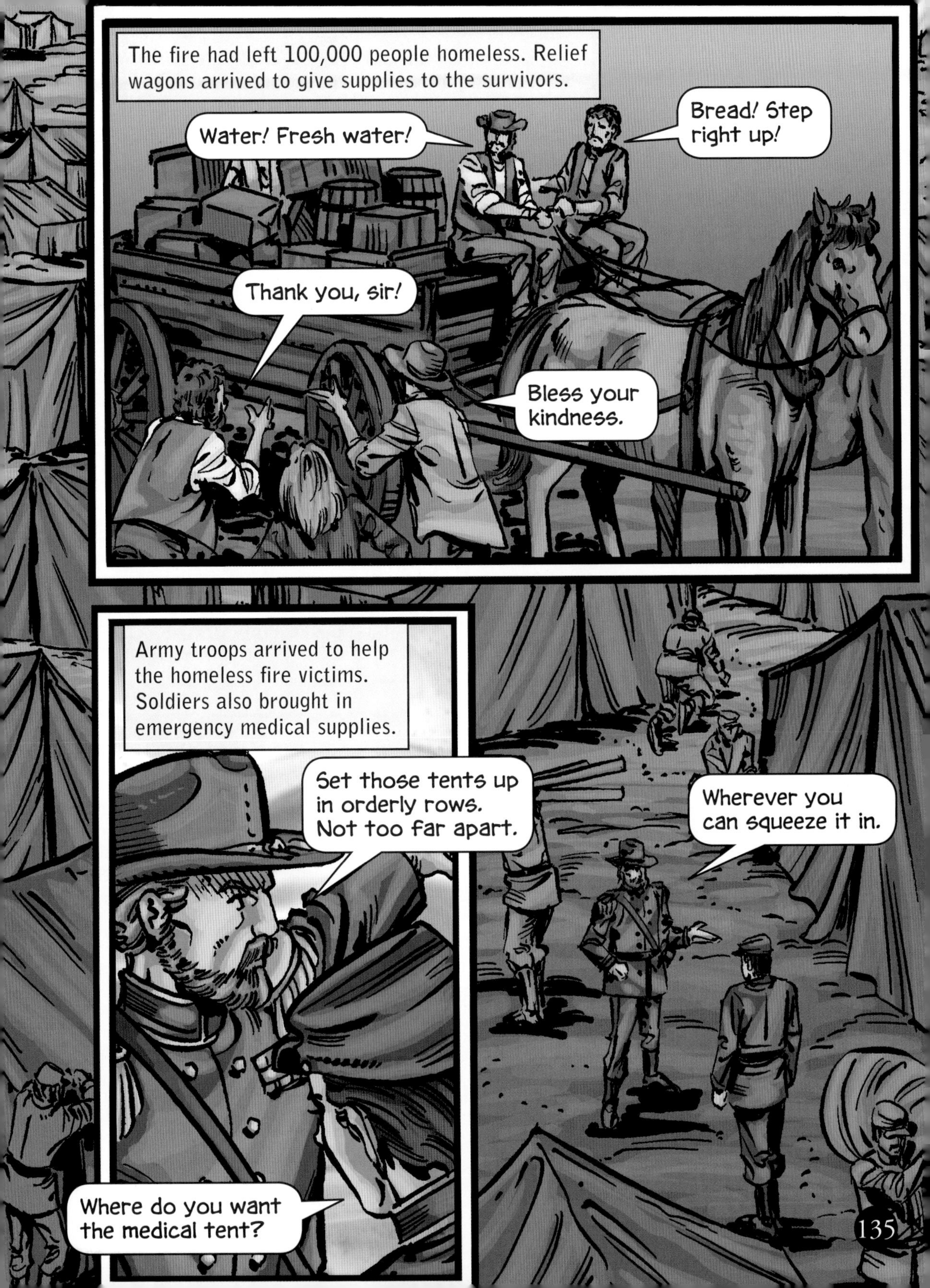
The fire had left 100,000 people homeless. Relief wagons arrived to give supplies to the survivors.
Water! Fresh water!
Bread! Step right up!
Thank you, sir!
Bless your kindness.
Army troops arrived to help the homeless fire victims. Soldiers also brought in emergency medical supplies.
Set those tents up in orderly rows. Not too far apart.
Wherever you can squeeze it in.
Where do you want the medical tent?

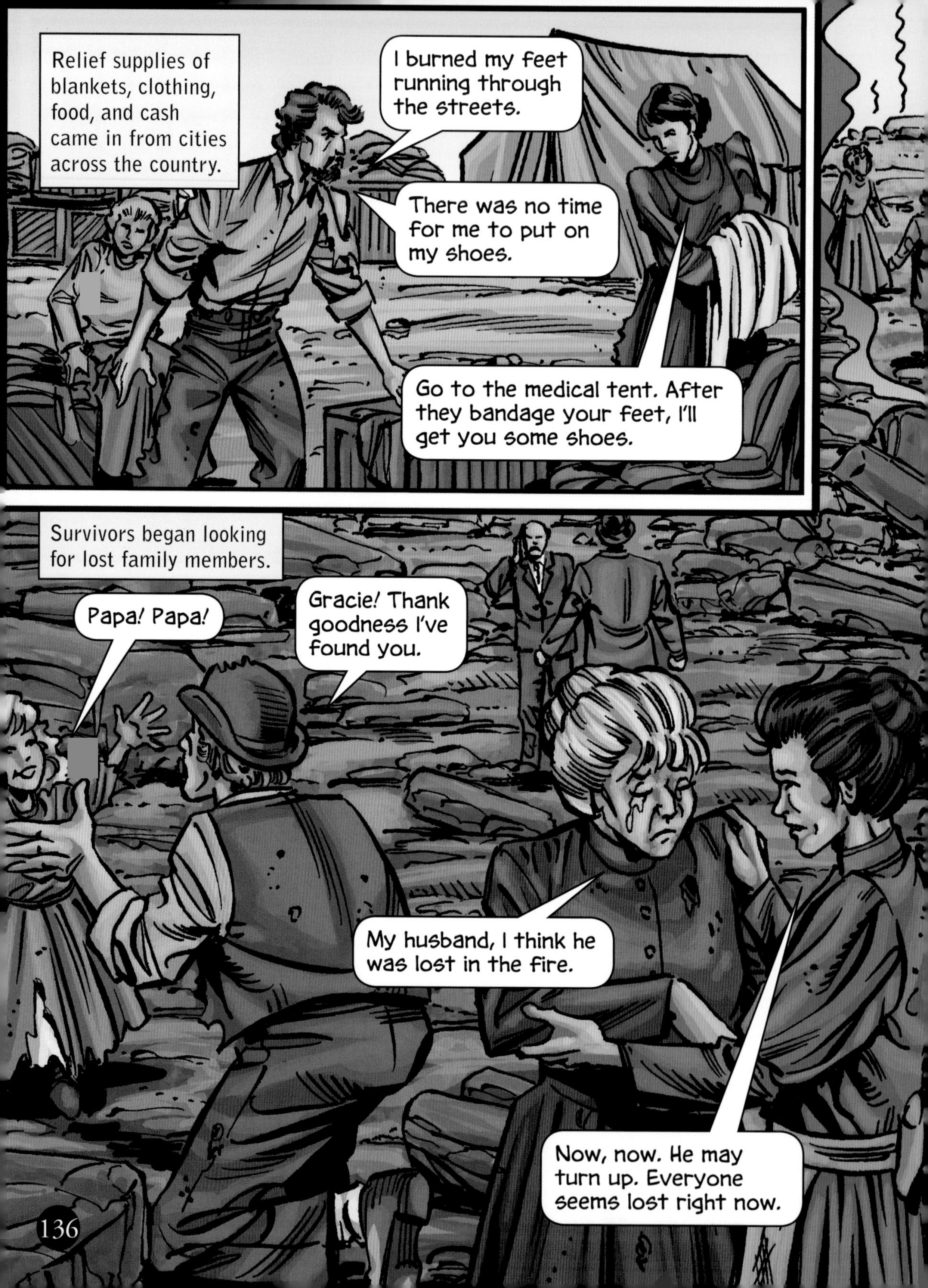
Relief supplies of blankets, clothing, food, and cash came in from cities across the country.
I burned my feet running through the streets.
There was no time for me to put on my shoes.
Go to the medical tent. After they bandage your feet, I'll get you some shoes.
Survivors began looking for lost family members.
Papa! Papa!
Gracie! Thank goodness I've found you.
My husband, I think he was lost in the fire.
Now, now. He may turn up. Everyone seems lost right now.

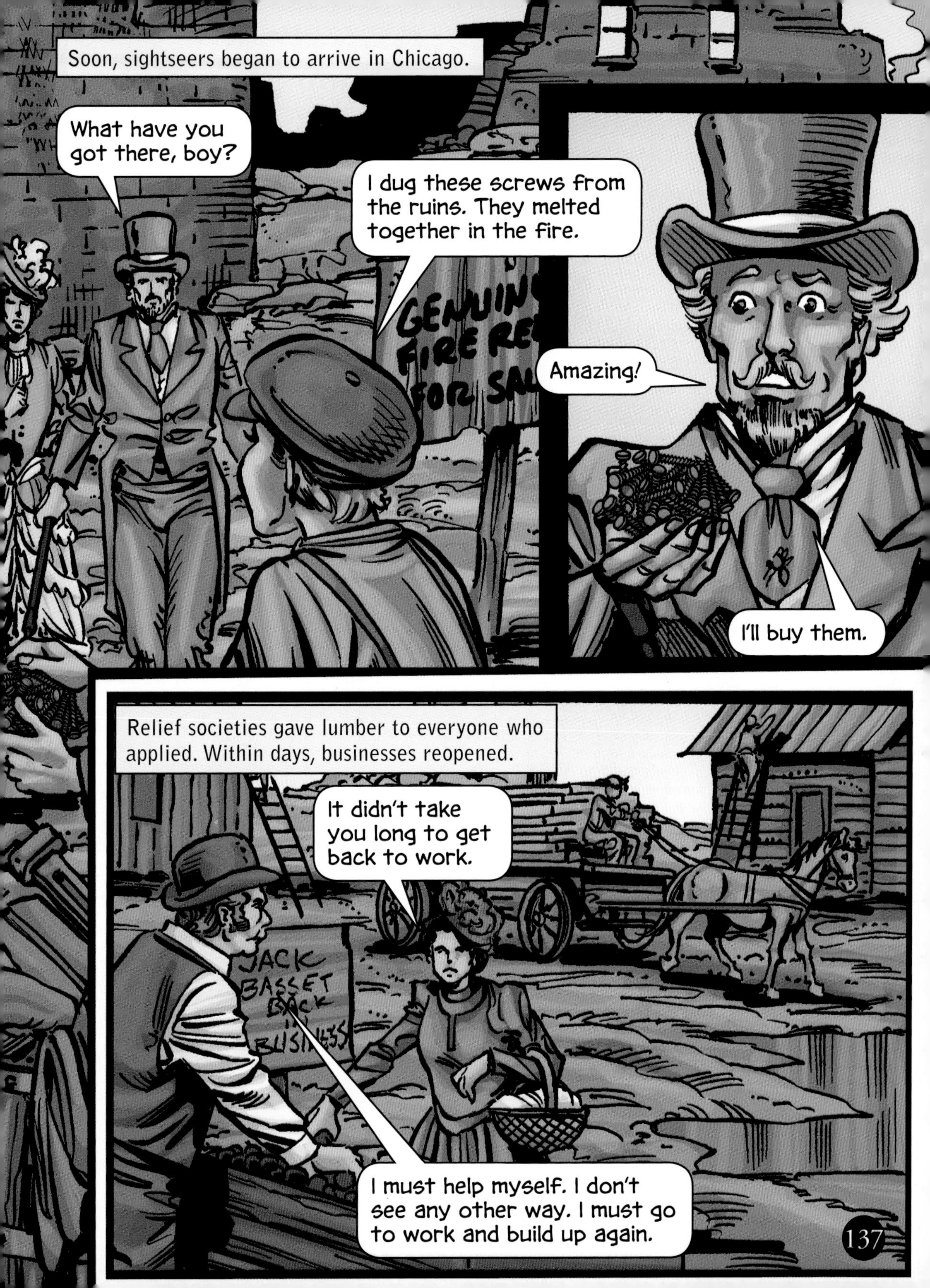

Soon, sightseers began to arrive in Chicago.
What have you got there, boy?
I dug these screws from the ruins. They melted together in the fire.
GENUINE FIRE RE... FOR SA...
Amazing!
I'll buy them.
Relief societies gave lumber to everyone who applied. Within days, businesses reopened.
It didn't take you long to get back to work.
JACK BASSET BACK IN BUSINESS
I must help myself. I don't see any other way. I must go to work and build up again.

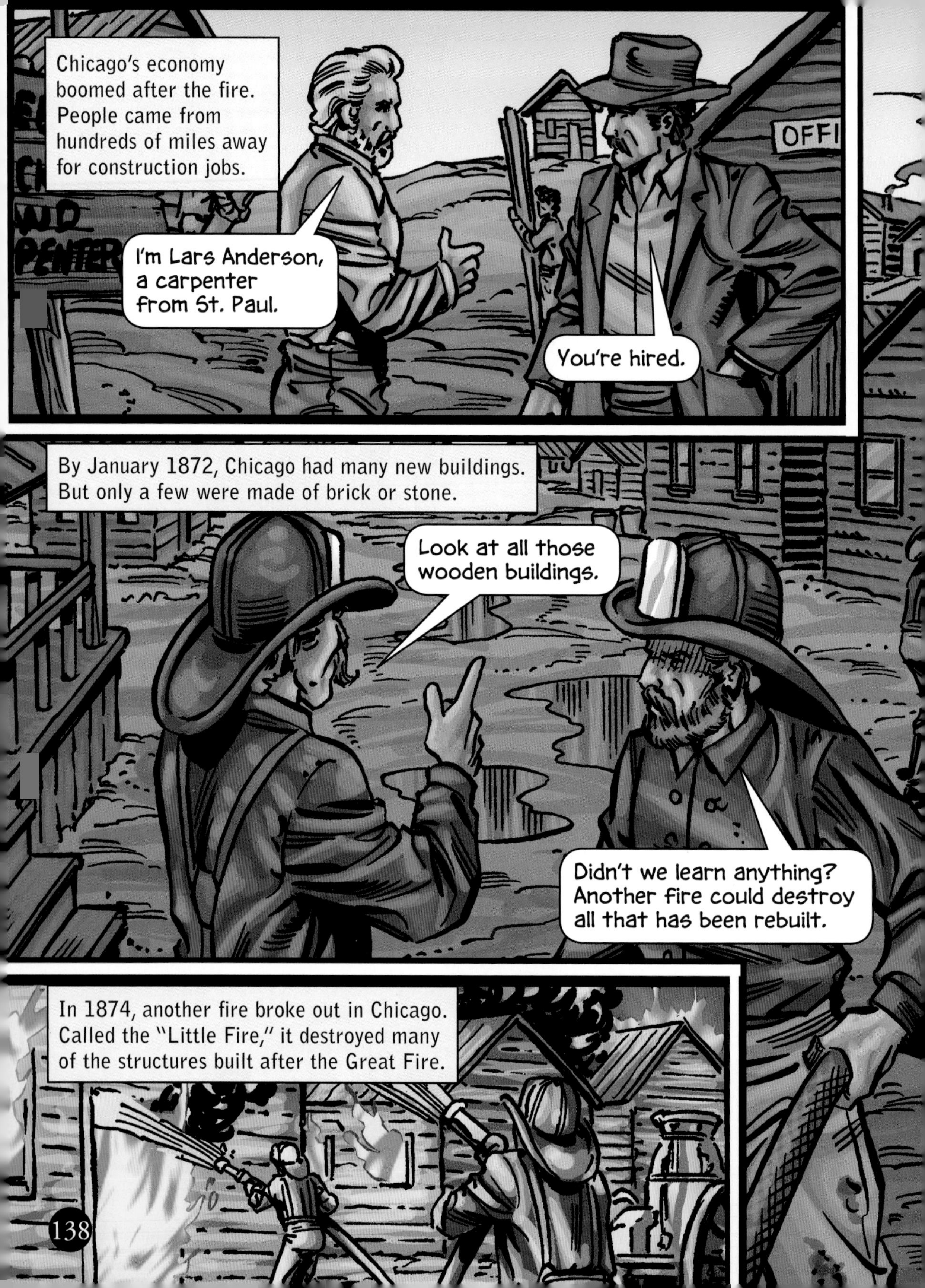
Chicago's economy boomed after the fire. People came from hundreds of miles away for construction jobs.
I'm Lars Anderson, a carpenter from St. Paul.
You're hired.
By January 1872, Chicago had many new buildings. But only a few were made of brick or stone.
Look at all those wooden buildings.
Didn't we learn anything? Another fire could destroy all that has been rebuilt.
In 1874, another fire broke out in Chicago. Called the "Little Fire," it destroyed many of the structures built after the Great Fire.

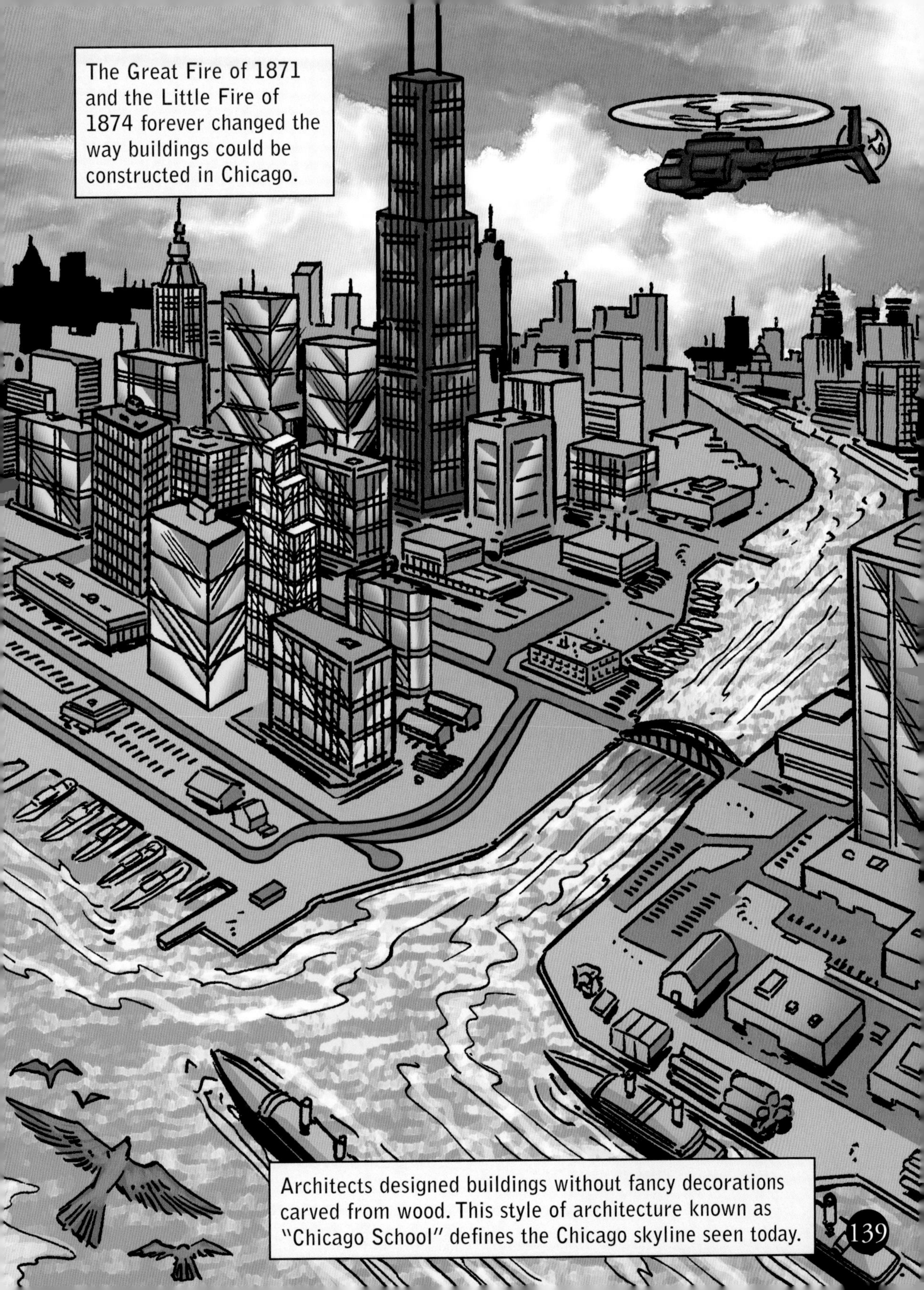
The Great Fire of 1871 and the Little Fire of 1874 forever changed the way buildings could be constructed in Chicago.
Architects designed buildings without fancy decorations carved from wood. This style of architecture known as "Chicago School" defines the Chicago skyline seen today.

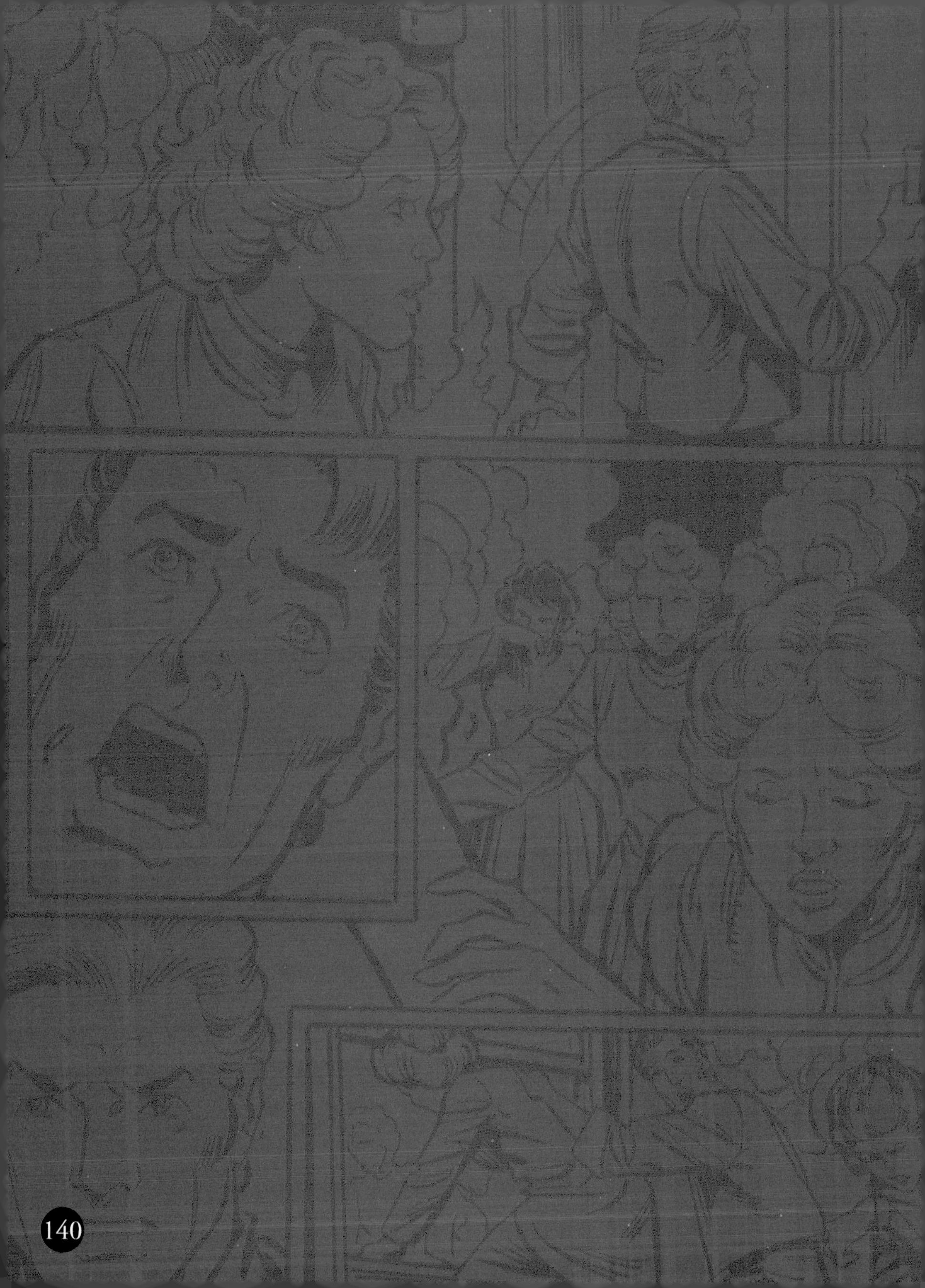

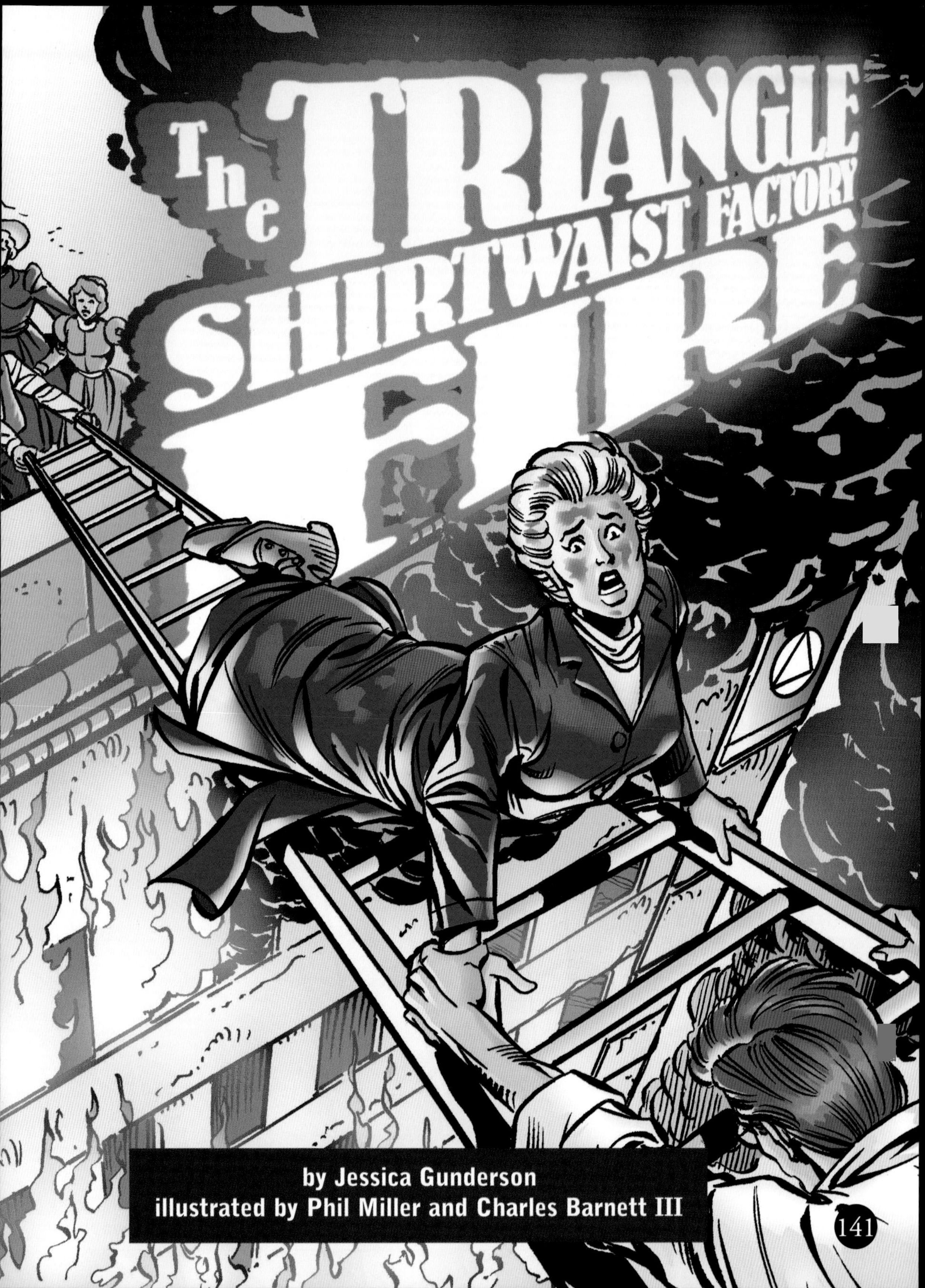
The TRIANGLE SHIRTWAIST FACTORY FIRE

by Jessica Gunderson
illustrated by Phil Miller and Charles Barnett III

Chapter 1
STRIKE!

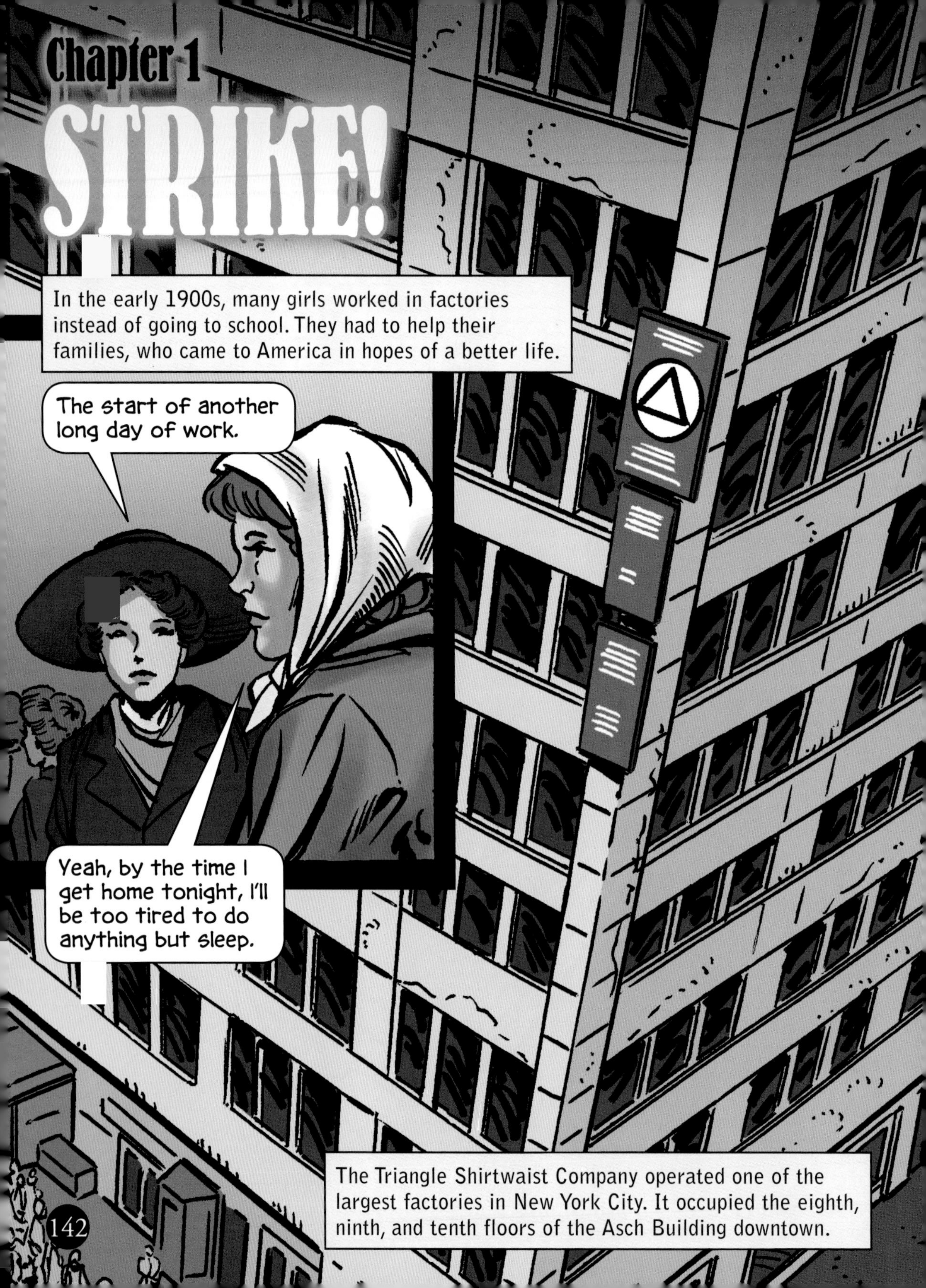
In the early 1900s, many girls worked in factories instead of going to school. They had to help their families, who came to America in hopes of a better life.
The start of another long day of work.
Yeah, by the time I get home tonight, I'll be too tired to do anything but sleep.
The Triangle Shirtwaist Company operated one of the largest factories in New York City. It occupied the eighth, ninth, and tenth floors of the Asch Building downtown.

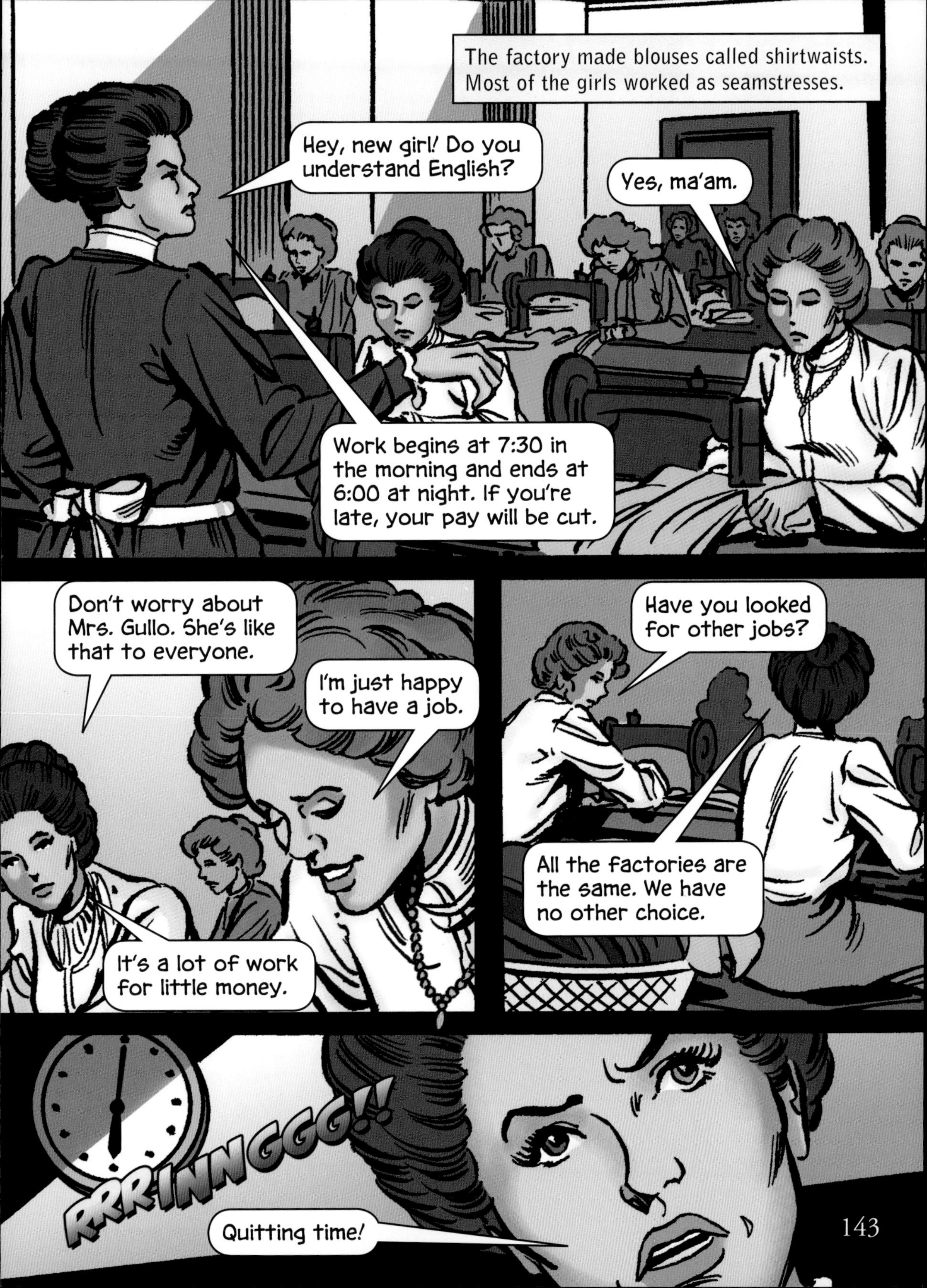
The factory made blouses called shirtwaists. Most of the girls worked as seamstresses.
Hey, new girl! Do you understand English?
Yes, ma'am.
Work begins at 7:30 in the morning and ends at 6:00 at night. If you're late, your pay will be cut.
Don't worry about Mrs. Gullo. She's like that to everyone.
I'm just happy to have a job.
It's a lot of work for little money.
Have you looked for other jobs?
All the factories are the same. We have no other choice.
RRRINNGGG!!
Quitting time!

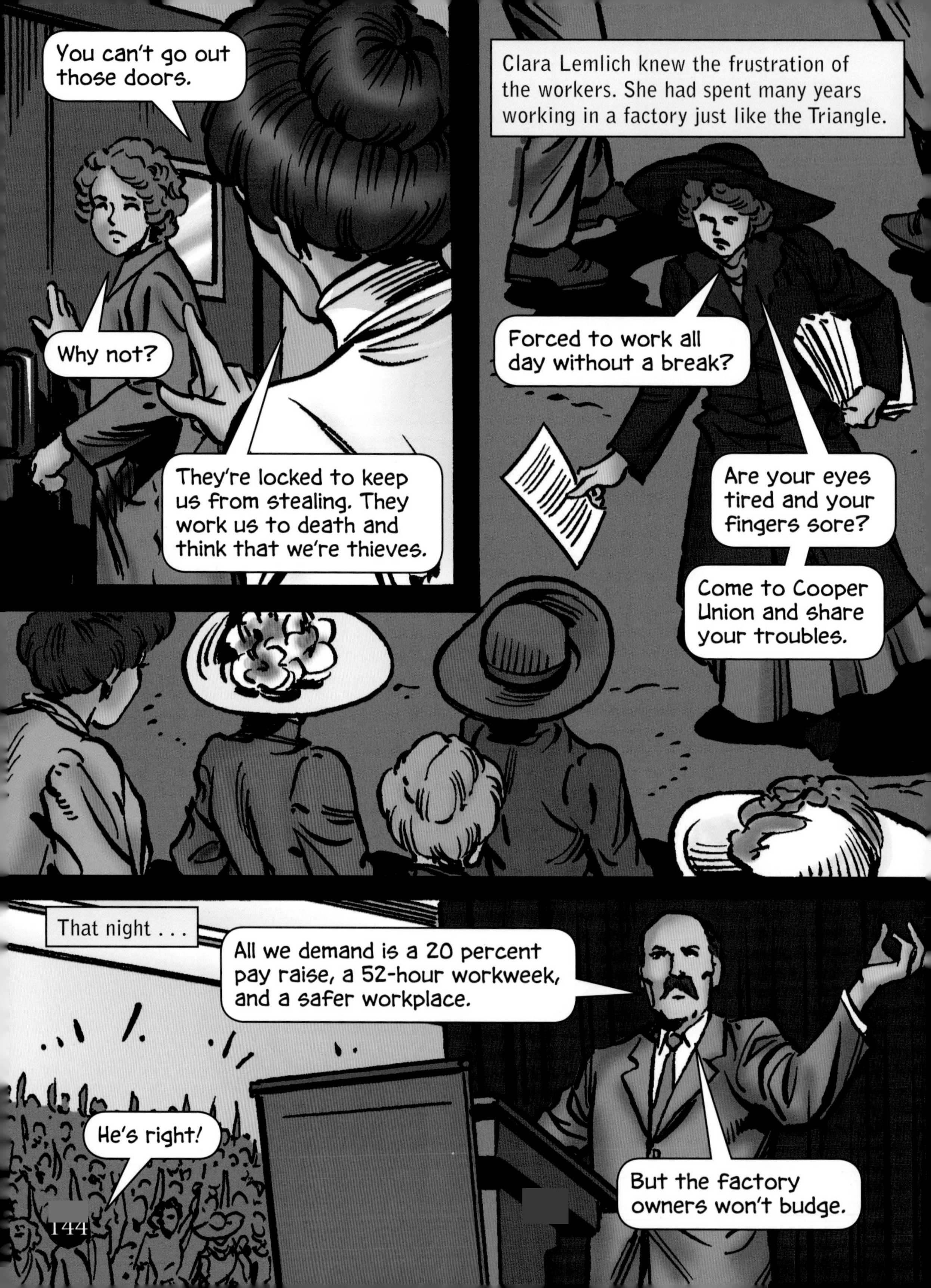
You can't go out those doors.
Why not?
They're locked to keep us from stealing. They work us to death and think that we're thieves.
Clara Lemlich knew the frustration of the workers. She had spent many years working in a factory just like the Triangle.
Forced to work all day without a break?
Are your eyes tired and your fingers sore?
Come to Cooper Union and share your troubles.
That night . . .
All we demand is a 20 percent pay raise, a 52-hour workweek, and a safer workplace.
He's right!
But the factory owners won't budge.

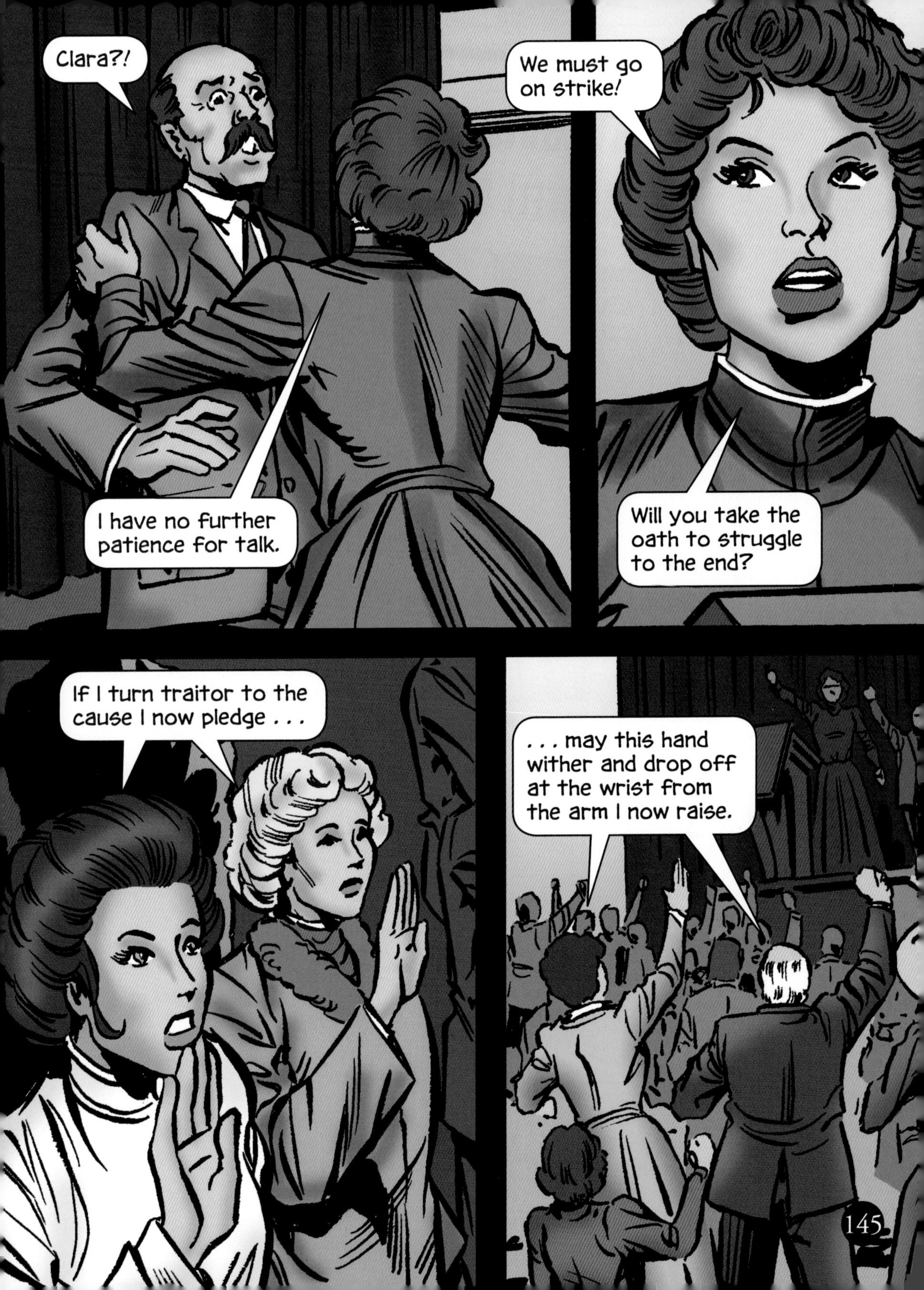
Clara?!
I have no further patience for talk.
We must go on strike!
Will you take the oath to struggle to the end?
If I turn traitor to the cause I now pledge . . .
. . . may this hand wither and drop off at the wrist from the arm I now raise.

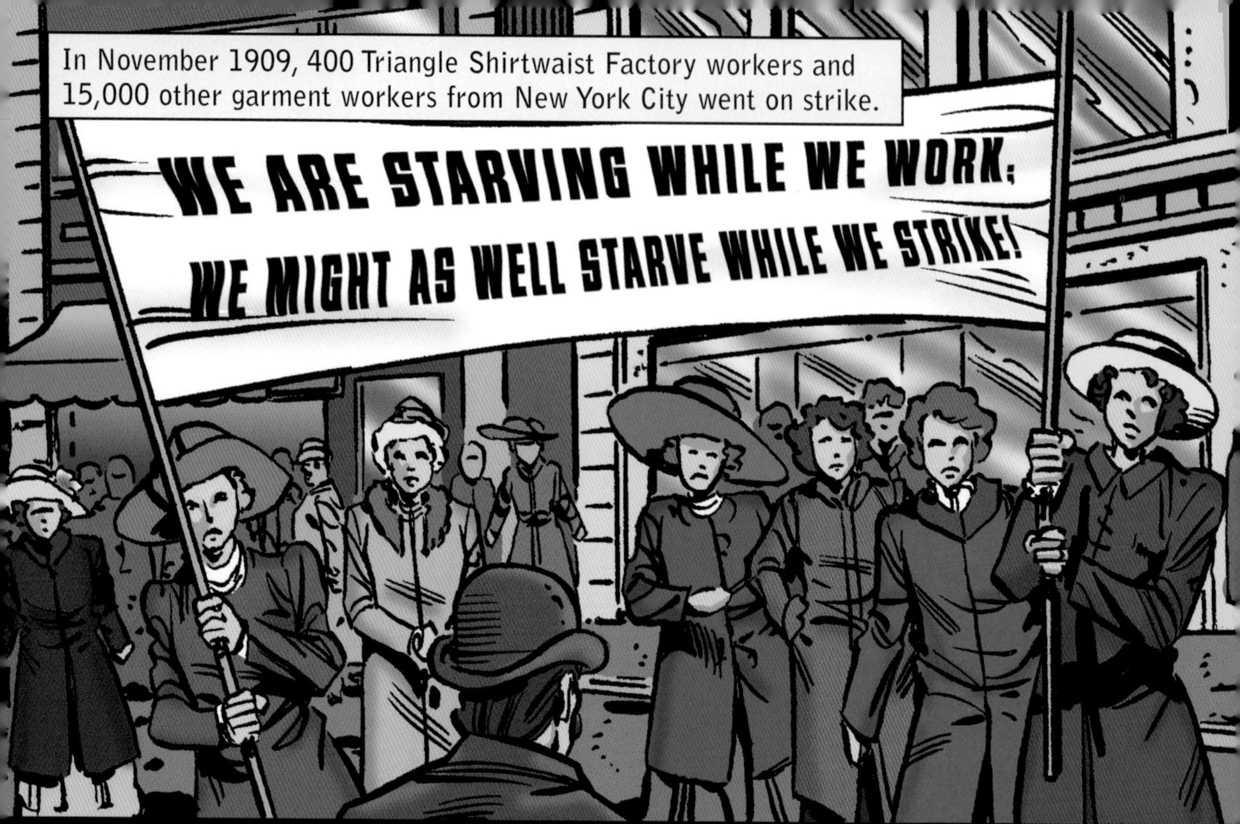
In November 1909, 400 Triangle Shirtwaist Factory workers and 15,000 other garment workers from New York City went on strike.
WE ARE STARVING WHILE WE WORK; WE MIGHT AS WELL STARVE WHILE WE STRIKE!

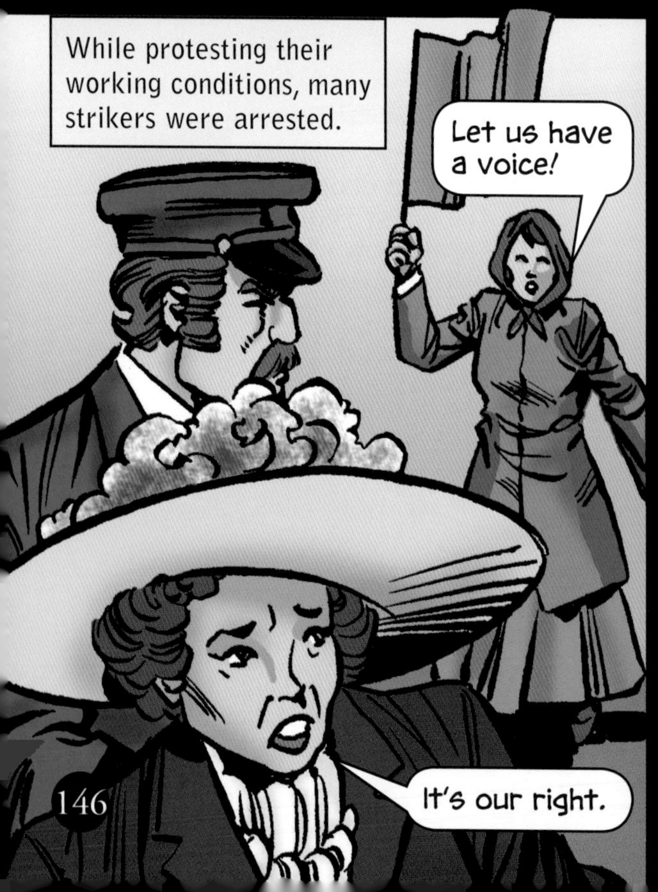
While protesting their working conditions, many strikers were arrested.
Let us have a voice!
It's our right.

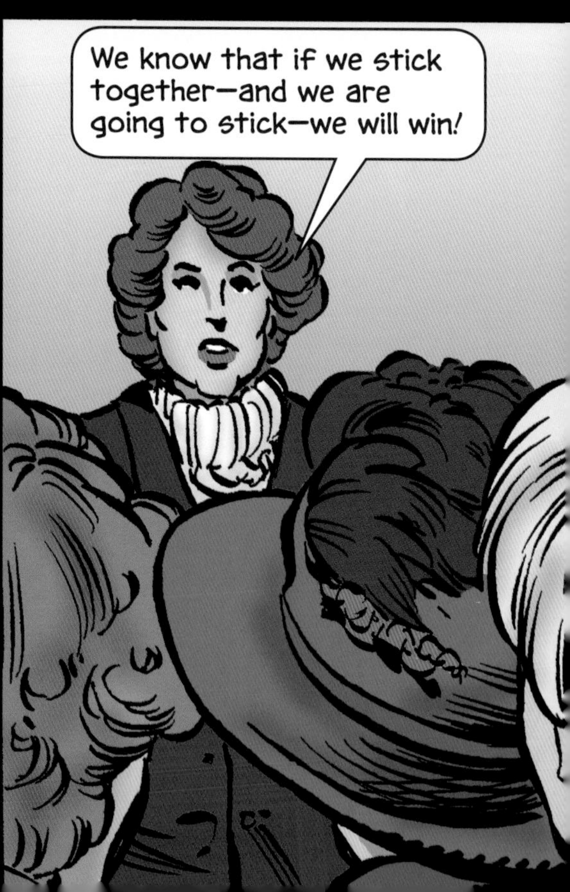
We know that if we stick together—and we are going to stick—we will win!

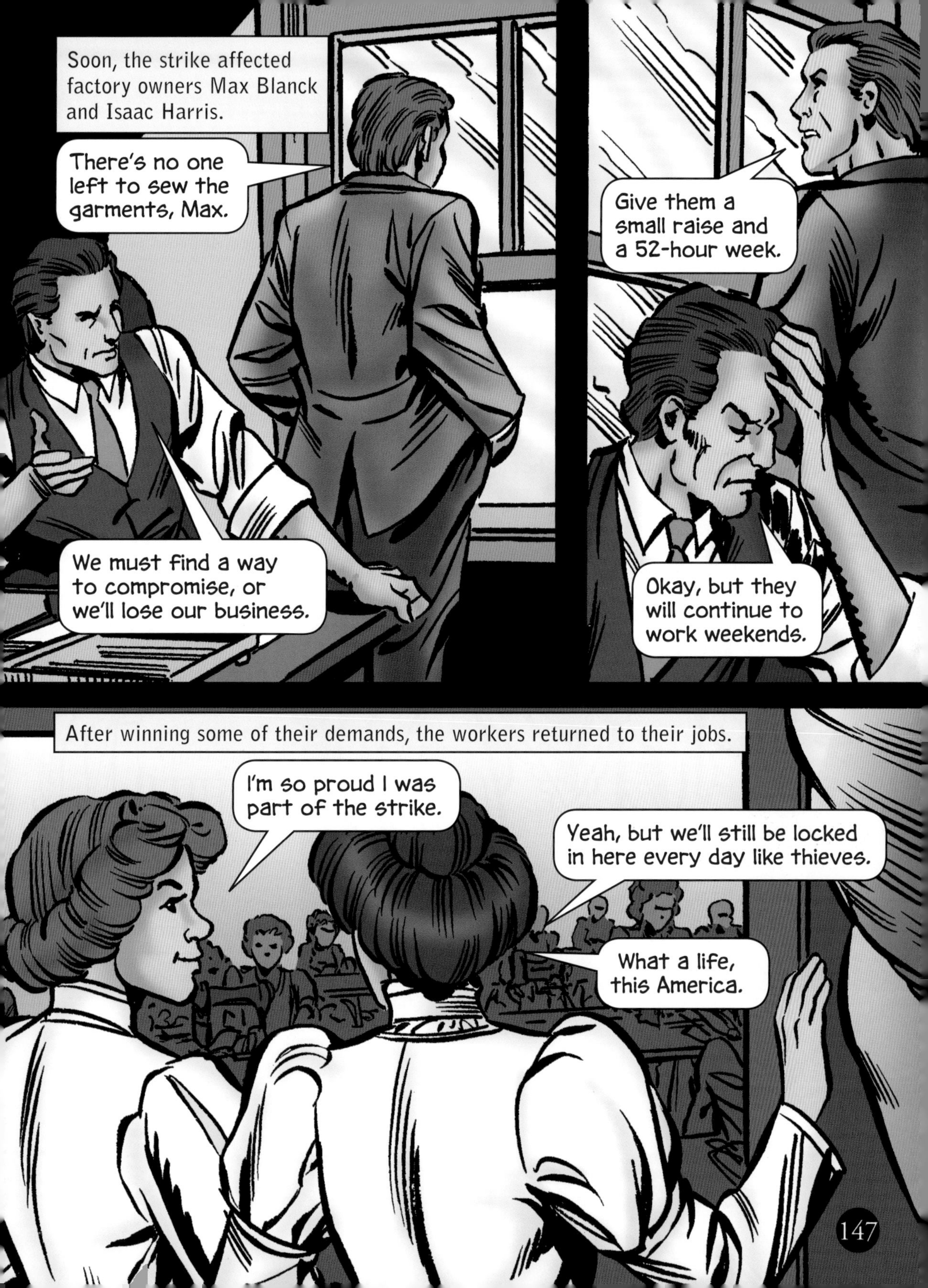
Soon, the strike affected factory owners Max Blanck and Isaac Harris.
There's no one left to sew the garments, Max.
We must find a way to compromise, or we'll lose our business.
Give them a small raise and a 52-hour week.
Okay, but they will continue to work weekends.
After winning some of their demands, the workers returned to their jobs.
I'm so proud I was part of the strike.
Yeah, but we'll still be locked in here every day like thieves.
What a life, this America.

Chapter 2
TRAPPED IN FLAMES

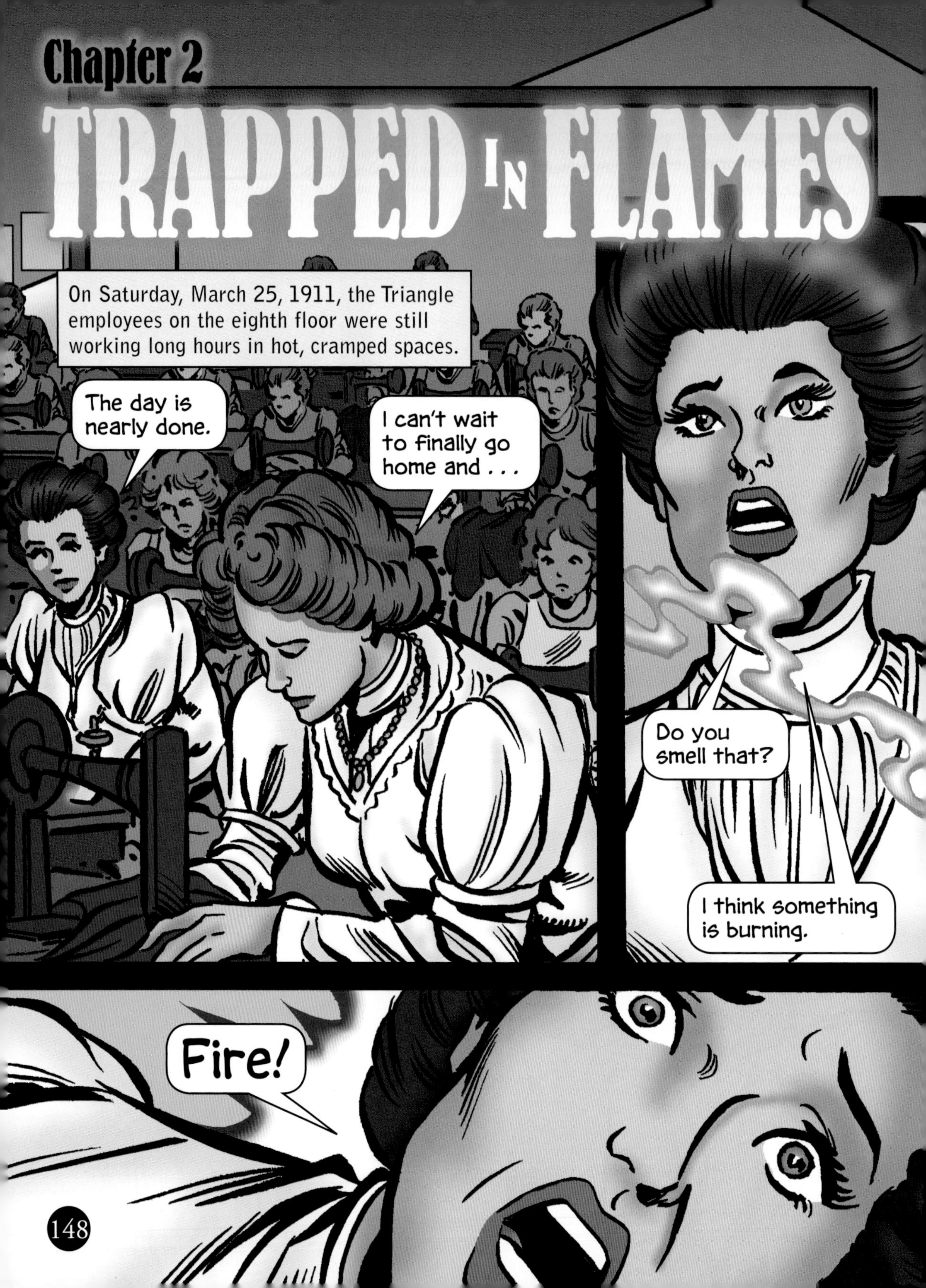

On Saturday, March 25, 1911, the Triangle employees on the eighth floor were still working long hours in hot, cramped spaces.
The day is nearly done.
I can't wait to finally go home and . . .
Do you smell that?
I think something is burning.
Fire!

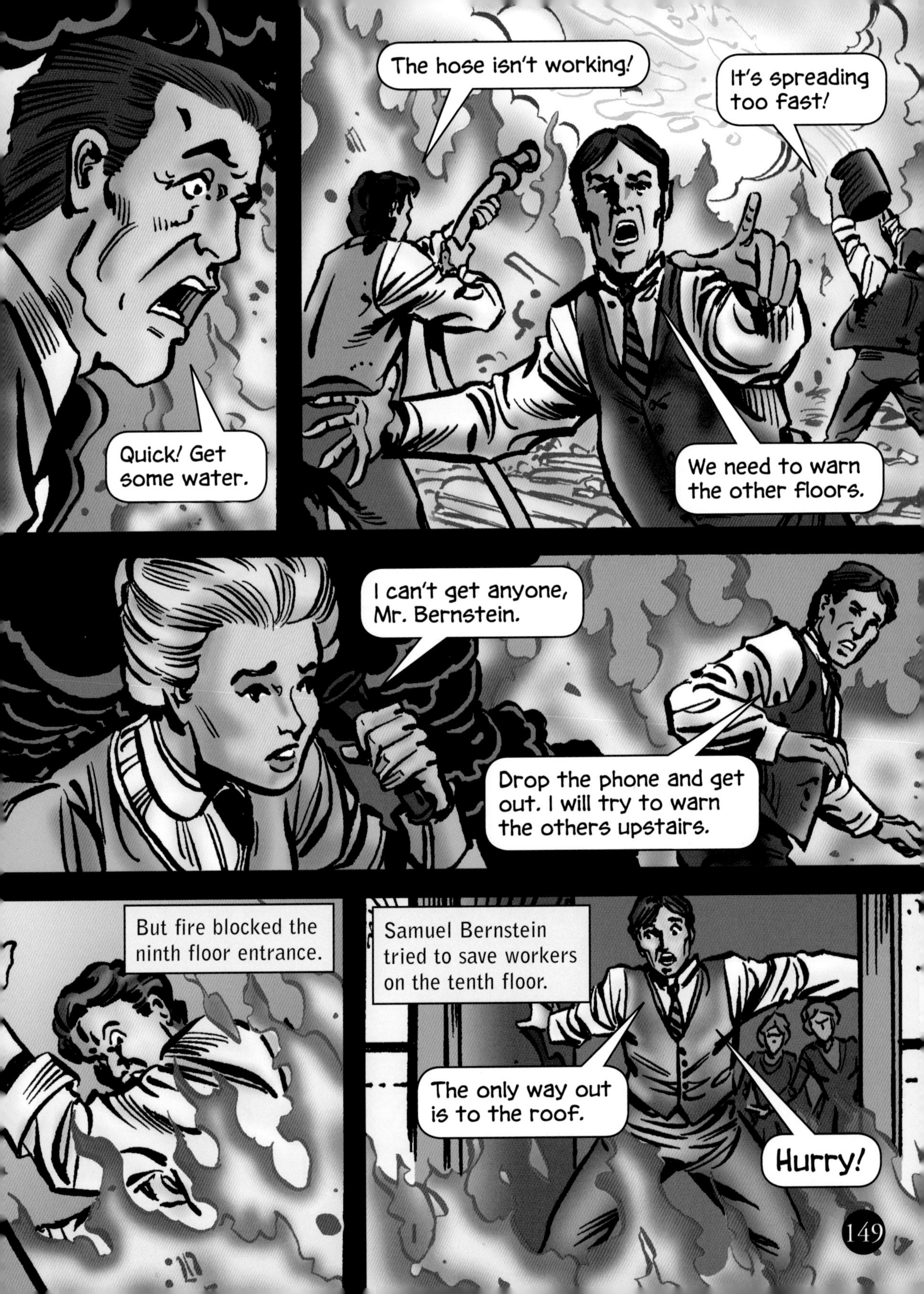
Quick! Get some water.
The hose isn't working!
It's spreading too fast!
We need to warn the other floors.
I can't get anyone, Mr. Bernstein.
Drop the phone and get out. I will try to warn the others upstairs.
But fire blocked the ninth floor entrance.
Samuel Bernstein tried to save workers on the tenth floor.
The only way out is to the roof.
Hurry!

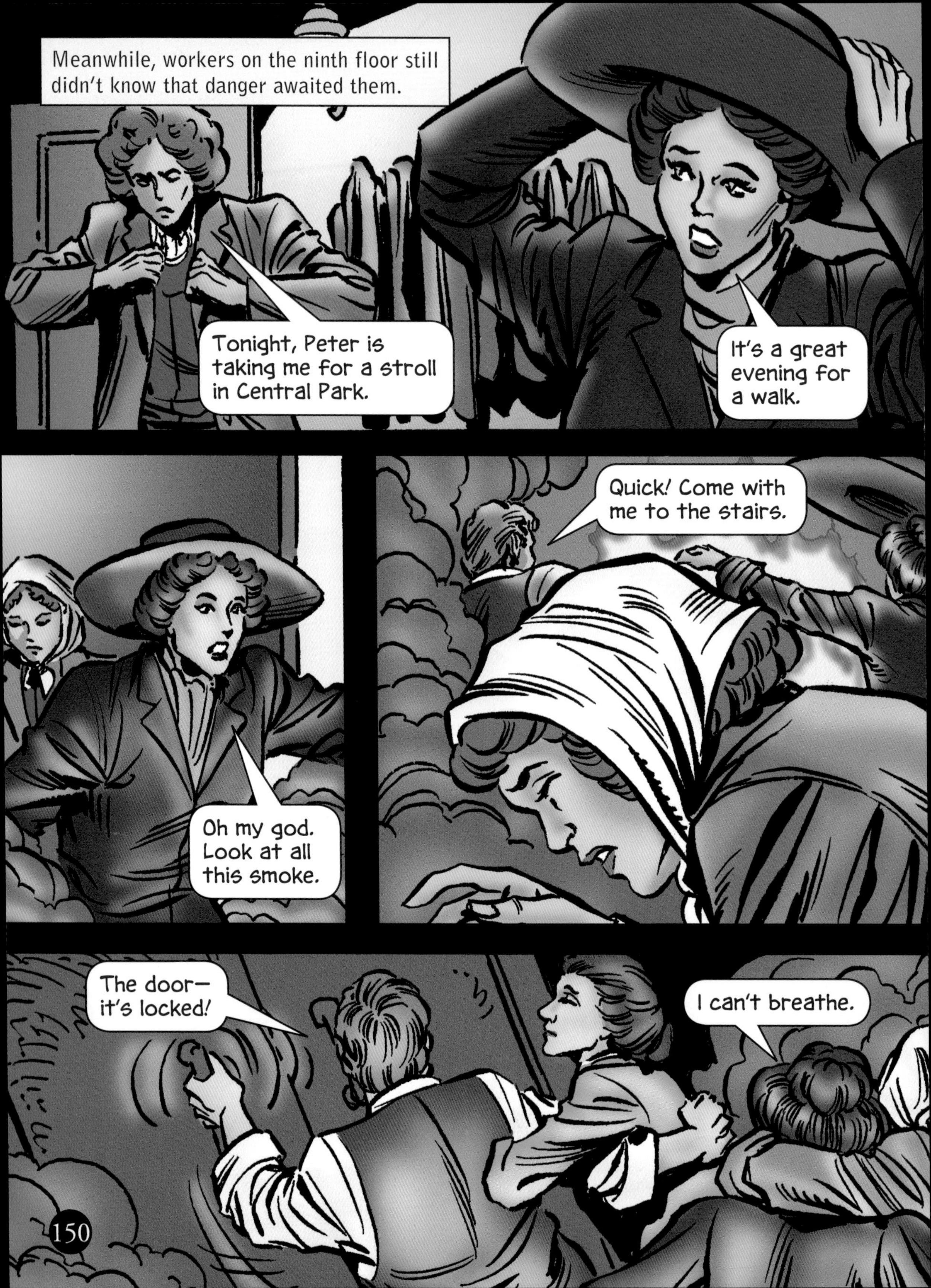

Meanwhile, workers on the ninth floor still didn't know that danger awaited them.
Tonight, Peter is taking me for a stroll in Central Park.
It's a great evening for a walk.
Oh my god. Look at all this smoke.
Quick! Come with me to the stairs.
The door— it's locked!
I can't breathe.

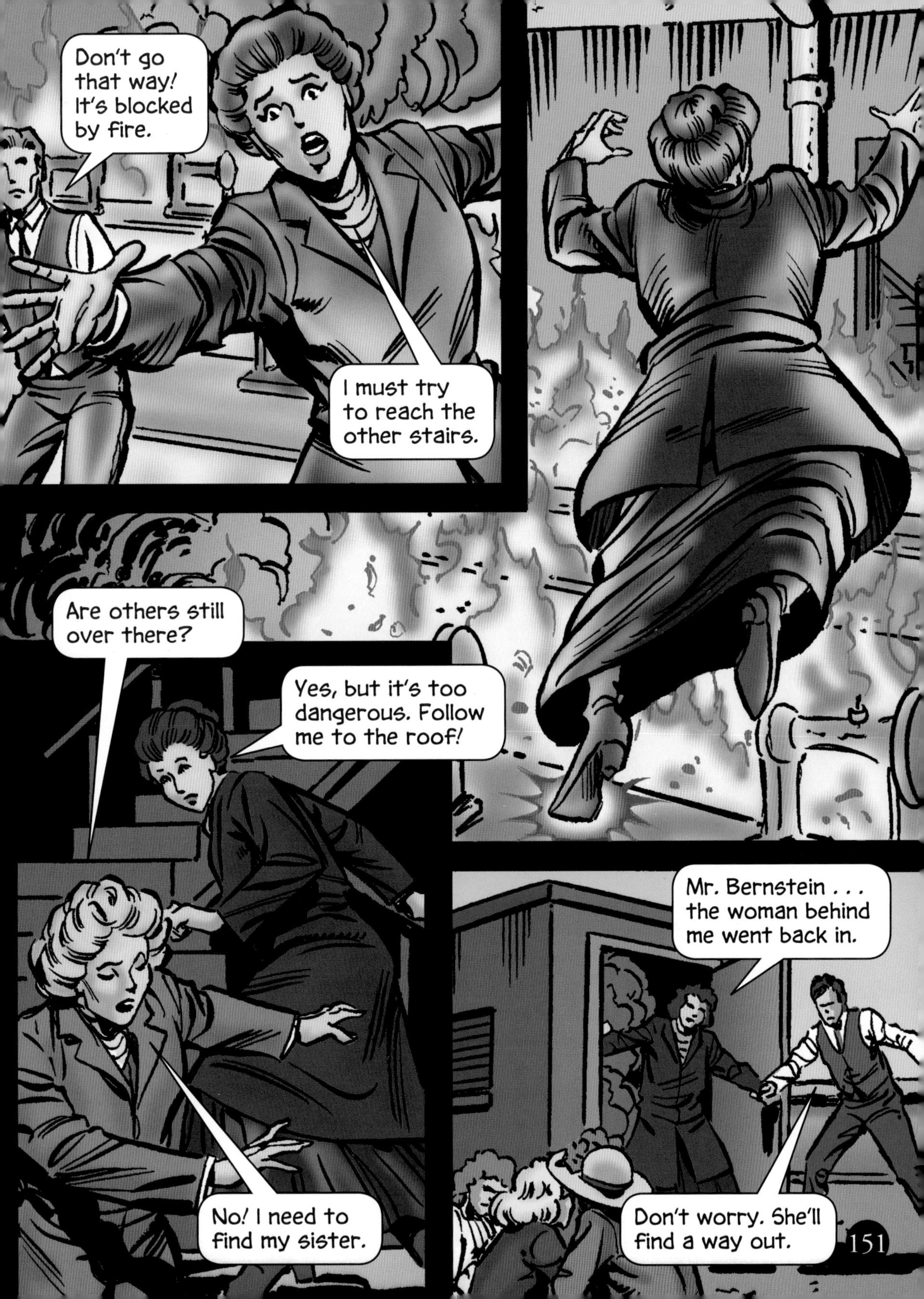
Don't go that way! It's blocked by fire.
I must try to reach the other stairs.
Are others still over there?
Yes, but it's too dangerous. Follow me to the roof!
No! I need to find my sister.
Mr. Bernstein . . . the woman behind me went back in.
Don't worry. She'll find a way out.

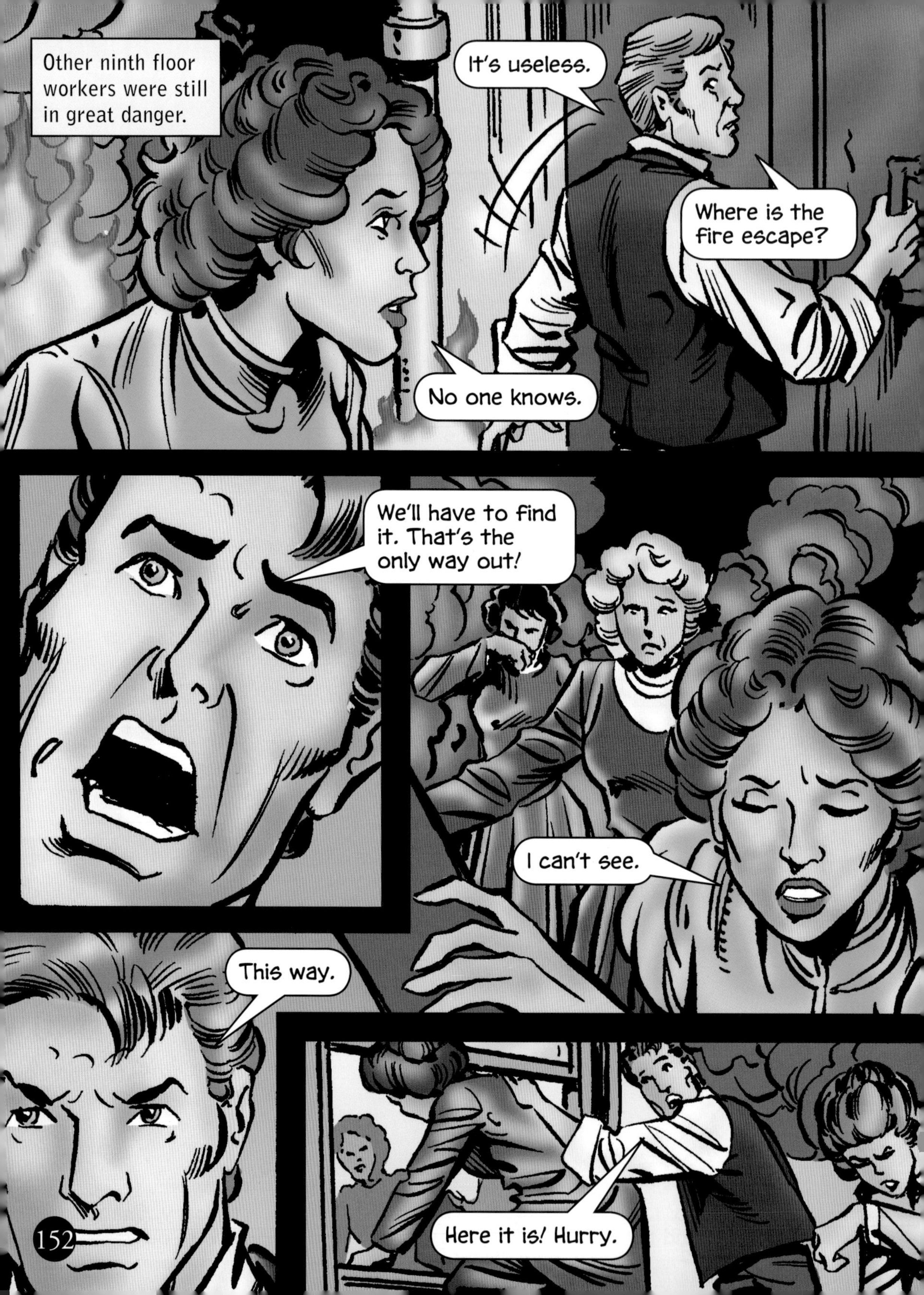
Other ninth floor workers were still in great danger.
It's useless.
Where is the fire escape?
No one knows.
We'll have to find it. That's the only way out!
I can't see.
This way.
Here it is! Hurry.

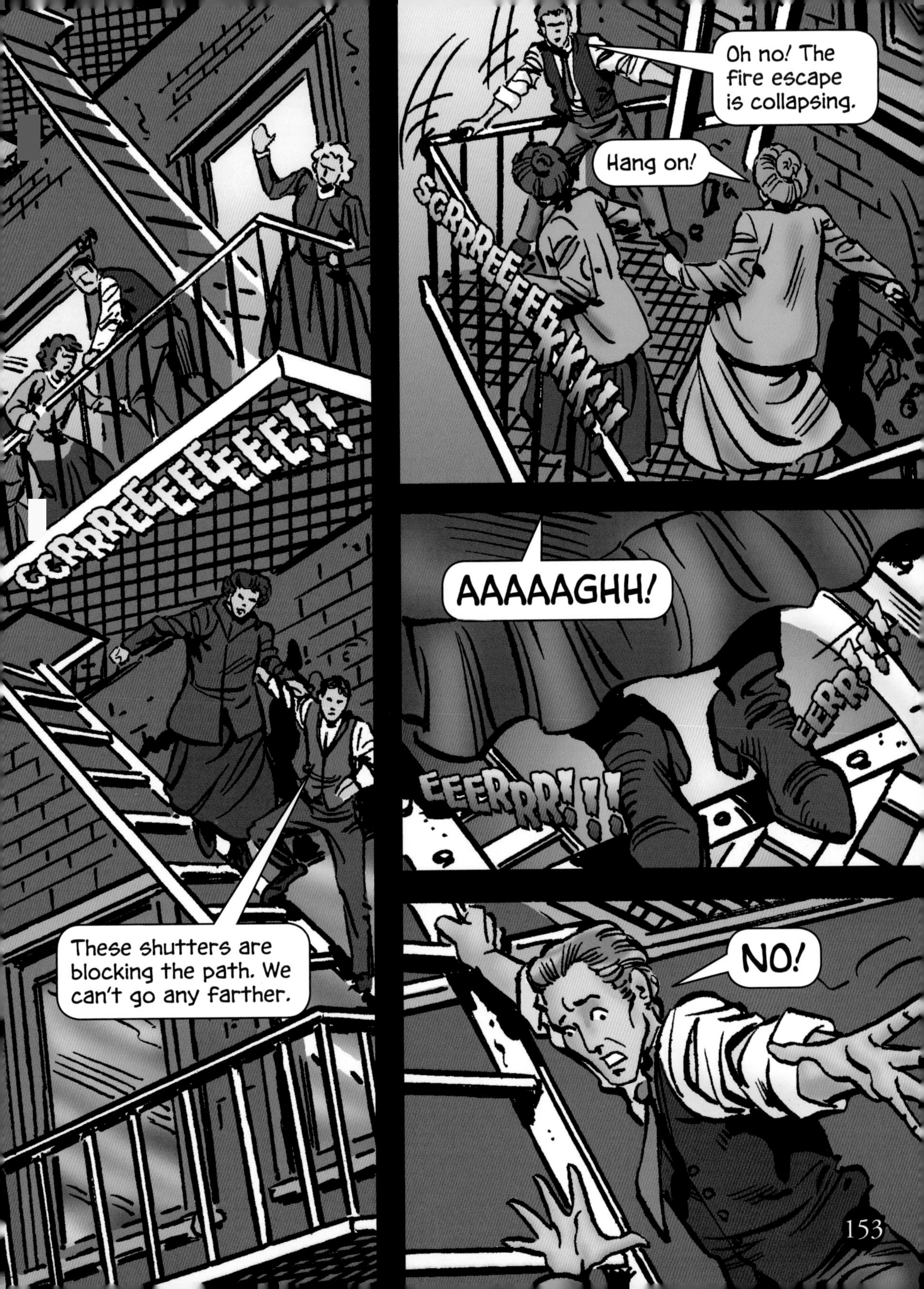

GGRRREEEEEEEEEE!!!
These shutters are blocking the path. We can't go any farther.
Oh no! The fire escape is collapsing.
Hang on!
SCRRREEEEEEKKK!!!
AAAAAGHH!
EEERRR!!!
EEERRR!!!
NO!

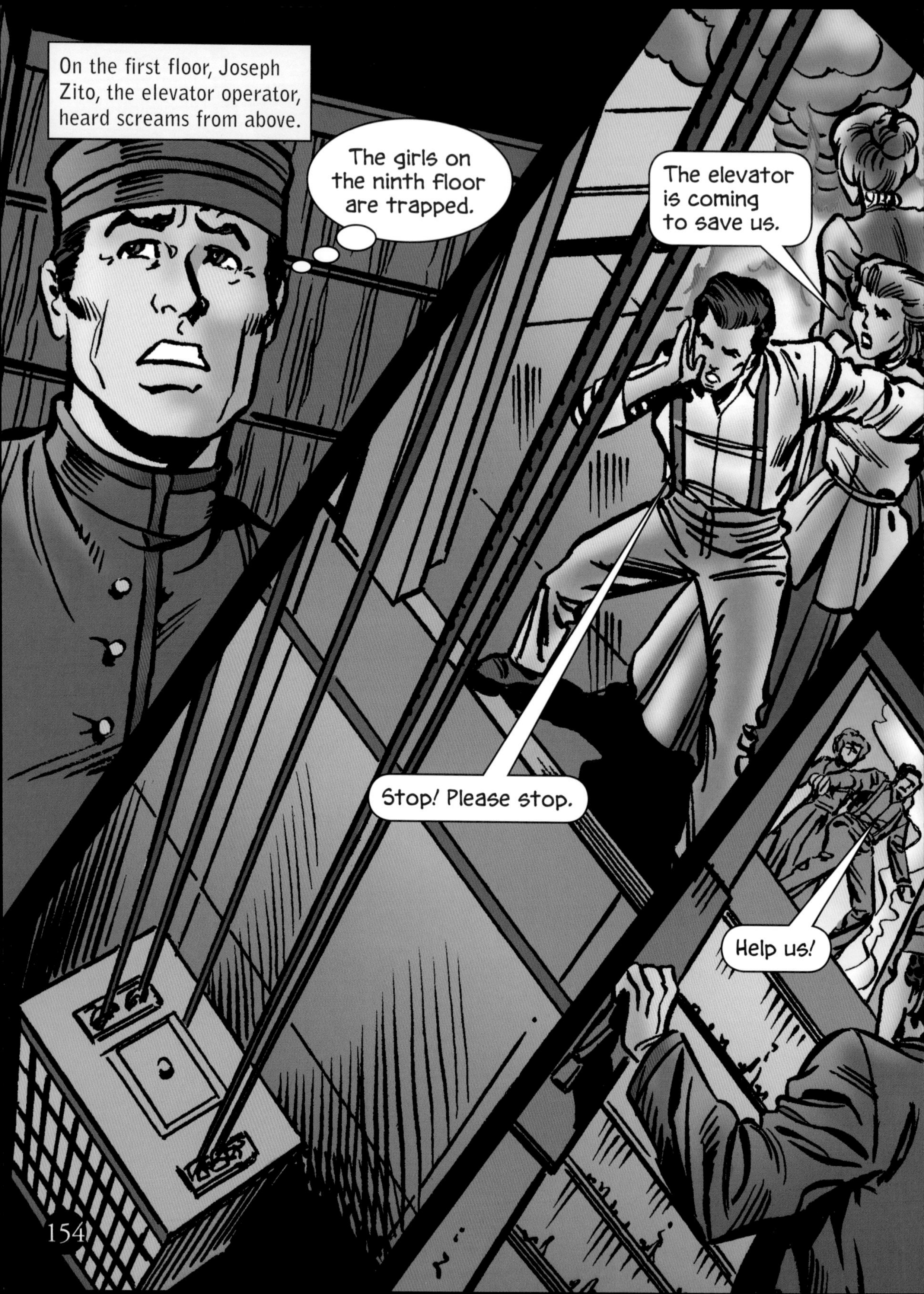
On the first floor, Joseph Zito, the elevator operator, heard screams from above.
The girls on the ninth floor are trapped.
The elevator is coming to save us.
Stop! Please stop.
Help us!

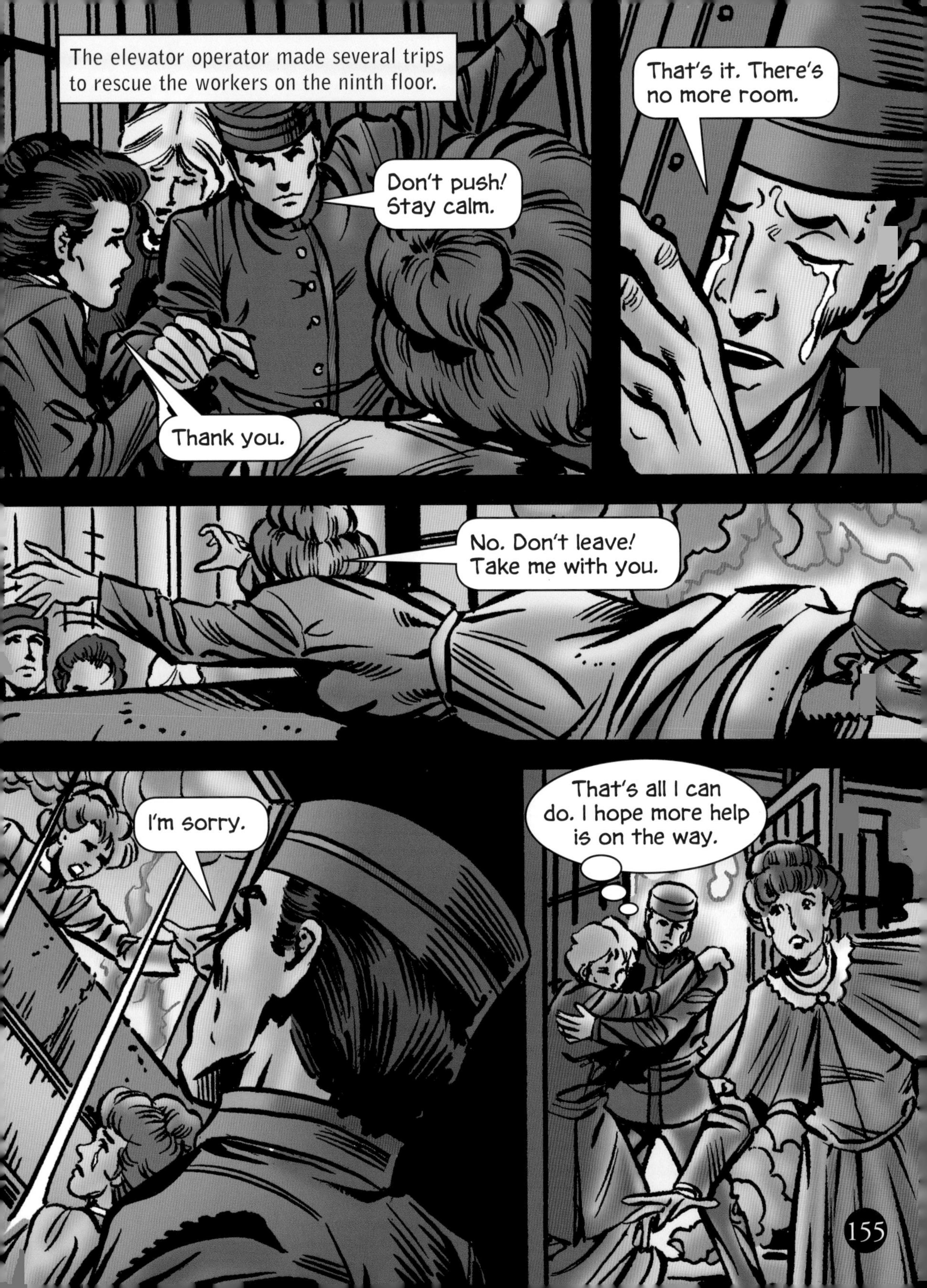

The elevator operator made several trips to rescue the workers on the ninth floor.
Don't push! Stay calm.
Thank you.
That's it. There's no more room.
No. Don't leave! Take me with you.
I'm sorry.
That's all I can do. I hope more help is on the way.

Chapter 3
THE RESCUE

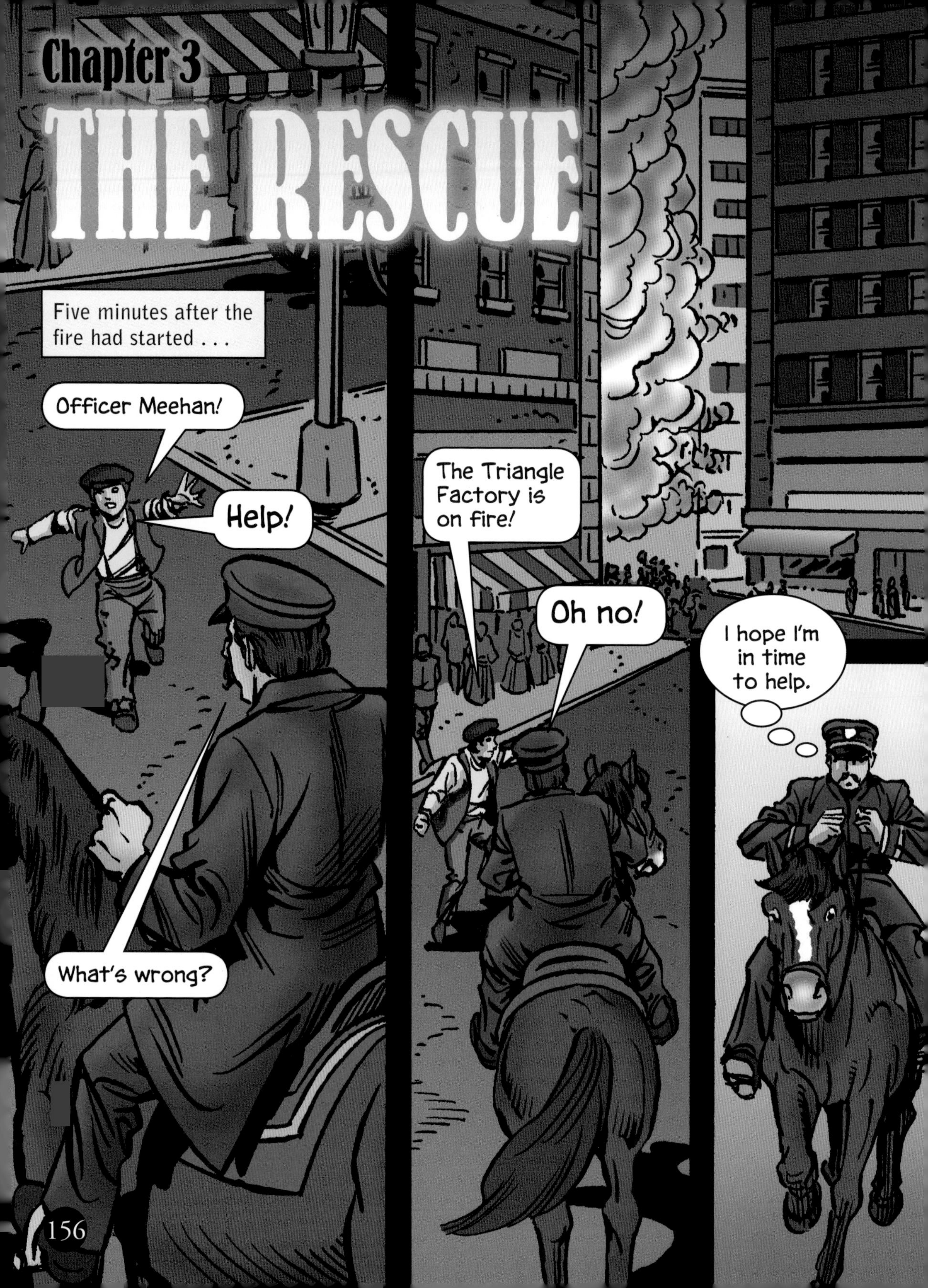
Five minutes after the fire had started . . .
Officer Meehan!
Help!
What's wrong?
The Triangle Factory is on fire!
Oh no!
I hope I'm in time to help.

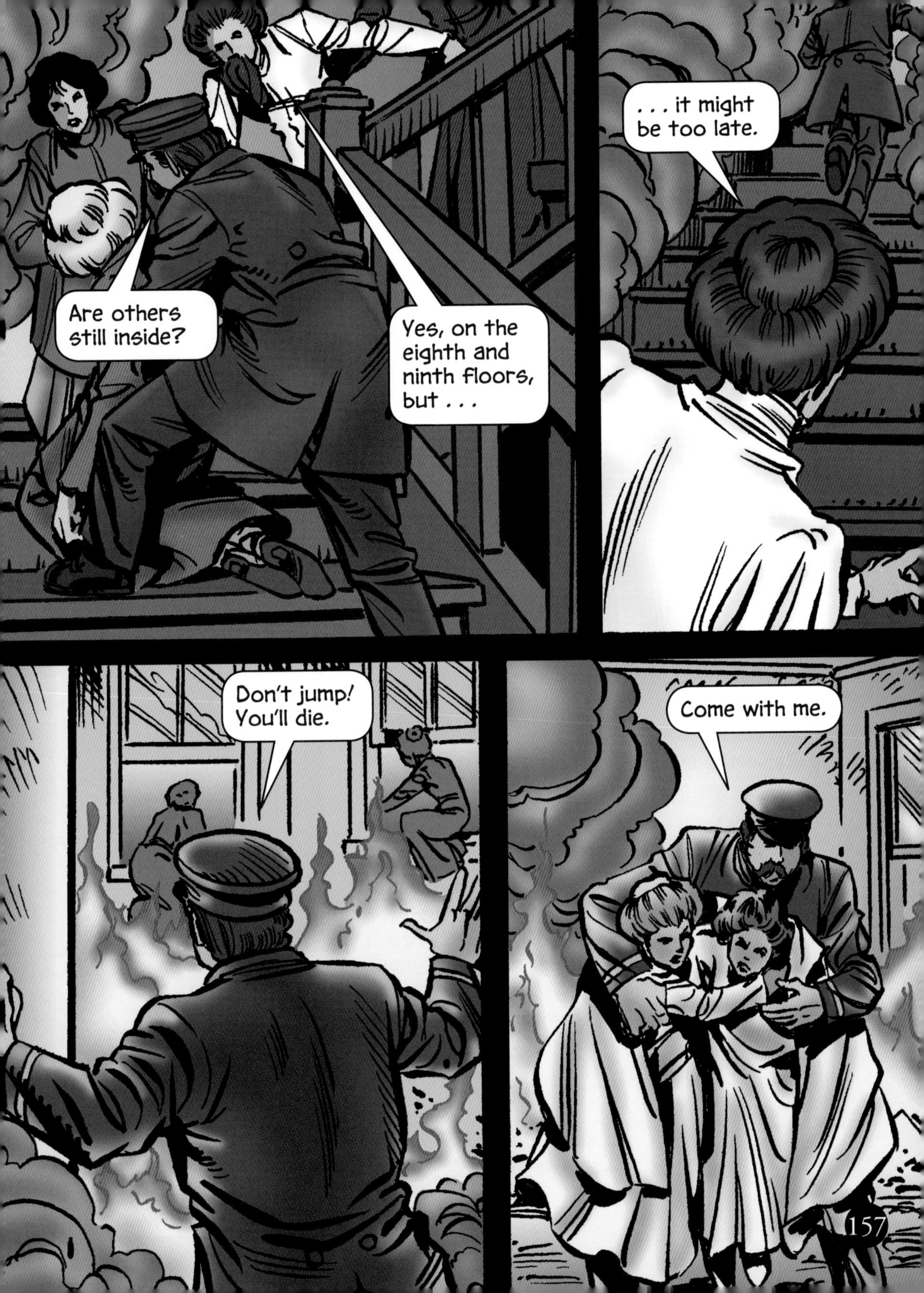
Are others still inside?
Yes, on the eighth and ninth floors, but . . .
. . . it might be too late.
Don't jump! You'll die.
Come with me.

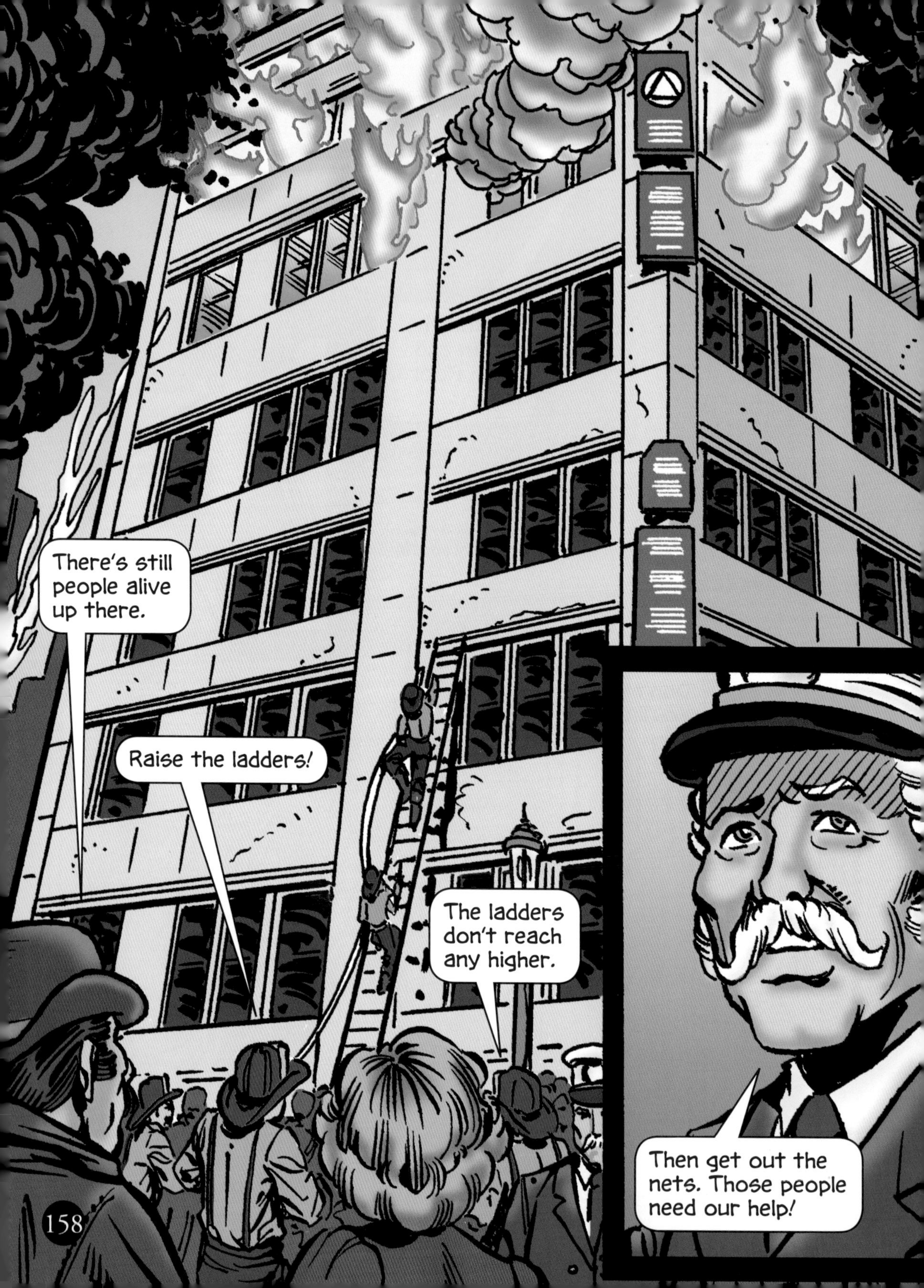
There's still people alive up there.
Raise the ladders!
The ladders don't reach any higher.
Then get out the nets. Those people need our help!

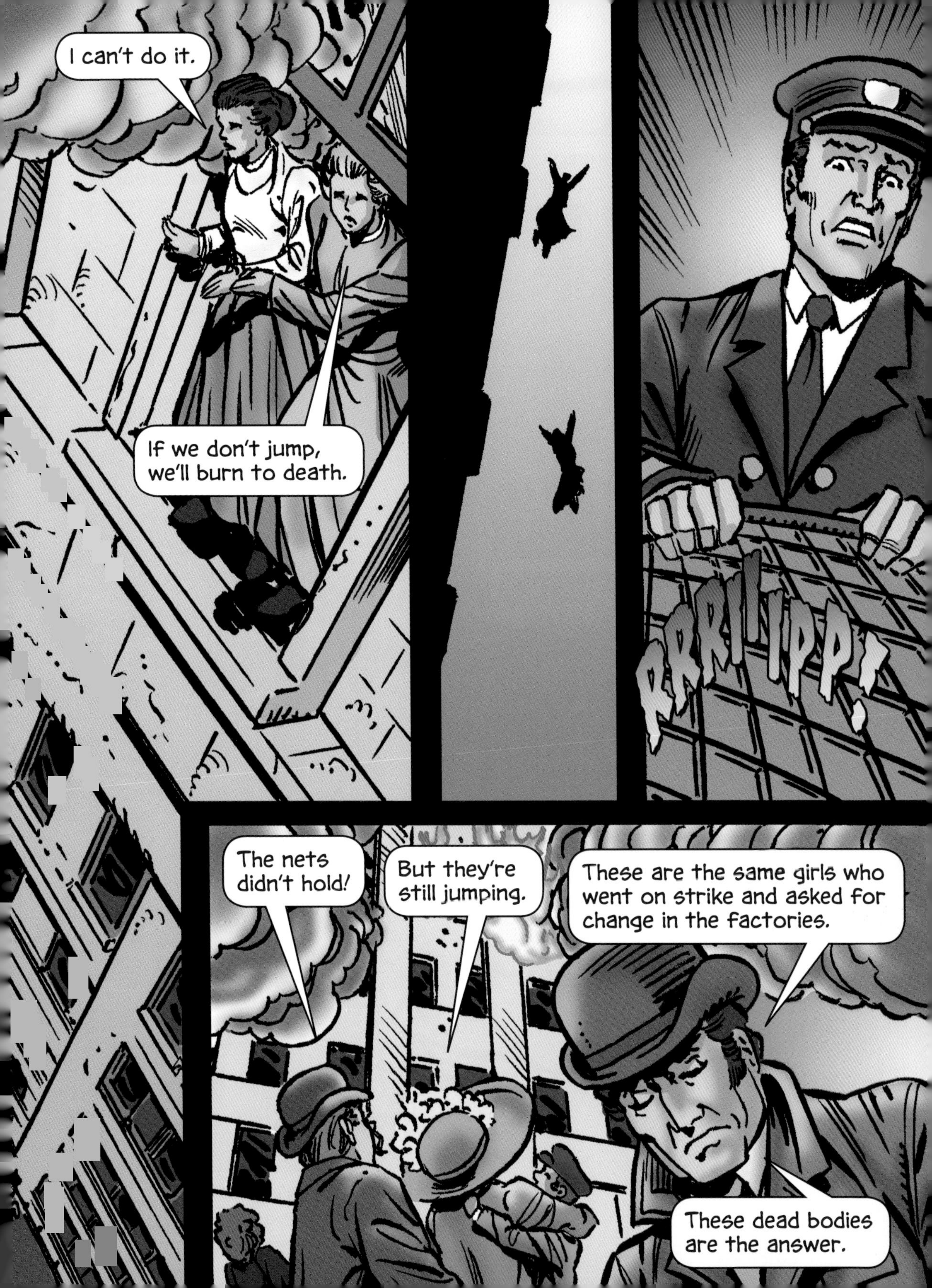
I can't do it.
If we don't jump, we'll burn to death.
RRRIIIPP!
The nets didn't hold!
But they're still jumping.
These are the same girls who went on strike and asked for change in the factories.
These dead bodies are the answer.

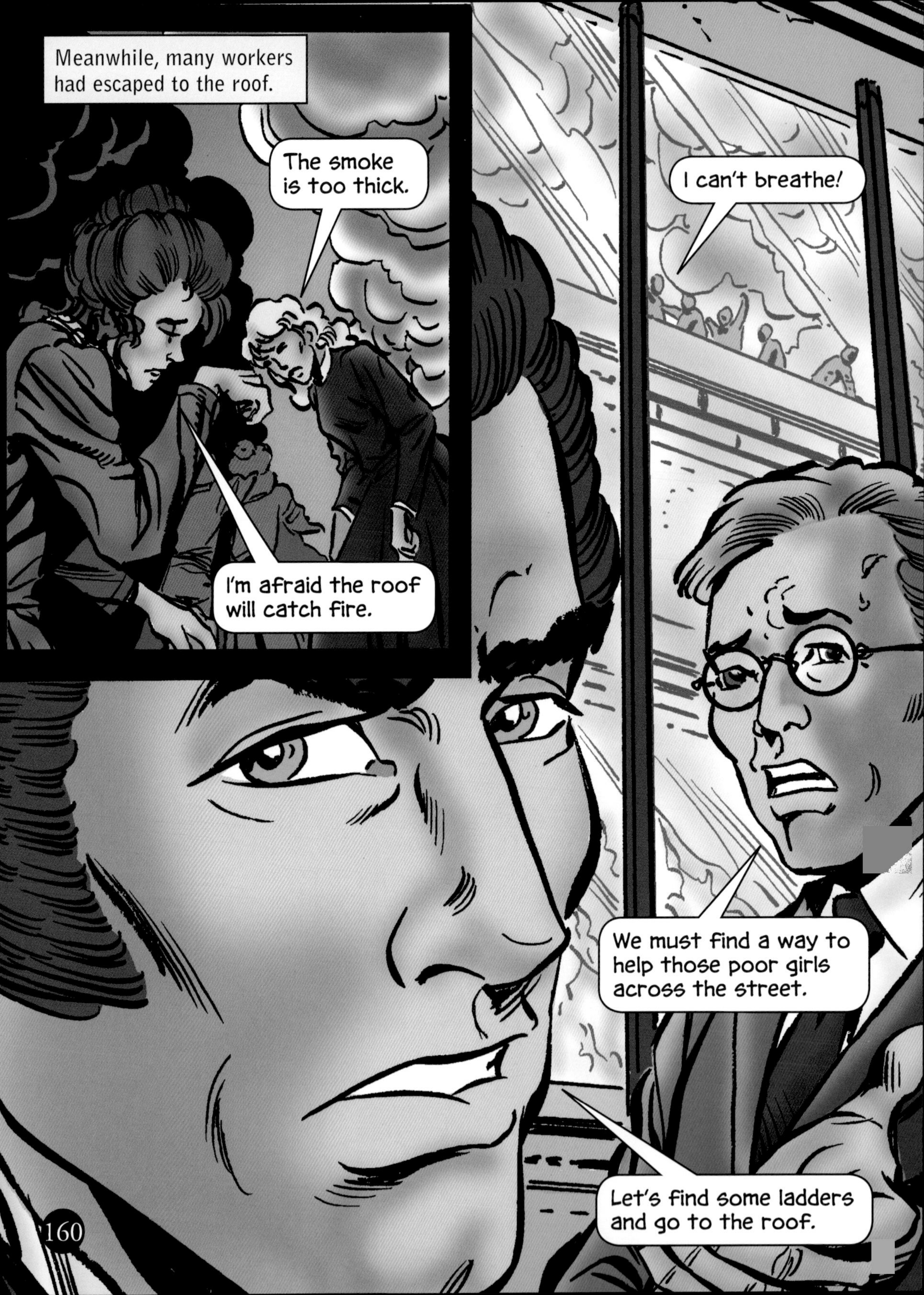
Meanwhile, many workers had escaped to the roof.
The smoke is too thick.
I'm afraid the roof will catch fire.
I can't breathe!
We must find a way to help those poor girls across the street.
Let's find some ladders and go to the roof.

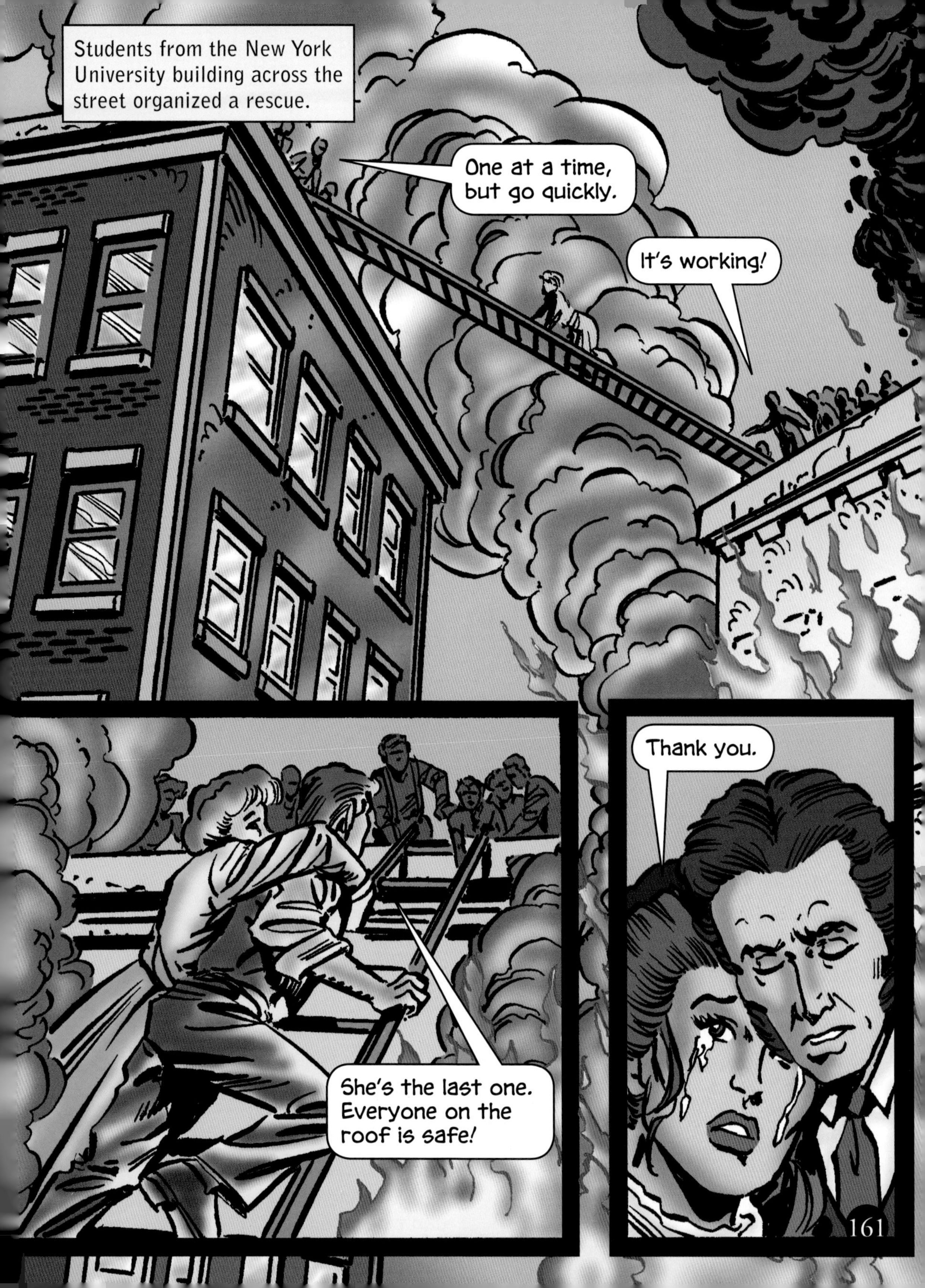
Students from the New York University building across the street organized a rescue.
One at a time, but go quickly.
It's working!
She's the last one. Everyone on the roof is safe!
Thank you.

Chapter 4
FROM THE ASHES

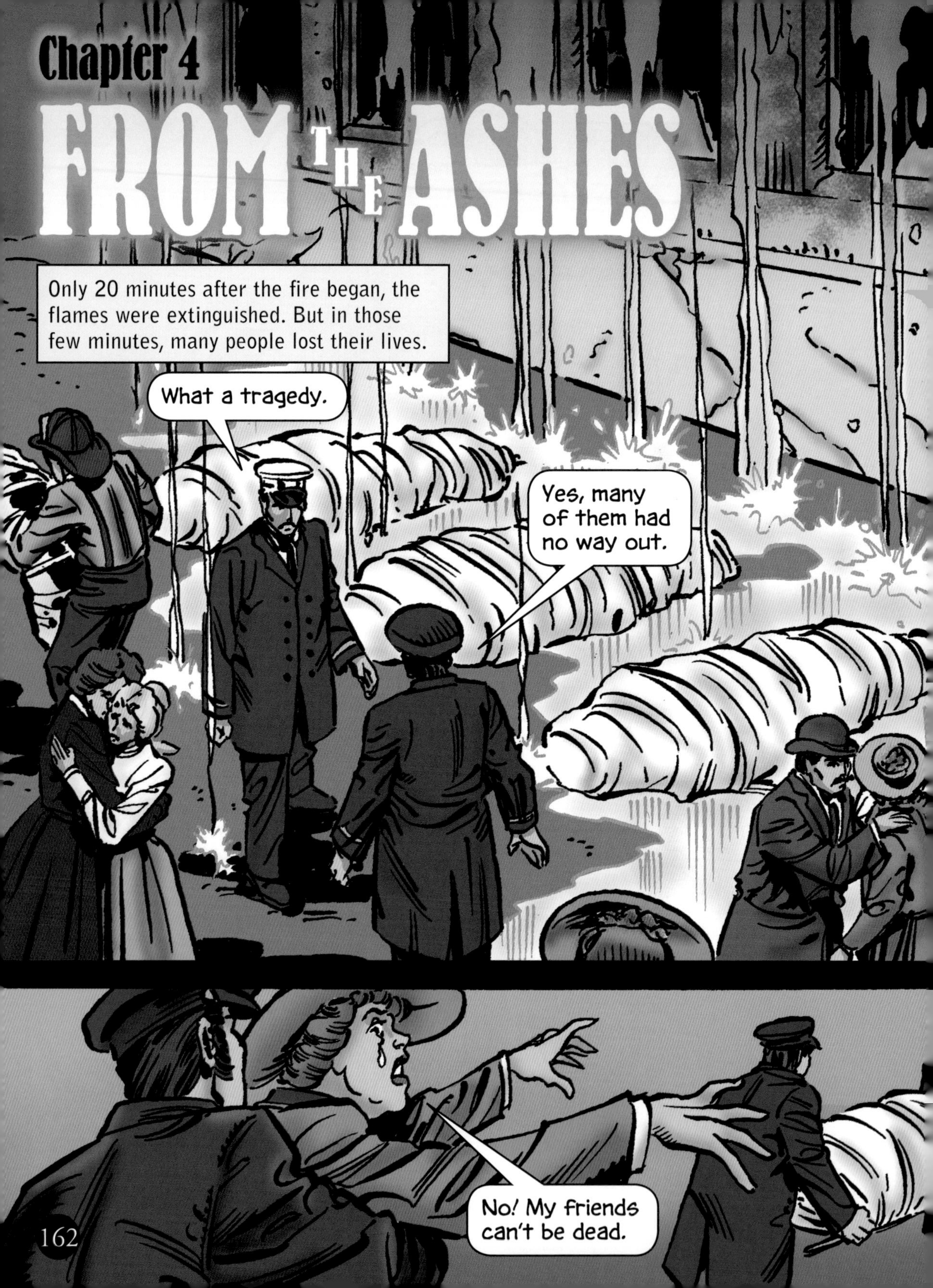
Only 20 minutes after the fire began, the flames were extinguished. But in those few minutes, many people lost their lives.
What a tragedy.
Yes, many of them had no way out.
No! My friends can't be dead.

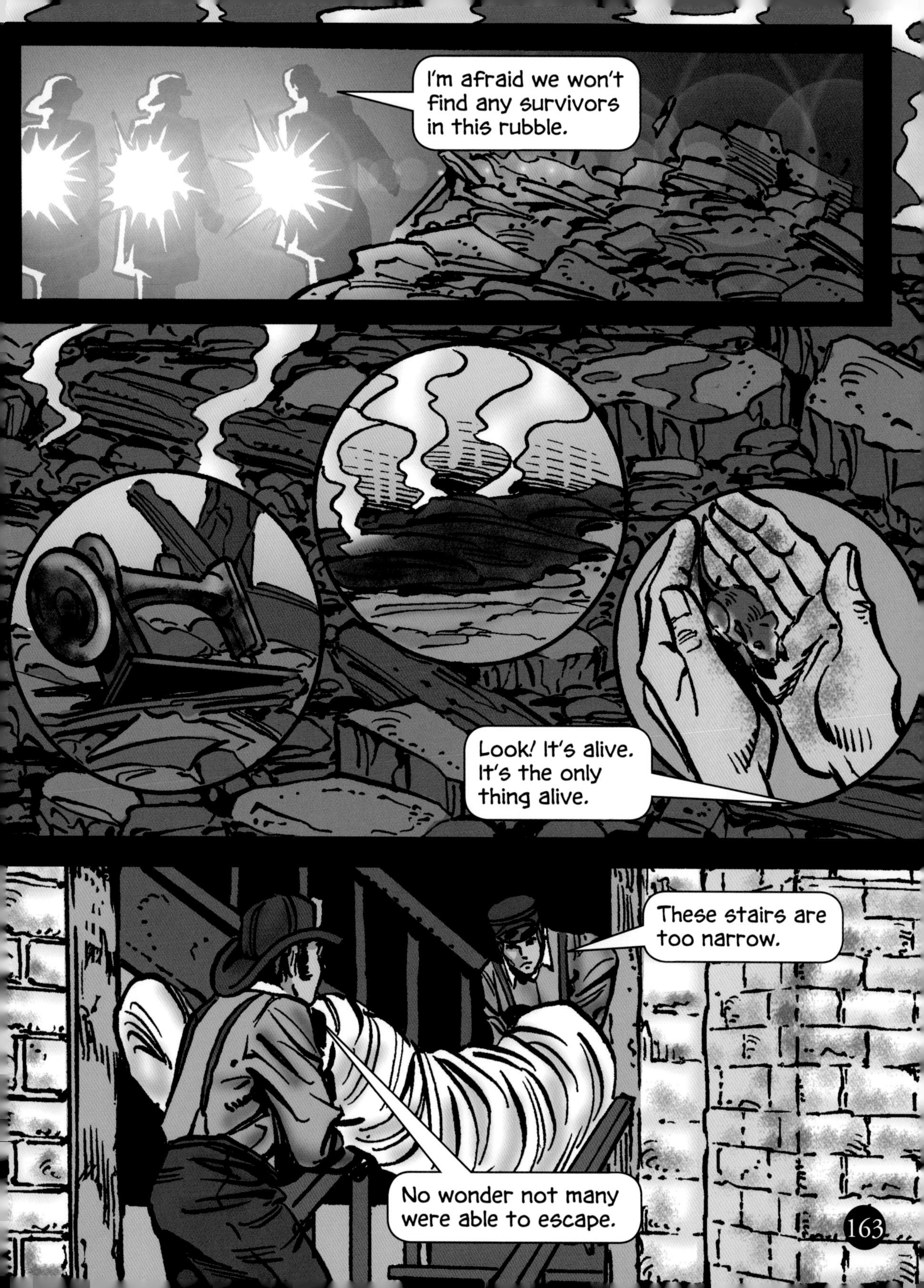
I'm afraid we won't find any survivors in this rubble.
Look! It's alive. It's the only thing alive.
These stairs are too narrow.
No wonder not many were able to escape.

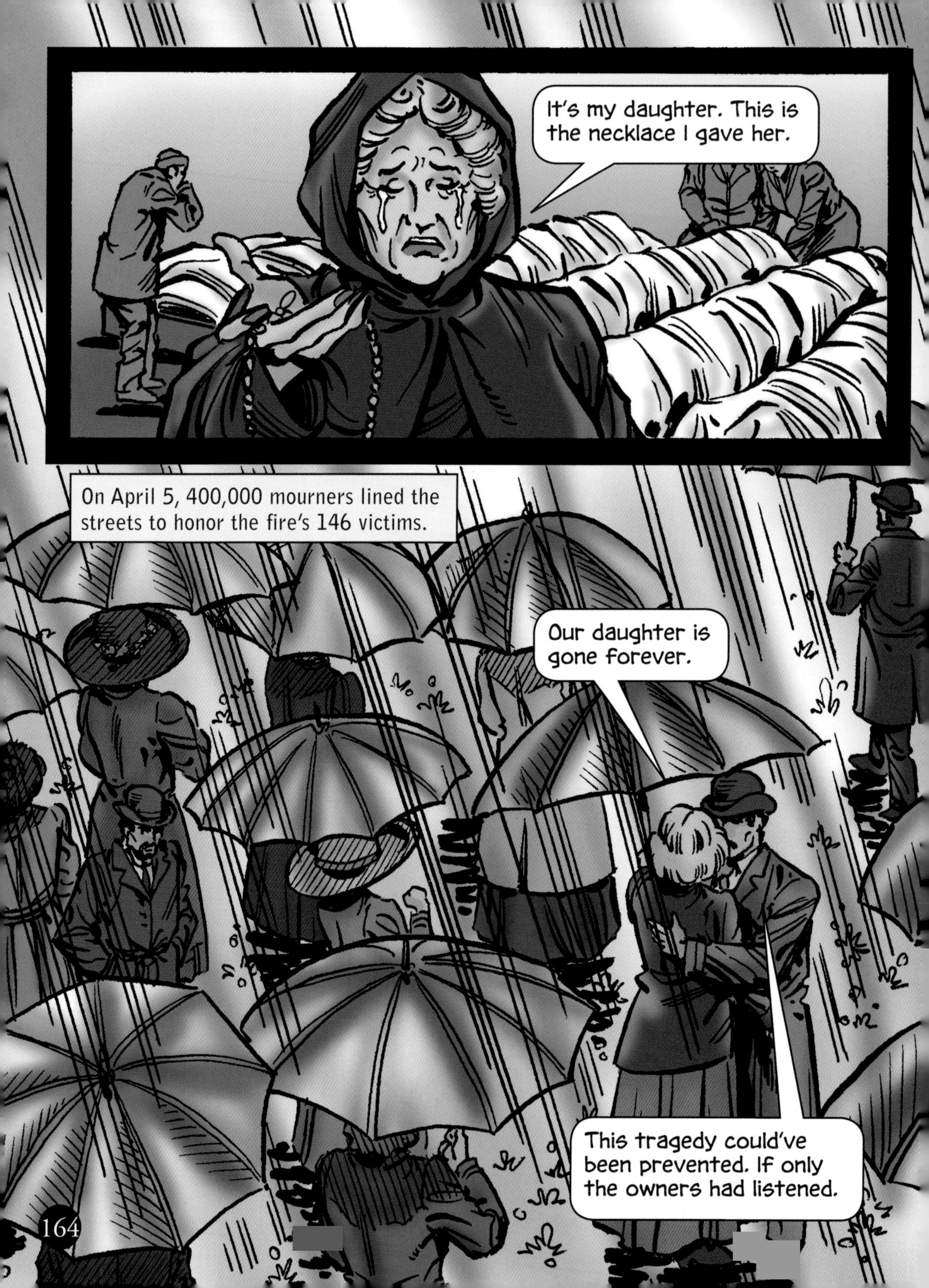
It's my daughter. This is the necklace I gave her.
On April 5, 400,000 mourners lined the streets to honor the fire's 146 victims.
Our daughter is gone forever.
This tragedy could've been prevented. If only the owners had listened.

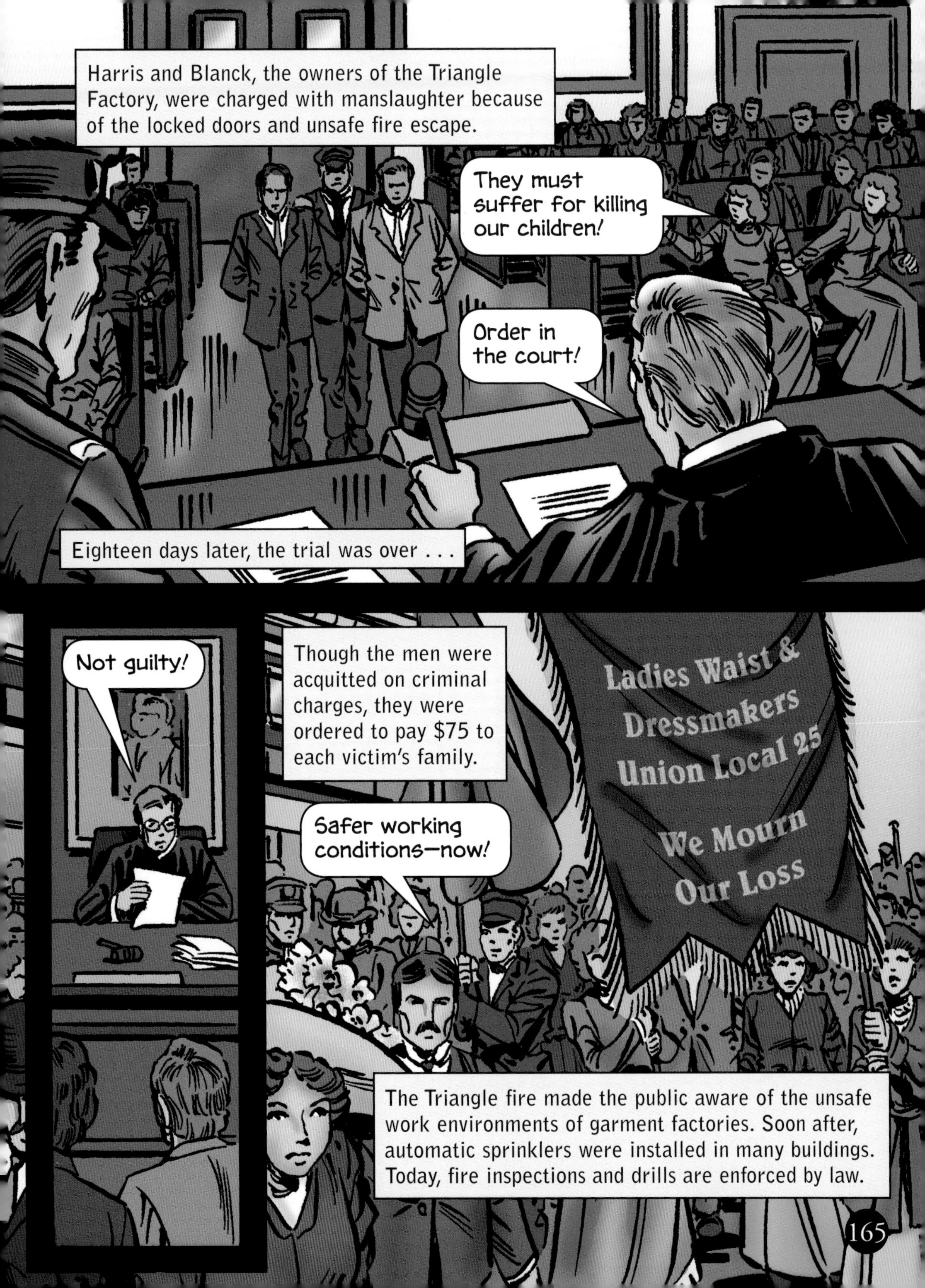
Harris and Blanck, the owners of the Triangle Factory, were charged with manslaughter because of the locked doors and unsafe fire escape.
They must suffer for killing our children!
Order in the court!
Eighteen days later, the trial was over . . .
Not guilty!
Though the men were acquitted on criminal charges, they were ordered to pay $75 to each victim's family.
Ladies Waist & Dressmakers Union Local 25 We Mourn Our Loss
Safer working conditions—now!
The Triangle fire made the public aware of the unsafe work environments of garment factories. Soon after, automatic sprinklers were installed in many buildings. Today, fire inspections and drills are enforced by law.

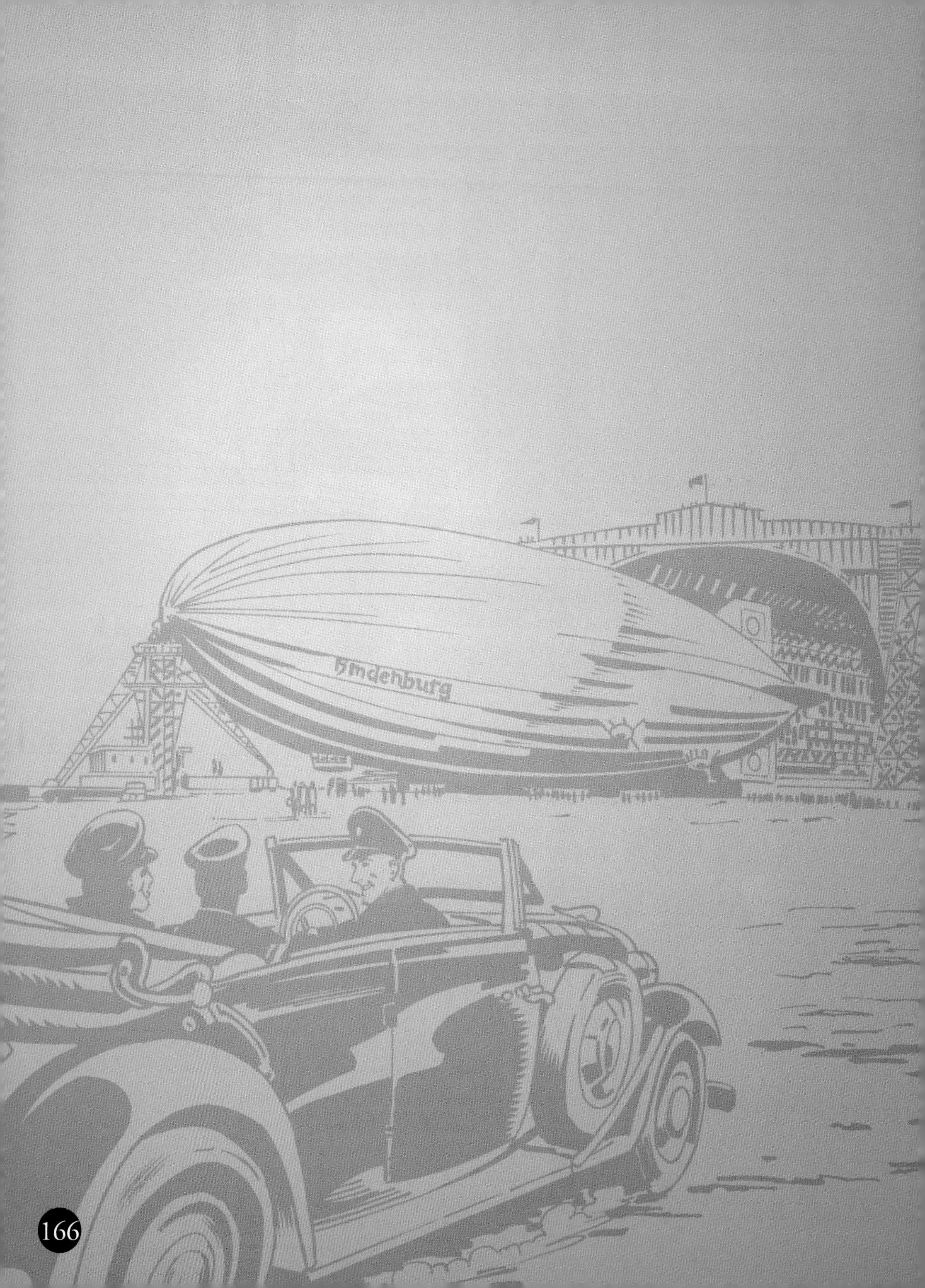
Hindenburg

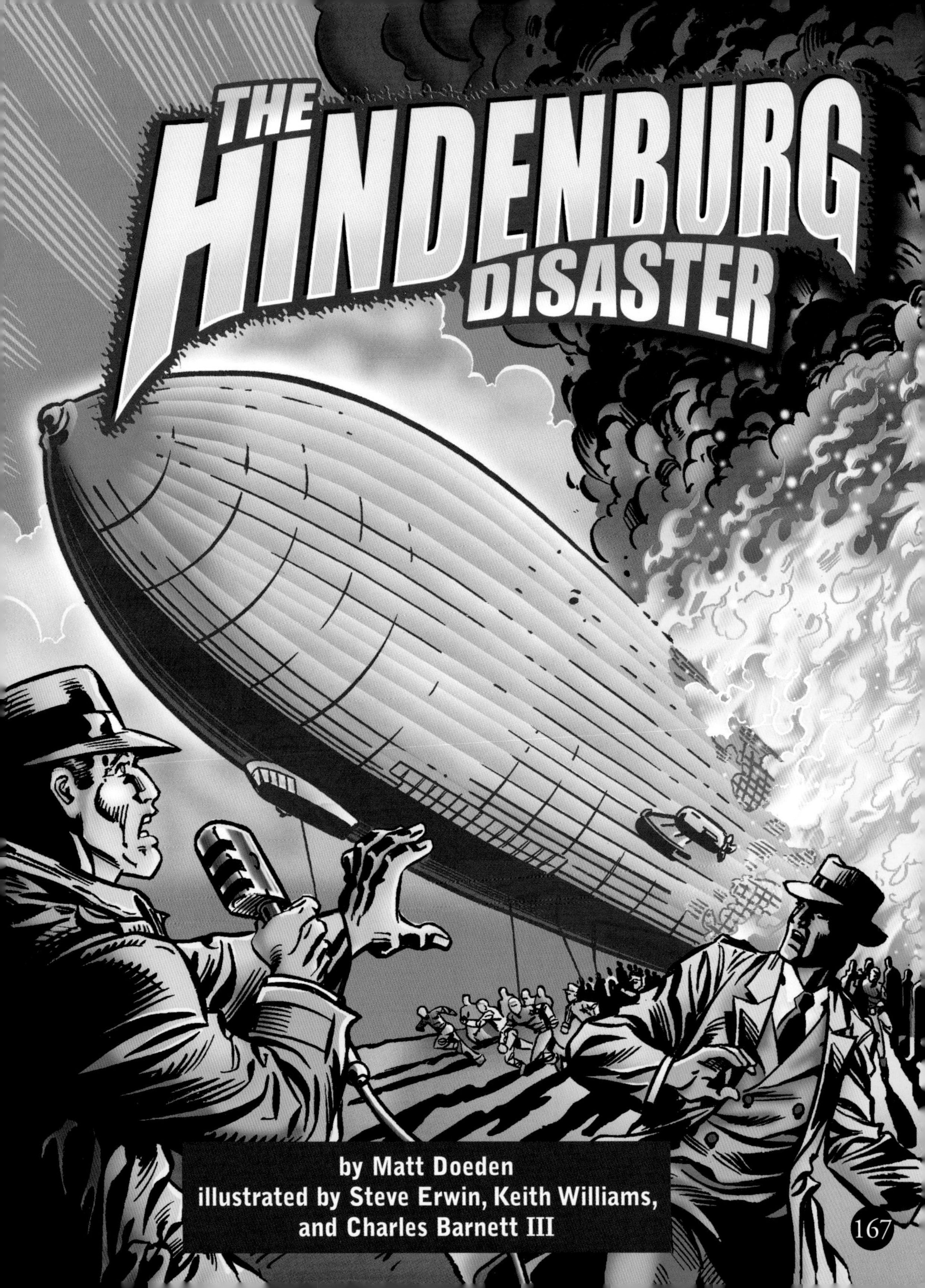

THE HINDENBURG DISASTER

by Matt Doeden
illustrated by Steve Erwin, Keith Williams, and Charles Barnett III

CHAPTER 1 TAKING FLIGHT

On May 3, 1937, three men approached the Hindenburg at the Frankfurt Airfield in Germany. The men were Captain Max Pruss, First Officer Albert Sammt, and Second Officer Heinrich Bauer. They were preparing for a journey across the Atlantic Ocean to Lakehurst, New Jersey. The trip was scheduled to last three days.

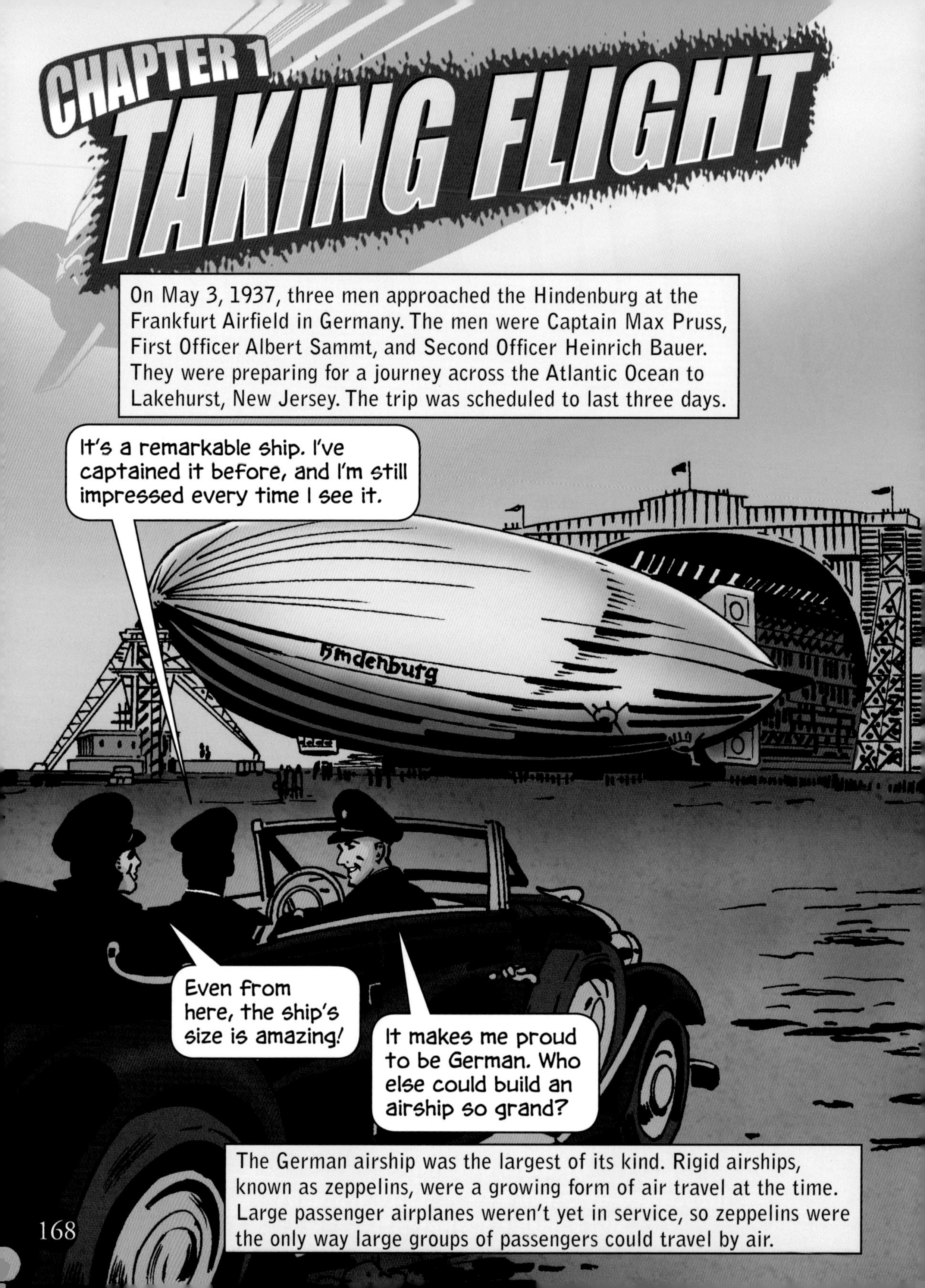
It's a remarkable ship. I've captained it before, and I'm still impressed every time I see it.
Hindenburg
Even from here, the ship's size is amazing!
It makes me proud to be German. Who else could build an airship so grand?

The German airship was the largest of its kind. Rigid airships, known as zeppelins, were a growing form of air travel at the time. Large passenger airplanes weren't yet in service, so zeppelins were the only way large groups of passengers could travel by air.

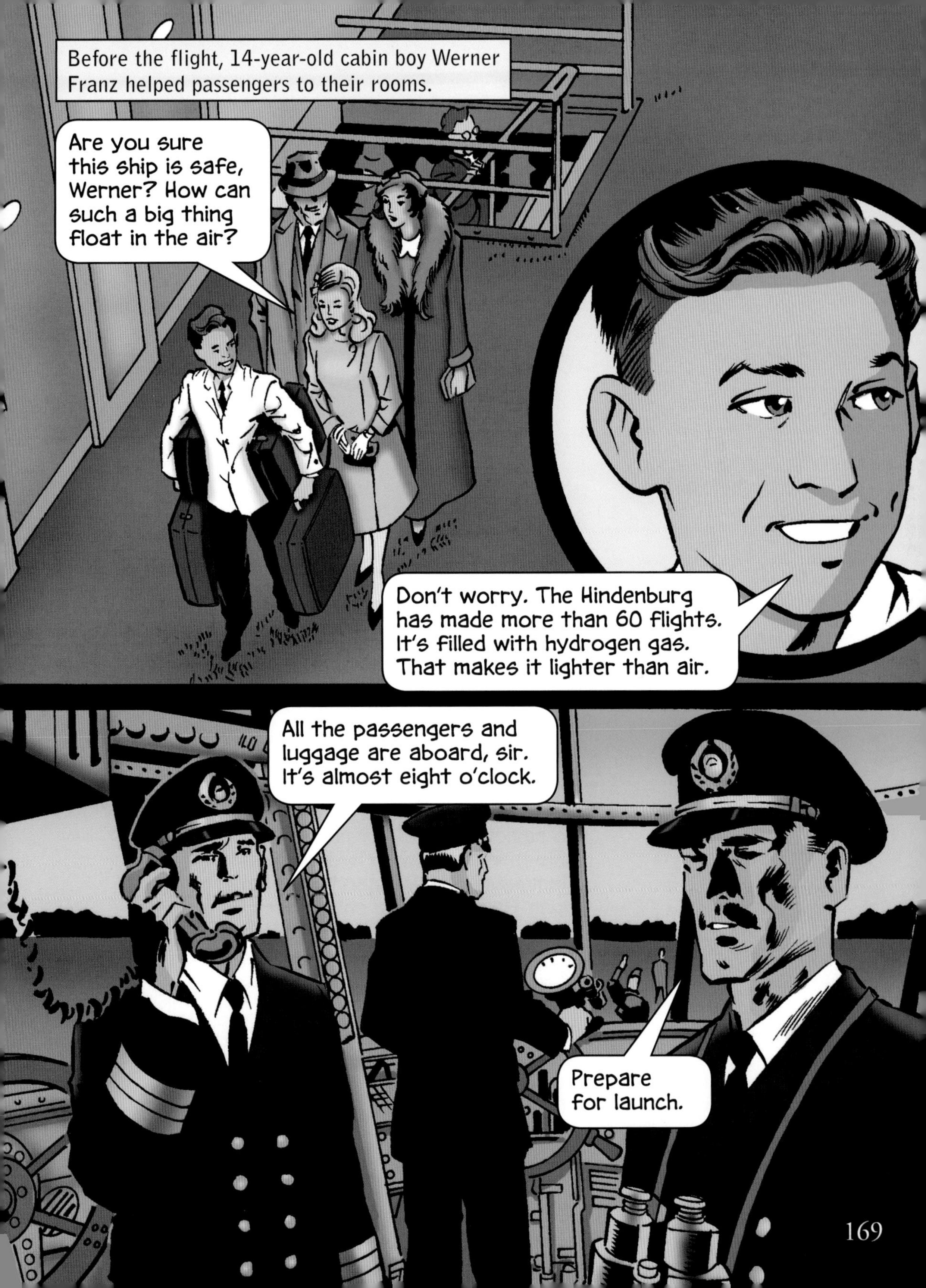
Before the flight, 14-year-old cabin boy Werner Franz helped passengers to their rooms.
Are you sure this ship is safe, Werner? How can such a big thing float in the air?
Don't worry. The Hindenburg has made more than 60 flights. It's filled with hydrogen gas. That makes it lighter than air.
All the passengers and luggage are aboard, sir. It's almost eight o'clock.
Prepare for launch.

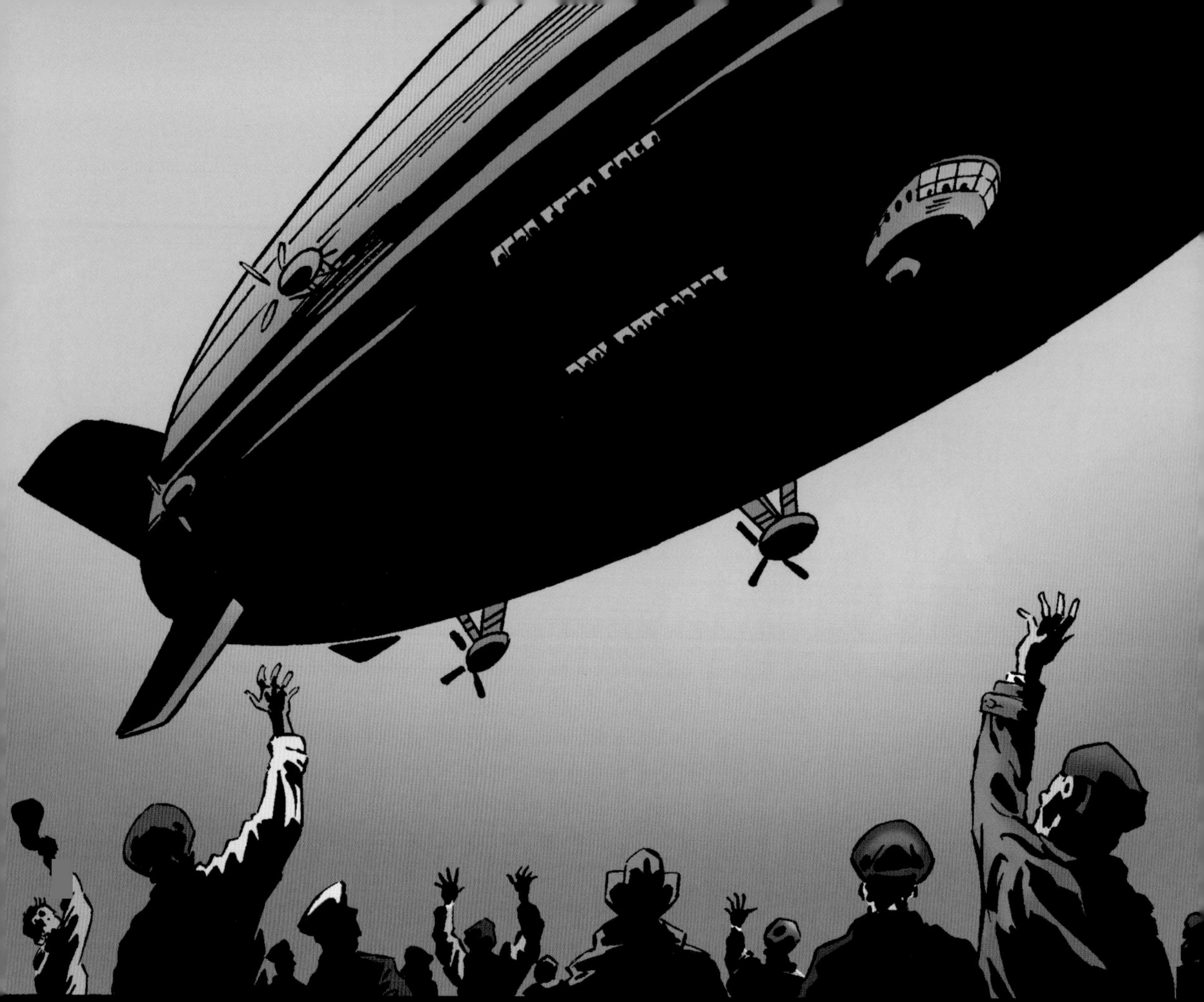

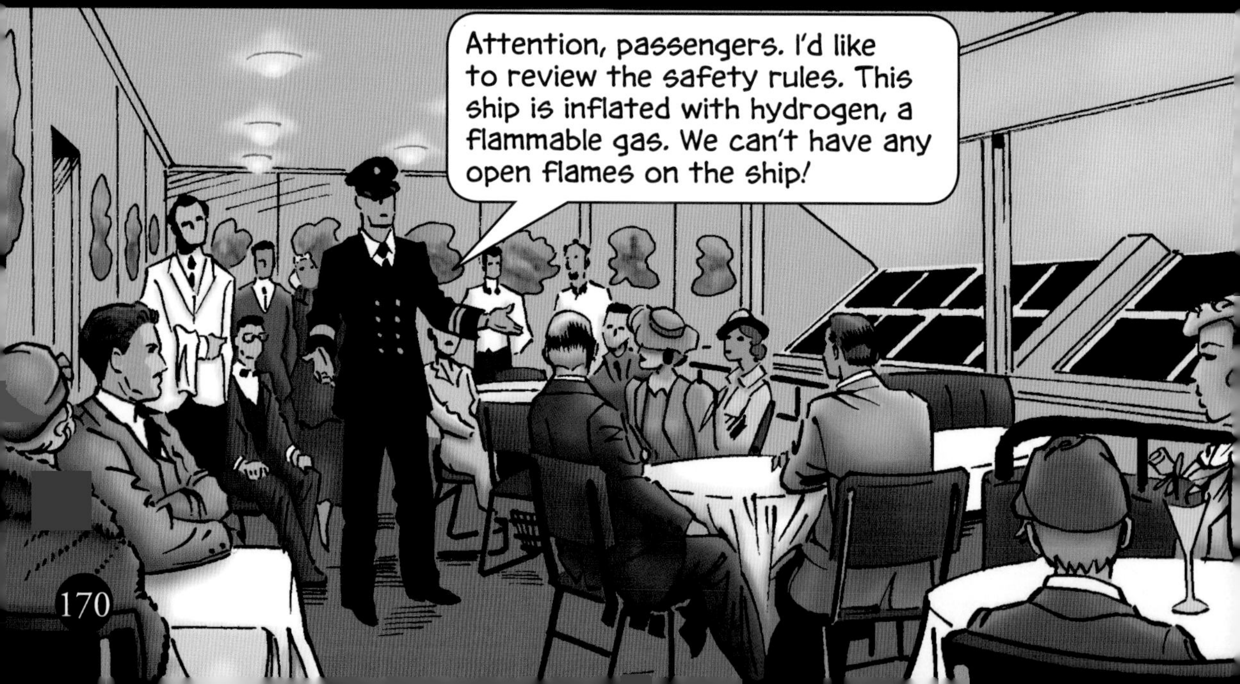
Attention, passengers. I'd like to review the safety rules. This ship is inflated with hydrogen, a flammable gas. We can't have any open flames on the ship!

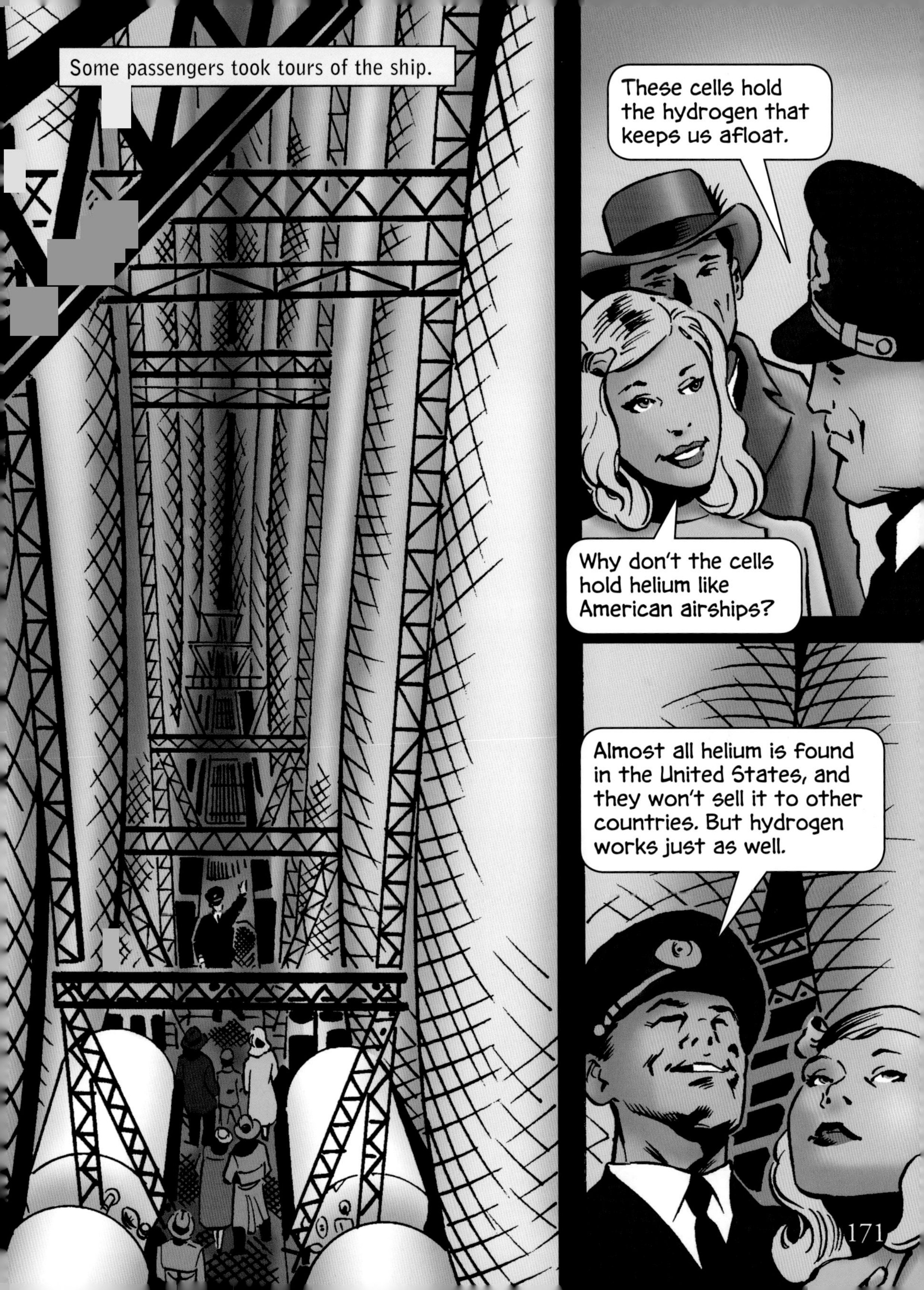

Some passengers took tours of the ship.
These cells hold the hydrogen that keeps us afloat.
Why don't the cells hold helium like American airships?
Almost all helium is found in the United States, and they won't sell it to other countries. But hydrogen works just as well.

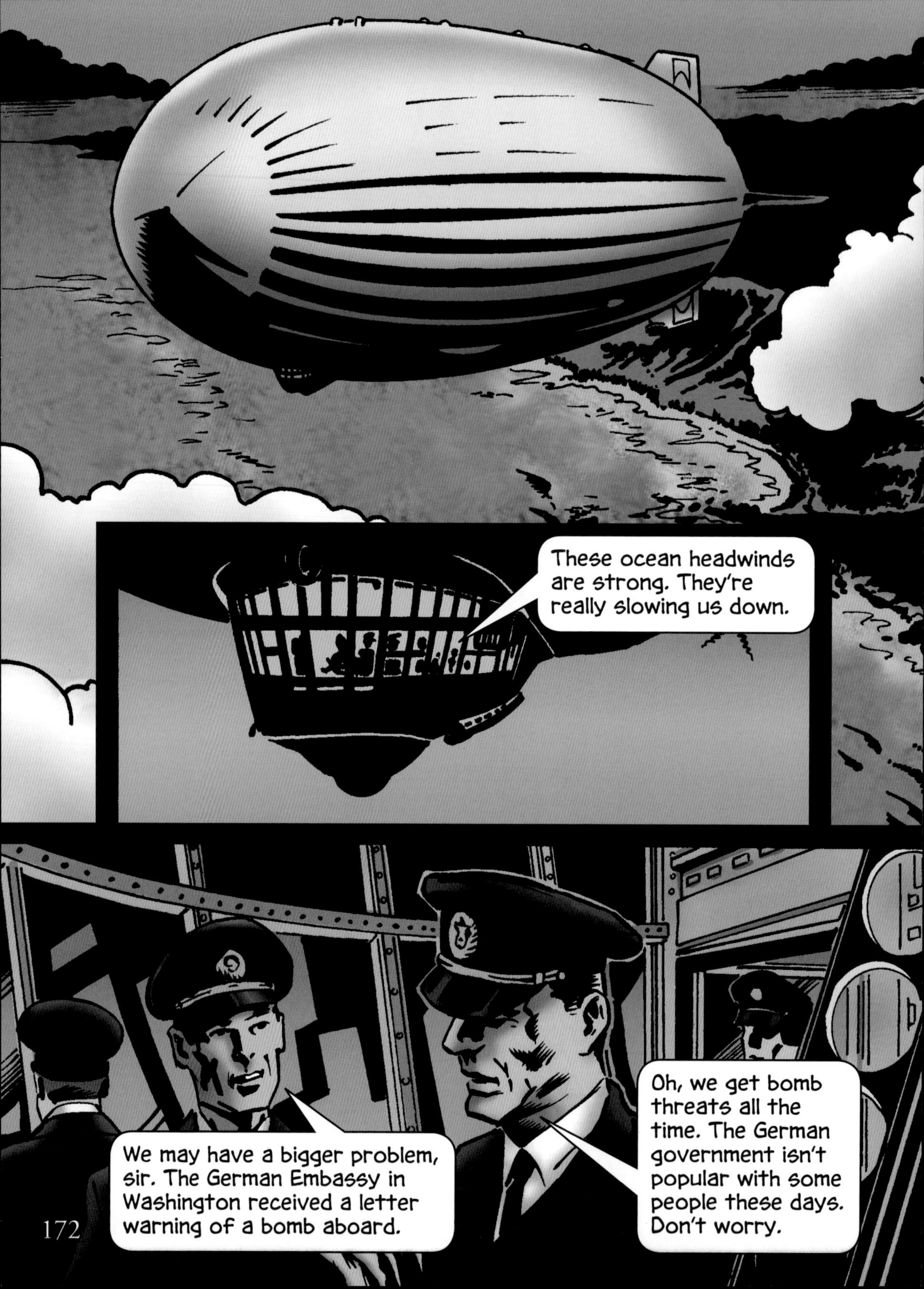
These ocean headwinds are strong. They're really slowing us down.
We may have a bigger problem, sir. The German Embassy in Washington received a letter warning of a bomb aboard.
Oh, we get bomb threats all the time. The German government isn't popular with some people these days. Don't worry.

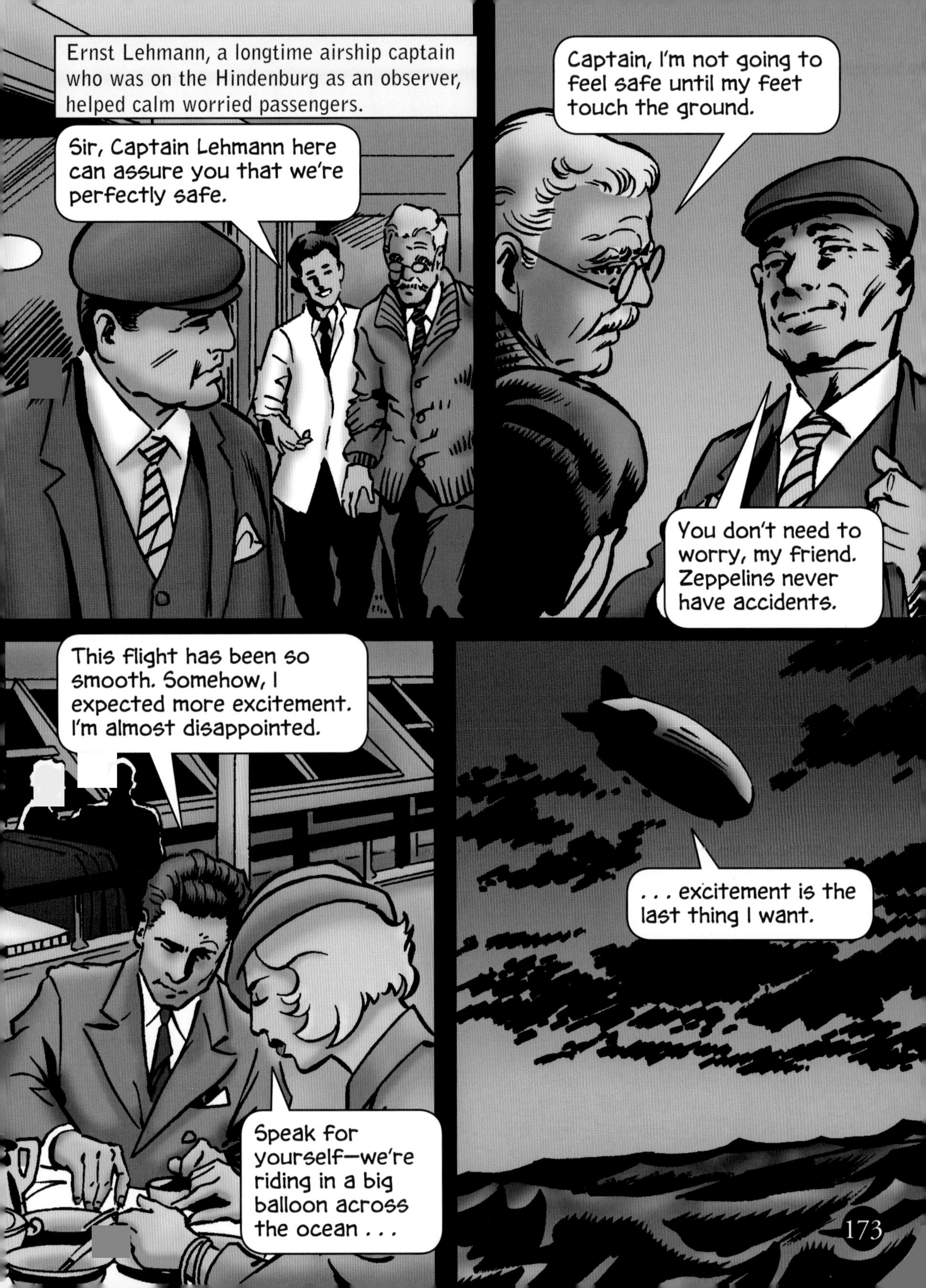
Ernst Lehmann, a longtime airship captain who was on the Hindenburg as an observer, helped calm worried passengers.
Sir, Captain Lehmann here can assure you that we're perfectly safe.
Captain, I'm not going to feel safe until my feet touch the ground.
You don't need to worry, my friend. Zeppelins never have accidents.
This flight has been so smooth. Somehow, I expected more excitement. I'm almost disappointed.
Speak for yourself—we're riding in a big balloon across the ocean . . .
. . . excitement is the last thing I want.

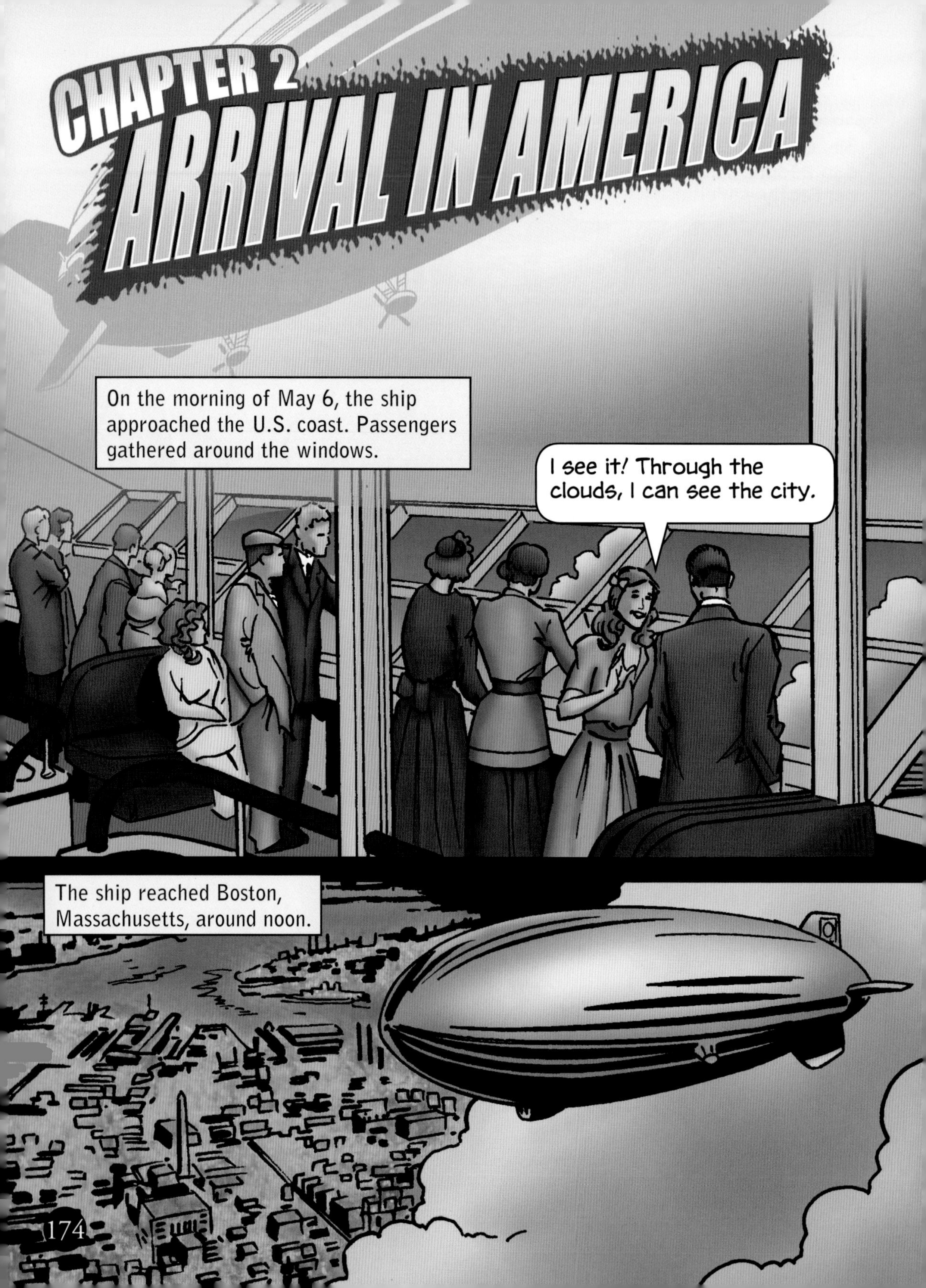
CHAPTER 2
ARRIVAL IN AMERICA
On the morning of May 6, the ship approached the U.S. coast. Passengers gathered around the windows.
I see it! Through the clouds, I can see the city.
The ship reached Boston, Massachusetts, around noon.

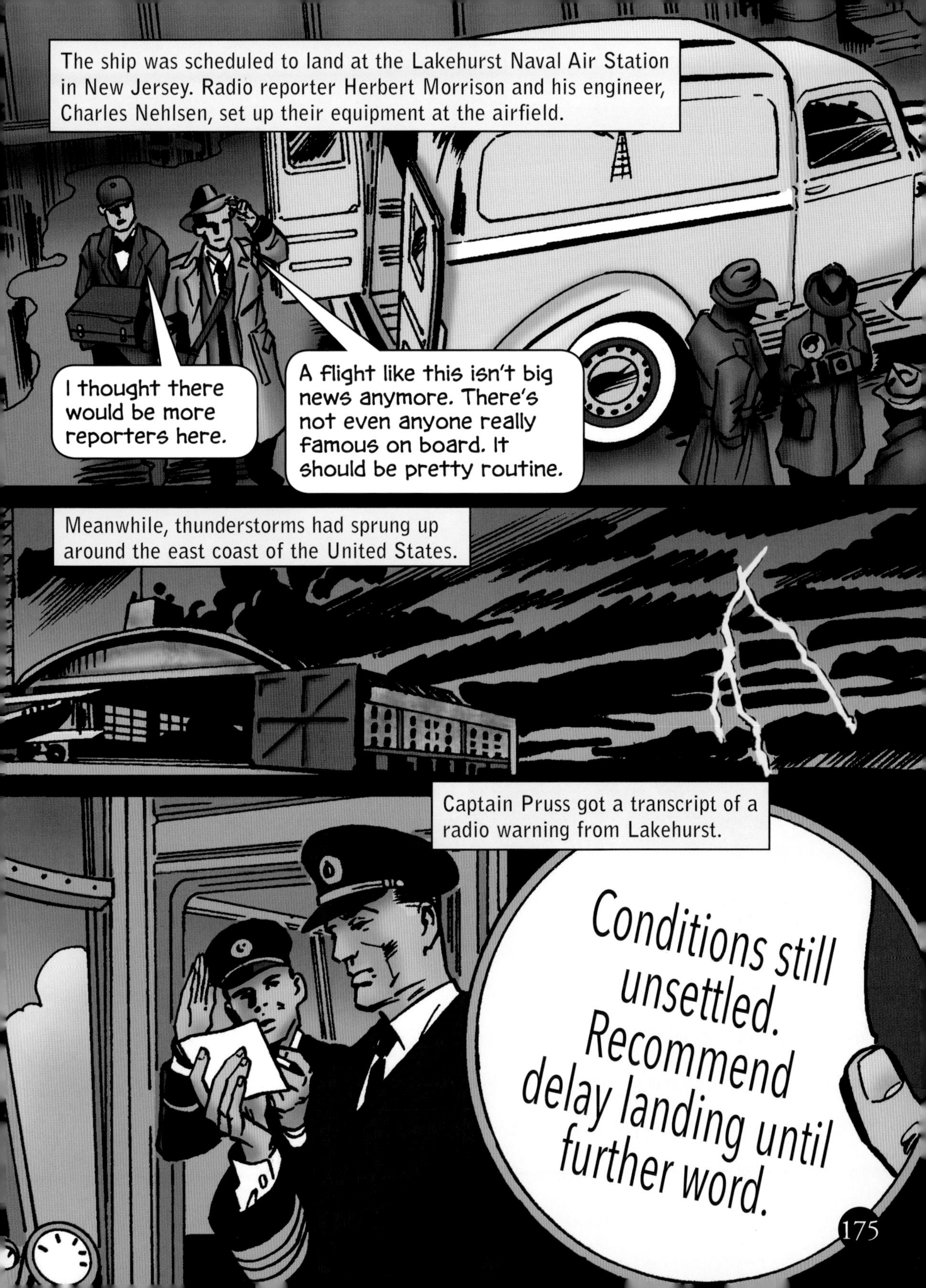
The ship was scheduled to land at the Lakehurst Naval Air Station in New Jersey. Radio reporter Herbert Morrison and his engineer, Charles Nehlsen, set up their equipment at the airfield.
I thought there would be more reporters here.
A flight like this isn't big news anymore. There's not even anyone really famous on board. It should be pretty routine.
Meanwhile, thunderstorms had sprung up around the east coast of the United States.
Captain Pruss got a transcript of a radio warning from Lakehurst.
Conditions still unsettled. Recommend delay landing until further word.

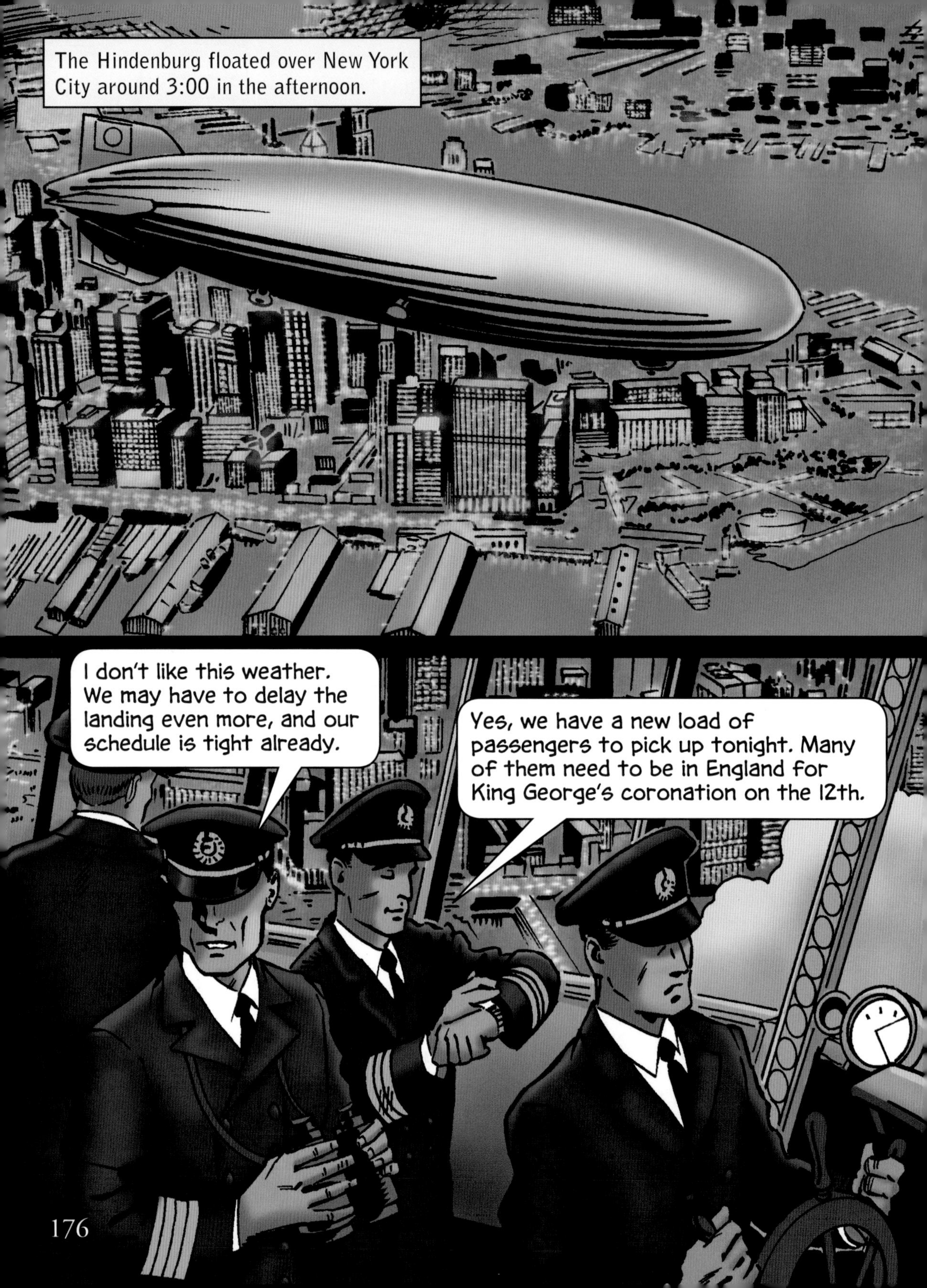

The Hindenburg floated over New York City around 3:00 in the afternoon.
I don't like this weather. We may have to delay the landing even more, and our schedule is tight already.
Yes, we have a new load of passengers to pick up tonight. Many of them need to be in England for King George's coronation on the 12th.

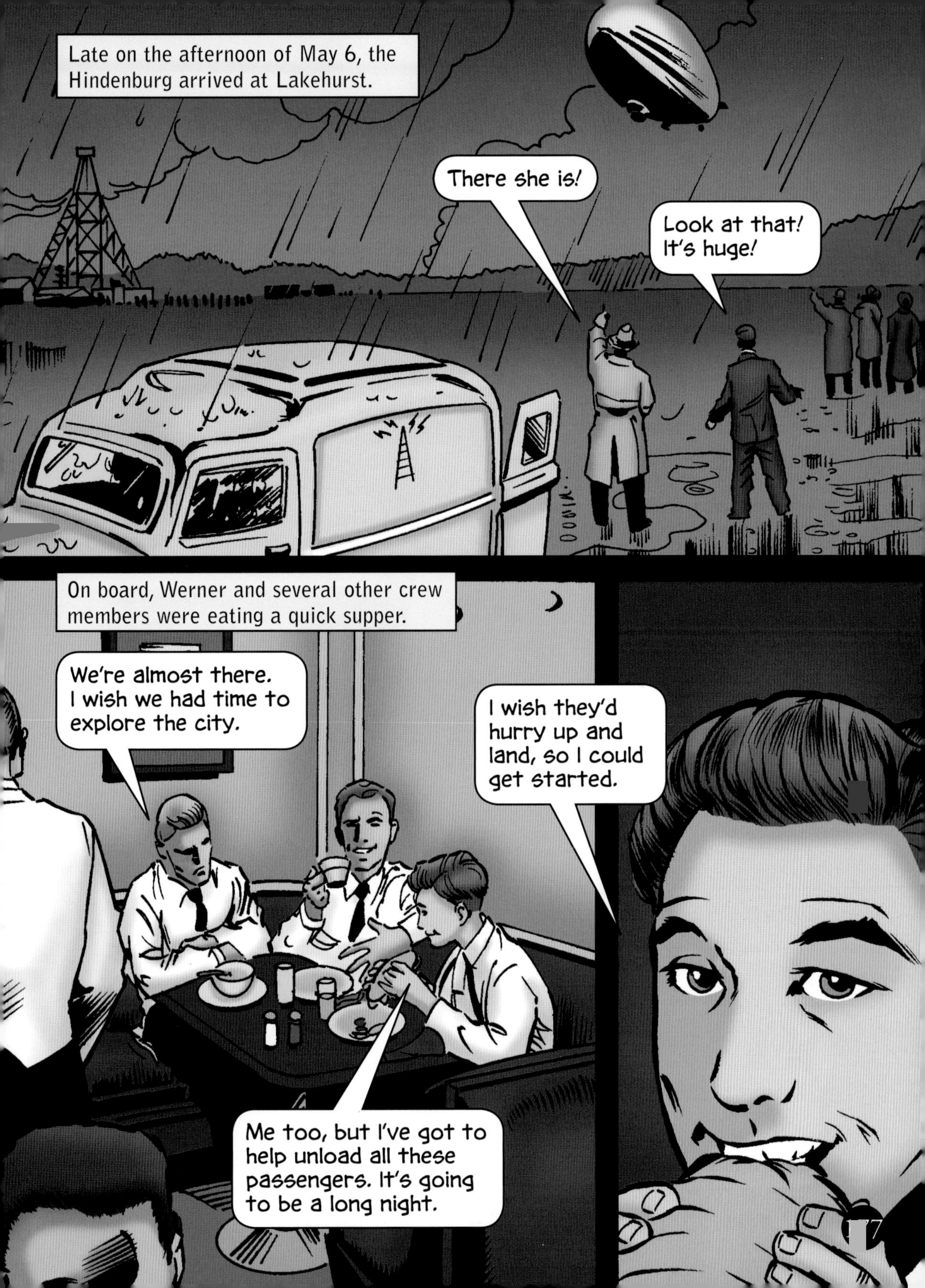
Late on the afternoon of May 6, the Hindenburg arrived at Lakehurst.
There she is!
Look at that! It's huge!
On board, Werner and several other crew members were eating a quick supper.
We're almost there. I wish we had time to explore the city.
Me too, but I've got to help unload all these passengers. It's going to be a long night.
I wish they'd hurry up and land, so I could get started.

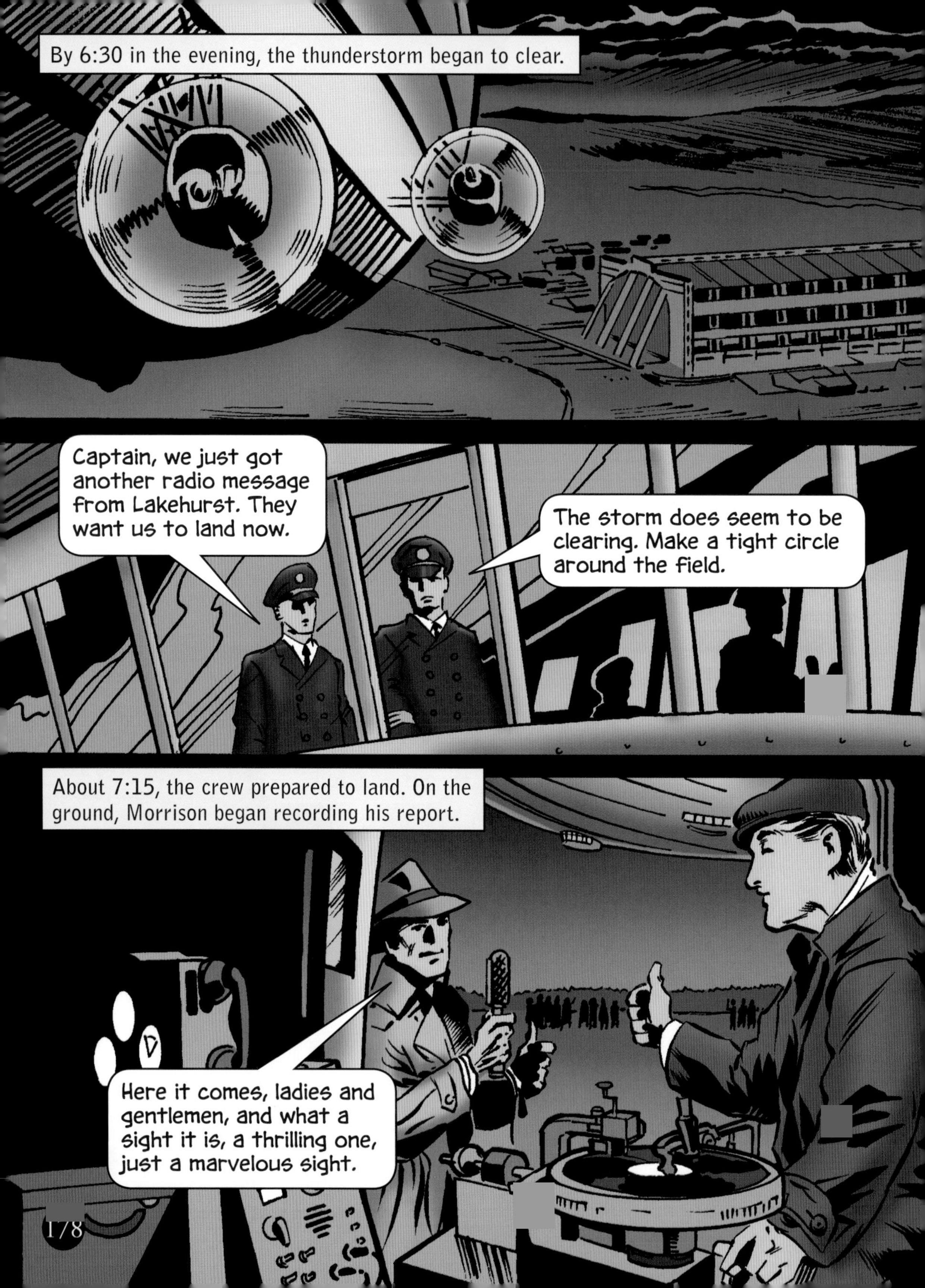

By 6:30 in the evening, the thunderstorm began to clear.
Captain, we just got another radio message from Lakehurst. They want us to land now.
The storm does seem to be clearing. Make a tight circle around the field.
About 7:15, the crew prepared to land. On the ground, Morrison began recording his report.
Here it comes, ladies and gentlemen, and what a sight it is, a thrilling one, just a marvelous sight.

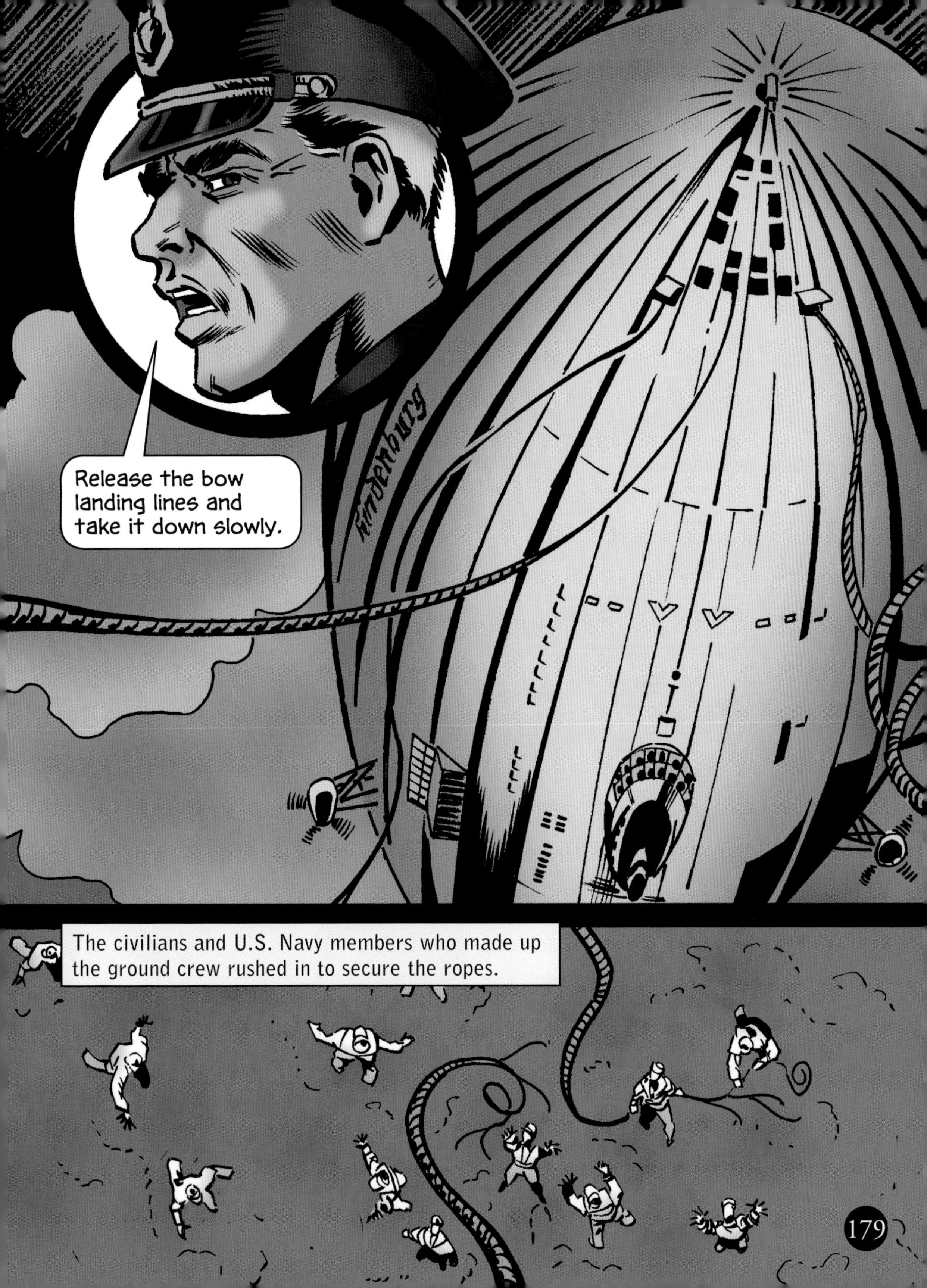
Release the bow landing lines and take it down slowly.
Hindenburg
The civilians and U.S. Navy members who made up the ground crew rushed in to secure the ropes.

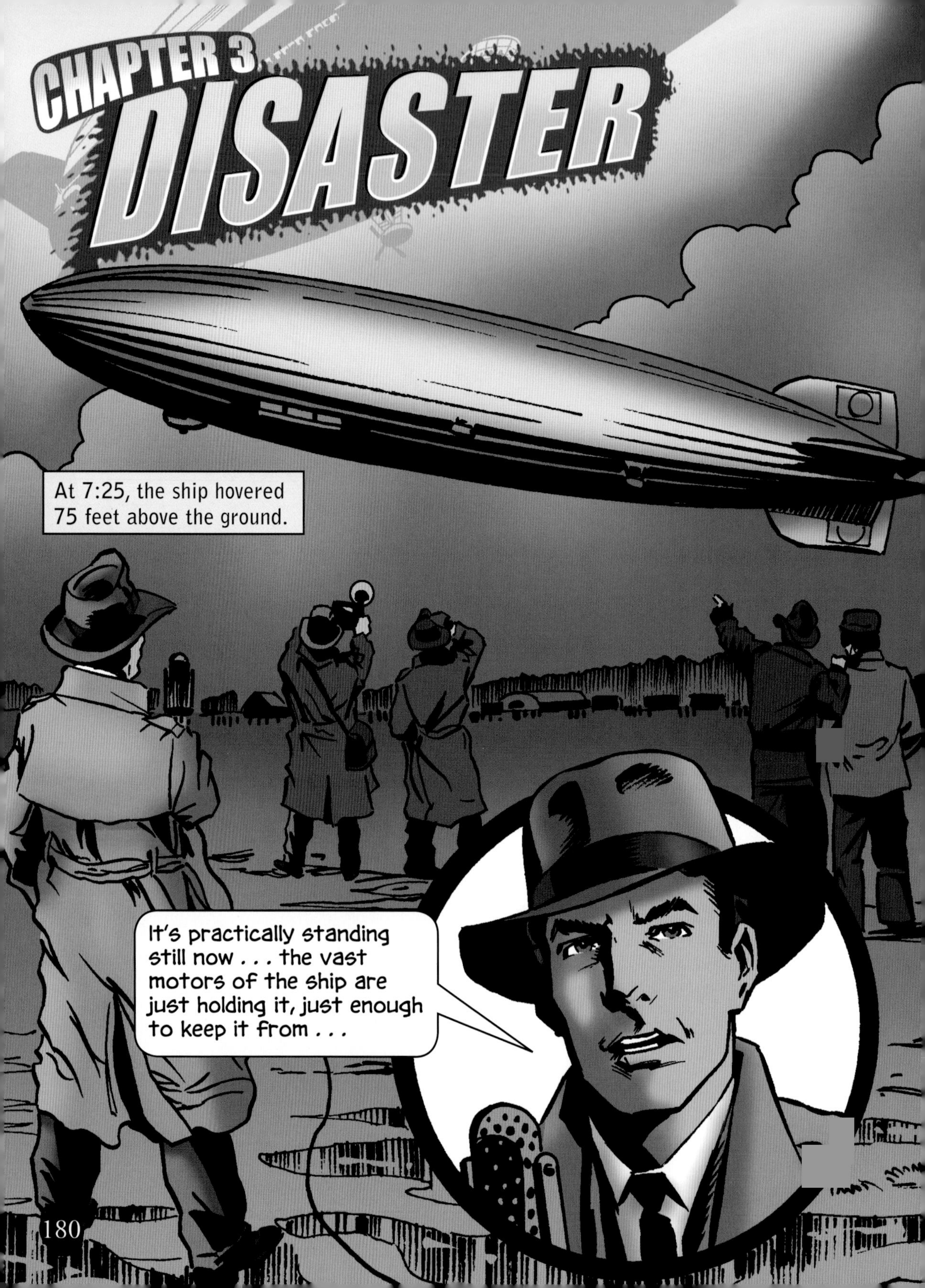
CHAPTER 3
DISASTER
At 7:25, the ship hovered 75 feet above the ground.
It's practically standing still now . . . the vast motors of the ship are just holding it, just enough to keep it from . . .

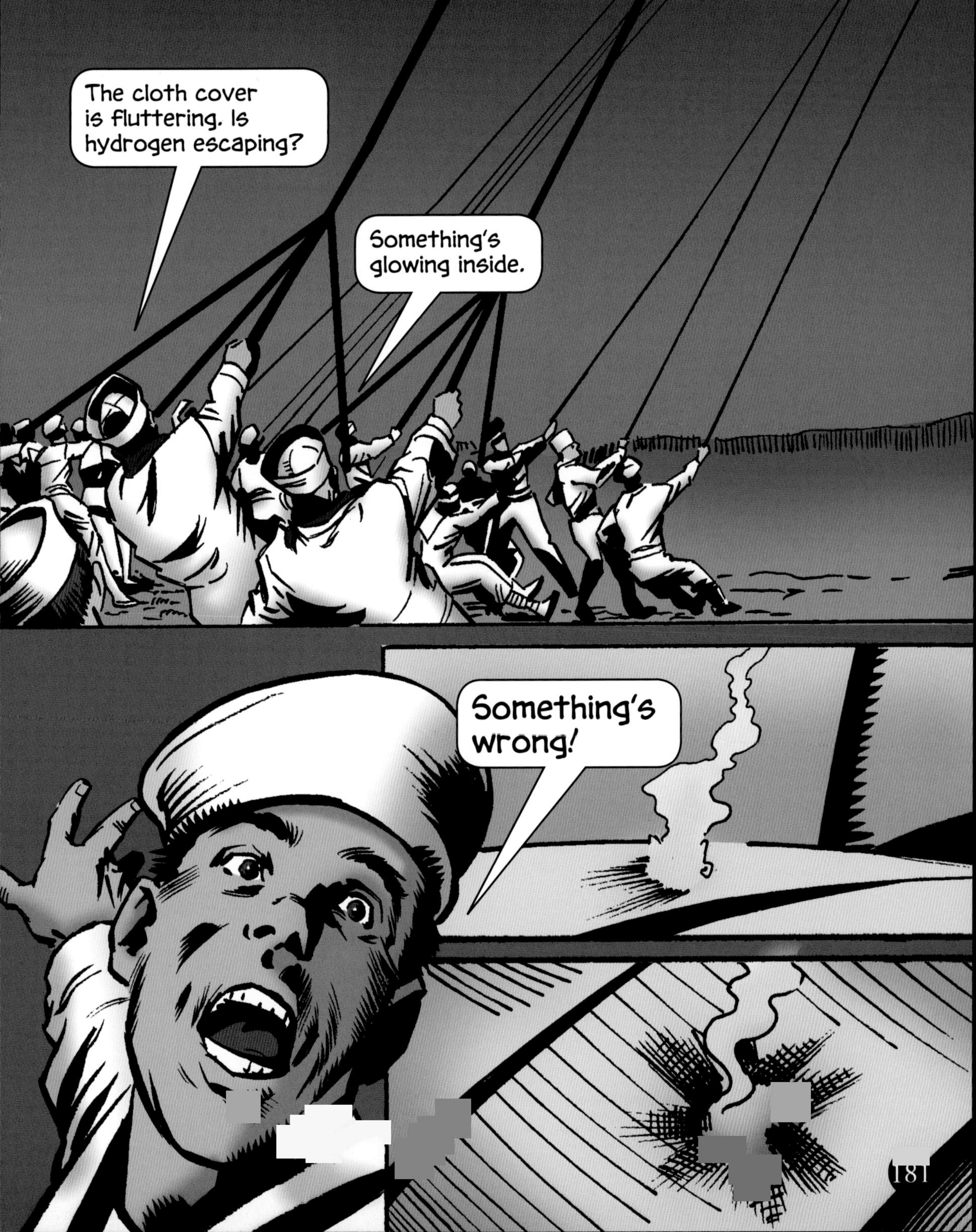
The cloth cover is fluttering. Is hydrogen escaping?
Something's glowing inside.
Something's wrong!

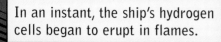

In an instant, the ship's hydrogen cells began to erupt in flames.

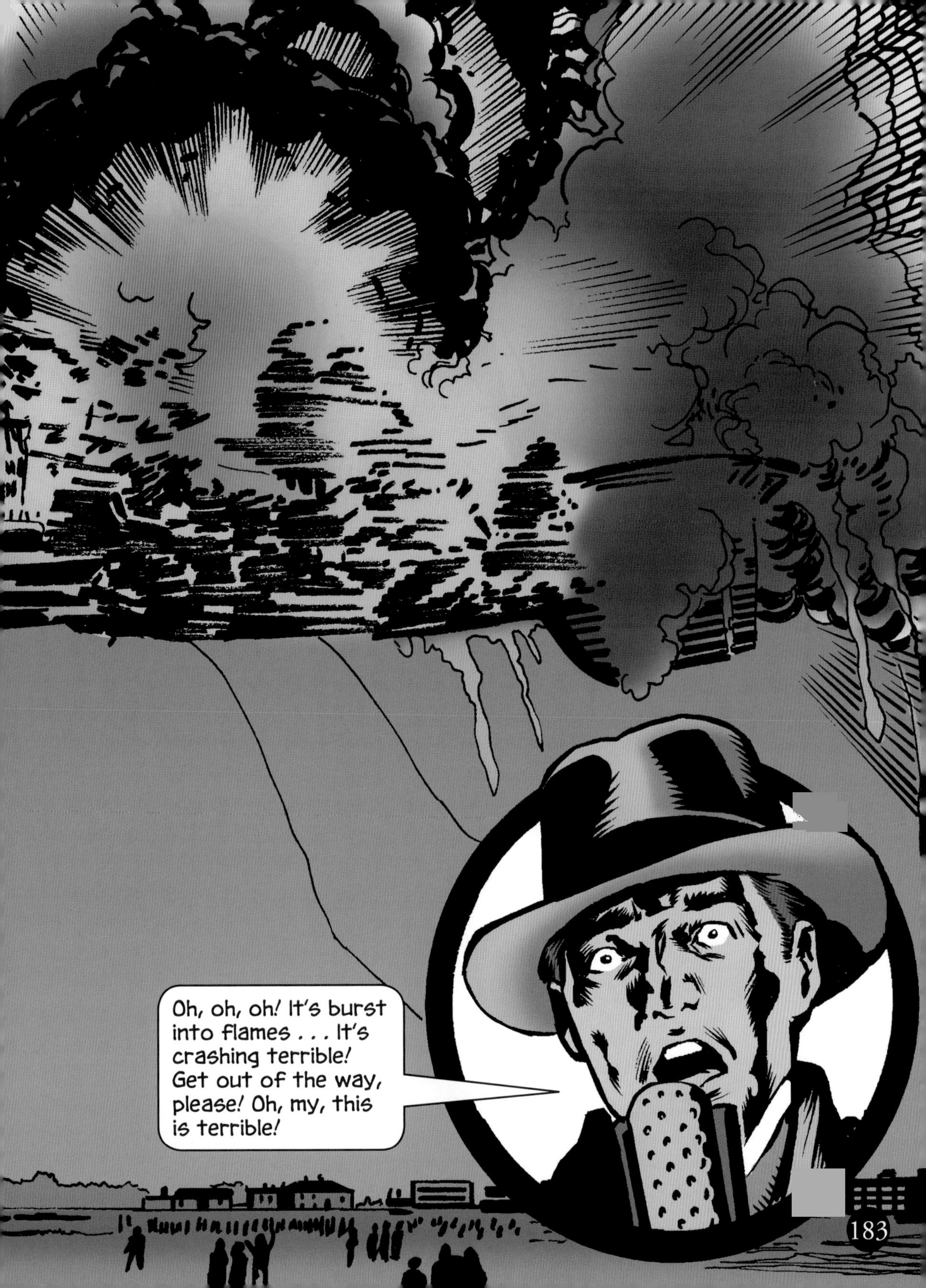
Oh, oh, oh! It's burst into flames . . . It's crashing terrible! Get out of the way, please! Oh, my, this is terrible!

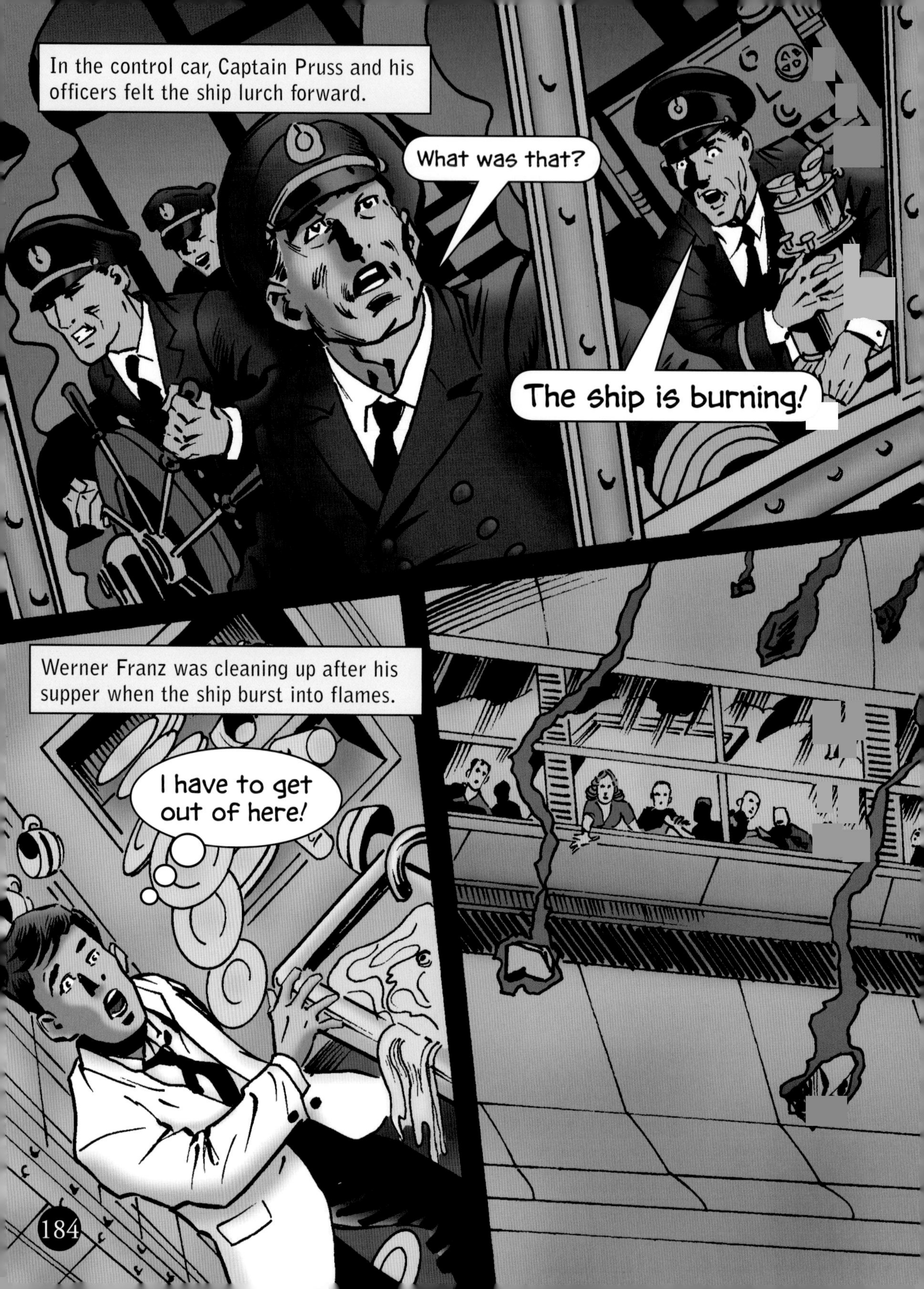
In the control car, Captain Pruss and his officers felt the ship lurch forward.
What was that?
The ship is burning!
Werner Franz was cleaning up after his supper when the ship burst into flames.
I have to get out of here!

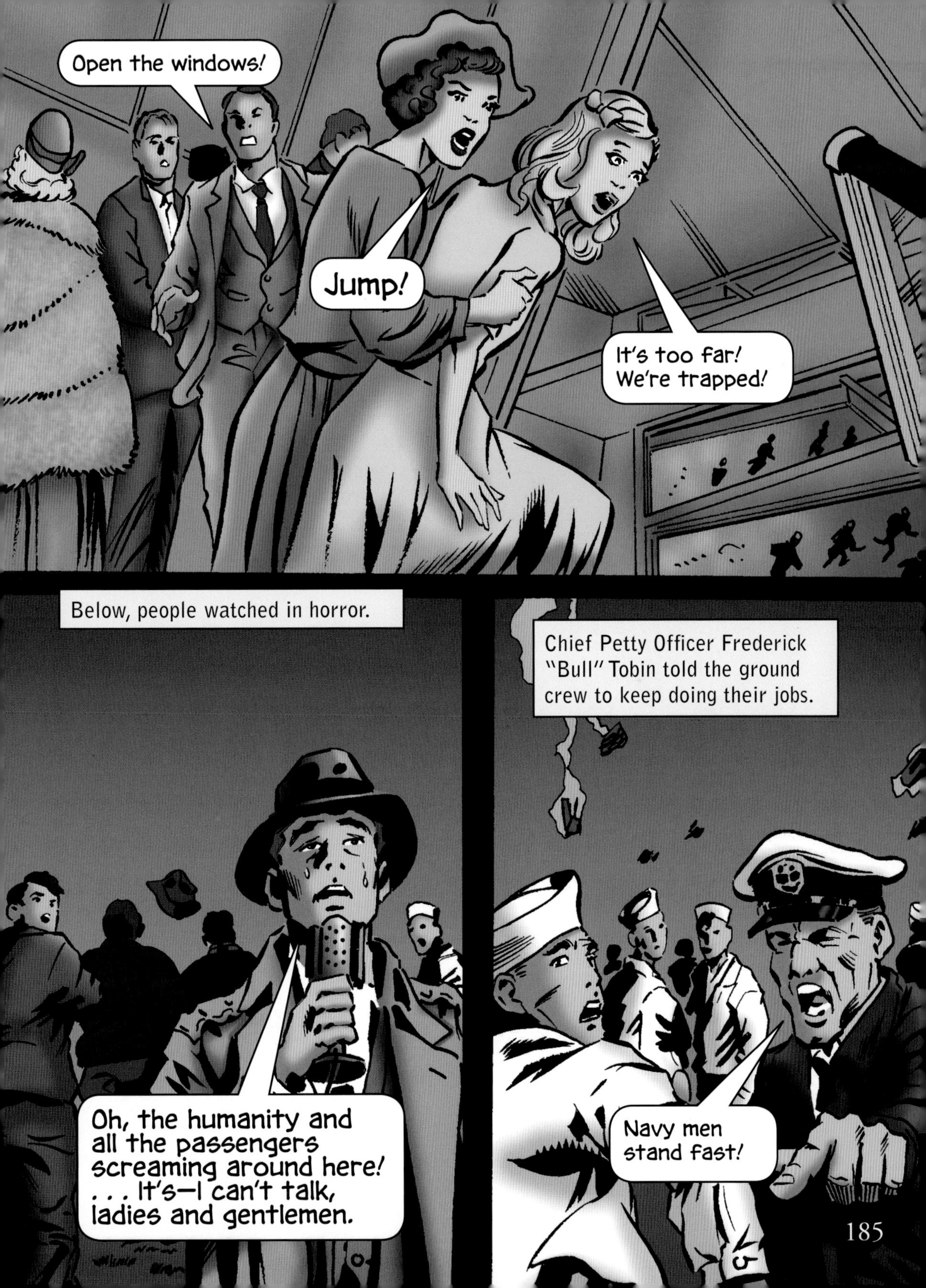
Open the windows!
Jump!
It's too far! We're trapped!
Below, people watched in horror.
Oh, the humanity and all the passengers screaming around here! . . . It's—I can't talk, ladies and gentlemen.
Chief Petty Officer Frederick "Bull" Tobin told the ground crew to keep doing their jobs.
Navy men stand fast!

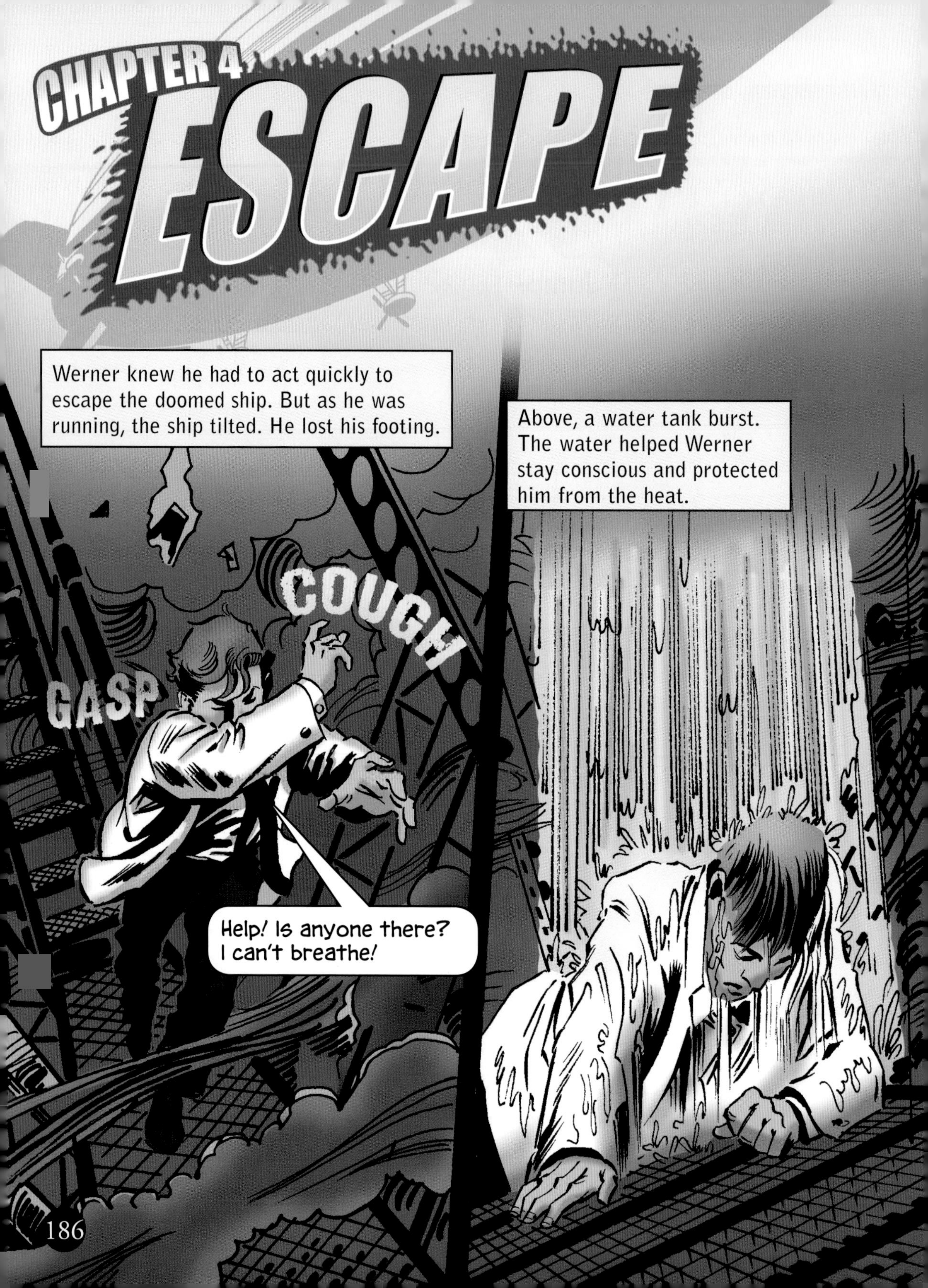
CHAPTER 4
ESCAPE
Werner knew he had to act quickly to escape the doomed ship. But as he was running, the ship tilted. He lost his footing.
COUGH
GASP
Help! Is anyone there? I can't breathe!
Above, a water tank burst. The water helped Werner stay conscious and protected him from the heat.

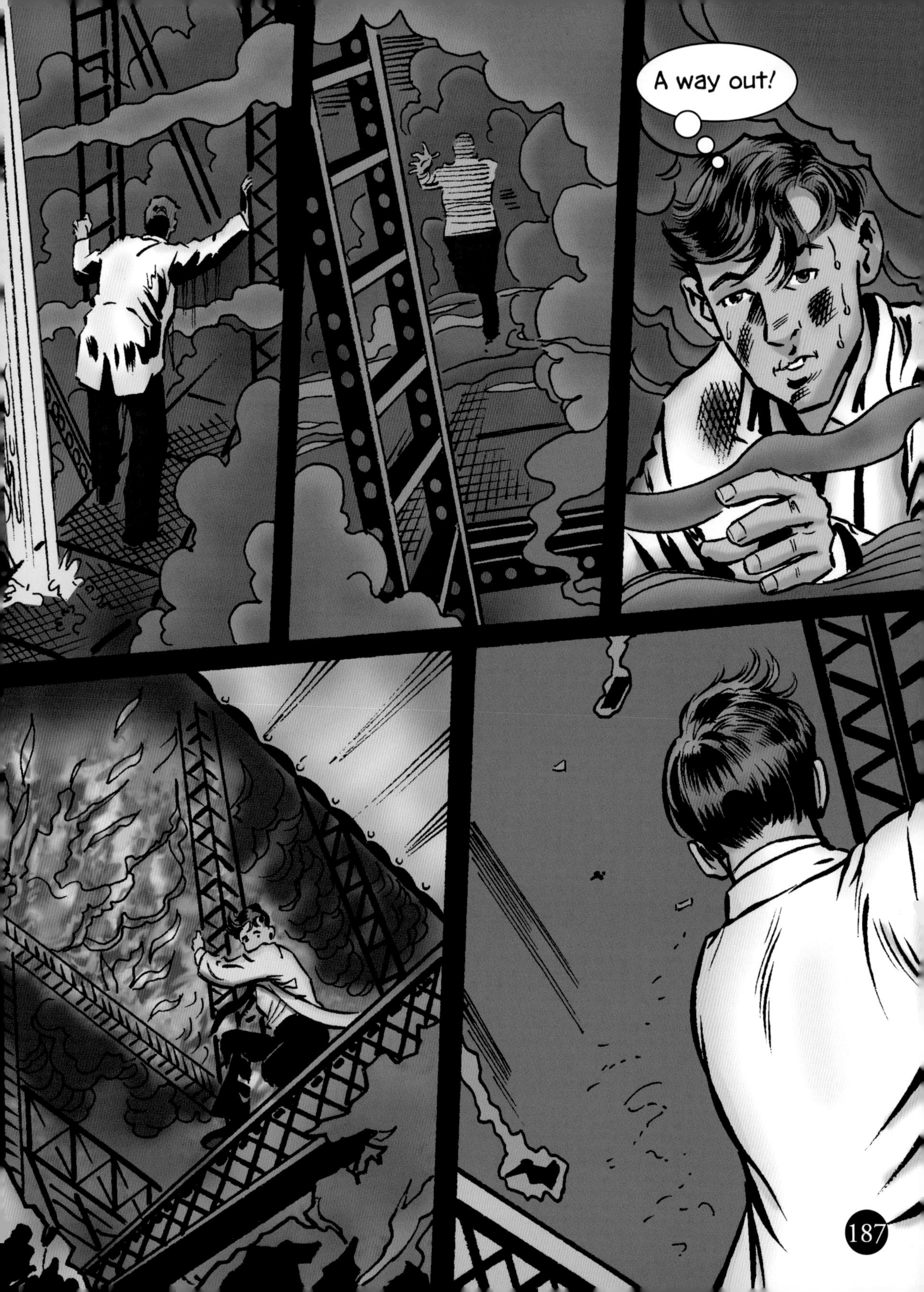
A way out!

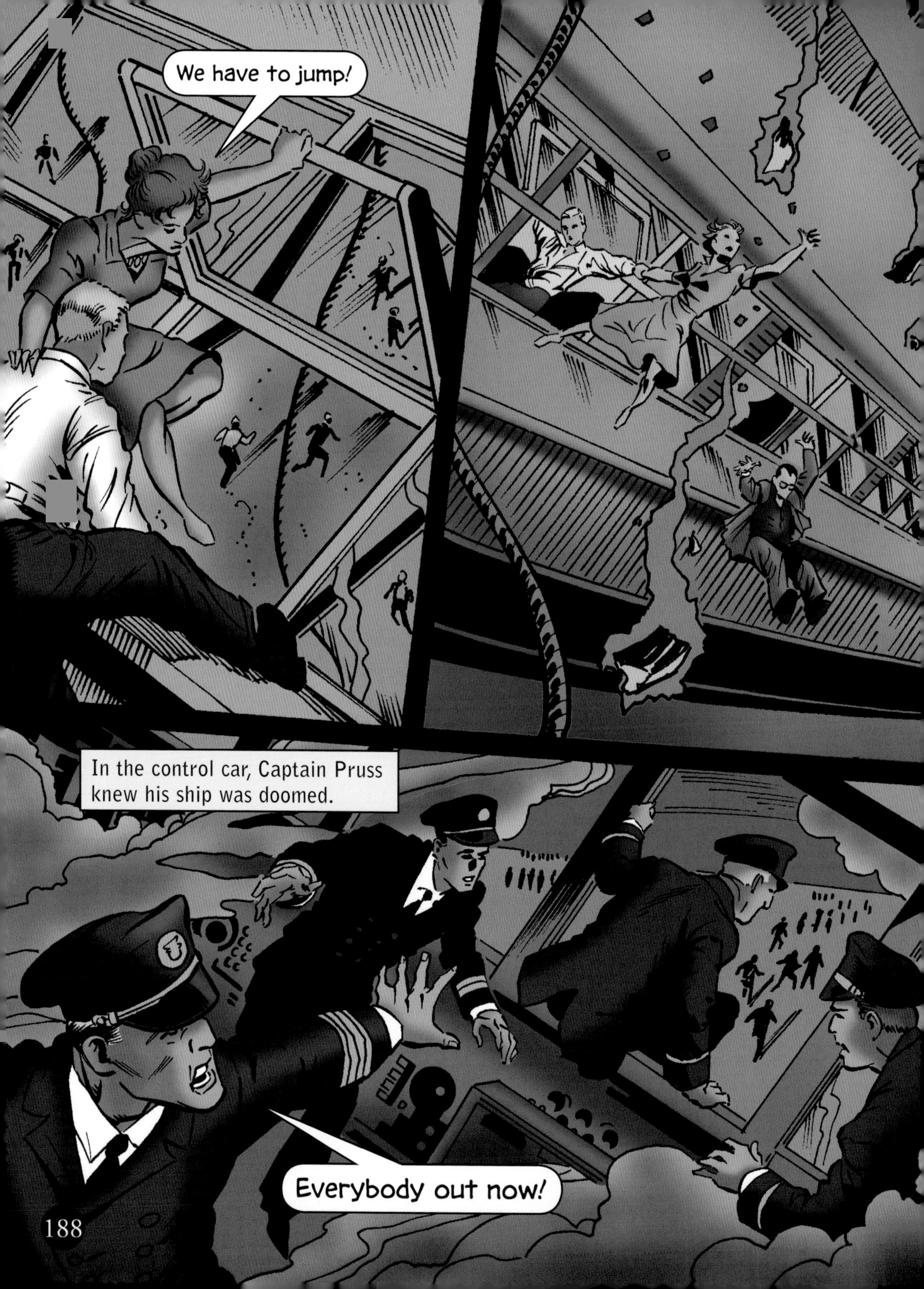
We have to jump!
In the control car, Captain Pruss knew his ship was doomed.
Everybody out now!

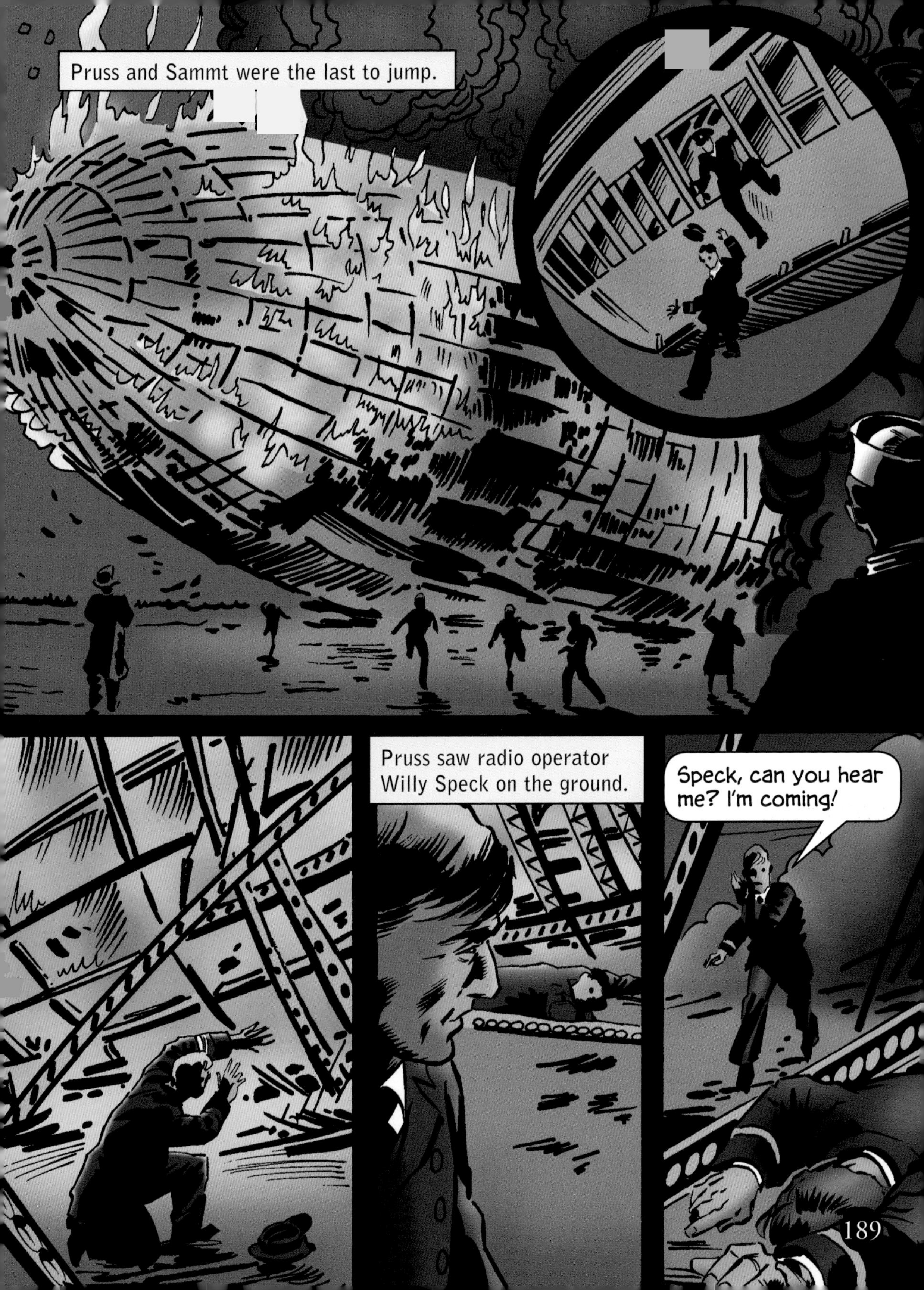
Pruss and Sammt were the last to jump.
Pruss saw radio operator Willy Speck on the ground.
Speck, can you hear me? I'm coming!

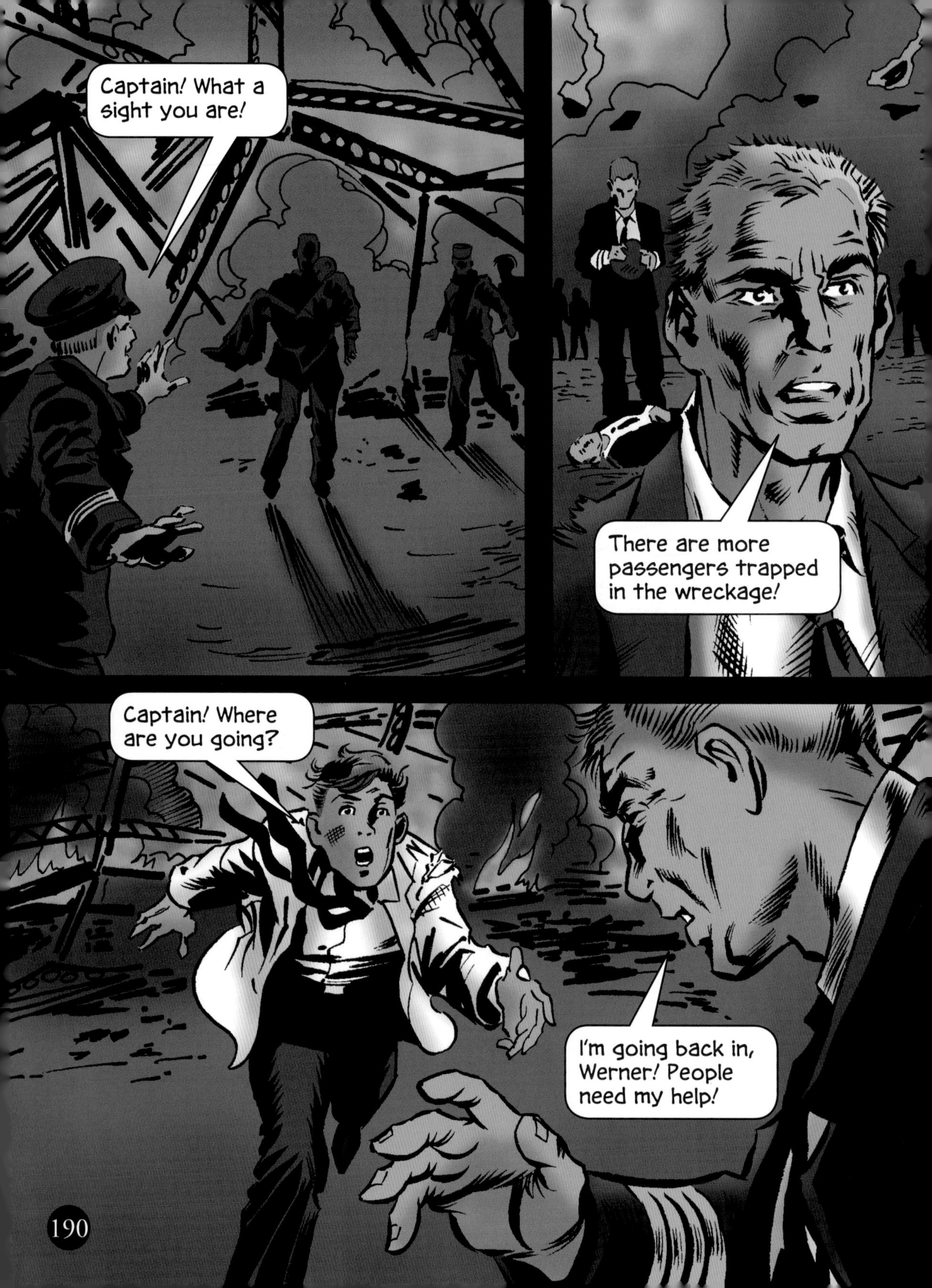
Captain! What a sight you are!
There are more passengers trapped in the wreckage!
Captain! Where are you going?
I'm going back in, Werner! People need my help!

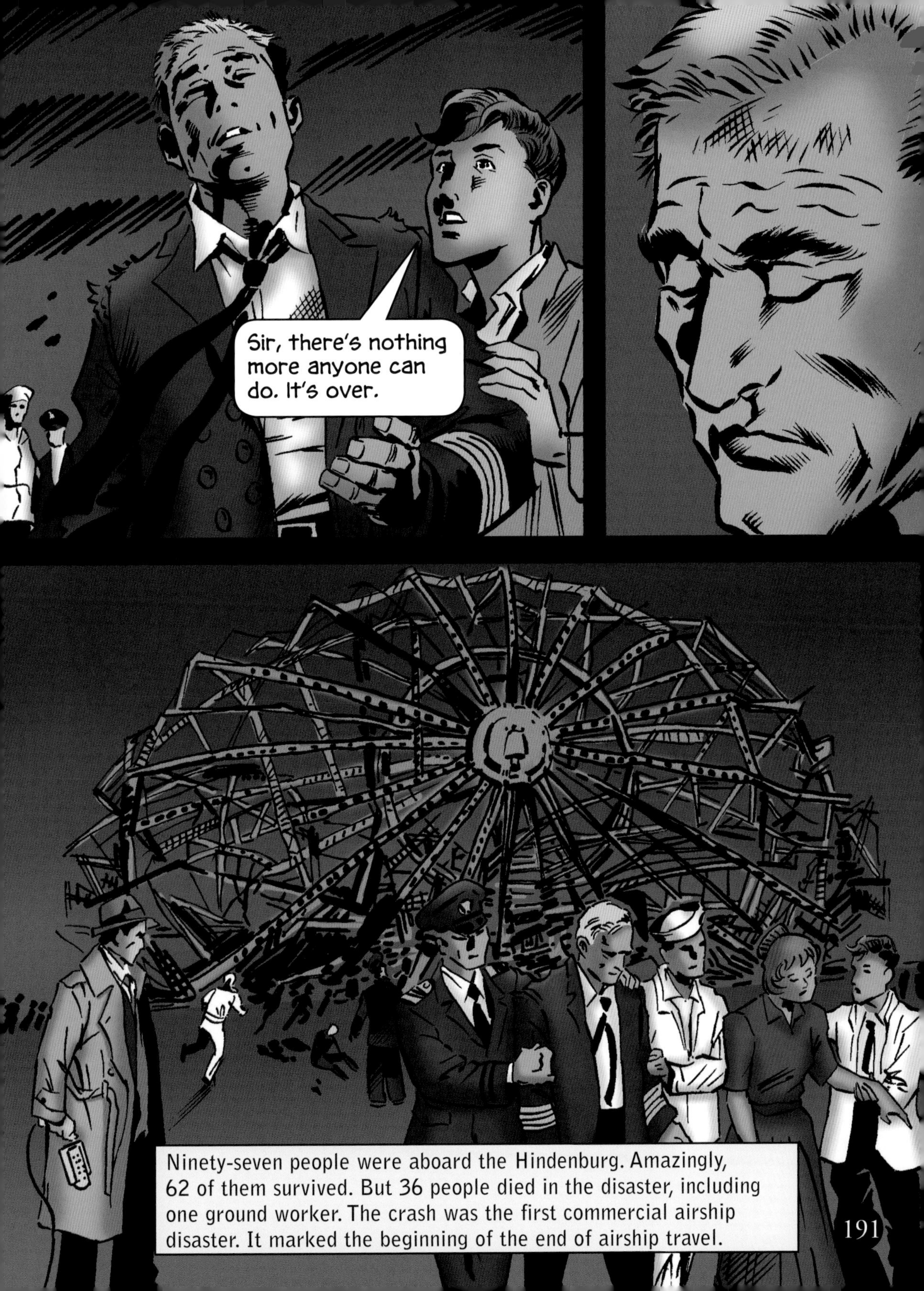
Sir, there's nothing more anyone can do. It's over.
Ninety-seven people were aboard the Hindenburg. Amazingly, 62 of them survived. But 36 people died in the disaster, including one ground worker. The crash was the first commercial airship disaster. It marked the beginning of the end of airship travel.

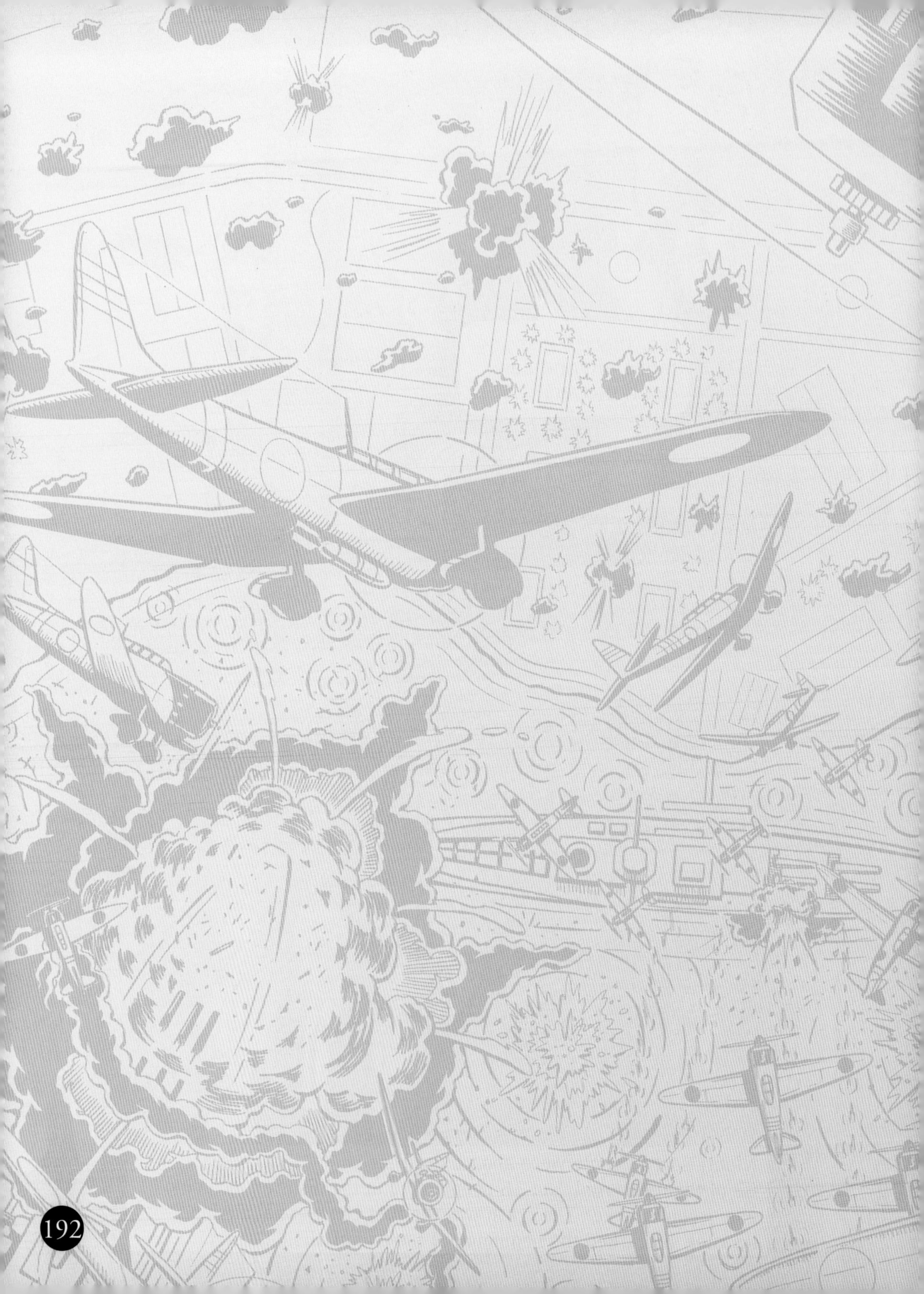

The Attack on Pearl Harbor

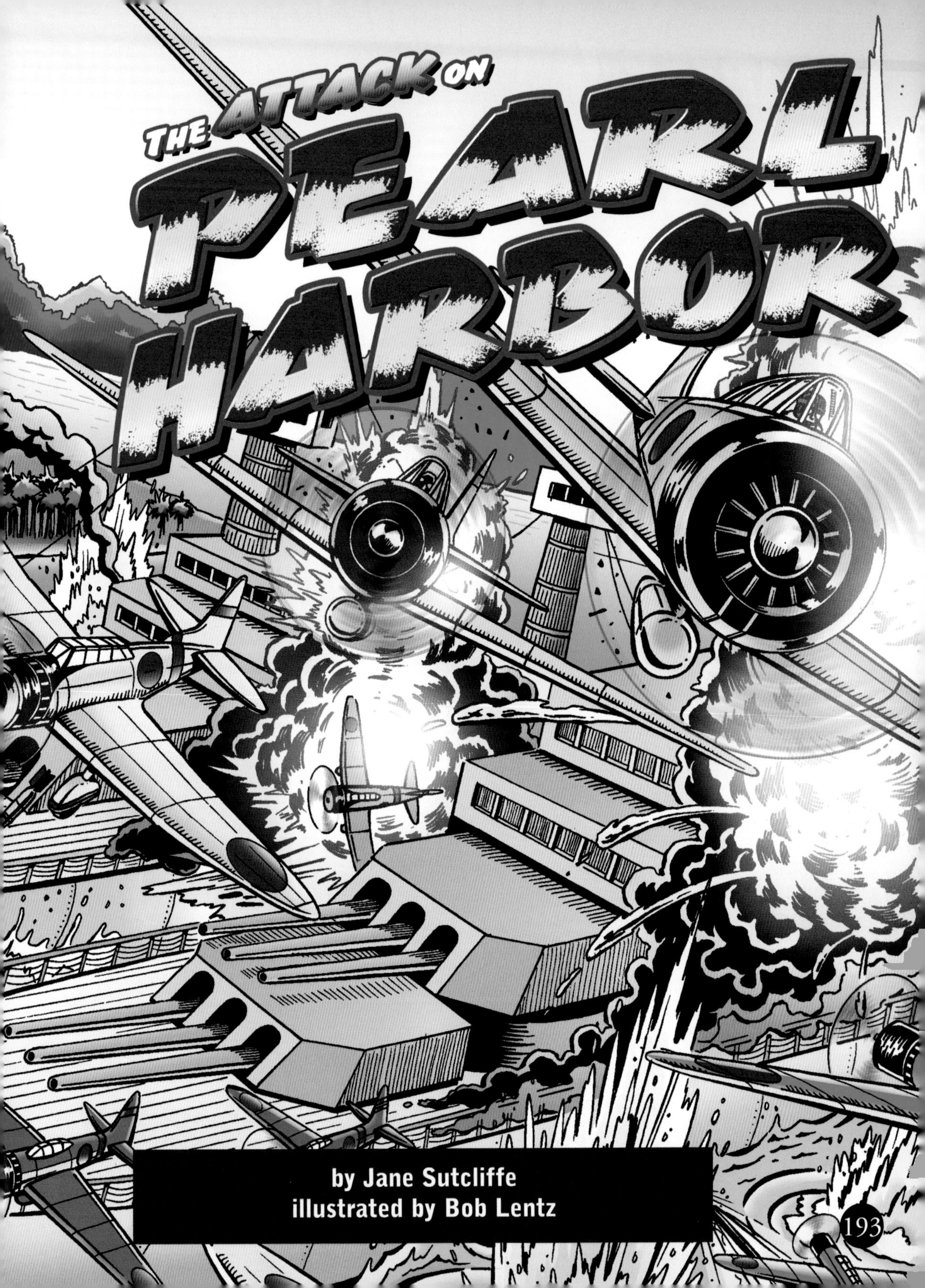

by Jane Sutcliffe
illustrated by Bob Lentz

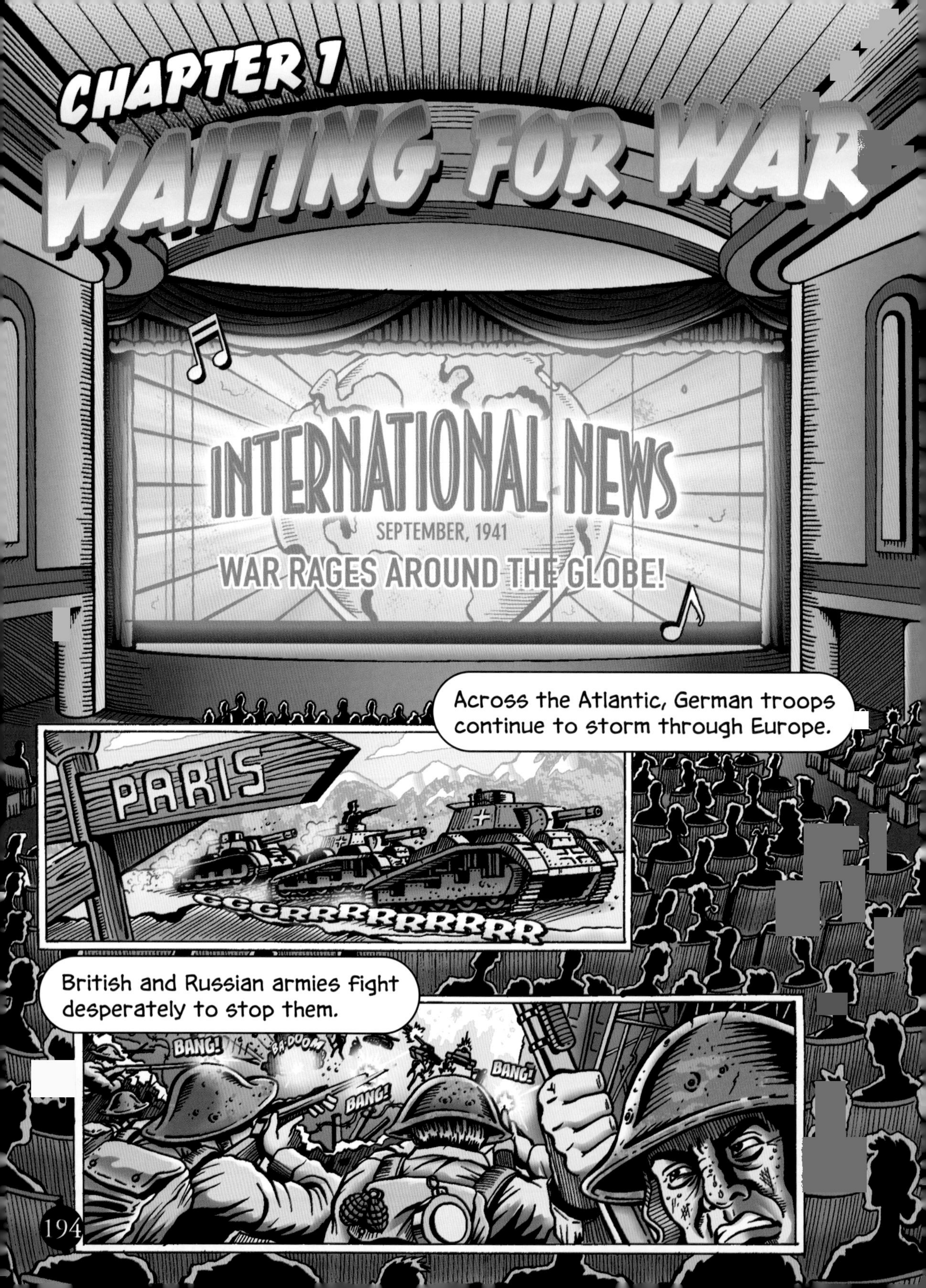
CHAPTER 1
WAITING FOR WAR
INTERNATIONAL NEWS
SEPTEMBER, 1941
WAR RAGES AROUND THE GLOBE!
Across the Atlantic, German troops continue to storm through Europe.
PARIS
GGGRRRRRRRRRRR
British and Russian armies fight desperately to stop them.
BANG!
BA-DOOM
BANG!
BANG!

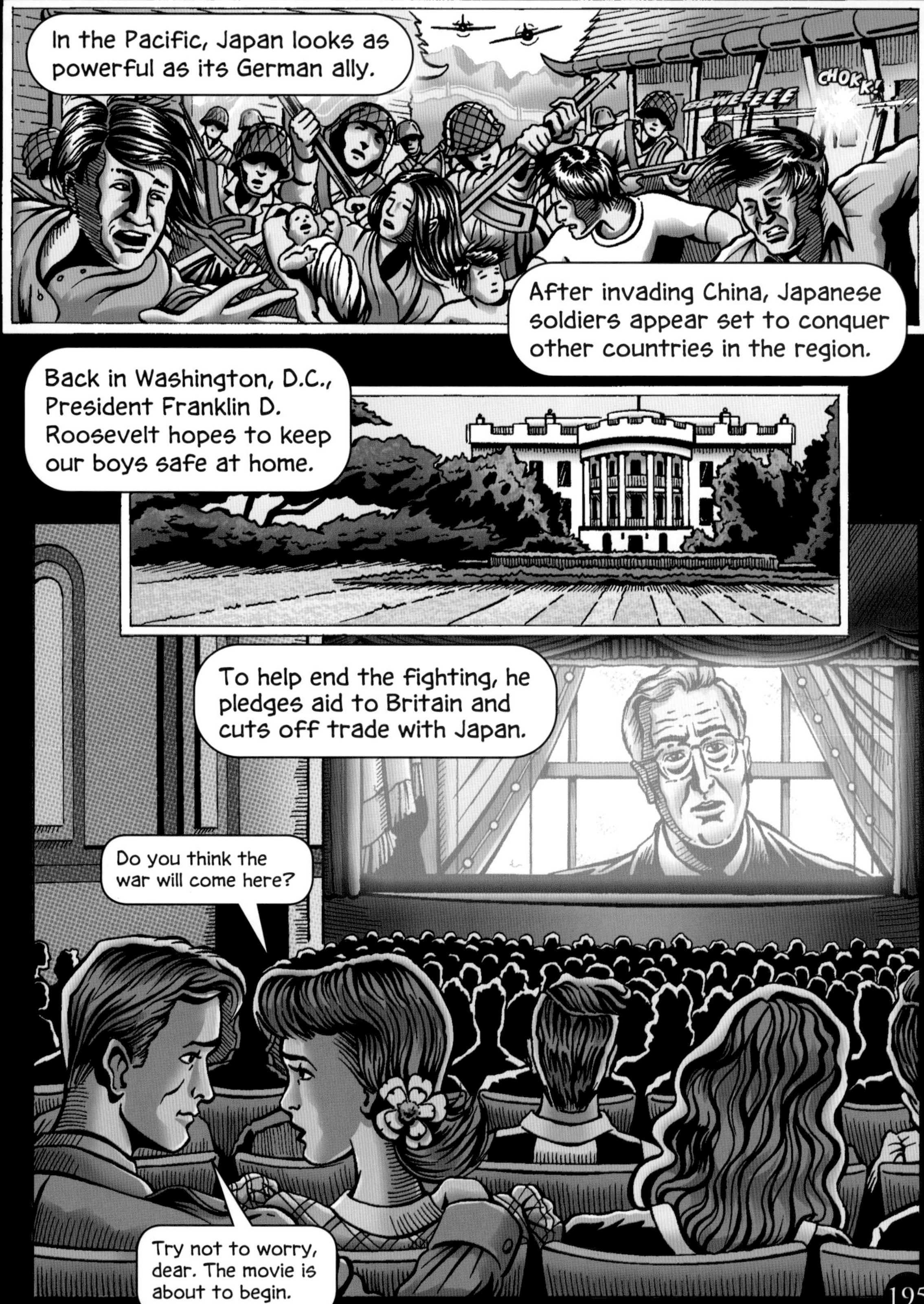

In the Pacific, Japan looks as powerful as its German ally.
CHOKK!
After invading China, Japanese soldiers appear set to conquer other countries in the region.
Back in Washington, D.C., President Franklin D. Roosevelt hopes to keep our boys safe at home.
To help end the fighting, he pledges aid to Britain and cuts off trade with Japan.
Do you think the war will come here?
Try not to worry, dear. The movie is about to begin.

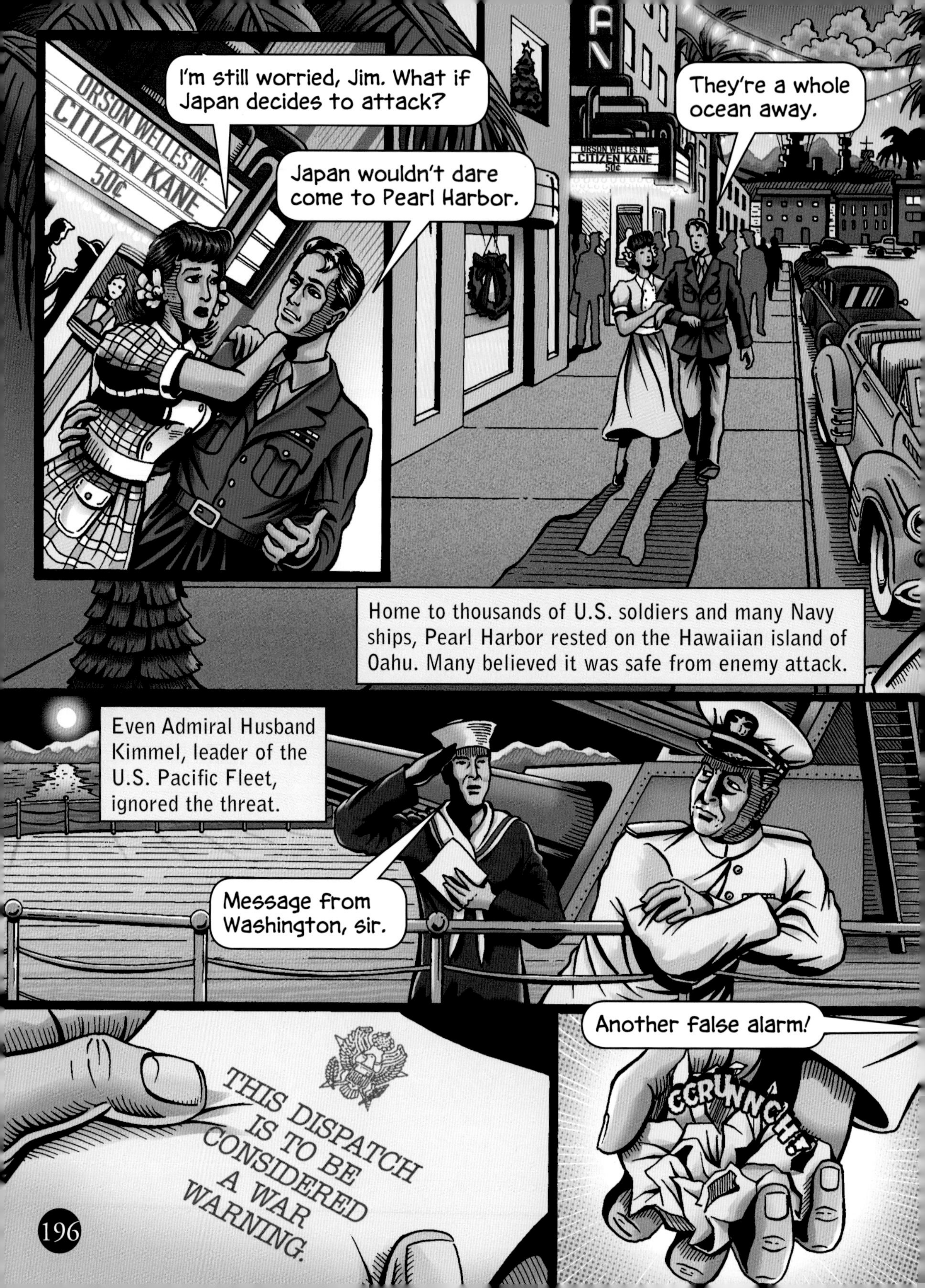
ORSON WELLES IN: CITIZEN KANE 50¢
I'm still worried, Jim. What if Japan decides to attack?
Japan wouldn't dare come to Pearl Harbor.
They're a whole ocean away.
Home to thousands of U.S. soldiers and many Navy ships, Pearl Harbor rested on the Hawaiian island of Oahu. Many believed it was safe from enemy attack.
Even Admiral Husband Kimmel, leader of the U.S. Pacific Fleet, ignored the threat.
Message from Washington, sir.
THIS DISPATCH IS TO BE CONSIDERED A WAR WARNING.
Another false alarm!
CCRUNNCH!

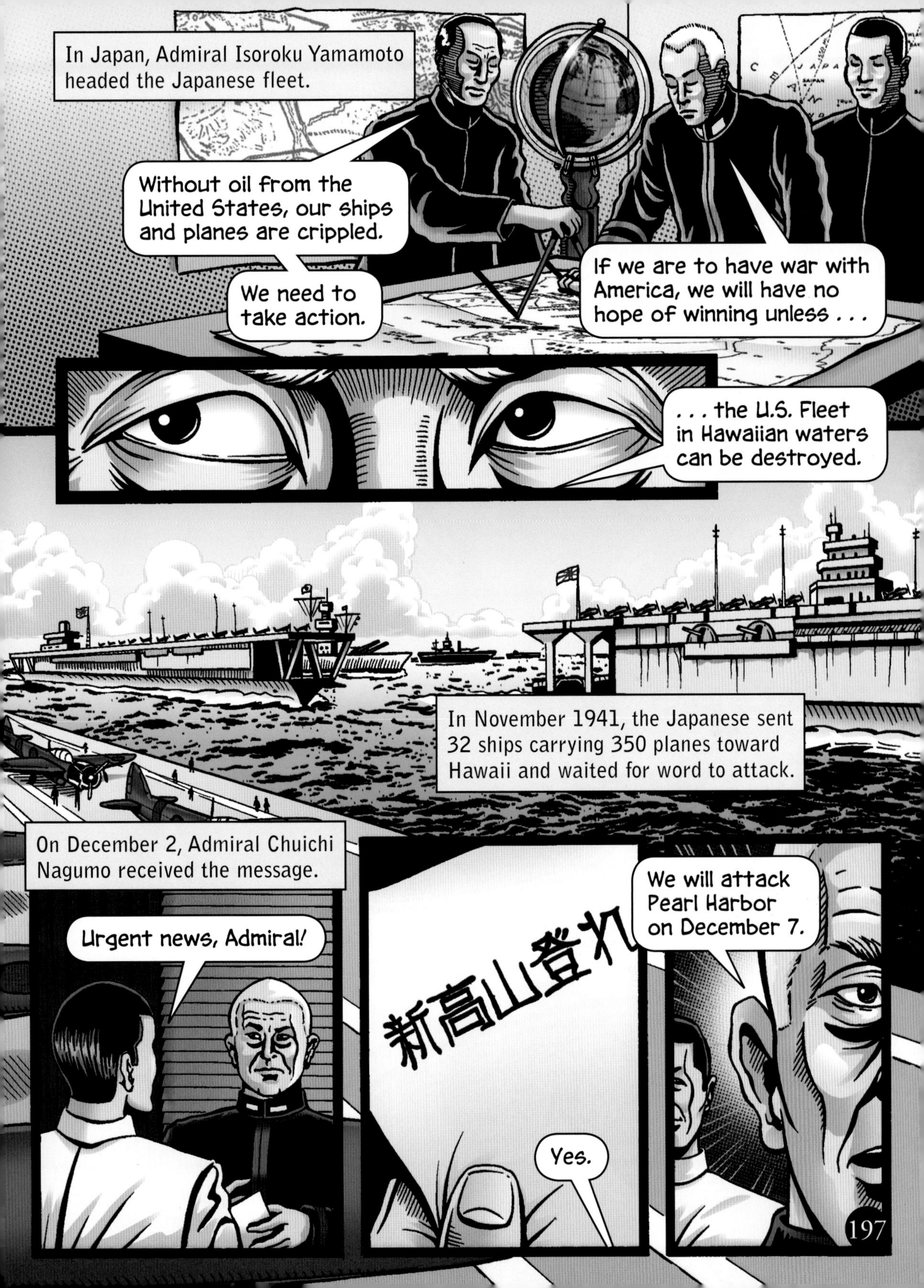

In Japan, Admiral Isoroku Yamamoto headed the Japanese fleet.
Without oil from the United States, our ships and planes are crippled.
We need to take action.
If we are to have war with America, we will have no hope of winning unless . . .
. . . the U.S. Fleet in Hawaiian waters can be destroyed.
In November 1941, the Japanese sent 32 ships carrying 350 planes toward Hawaii and waited for word to attack.
On December 2, Admiral Chuichi Nagumo received the message.
Urgent news, Admiral!
新高山登れ
Yes.
We will attack Pearl Harbor on December 7.

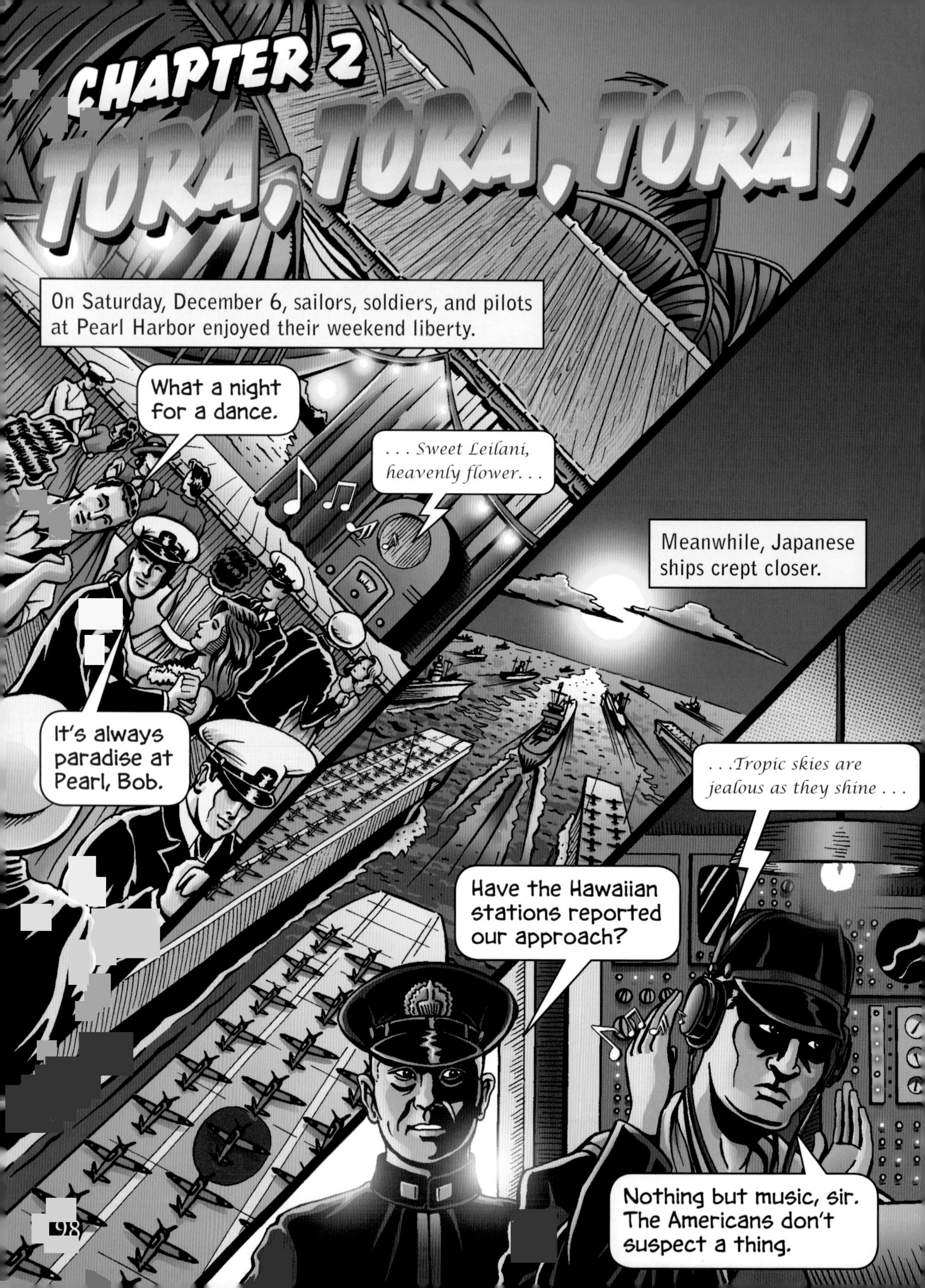
CHAPTER 2
TORA, TORA, TORA!
On Saturday, December 6, sailors, soldiers, and pilots at Pearl Harbor enjoyed their weekend liberty.
What a night for a dance.
. . . Sweet Leilani, heavenly flower. . .
It's always paradise at Pearl, Bob.
Meanwhile, Japanese ships crept closer.
. . .Tropic skies are jealous as they shine . . .
Have the Hawaiian stations reported our approach?
Nothing but music, sir. The Americans don't suspect a thing.

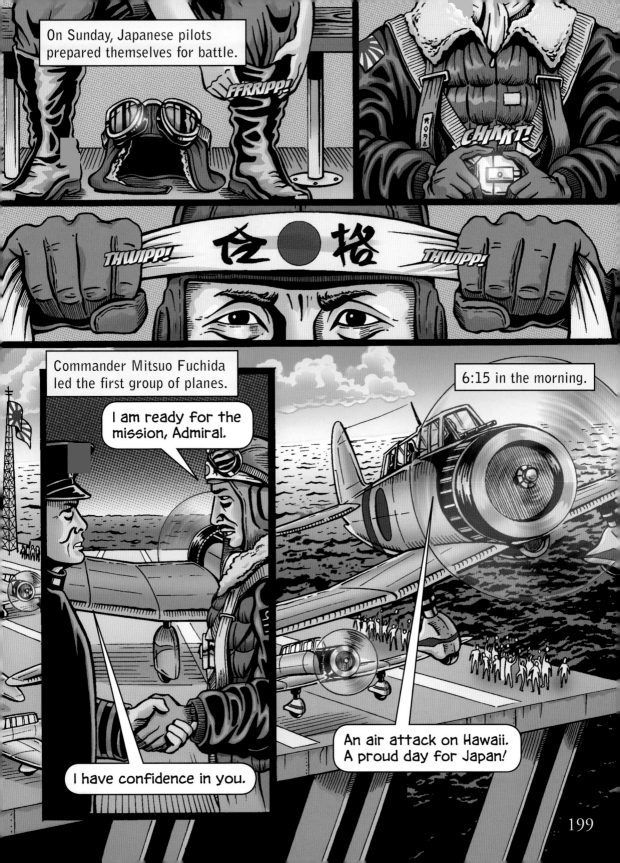

On Sunday, Japanese pilots prepared themselves for battle.

FFRRIPP!

CHIKKT!

THWIPP!   THWIPP!

合 格

Commander Mitsuo Fuchida led the first group of planes.

I am ready for the mission, Admiral.

I have confidence in you.

6:15 in the morning.

An air attack on Hawaii. A proud day for Japan!

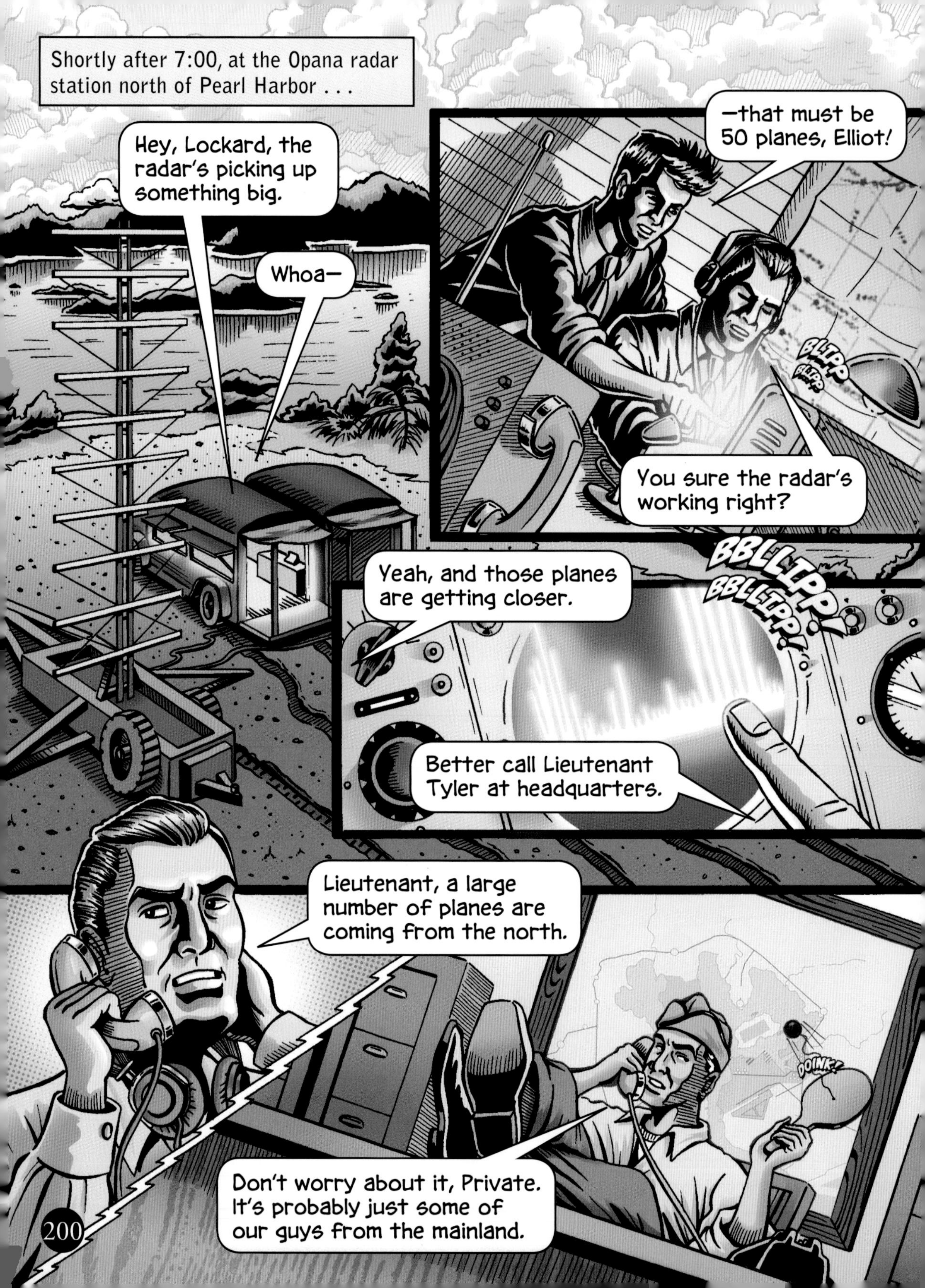

Shortly after 7:00, at the Opana radar station north of Pearl Harbor . . .
Hey, Lockard, the radar's picking up something big.
Whoa—
—that must be 50 planes, Elliot!
BLIPP
BLIPP
You sure the radar's working right?
BBLLIPP!
BBLLIPP!
Yeah, and those planes are getting closer.
Better call Lieutenant Tyler at headquarters.
Lieutenant, a large number of planes are coming from the north.
DOINK!
Don't worry about it, Private. It's probably just some of our guys from the mainland.

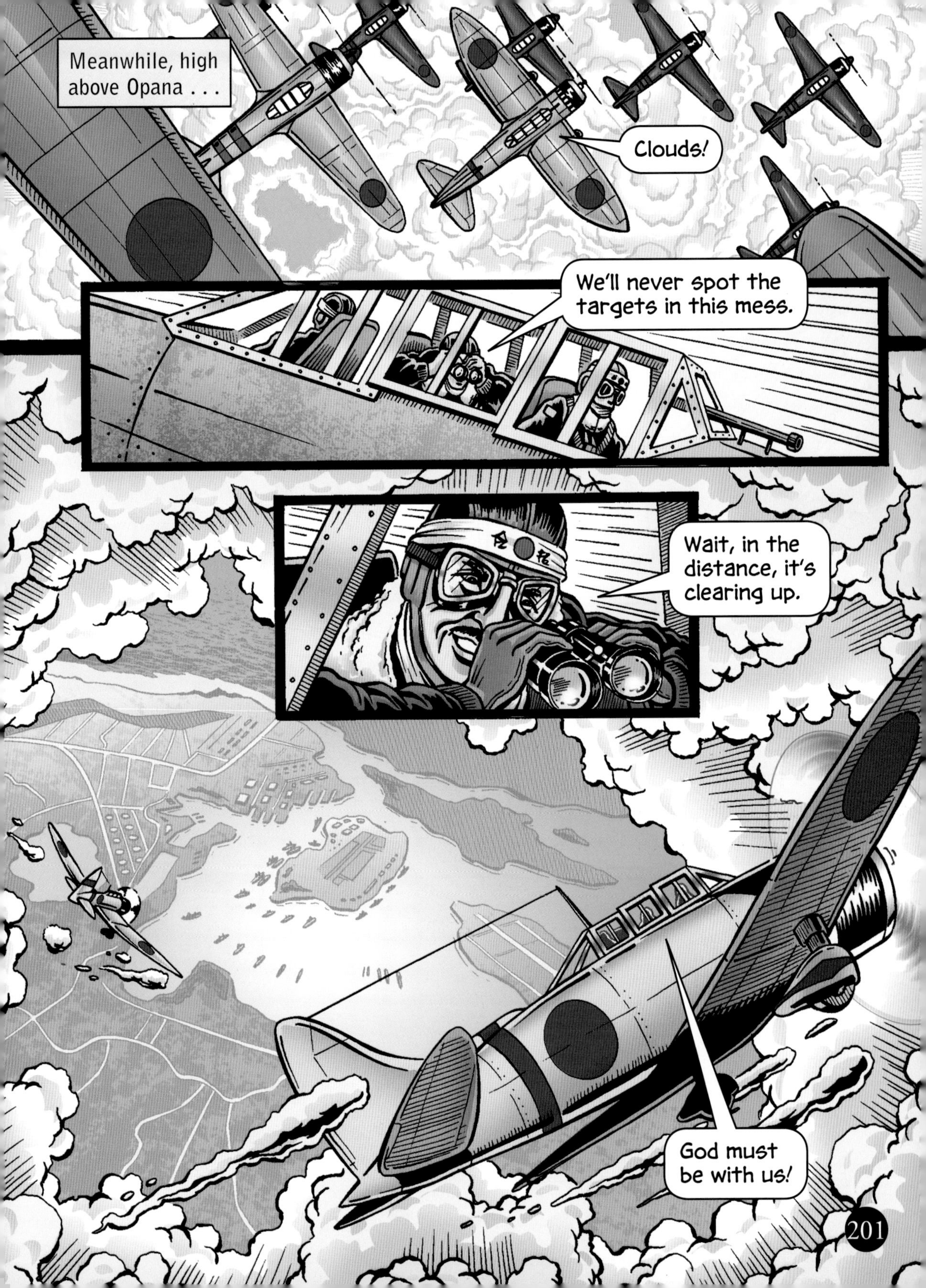
Meanwhile, high above Opana . . .
Clouds!
We'll never spot the targets in this mess.
Wait, in the distance, it's clearing up.
God must be with us!

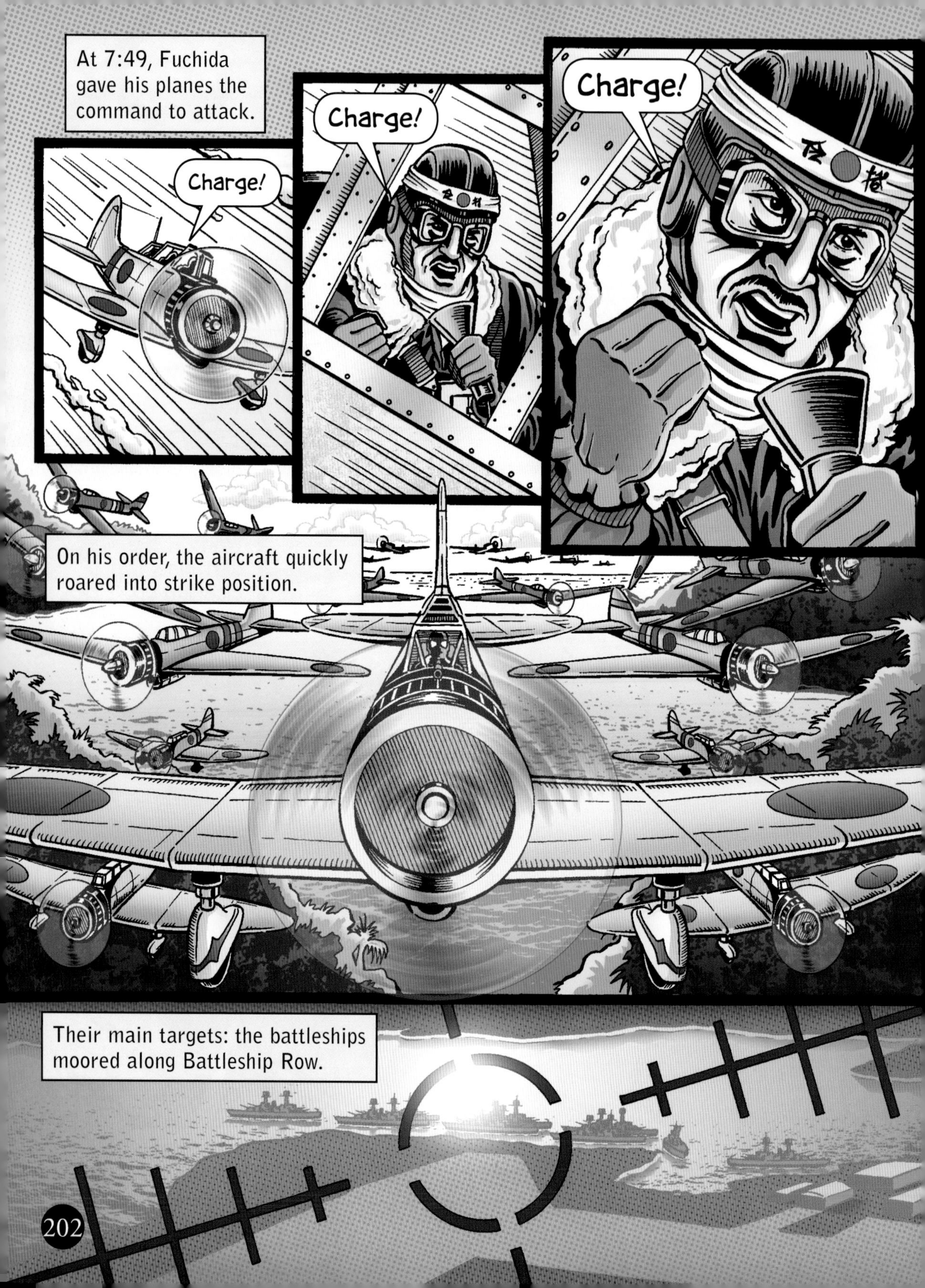
At 7:49, Fuchida gave his planes the command to attack.
Charge!
Charge!
Charge!
On his order, the aircraft quickly roared into strike position.
Their main targets: the battleships moored along Battleship Row.

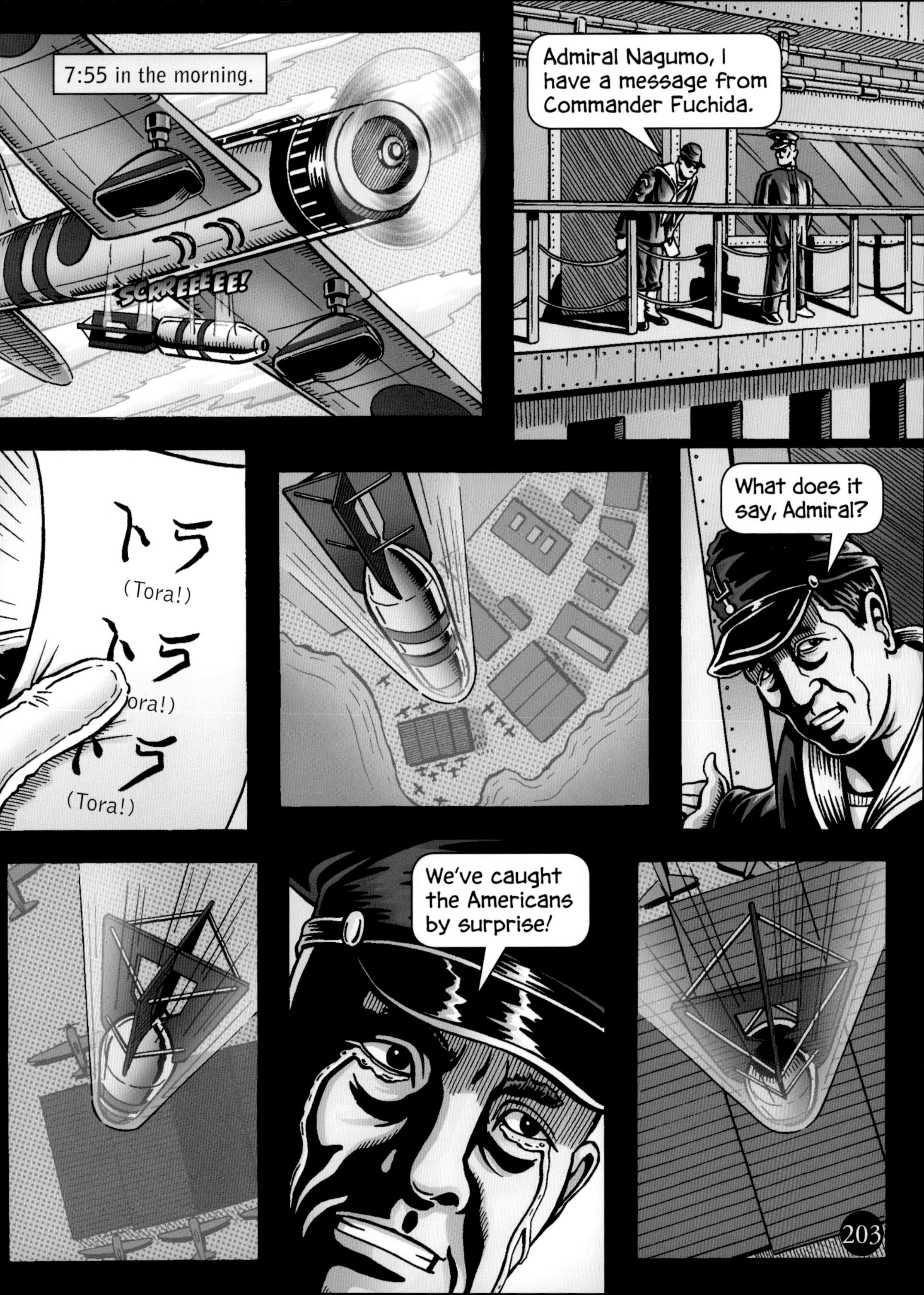
7:55 in the morning.
SCREEEEE!
Admiral Nagumo, I have a message from Commander Fuchida.
トラ
(Tora!)
トラ
ラ
(Tora!)
What does it say, Admiral?
We've caught the Americans by surprise!

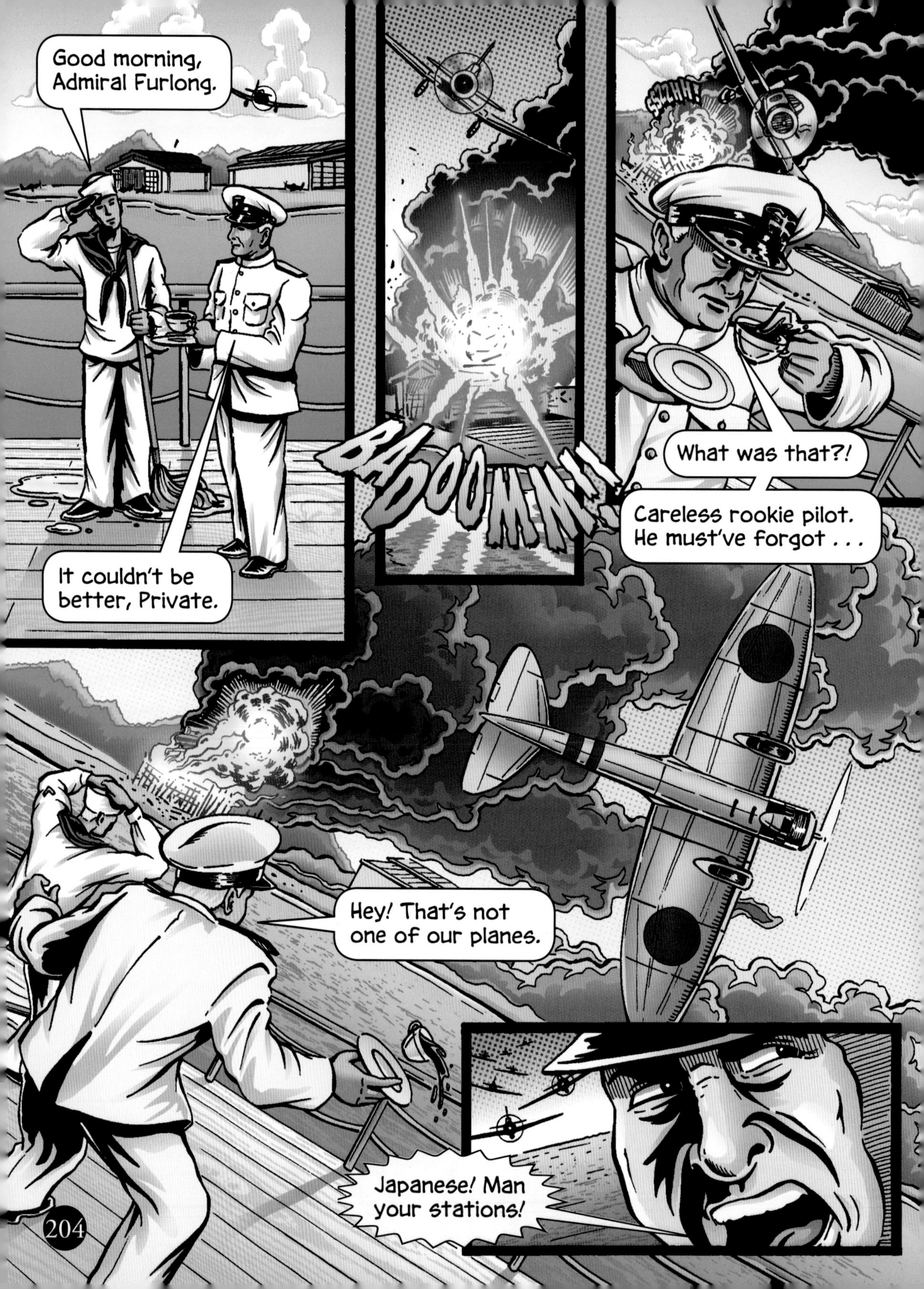
Good morning, Admiral Furlong.
It couldn't be better, Private.
BADOOMM!!
SSZZHH!
What was that?!
Careless rookie pilot. He must've forgot . . .
Hey! That's not one of our planes.
Japanese! Man your stations!

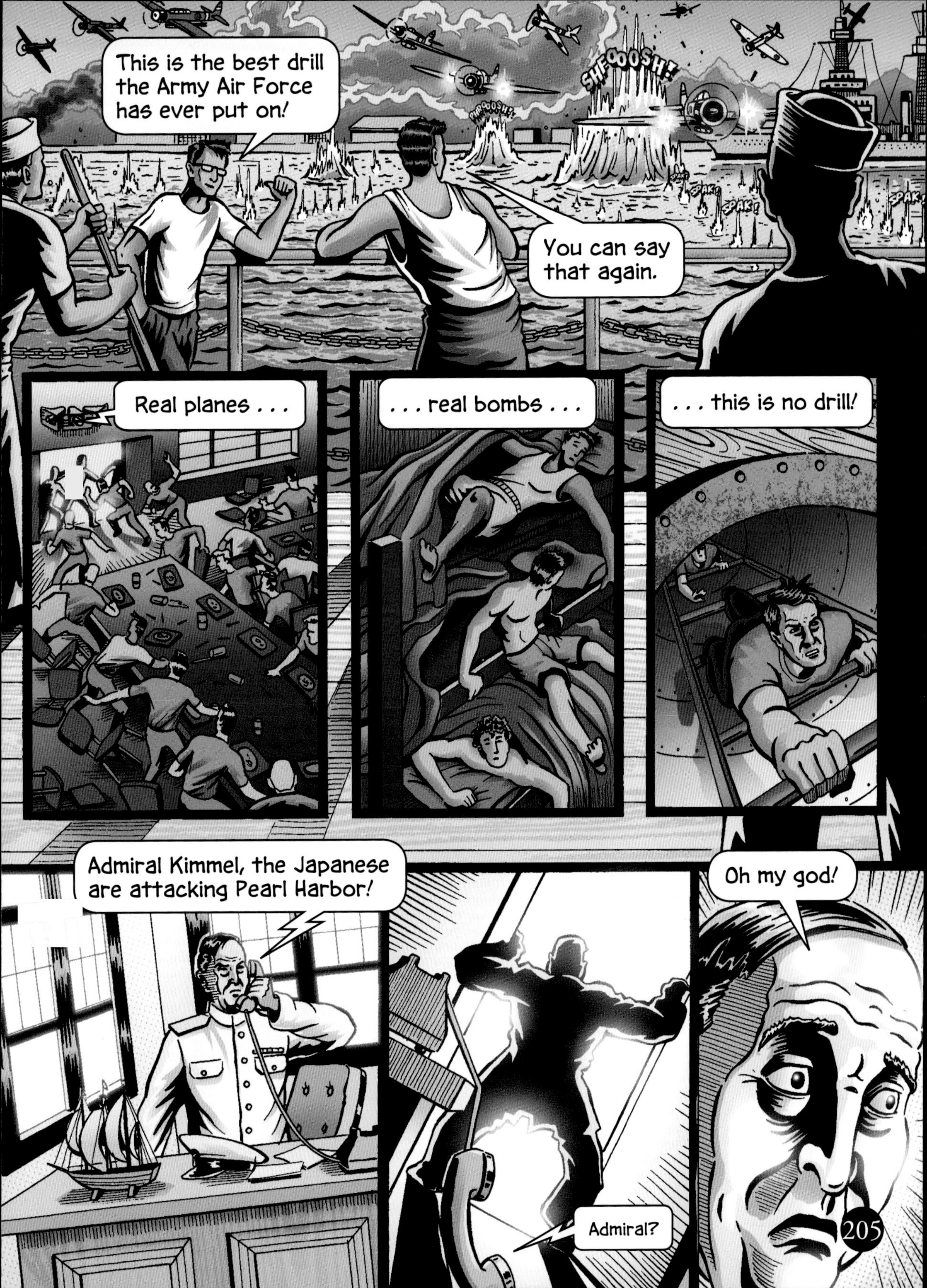
This is the best drill the Army Air Force has ever put on!
SHFOOOSH!
You can say that again.
SPAK!
Real planes . . .
. . . real bombs . . .
. . . this is no drill!
Admiral Kimmel, the Japanese are attacking Pearl Harbor!
Oh my god!
Admiral?

CHAPTER 3
BATTLE STATIONS!

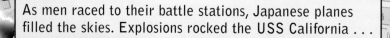

As men raced to their battle stations, Japanese planes filled the skies. Explosions rocked the USS California . . .

KABOOM!

BLAMM!

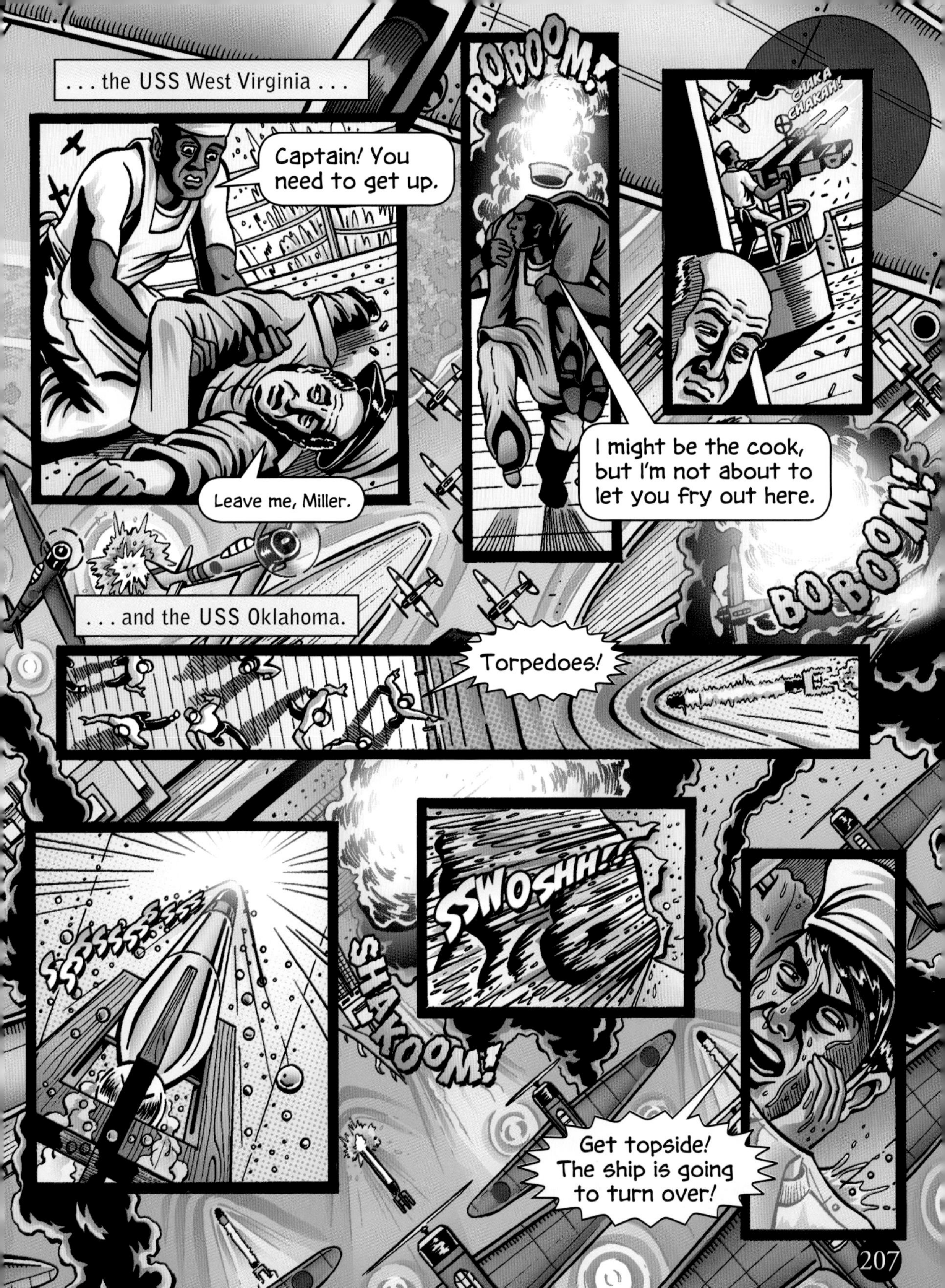
. . . the USS West Virginia . . .
Captain! You need to get up.
Leave me, Miller.
BOBOOM!
I might be the cook, but I'm not about to let you fry out here.
CHAKA CHAKAH!
BOBOOM!
. . . and the USS Oklahoma.
Torpedoes!
SSSSSSSSSS
SHAKOOM!
SSWOSHH!!
Get topside! The ship is going to turn over!

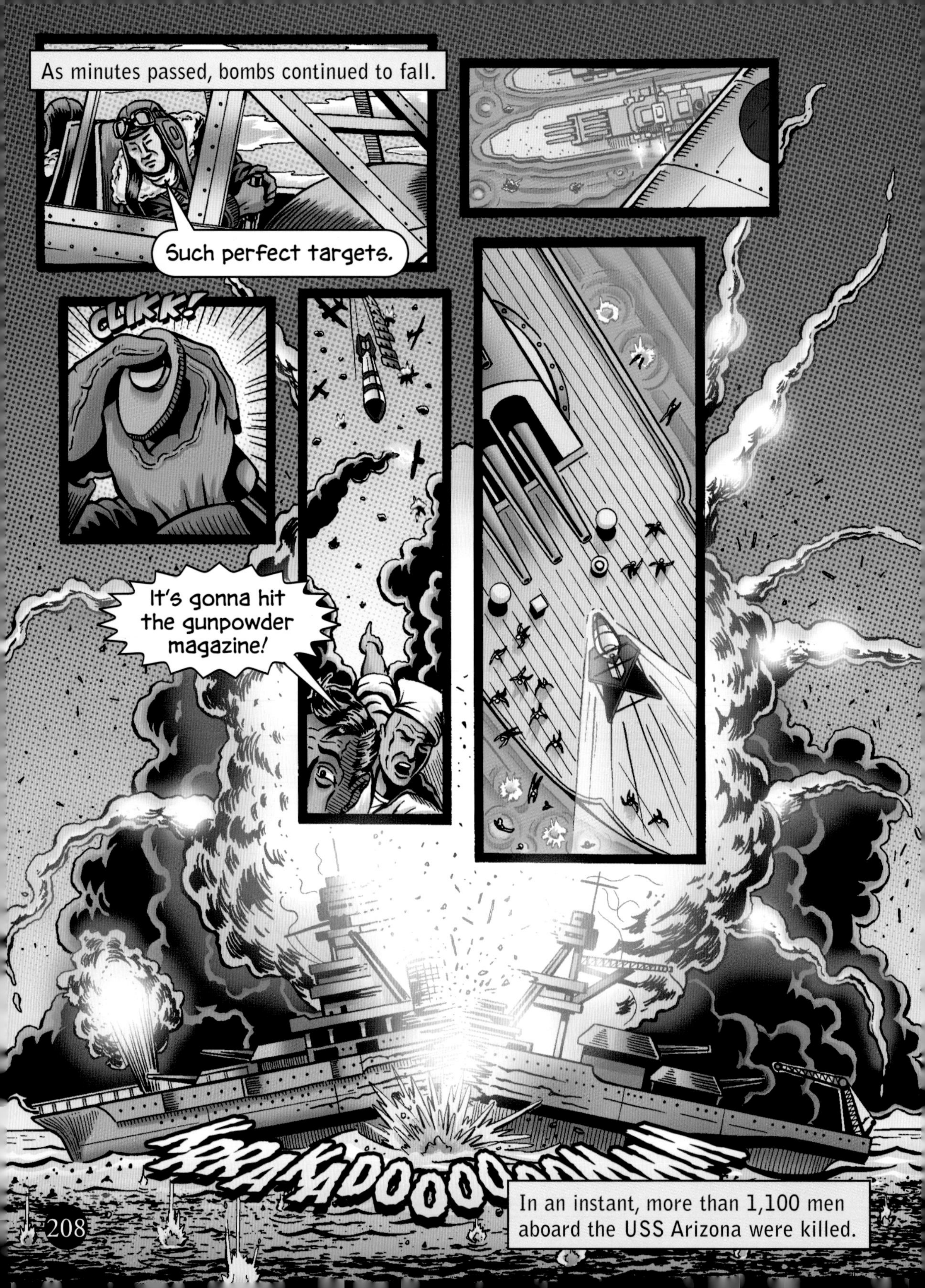

As minutes passed, bombs continued to fall.
Such perfect targets.
CLIKK!
It's gonna hit the gunpowder magazine!
In an instant, more than 1,100 men aboard the USS Arizona were killed.

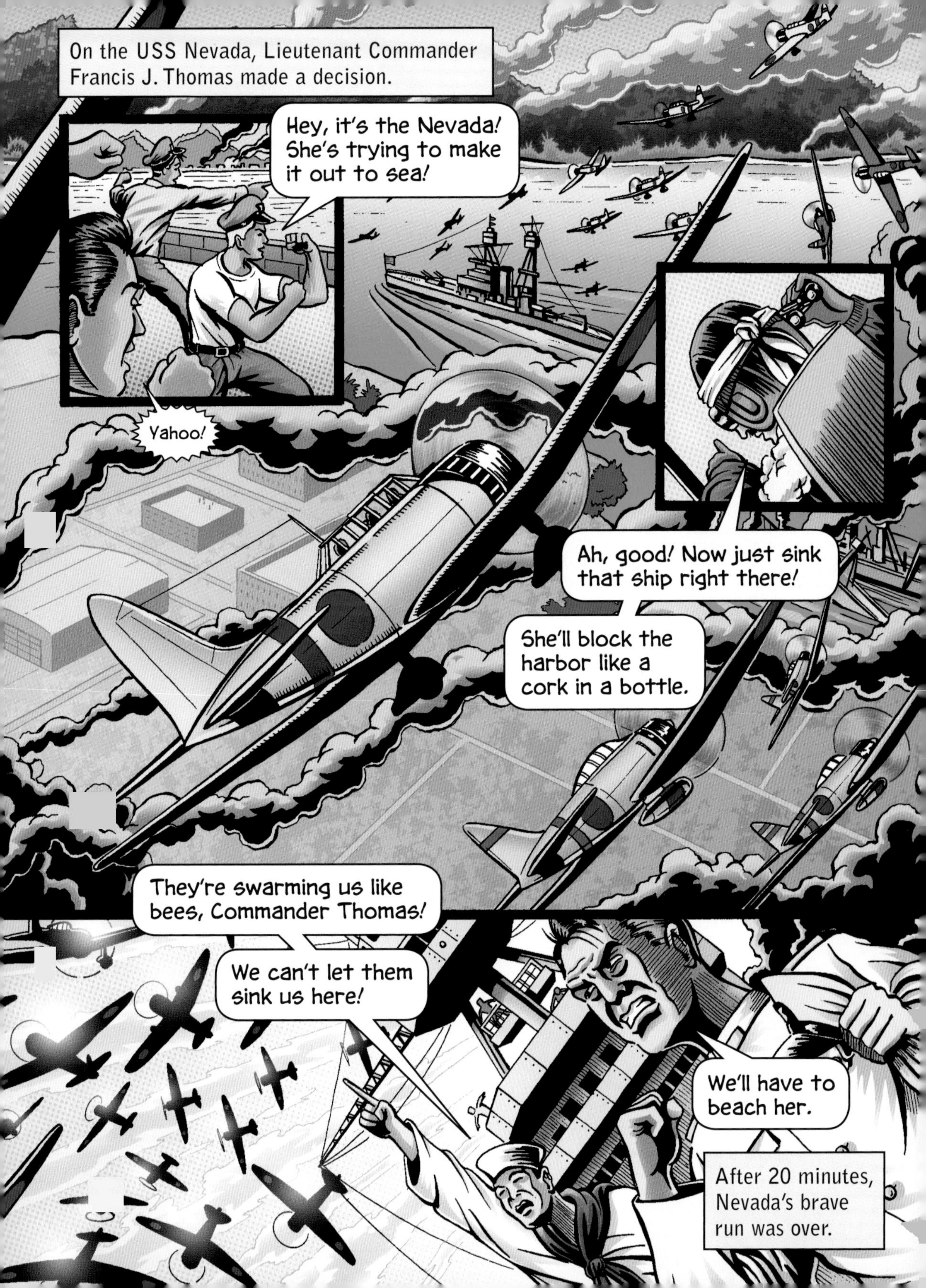
On the USS Nevada, Lieutenant Commander Francis J. Thomas made a decision.
Hey, it's the Nevada! She's trying to make it out to sea!
Yahoo!
Ah, good! Now just sink that ship right there!
She'll block the harbor like a cork in a bottle.
They're swarming us like bees, Commander Thomas!
We can't let them sink us here!
We'll have to beach her.
After 20 minutes, Nevada's brave run was over.

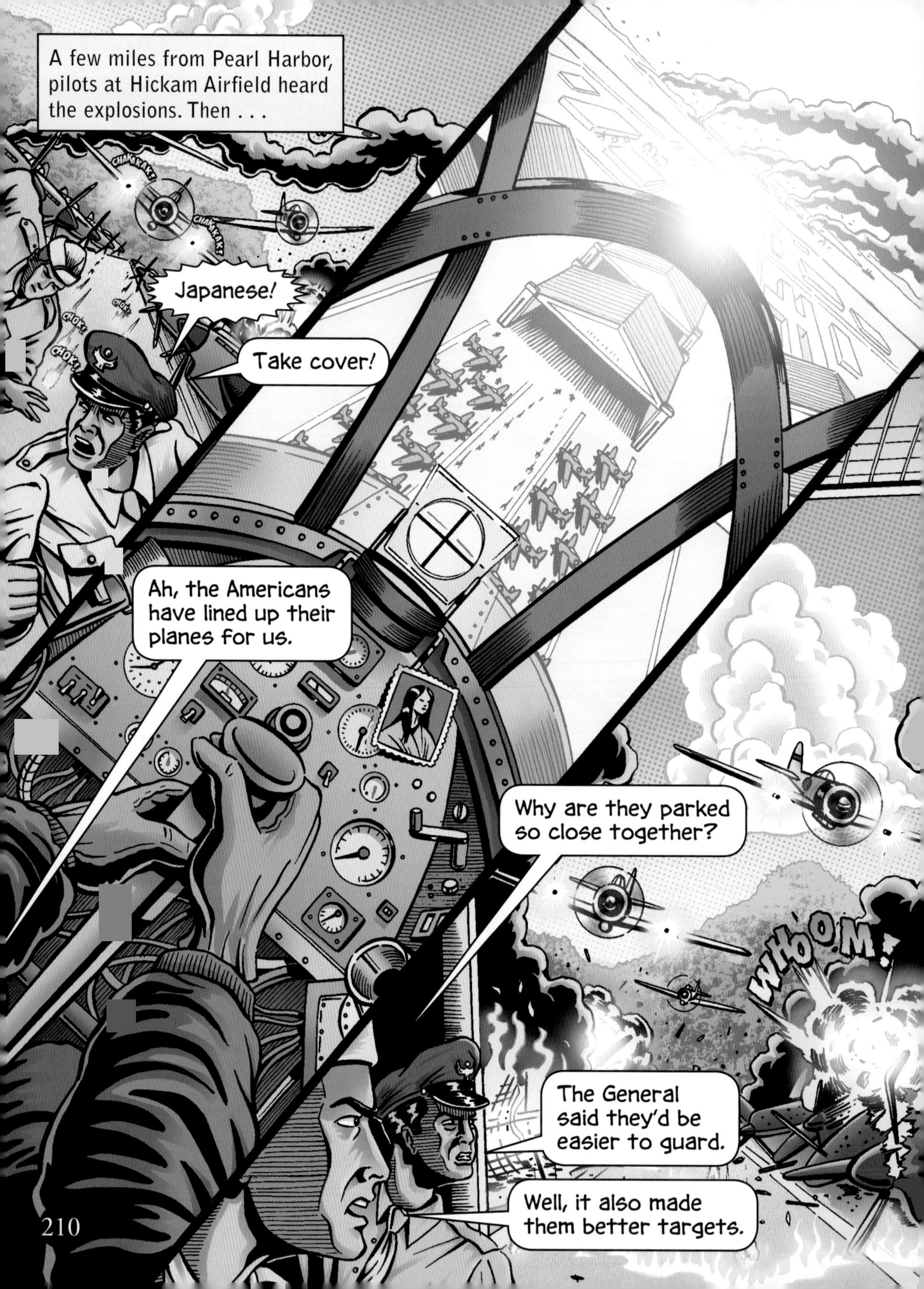

A few miles from Pearl Harbor, pilots at Hickam Airfield heard the explosions. Then . . .
CHAKAKAK!
CHAKAKAK!
Japanese!
CHOK!
CHOK!
CHOK!
Take cover!
Ah, the Americans have lined up their planes for us.
Why are they parked so close together?
WHOOM!
The General said they'd be easier to guard.
Well, it also made them better targets.

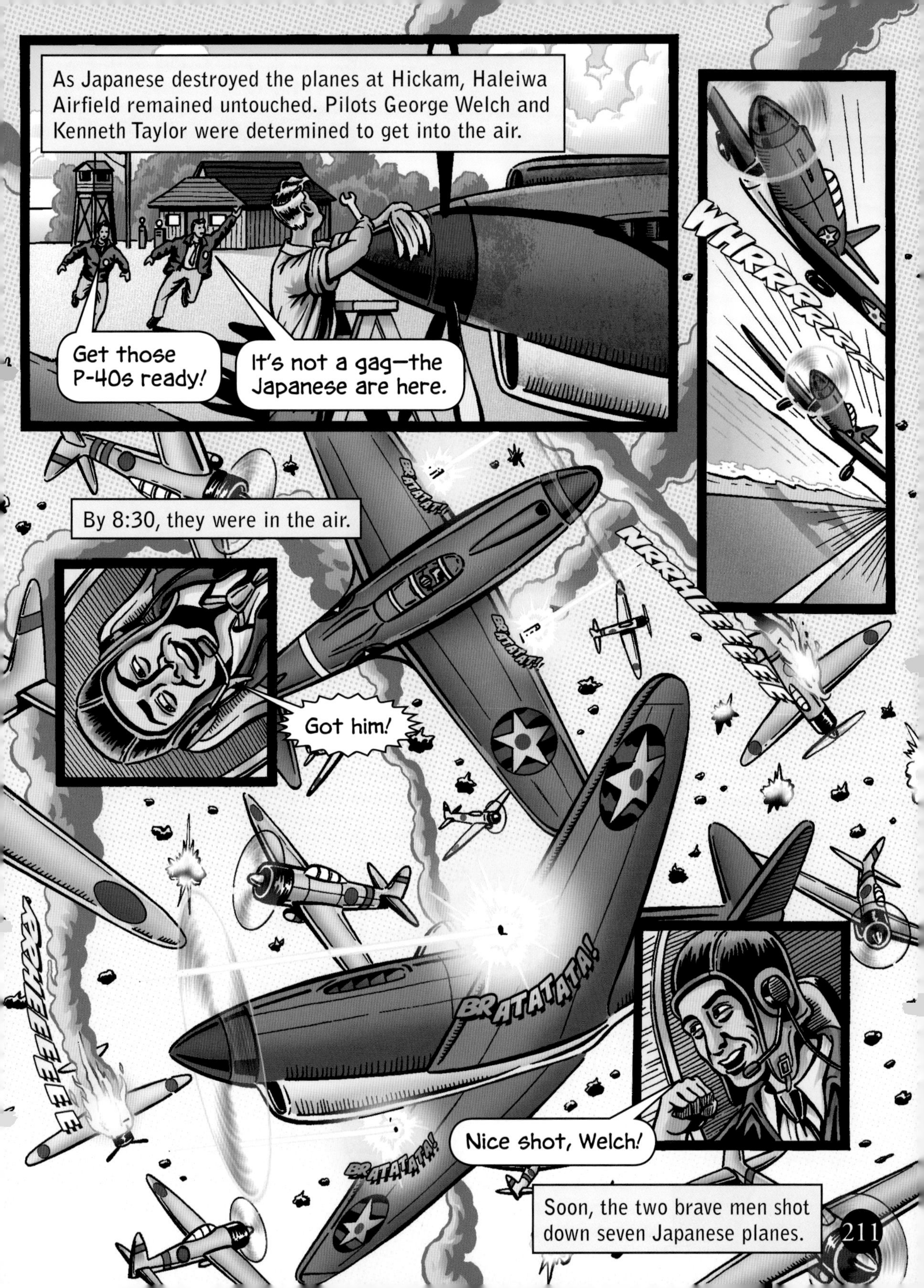
As Japanese destroyed the planes at Hickam, Haleiwa Airfield remained untouched. Pilots George Welch and Kenneth Taylor were determined to get into the air.
Get those P-40s ready!
It's not a gag—the Japanese are here.
WHRRRRR
NRRHEEEEEE
By 8:30, they were in the air.
BRATATAT!
Got him!
BRATATATA!
Nice shot, Welch!
BRATATATA!
Soon, the two brave men shot down seven Japanese planes.

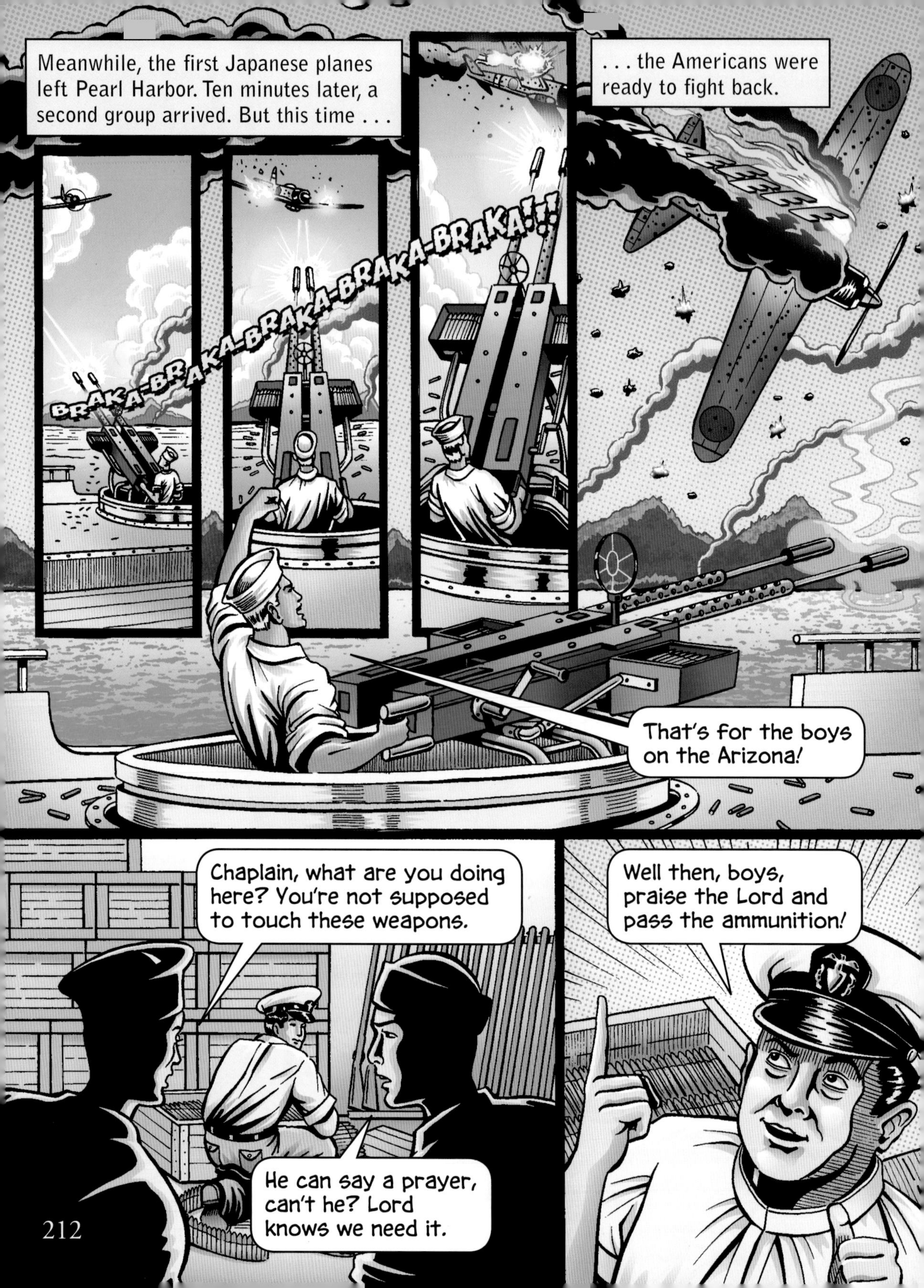
Meanwhile, the first Japanese planes left Pearl Harbor. Ten minutes later, a second group arrived. But this time . . .
. . . the Americans were ready to fight back.
BRAKA-BRAKA-BRAKA-BRAKA-BRAKA!!!
That's for the boys on the Arizona!
Chaplain, what are you doing here? You're not supposed to touch these weapons.
He can say a prayer, can't he? Lord knows we need it.
Well then, boys, praise the Lord and pass the ammunition!

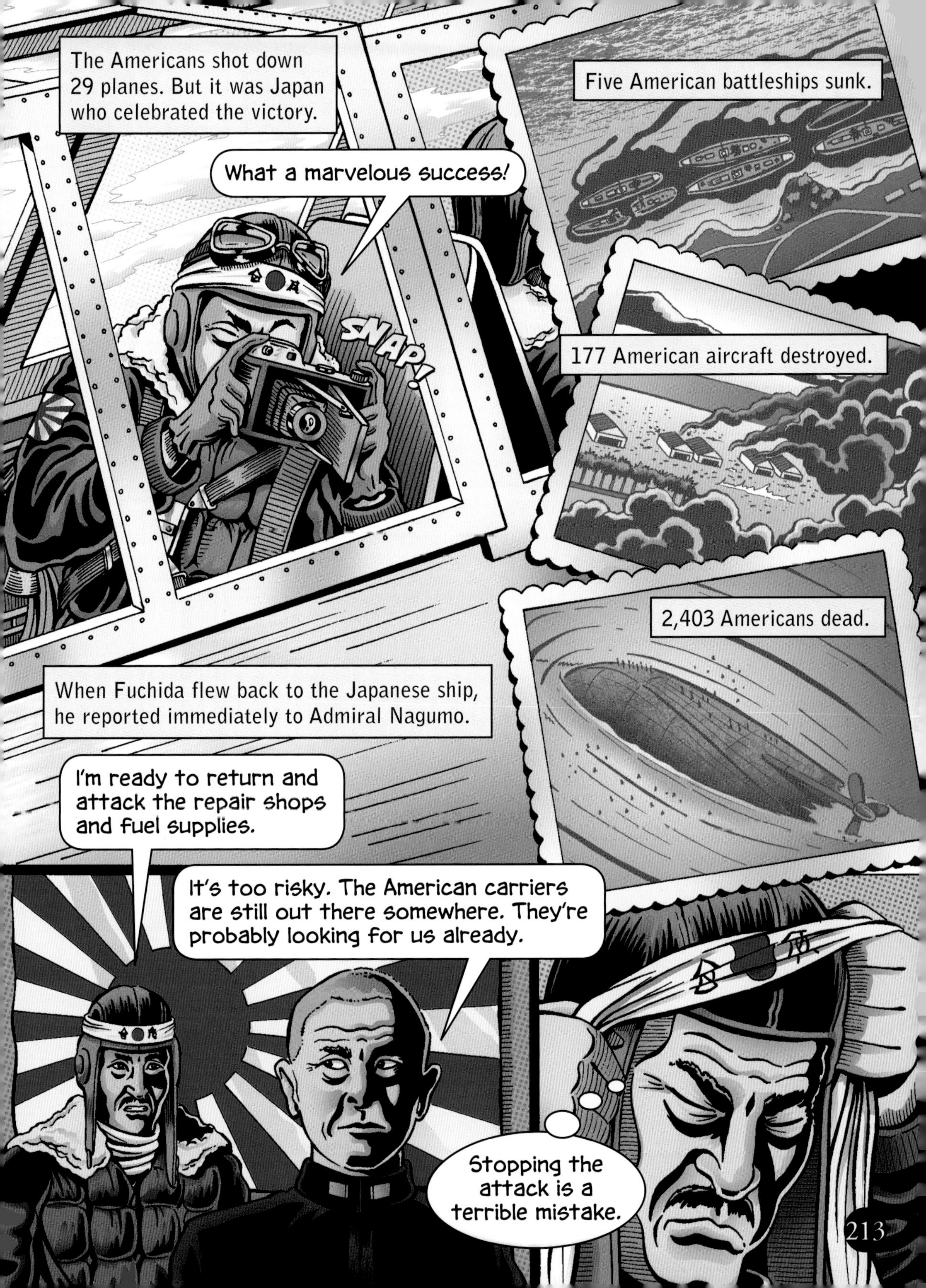
The Americans shot down 29 planes. But it was Japan who celebrated the victory.
What a marvelous success!
SNAP!
Five American battleships sunk.
177 American aircraft destroyed.
2,403 Americans dead.
When Fuchida flew back to the Japanese ship, he reported immediately to Admiral Nagumo.
I'm ready to return and attack the repair shops and fuel supplies.
It's too risky. The American carriers are still out there somewhere. They're probably looking for us already.
Stopping the attack is a terrible mistake.

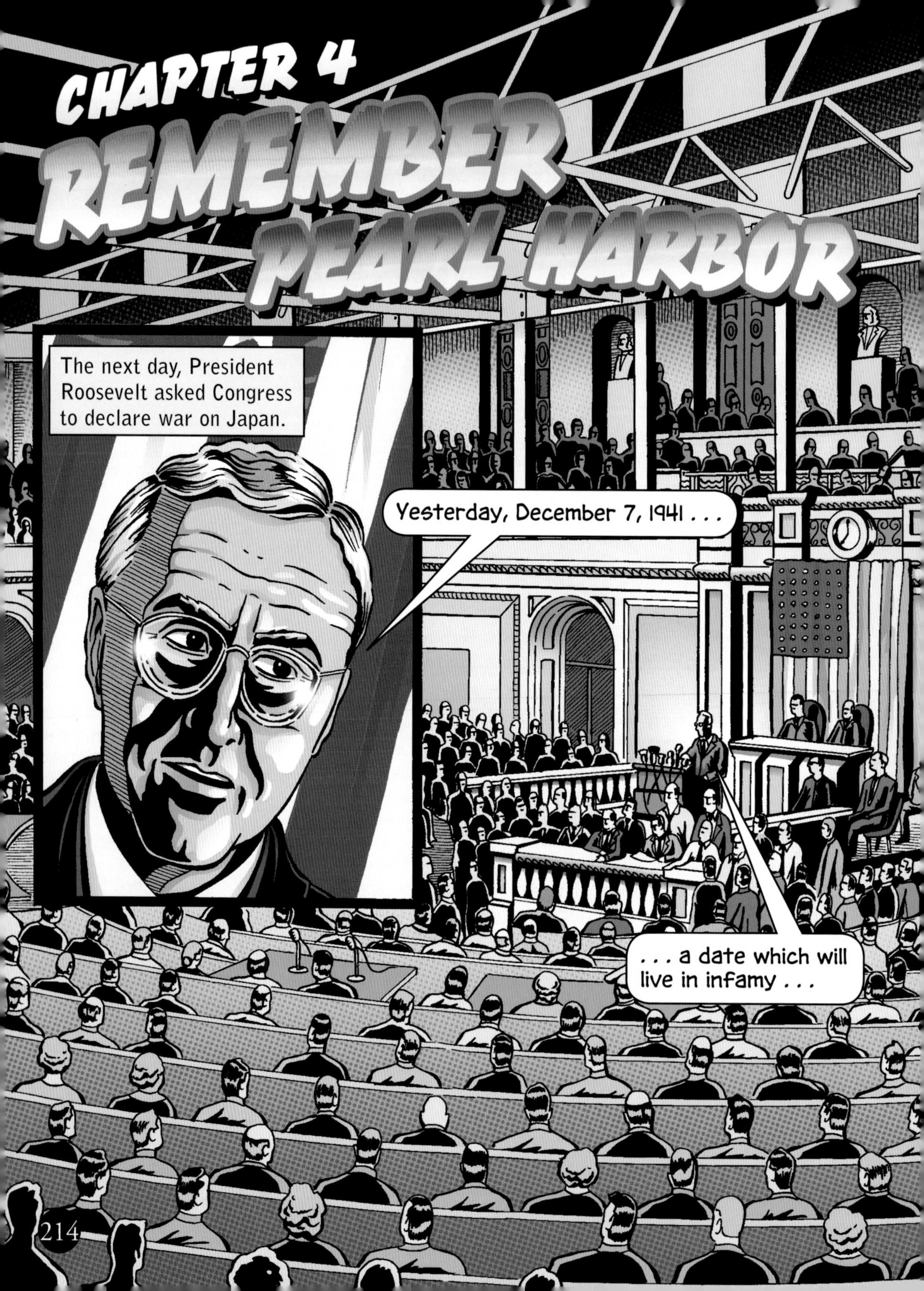

CHAPTER 4
REMEMBER PEARL HARBOR
The next day, President Roosevelt asked Congress to declare war on Japan.
Yesterday, December 7, 1941 . . .
. . . a date which will live in infamy . . .

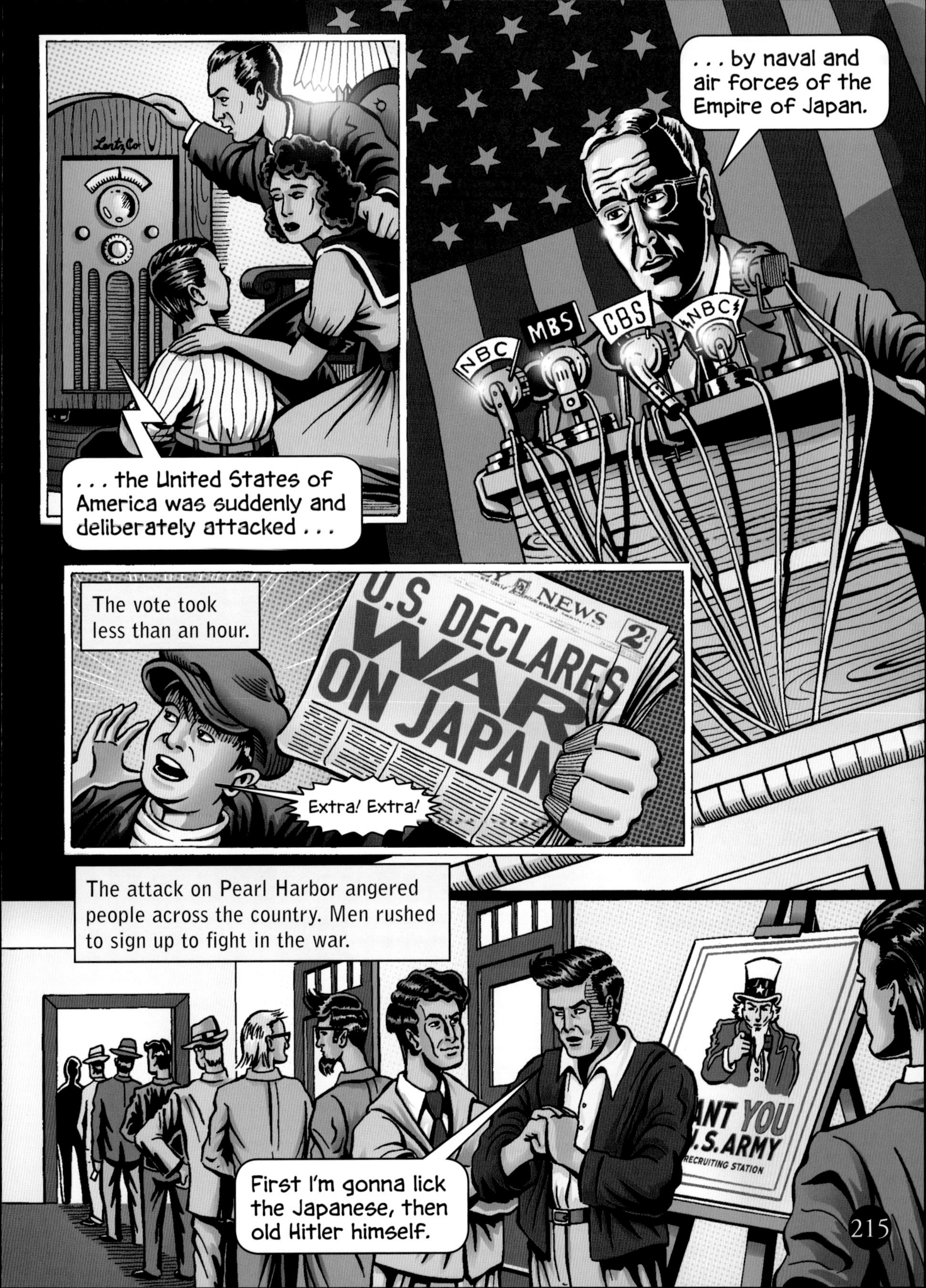

. . . the United States of America was suddenly and deliberately attacked . . .
. . . by naval and air forces of the Empire of Japan.
NBC
MBS
CBS
NBC
The vote took less than an hour.
NEWS
2¢
U.S. DECLARES WAR ON JAPAN
Extra! Extra!
The attack on Pearl Harbor angered people across the country. Men rushed to sign up to fight in the war.
ANT YOU
.S. ARMY
RECRUITING STATION
First I'm gonna lick the Japanese, then old Hitler himself.

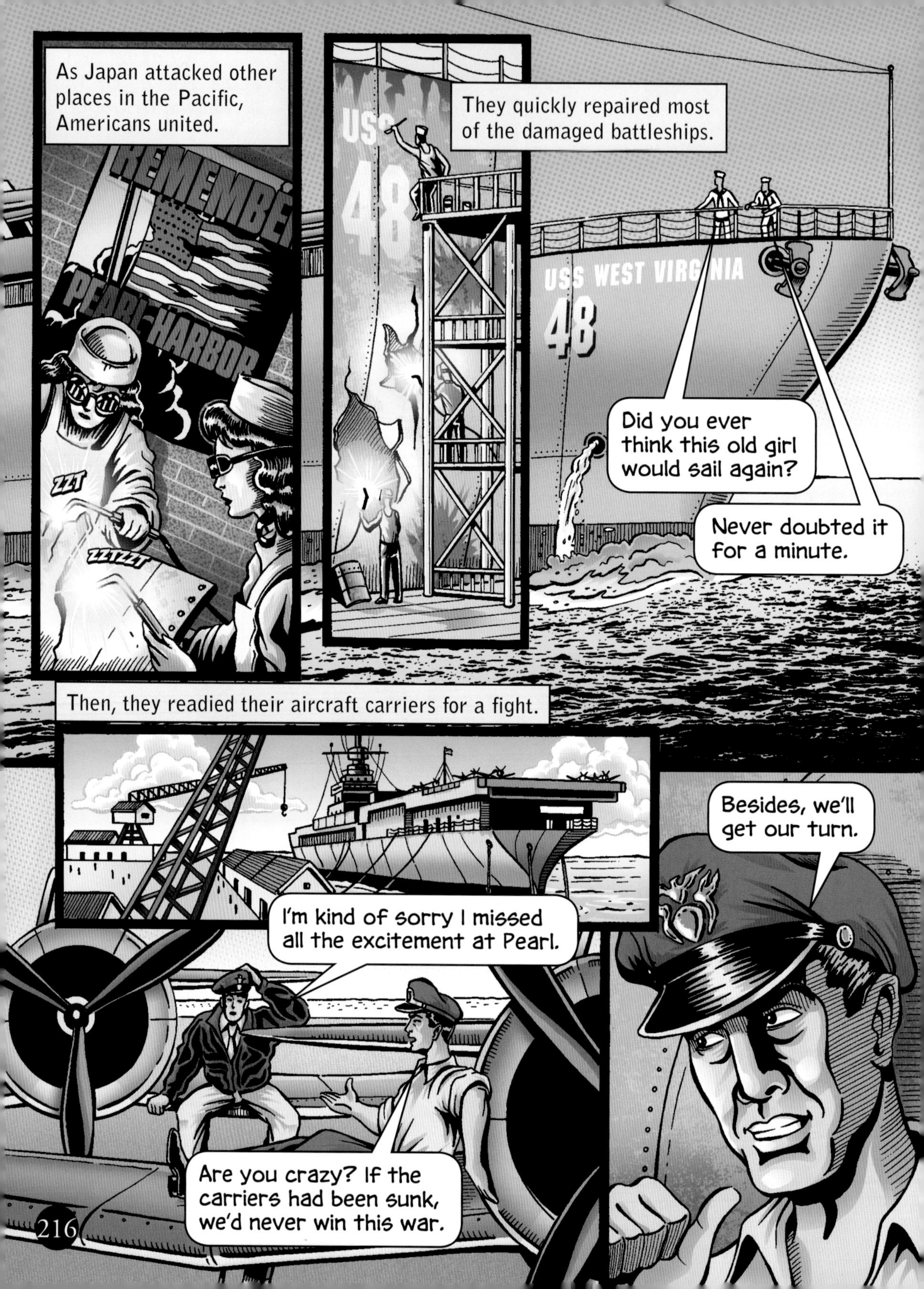

As Japan attacked other places in the Pacific, Americans united.
REMEMBER PEARL HARBOR
ZZT
ZZTZZT
They quickly repaired most of the damaged battleships.
USS 48
USS WEST VIRGINIA
48
Did you ever think this old girl would sail again?
Never doubted it for a minute.
Then, they readied their aircraft carriers for a fight.
I'm kind of sorry I missed all the excitement at Pearl.
Are you crazy? If the carriers had been sunk, we'd never win this war.
Besides, we'll get our turn.

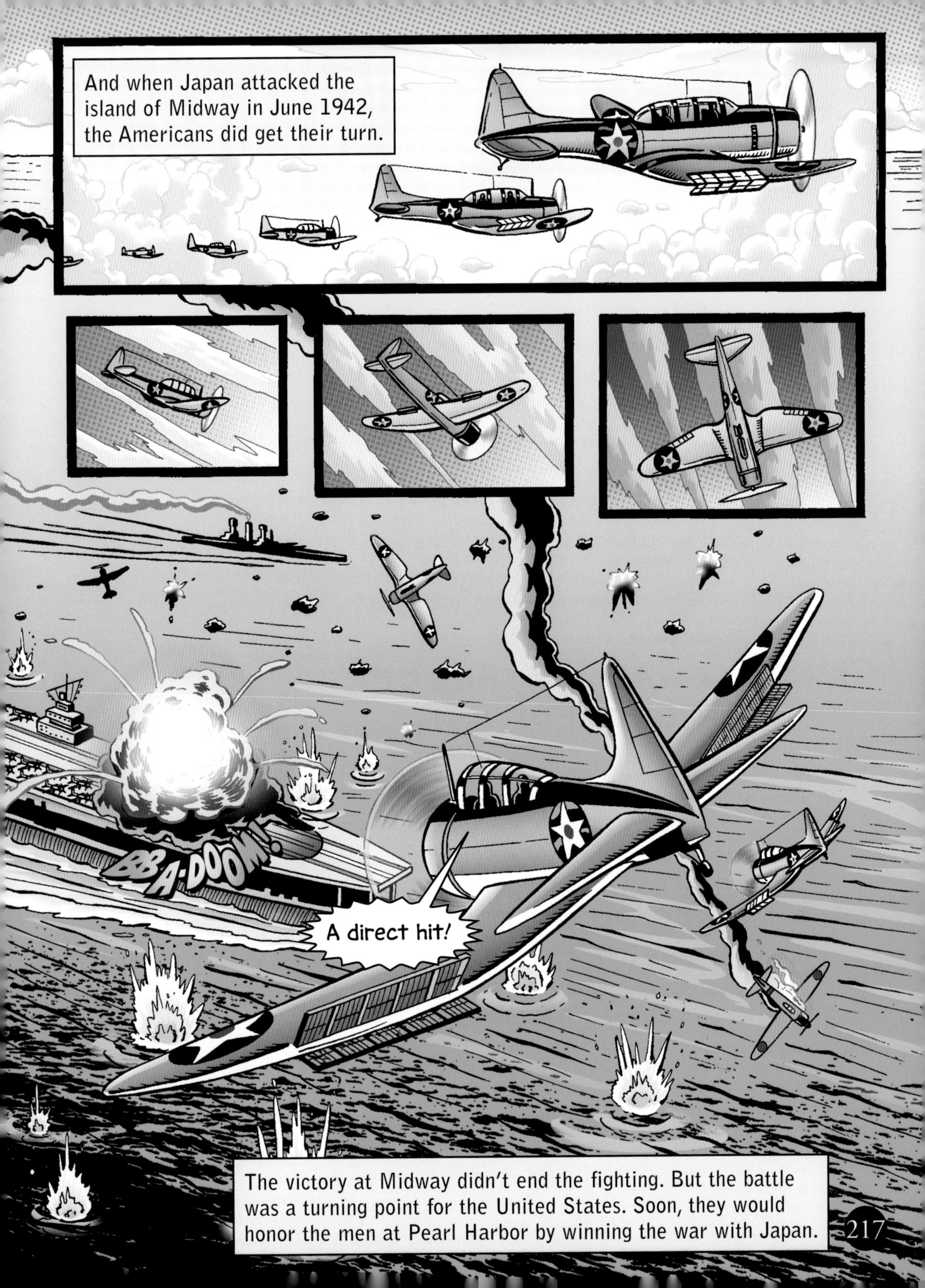
And when Japan attacked the island of Midway in June 1942, the Americans did get their turn.
BBBA-DOOM!
A direct hit!
The victory at Midway didn't end the fighting. But the battle was a turning point for the United States. Soon, they would honor the men at Pearl Harbor by winning the war with Japan.

MORE ABOUT...

THE DONNER PARTY

- The Donner Party consisted of 87 people and 23 wagons. Only 29 of the 87 people in the Donner Party were men, age 15 or older. The rest were women and children. In all, 41 people died during the Donner Party's journey to California. Thirty-six people died in the mountains during the winter. Of those who died, 32 were male and nine were female.

- The group of snowshoers later became known as the Forlorn Hope. Two of the Forlorn Hope survivors, William Eddy and William Foster, volunteered to join one of the four relief parties that went to the Donner Party camps.

- Parts of the Sierra Nevada have been renamed for the Donner Party. Truckee Lake is now called Donner Lake. The mountain summit is called Donner Summit. The rocky path over the summit is named Donner Pass.

SHACKLETON AND THE LOST ANTARCTIC EXPEDITION

- In 1901, Shackleton left on his first trip to Antarctica. The National Antarctic Expedition was led by British naval officer Robert Falcon Scott. Scott and Shackleton attempted to find a way to the South Pole. They fell short of their goal by 450 miles.

- In 1907, Shackleton led an expedition to reach the South Pole. He came within 97 miles of his goal. Shackleton turned back because he and his men were nearly out of supplies. Even though he failed to reach the South Pole, Shackleton was considered a hero for trying. The British king knighted him Sir Ernest Shackleton. Shackleton published a book, *The Heart of the Antarctic*, about his expedition.

- In 1921, Shackleton left on what would be his last expedition. While staying on South Georgia, he died of heart failure on January 5, 1922, at age 47. He was buried on South Georgia.

THE APOLLO 13 MISSION

- Only five minutes after launch, the Apollo 13 mission nearly ended. The first stage of the Saturn V rocket had fallen off, and the second-stage engines were burning smoothly. Then suddenly, one of the engines shut down. Flight controllers at Mission Control acted quickly. They burned the remaining engines a little longer and saved the mission.

- During the rescue, Lovell, Haise, and Swigert limited their drinking water. By the end of the mission, each member of the crew was severely dehydrated. Commander Jim Lovell lost nearly 14 pounds. The crew lost a total of 31.5 pounds during their nearly 6 days in space.

- After a long investigation, the Apollo 13 Accident Review Board identified the cause of the explosion. Damaged wires shorted out and caught fire inside oxygen tank 2. Within seconds, the tank exploded. The explosion damaged oxygen tank 1 and part of the service module.

THE CHALLENGER EXPLOSION

- A commission report determined that O-ring failure was the cause of Challenger's explosion. Cold weather was noted as a factor in the O-ring failure.

- The fleet of space shuttles was grounded for more than two years after Challenger's explosion. New safety features were added to the shuttle and engineers developed better seals for the rocket boosters.

- The families of the Challenger astronauts worked together to create Challenger Centers. These educational centers around the country let students learn about space and teamwork by simulating space missions.

THE GREAT CHICAGO FIRE OF 1871

- At the time of the Great Fire, Chicago was the fourth largest city in the United States. About 334,000 people lived in the city. The Great Fire killed about 300 people and left another 100,000 homeless. The Great Fire destroyed property valued at $192,000,000.

- In 1871, telephones, radios, and televisions did not exist. Most people in Chicago did not know about the fire until they saw the flames or neighbors knocked on their doors. Telegraph messages sent word of Chicago's fire to other cities. Fire engines from nearby towns could not arrive in time to help fight the fire.

- How did the Great Fire start? No one is sure, but we do know it started in the O'Leary barn. Many myths and legends suggest Catherine O'Leary's cow kicked over a lantern that started the fire. But Patrick and Catherine O'Leary were in bed when the fire started. Many people unfairly accused the O'Learys of causing Chicago's Great Fire.

THE TRIANGLE SHIRTWAIST FACTORY FIRE

- No one knows what caused the Triangle Shirtwaist Factory fire of 1911. Some people believe a match or lit cigar ignited a pile of rags on the eighth floor.

- In 1911, laws requiring fire drills didn't exist in New York. Most workers at the Triangle Factory had never practiced how to escape the building during a fire. Today, businesses need to have fire alarms and an emergency action plan. The plan must include safe exit routes for employees.

- After the Triangle fire, the New York State Factory Investigating Commission was created. Commission members spent three years investigating factories in the area. They made 60 suggestions to improve workplace safety. Most of their recommendations were quickly adopted, including the addition of automatic sprinklers in buildings more than seven stories tall and doubling the number of fire inspectors. They also suggested new rules for lighting, ventilation, washrooms, and dangerous equipment.

THE HINDENBURG DISASTER

- Zeppelins were named for airship designer Count Ferdinand von Zeppelin, a former German Army officer. Zeppelin had the idea to use a rigid metal frame and cloth outer cover to enclose a group of separate balloons, or gas cells. Many of the great airships followed Zeppelin's design.

- The Hindenburg was 804 feet (245 meters) long and held 72 passengers. The cost of a round-trip flight was $720.

- No one ever proved what caused the disaster. Many people think it may have been a spark from static electricity in the air. Others suggest that there was a bomb on board the ship. Another idea is that when the ship's landing lines hit the ground, they grounded the electrically charged airship and caused a spark to jump to the ship.

THE ATTACK ON PEARL HARBOR

- Before December 7, many U.S. officers believed Pearl Harbor couldn't be successfully attacked by air. They thought the harbor was too shallow for aerial torpedoes to work. The Japanese, however, had attached wooden tail fins to their torpedoes. The fins made aerial torpedoes a powerful weapon for Japan and devastated the U.S. Pacific Fleet.

- During the Japanese attack, Doris "Dorie" Miller was a cook aboard the USS *West Virginia*. As bombs rained down, Miller carried the ship's injured captain to safety. He then grabbed an anti-aircraft machine gun and started firing, even though he had no training. For his courage, Miller became the first Black person to receive the Navy Cross. This honor is one of the highest awards for courage given by the U.S. military.

- In 1962, a national memorial opened at Pearl Harbor, Hawaii. The memorial rests above the sunken USS *Arizona*, which remains a tomb for hundreds of soldiers who died on December 7, 1941. Today, visitors can take a boat to the memorial and pay their respects to these fallen heroes.

Contributor Credits

The Donner Party

Art Director: Jason Knudson
Graphic Designers: Bob Lentz and Thomas Emery
Production Artist: Alison Thiele
Storyboard Artist: Jason Knudson
Colorist: Benjamin Hunzeker
Editor: Christine Peterson
Consultant: Kristin Johnson, Librarian Salt Lake Community College, Salt Lake City, Utah, Editor, Unfortunate Emigrants: Narratives of the Donner Party

Direct Quotations
Page 10, from a letter written by Tamsen Donner dated May, 11, 1846 (http://members.aol.com/DanMRosen/donner/may46.htm).
Page 18, from The Expedition of the Donner Party and its Tragic Fate by Eliza P. Donner Houghton (Chicago: A. C. McClurg & Co., 1911).
Page 24, from Mary Graves' account of Forlorn Hope as published in History of the Donner Party, A Tragedy of the Sierra by C. F. McGlashan, (Stanford University, California: Stanford University Press, 1940).
Page 30, from a statement given by Donner Party rescuer Daniel Rhoads in 1873 (http://www.geocities.com/Heartland/Ranch/5417/GenReports/DanielR.htm#bancroft).

Shackleton and the Lost Antarctic Expedition

Art Direction and Design: Jason Knudson
Storyboard Artist: B. A. Hoena
Production Designer: Alison Thiele
Colorist: Benjamin Hunzeker
Editor: Erika L. Shores
Consultant: Robert Headland, Archivist and Curator, Scott Polar Research Institute, University of Cambridge, United Kingdom

Direct Quotations
Pages 38, 42, from crewmembers' diaries as quoted in Endurance: Shackleton's Incredible Voyage by Alfred Lansing, (Wheaton, Ill.: Tyndale House, 1999).

Pages 44, 47 (bottom), 21, from crewmembers' diaries and letters as quoted in The Endurance: Shackleton's Legendary Antarctic Expedition by Caroline Alexander, (New York: Alfred E. Knopf, 1998).
Pages 47 (top), 58, 59, from South: A Memoir of the Endurance Voyage by Ernest Shackleton, (New York: Carroll & Graf, 1998).

The Apollo 13 Mission

Art Direction: Jason Knudson
Graphic Designers: Juliette Peters and Jason Knudson
Production Designer: Alison Thiele
Colorist: Kim Brown
Editor: Tom Adamson
Consultant: James Gerard, Aerospace Education Specialist, Kennedy Space Center

Direct Quotations
Pages 63, 65, 67, 68, 69, 71, 81, 82, 83, 84, from Apollo 13 PAO Mission Commentary transcript (http://www.jsc.nasa.gov/history/mission_trans/apollo13.htm).
Pages 72 (top panel), 73, 80, quoted in Failure Is Not an Option by Gene Kranz (New York: Simon & Schuster, 2000).
Pages 72 (bottom panel), 75, 77, 78, quoted in Lost Moon by Jim Lovell (Boston: Houghton Mifflin, 1994).

The Challenger Explosion

Art Direction and Design: Jason Knudson
Storyboard Artist: Alison Thiele
Editor: Christopher Harbo
Consultant: James Gerard, Aerospace Education Specialist, Kennedy Space Center

Direct Quotations
Page 89, from "Remarks of the Vice President Announcing the Winner of the Teacher in Space Project," 1985 (http://www.reagan.utexas.edu/archives/speeches/1985/71985a.htm).
Page 98, from Report of the Presidential Commission on the Space Shuttle Challenger

Accident, 1986 (http://history.nasa.gov/
rogersrep/51lcover.htm).
Pages 102 (bottom, both), 103 (bottom), from
"Transcript of the Challenger Crew Comments
from the Operational Recorder.", 1986 (http://
history.nasa.gov/transcript.htm).
Pages 102 (top), 106 from "Flight Director and
NASA Select Audio Mix." Spaceflight Now: The
Challenger Accident, 1986 (http://spaceflightnow.
com/challenger/Video/loops_qt.html).
Page 111 (both), from "Explosion of the Space
Shuttle Challenger Address to the Nation. January
28, 1986." by President Ronald W. Reagan, 1986
(http://history.nasa.gov/reagan12886 html).

The Great Chicago Fire of 1871
Art Direction and Design: Bob Lentz
Storyboard and Production Artist: Alison Thiele
Colorist: Matt Webb
Editor: Donald Lemke
Consultant: Richard F. Bales, author The Great
Chicago Fire and the Myth of Mrs. O'Leary's Cow

The Triangle Shirtwaist Factory Fire
Art Direction and Design: Bob Lentz
Production Designer: Alison Thiele
Colorist: Buzz Setzer
Editor: Donald Lemke
Consultant: Clete Daniel, Professor of American
Labor History, School of Industrial and Labor
Relations, Cornell University, Ithaca, New York

Direct Quotations
Page 145, from Clara Lemlich's speech at Cooper
Union, November 22, 1909, as quoted in Dave Von
Drehle's Triangle: The Fire that Changed America
(New York: Atlantic Monthly Press, 2003).
Page 146, from a speech on November 24, 1909,
by Clara Lemlich, as quoted in Dave Von Drehle's
Triangle: The Fire that Changed America (New
York: Atlantic Monthly Press, 2003).
Page 159, from an article originally published in
the Call, November 23, 1909, as transcribed on
Cornell University School of Industrial and Labor
Relations' Kheel Center website (http://www.
ilr.cornell.edu/trianglefire/texts/stein_ootss/
ootss_sg.html).

The Hindenburg Disaster
Art Director: Jason Knudson
Graphic Designers: Jason Knudson and Jennifer
Bergstrom

Production Designer: Alison Thiele
Storyboard Artist: Bob Lentz
Colorist: Kristen Denton
Editor: Angie Kaelberer
Consultant: Eric Brothers, The Lighter-Than-Air
Society

Direct Quotations
Page 175, from the Hindenburg disaster files,
Federal Bureau of Investigation (http://foia.fbi.
gov/foiaindex/hindburg.htm).
Pages 178, 180, 183, 185, from the description of
the crash of the Hindenburg, National Archives
Sound Recording, Herbert Morrison reporting,
1937.

The Attack on Pearl Harbor
Art Director and Designer: Bob Lentz
Editor: Donald Lemke
Consultant: William L. O'Neill, Professor of
History, Rutgers University

Direct Quotations
Pages 197, 204, from Investigation of the Pearl
Harbor Attack: Report Pursuant to S. Con. Res. 27,
79th Congress by U. S. Congress. Joint Committee
on the Investigation of the Pearl Harbor Attack
(Washington: U.S. Govt. Print. Off., 1946).
Pages 199, 209, from Gordon William Prange's
interview with Commander Mitsuo Fuchida,
December 10, 1963, as quoted in December 7,
1941: The Day the Japanese Attacked Pearl Harbor
by Gordon William Prange (New York: McGraw-
Hill, 1988).
Page 205, from a letter to Gordon William Prange
from Robert G. Crouse, November 24, 1964, as
quoted in December 7, 1941: The Day the Japanese
Attacked Pearl Harbor by Gordon William Prange
(New York: McGraw-Hill, 1988).
Page 207, from Gordon William Prange's
interview with 1st Class Boatswain's Mate
Howard C. French, August 11, 1964, as quoted in
December 7, 1941: The Day the Japanese Attacked
Pearl Harbor by Gordon William Prange (New
York: McGraw-Hill, 1988).
Pages 214–215, from Franklin D. Roosevelt's Joint
Address to Congress Leading to a Declaration of
War Against Japan, December 8, 1941, archived
at Franklin D. Roosevelt Presidential Library and
Museum (http://www.fdrlibrary.marist.edu/
oddec7.html).

LOOKING FOR MORE?

Learn about five crucial days that changed history forever in this graphic novel collection from Capstone!

24 HOUR HISTORY
THE COMPLETE GRAPHIC NOVEL COLLECTION
capstone

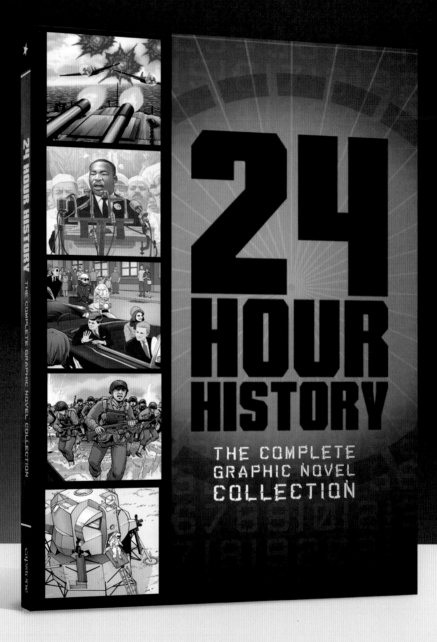